The Communist Judicial System
in China, 1927-1976

The Communist Judicial System in China, 1927-1976

Building on Fear

Qiang Fang

Routledge
Taylor & Francis Group
LONDON AND NEW YORK

First published in 2021 by Amsterdam University Press Ltd.

Published 2025 by Routledge
4 Park Square, Milton Park, Abingdon, Oxon OX14 4RN
605 Third Avenue, New York, NY 10158

Routledge is an imprint of the Taylor & Francis Group, an informa business

ISBN: 9789463729451 (hbk)
ISBN: 9781041187486 (pbk)
ISBN: 9781003705598 (ebk)
NUR 823

Cover image: The People's Court of the Shanghai Pudong New District [上海市浦东新区人民法院]
Photographer: Wang Jin

Cover design: Coördesign, Leiden

DOI: 10.5117/9789463729451

For Product Safety Concerns and Information please contact our EU representative:
GPSR@taylorandfrancis.com
Taylor & Francis Verlag GmbH, Kaufingerstraße 24, 80331 München, Germany

Table of Contents

List of Tables

Dedicated to my parents

Acknowledgement

In 2009, when I was revising my first book on the Chinese complaint systems, I went to the Shanghai Municipal Archives, arguably the best and most open official archive in China today, to read archives pertaining to law, police, and court in both the Republic of China and the People's Republic of China. But my eye was suddenly caught by a plethora of archives on the Shanghai People's Court in the 1950s. After spending a couple of weeks in the archives, I found that the archives of the Shanghai People's Court had never been studied before and could be a very good research topic for my second book. Fortunately, the Chinese government policy was relatively tolerant at that time and there was no limit for me to photocopy almost whatever archives I wanted, albeit all copies had to be approved in advance and stamped by officials in the archives. The situation became drastically hostile and stricter after 2013 as the Shanghai Municipal Archives began to limit the number of photocopies to at most one third of each archive. Given the fact that many archives contained pages ranging from ten to more than one hundred, it would be rather cumbersome for researchers to type or write down what they needed. Making matters worse, archives related to politically sensitive issues such as the people's court, police, death penalties, or political campaigns would no longer be approved to be read, much less photocopied. Fortunately, prior to the new draconian policy, I had already gleaned the bulk of legal archives I could find. I am still grateful to the staffs in the Shanghai Municipal Archives for their assistance.

While I have been distracted by some other duties since 2010, I manage to write about one chapter each year and present it at the annual conferences organized by the American Historical Association (AHA), the academic gathering organized by Chinese Historians in the United States (CHUS), or the Association of Chinese Professors in Social Sciences (ACPSS). In the summer of 2019, I was invited by Professor Yang Songtao to present part of my book in the law school at Henan University where I had received many valuable suggestions and comments from Professor Yang, Chen Shuang, a history professor at the University of Iowa, and some students.

This book has also benefited greatly from official documents and archives collected by Professor Cao Shuji and the history department at Shanghai Jiaotong University. Most notable ones are the court and police archives of Liangshan, Jiaxing, and Neixiang counties from the early 1950s to the end of the Cultural Revolution. The University Service Center for China Studies at the Chinese University of Hong Kong holds one of the most comprehensive collections of the PRC in the world including many local legal gazettes and documents. Some staffs in the center have been very friendly and helpful during my visits there. The staffs at the Taiwan Academia Sinica library and professors such as Lai Hui-min at the Institute of Modern History have also been very kind to me.

I am thankful for the generous grants from the University of Minnesota and the University of Minnesota Duluth that allowed me to conduct archival research in China, Hong Kong, and Taiwan.

In particular, I greatly appreciate the editing and comments made by my mentor, Professor Roger Des Forges, who has in the past two decades continued to offer his invaluable help and guidance to me. He has read through the whole manuscript and made many insightful and important comments. My appreciation also extends to the two AUP reviewers whose highly meticulous and valuable suggestions and corrections have helped further improve the writing, logic, and argument of this book in many ways.

I sincerely wish to thank Dr. Saskia Gieling, senior editor at AUP, for her strong interest, support, encouragement, and timely help in this book. Professor Chen Linghai at East China University of Politics and Law has provided me with not only many useful books for this book but also some beautiful photos including the one used for the cover.

Writing and completing this book has not been possible without the immense devotion and encouragement from my beloved wife Duan Jing and the joy and peace brought by my two sons, Harold (Hanru) and Gerald (Junru). Covid-19 has allowed me to stay with my family while teaching class and completing the revision of this book. Decades from now, I am sure this period will be reminisced as my happiest time in life.

Qiang Fang
January 2021

Acronyms

CCP	Chinese Communist Party
COCR	Central Organization of the Cultural Revolution
GMD	Nationalist Party
OLC	Organic Law of the People's Court
PRC	People's Republic of China
ROC	Republic of China
SPC	Shanghai People's Court
SPSB	State Political Security Bureau
SRPS	Six Regulations of Public Security

Introduction

Abstract
The book starts with recent cases in which several prominent Chinese dissidents have been punished under the crime of threatening state security. The Introduction then examines the long history of governmental imposition of draconian penalties on people for fear that they may threaten the rulers or ruling parties. The Communist judicial system in China is a hodgepodge that is a mixture of Soviet laws, Republican laws, and traditional Chinese legal norms. Throughout the Mao era, Communist judges had been swung from "left (law was a tool of the Party)" to "right (upholding basic legal principles)." During political campaigns, judges were required to stick to central policies to punish so-called political enemies severely. When the campaign subsided, many judges including top judicial officials began stressing legal principles.

Keywords: building on fear, legal hodgepodge, judicial pendulum

Building on Fear

In December 2017, the Second Tianjin Intermediate Court sentenced Wu Gan, whose internet nickname was "Super Vulgar Butcher," to eight years in prison. The verdict accused Wu of "seriously threatening state security and social stability," a crime synonymous with "counterrevolutionary" in the era of Mao Zedong (c. 1927-1976). Among his main "crimes" were providing legal support to victims of local government abuses, expressing anti-government rhetoric on the internet, "[O]rganizing boisterous protests outside courthouses and government offices," and conducting illegal demonstrations.[1] Among many Westerners, Wu Gan is not as famous as other Chinese political dissidents such as Liu Xiaobo, the 2010 Nobel Peace Prize

1 Chris Buckley, "Chinese Activist Sentenced to 8 Years in Prison for Shaming Officials" in *The New York Times*, December 26, 2017.

Fang, Qiang, *The Communist Judicial System in China, 1927-1976: Building on Fear.*
Taylor & Francis Group 2021
DOI: 10.5117/9789463729451_INTRO

winner, and Fang Lizhi, a leading figure in the 1986 student demonstrations.[2] Since 2008, the Chinese Communist Party (CCP) has beefed up crackdowns against outspoken political critics and Wu Gan was just one of the many minor targets. Liu Xiaobo was sentenced to eleven years of imprisonment in 2009 for his championing of a "democratic charter." In 2014, a Beijing court convicted Xu Zhiyong, a civil rights lawyer, for "gathering a crowd to disturb public order" and sentenced him to four years in prison.[3] In June 2016, two dissidents in Zhejiang who had tried to promote a political party and "published prodemocracy essays on overseas websites" were harshly punished with eleven years in prison.[4]

The People's Republic's campaigns against political dissenters and critics are by no means limited to the provinces of the mainland. The Party's long arm has extended to territories considered to be part of China or even to other countries. In late 2016, for example, several booksellers were kidnapped by Chinese agents in Hong Kong, a semi-autonomous city, and in Thailand, a fully independent foreign country. They were taken to China and interrogated about their plan to publish a gossip book about the private life of China's president Xi Jinping.[5] In the early summer of 2017, Lee Ming-cheh, a Taiwan activist attempting to assist China's democratic movements, was charged by a Chinese court for "colluding with individuals" in China and "establishing an illegal organization and implementing activities to subvert state power." For that alleged crime, Lee, in spite of being a Taiwan resident, would spend the next five years of his life in a Chinese prison.[6] Aside from political crackdowns, the CCP has appointed student spies to monitor college teachers' lectures. It has installed millions of surveillance cameras with facial-recognition technology to oversee lives of ordinary citizens.[7] Reports

2 For Liu Xiaobo see "China: Democratic Voice Liu Xiaobo Dies in Custody" in *Human Rights Watch*, July 13, 2017 https://www.hrw.org/news/2017/07/13/china-democratic-voice-liu-xiaobo-dies-custody; for Fang Lizhi see Fang Lizhi方励之, *Autobiography of Fang Lizhi* (*Fang LIzhi zizhuan*方励之传) (Taiwan: Tianxia yuanjian chubanshe, 2013).

3 Jonathan Kaiman, "China Upholds Four-year Sentence of Activist Xu Zhiyong" in *The Guardian*, April 11, 2014.

4 Chris Buckley, "2 Chinese Activists Sentenced to Over 10 Years on Subversion Charges" in *The New York Times*, June 20, 2016.

5 Michael Forsythe, "If China Meant to Chill Hong Kong Speech, Booksellers' Case Did the Job" in *The New York Times*, November 7, 2016.

6 Chris Horton and Chris Buckley, "China Charges Activist From Taiwan with 'Subverting State Power'" in *The New York Times*, May 29, 2017.

7 Javier C. Hernandez, "Professors, Beware. A 'Student Information Officer' Might be Watching" in *The New York Times*, November 1, 2019; Emile Dirkes and Sarah Cook, "China's Surveillance State Has Tens of Millions of New Targets" in *Foreign Policy*, October 21, 2019; https://foreignpolicy.com/2019/10/21/china-xinjiang-surveillance-state-police-targets/

also show that, in the past few years, the CCP has opened new fronts and attacked alien and untrustworthy religions such as Christianity and Islam by destroying churches and mosques.[8]

With millions of armed soldiers and police, why can the CCP and its judiciary not tolerate small-scale protests or moderate criticism? Why do the Communist courts inflict severe punishments on political activists whose numbers are scanty and evidence of "crimes" is flimsy? Why does the CCP hire students to spy on college professors? And what does the CCP really want to find out from millions of surveillance cameras? The best answer to these queries should and has to be the "fears" of the CCP: fear of insecurity, fear of people's uprising, and above all fear of losing power. According to British philosopher John Locke, "Fear is an uneasiness of the mind."[9] More recently, Corey Robin has argued about political fear, "It is not only the powerful who wield fear and the powerless who are afraid. People with power are themselves often seized by a fear of those without it."[10] In other words, the fear of losing power compels rulers or ruling parties to routinely seek to intimidate potential foes. During the French revolution, Napoleon Bonaparte rejected the peace proposal of other European countries because he understood that his power and intrepidity hinged on strength and war. "I am an upstart soldier," Napoleon said, "my domination will not survive the day when I cease to be strong, and therefore feared."[11] Like Napoleon, the CCP, haunted by its constant apprehension of losing power, would employ draconian laws and the judicial system as the instrument or "knife hilt" (*daobazi*) of the Party.[12] It considered any political crimes, however minor, as a threat to the Party's very survival.

In retrospect, most, if not all, rulers in China's long history, like the CCP, relentlessly exercised law and the judicial system to punish or even eliminate opponents or potential enemies who may threaten their power or security. As Herrlee G. Creel has remarked, Zhou Wuwang, the martial founder of the Zhou dynasty, frequently imposed the death penalty against

8 Steven Lee Myers, "A Crackdown on Islam Is Spreading Across China" in *The New York Times*, September 23, 2019.

9 John Locke, *An Essay Concerning Human Understanding* (London: H. Woodfall, 1768): 187.

10 Corey Robin, *Fear: The History of a Political Idea* (Oxford: Oxford University Press, 2006): 20.

11 Dennis Sherman and Joyce Salisbury, *The West in the World: A History of Western Civilization* (New York: McGraw Hill, 2011): 536; William H.C. Smith, *The Bonapartes: The History of a Dynasty* (London: A & C Black, 2007): 65.

12 For the judicial system being a knife hilt of the CCP see Qiang Fang and Xiaobing Li, *Power Versus Law in Modern China: Cities, Courts, and the Communist Party* (Lexington: University Press of Kentucky, 2017): Ch. 1.

lawbreakers, including his brothers, to consolidate his new dynasty and authoritarian rule. Wuwang's policies were later applauded by Lord Shang,[13] one of the most renowned legalists in ancient China who has been criticized as "the author of a despotic concept of law that placed the ruler at the pinnacle of the state."[14] Overwhelmed by fear of criticism, Liwang (890-828 BCE), another brutal and paranoid Zhou ruler, hired agents to monitor and execute whoever dared to speak ill of him. His extreme cruelty eventually triggered a mass rebellion that banished him.[15] Having conquered the other six states in 221 BCE, the First August Lord of the Qin (*qinshihuang*) imposed harsh punishments on newly identified crimes to deter any critics. Anyone who "accidentally or unintentionally cited" (*ouyu shishu*) Confucian texts could be put to death. Slanderers against the ruler or government could have their whole family executed. As a result of this law, hundreds of scholars reportedly were buried alive under the charge of defaming Qinshihuang.[16]

In the Western Jin (266-316), any subject or official who verbally or physically offended the ruler could be deemed a great traitor (*dani*) and, according to the Wei Code, could be chopped by half at the waist.[17] In the early Tang dynasty (618-907), the rulers promulgated the Tang Code whose impact on future periods was so great that as much as 30-40% of the code remained in the Great Qing code.[18] Many Tang rulers including Tang Taizong could respect judicial independence,[19] but Tang rulers inherited the Ten Serious Crimes of the Northern Qi (550-577) and changed them into the Ten Abominations. The first three abominations were all about rebellion, sedition, and betrayal. Violators of the first three abominations would be

13 Herrlee G. Creel, "Legal Institutions and Procedures during the Chou Dynasty" in Jerome A. Cohen, R. Randle Edwards, and Fu-mei Chang Chen, eds., *Essays on China's Legal Tradition* (Princeton: Princeton University Press, 1980), pp. 26-55: 53-55.

14 Karen Turner, "War, Punishment, and the Law of Nature in Early Chinese Concepts of the State" in *Harvard Journal of Asiatic Studies*, Vol. 53. No. 2 (Dec., 1993), pp. 285-324: 312.

15 Zuo Qiuming左丘明, *Discourses of the States* (*guoyu*国语) (Shanghai: Shanghai guji chubanshe, 2015): 45-46.

16 Sima Qian司马迁, *Historical Record* (*shiji*史记) (Beijing: Zhonghua shujü, 2014): 1.329.

17 Zhang Jinfan张晋藩, ed., *History of Chinese Judicial System* (*zhongguo sifa zhidushi*中国司法制度史) (Beijing: Renmin fayuan chubanshe, 2004): 65.

18 William P. Alford, *To Steal a Book is an Elegant Offense: Intellectual Property Law in Chinese* Civilization (Stanford: Stanford University Press, 1995): 22.

19 Many Han and Tang rulers respected judicial independence and the supremacy of the law. See Qiang Fang and Roger Des Forges, "Were Chinese Rulers Above the Law? Toward a Theory of the Rule of Law in Chinese History" in *Stanford Journal of International Law*, Vol. 44.1, 2007, pp. 101-146; also see Lin Qian林乾, *Power and Law in Traditional China* (*chuantong zhongguo dequan yufa*传统中国的权与法) (Beijing: Falü chubanshe, 2013): 194.

executed. People who refused to report the grave crimes to the government would be strangled.[20]

The political and military upheavals after the Tang prompted many rulers to adopt cruel punishments such as death by slicing (*lingchi*) for traitors. After losing large northern territories and two emperors to the Jin dynasty, Southern Song rulers were spooked by the prospect of losing power and they were said to have meted out more capital punishment by slicing than their predecessors had to strengthen their fragile dominion.[21] Zhu Yuanzhang, the commoner founder of the Ming dynasty (1368-1644), was a typical rags-to-riches model in Chinese history. Yet, his modest social origins may have made him fearful of being opposed and betrayed. During his reign, Zhu Yuanzhang had not only inherited harsh penalties from the Song targeting rebels and traitors but also launched major assaults against alleged treacherous and libelous officials that resulted in tens of thousands of deaths of innocent people.[22] In the late Ming period, weak rulers and bureaucratic factions resulted in harsh punishment and death of some officials from the Donglin faction and their opponents who were charged with allying with powerful eunuchs.[23]

In the last stage of the dynasty, Manchu rulers remained alert and anxious after overcoming rebels and Ming loyalists and taking power in Beijing in 1644. They continued to fear the prospects of resistance and rebellion on the part of the majority ethnic Han Chinese and they adopted severe laws and marshaled powerful forces to suppress evident and latent opponents. Jonathan Spence has analyzed the case of Zeng Jing, a Ming loyalist in the Yongzheng reign who failed to persuade a Han governor to rise against the Qing. While Yongzheng tried to use the Zeng Jing case to demonstrate his magnanimity, his son Qianlong put Zeng to a brutal death.[24]

20 Xue Yunsheng薛允升, *A Combined Edition of the Tang and Ming Codes* (*tangminglu hebian* 唐明律合编) (Beijing: Falü chubanshe, 1999): 2-3.

21 Kong Xue孔雪, "The Origin of Lingchi and its Development in the Song Dynasty (*lunlingchi zhixing deqiyuan jizai songdai defazhan*论凌迟之刑的起源及在宋代的发展)" in *Shixue yuekan* 史学集刊, Vol. 6, 2004, pp. 38-47; for a complete good study of *lingchi* see Timothy Brook, Jerome Bourgon, and Gregory Blue, *Death By a Thousand Cuts* (Cambridge, Ma: Harvard University Press, 2008).

22 Wang Tianyou王天有 and Xu Daling许大龄, *Sixteen Emperors of the Ming Dynasty* (*mingchao shiliudi*明朝十六帝) (Beijing: Zijincheng chubanshe, 1991): 1-38.

23 John Dardess, *Blood and History in China: The Donglin Faction and its Repression, 1620-1627* (Honolulu: University of Hawaii Press, 2002).

24 Jonathan Spence, *Treason by the Book: Traitors, Conspirators and Guardians of an Emperor* (London: Penguin Books, 2012).

With the establishment of a Republic in 1912 and the drafting of constitutions that guaranteed citizens' rights to speech and a political representation, the use of harsh penalties to deter and punish political foes was ostensibly obsolete. Indeed, Sun Yat-sen abolished official privileges, while Yuan Shikai and subsequent Republican leaders labored to create what might be called a "golden age" for aggrieved complainants.[25] In the late 1920s, however, members of a nascent Communist Party came into conflict with warlords and a young Nationalist Party (the Guomindang, or GMD). Some Communist leaders such as Li Dazhao lost their lives.[26] After the Nationalist Party split with the Communists in 1927, they founded a government under Chiang Kai-shek, which had from the very beginning engaged in prolonged and violent wars with the CCP. Unlike its counterpart in the early Republic, the judicial system of the GMD became increasingly politicized.[27] The specter of Communist subversion and a plot to monopolize power had always topped the GMD's concerns. In March 1928, the GMD legislature passed the Provisional Law Punishing Counterrevolutionaries to prevent efforts to overthrow the government or other political crimes. In the 1930s, the GMD promulgated more laws such as the Self-surrendering Law of the Communists that applied penalties ranging from ten-year incarceration to death against any person who plotted to disturb social security.[28] In Shanghai, GMD police collaborated with foreign concessions and local courts in campaigns arresting Communists. According to Frederic Wakeman Jr, courts in Shanghai concessions asked local police to arrest suspected Communists on a list sent by GMD provincial government. Moreover, GMD agents under spymaster Dai Li had virtually full power and impunity in detaining and torturing Communist suspects.[29]

From its inception, the CCP judicial system was built amid a life-and-death military struggle with the GMD. The CCP's overriding goal was survival on which the Party could create an army and judicial system. To ensure

25 Qiang Fang, *Chinese Complaint Systems: Natural Resistance* (Abingdon: Routledge, 2013): Ch. 5.

26 For a good study of Li Dazhao see Maurice Meisner, *Li Ta-Chao and the Origins of Chinese Marxism* (Cambridge, Ma: Harvard University Press, 1967).

27 For the politicization of the GMD judicial system see Xiaoqun Xu, *Trial of Modernity: Judicial Reform in Early Twentieth-Century China, 1901-1937* (Stanford: Stanford University Press, 2008).

28 Liu Hengwen刘恒妏, Revolution and Counterrevolution: A Study on the GMD Law in the Period of Nanjing Nationalist Government (*geming/fangeming: Nanjing guomin zhengfu shiqi guomindang defalü lunshu*革命/反革命：南京国明政府时期国民党的法律论述) in Wang Pengxiang王鹏翔, ed., *Legal Thoughts and Social Vicissitudes in 2008* (*2008 falü sixiang yushehui bianqian* 2008法律思想与社会变迁) (Taiwan: Academia Sinica, 2008): 255-304.

29 Frederic Wakeman, Jr., *Policing Shanghai, 1927-1937* (Berkeley: University of California Press, 1995): 176-177, 250-251.

its security, the CCP used its army and judicial system to brutally suppress alleged counterrevolutionary cliques and organizations. In 1942, as tensions with the GMD mounted, the CCP launched an internal struggle against suspected GMD and Japanese agents within the party. Like its dynastic and Republican predecessors, the Communists maintained and nurtured an ingrained and constant fear of opposition well beyond its victory in 1949.

From the Korean War (1950-1953) until the end of the Cultural Revolution (1966-1976), China experienced a number of major internal campaigns. Most of them stemmed from fears of external threats (the Korean War) and internal sabotage (of GMD agents or other class enemies). In the Anti-Rightist Movement alone (1957-1958), hundreds of thousands of alleged "rightists" or counterrevolutionaries were prosecuted, imprisoned, or forced to do hard labor. The Cultural Revolution has been described as the worst era in the PRC for legal practice, and its first two years (1966-1967) were filled with excessive and unchecked violence as well as a dysfunctional judicial system.[30] To make its judicial system more effective in combatting class enemies and averting counterrevolutionary sabotage, the Party in early 1968 moved to put the judicial system under military control. As a result, many political critics of Party leaders were convicted and punished with long imprisonment or even death. Even Mao's death in 1976 and the subsequent reforms failed to liberate the Party from the persistent fear of losing power. As we will find out in the Conclusion, the fear remains active in China today.

To be sure, harsh judicial policies and punishments triggered by fear of political disruption or subversion are not confined to China. In many countries, be they authoritarian or democratic, courts and police can sometimes be used to prosecute and punish suspects thought to be posing imminent or potential threats. A good example is the former Soviet Union ruled by Joseph Stalin. As Eugenia Belova and Paul Gregory have pointed out, most crimes for Stalin were against himself. In other words, for Stalin, almost any crime could generate uneasiness. To stave off his fear and potential threats, Stalin imposed expansive and ruthless terror. Even minor economic crimes such as petty theft or accidental misdemeanors could be severely punished.[31] In the Great Terror (1937-1938) alone, more than one million people died by execution or as a result of poor conditions in the Gulag.[32]

30 For more details about the law in the Cultural Revolution see Chapter 7.

31 Eugenia Belova and Paul Gregory, "Political Economy of Crime and Punishment under Stalin" in *Public Choice*, Vol. 140, No. 3/4 (Sep., 2009), pp. 463-478: 464.

32 James Harris, *The Great Terror: Stalin's Terror of the 1930s* (Oxford: Oxford University Press, 2016): 1.

From 1940 to his death, Stalin's terror continued as an average of 19,000 people lost their lives each year and the annual prison sentences were five times that of the US rate.[33] The Soviet judicial system that had since Lenin been a legitimate "tool for implementing" Bolshevik orders,[34] now became an active accomplice of the dictator Stalin who implemented the terror and arbitrary trials and punishments.[35]

Democratic countries including the United States are not at all immune from insecurity or the fear of subversion, by communism for instance. In extreme times, democratic governments could still employ rigorous laws and the established judicial system against alleged anarchists or subversives. One of the best cases was the spread of McCarthyism during the early 1950s when the "fear of communism" spread widely among millions of ordinary citizens in the United States. At the height of the Cold War, almost any Communist or even any critic of the US government could be viewed as a Soviet agent. In 1947, President Truman announced a federal loyalty program that virtually made "both domestic and international communism the enemy of American democracy."[36] University professors advocating socialism or even liberalism would be warned or laid off.[37] Seeing communism as "a phantom that conjured a myriad of demonic images," lawmakers in the Capitol created the House Un-American Activities Committee to interrogate witnesses and impugn citizens' loyalty to the country.[38] The anti-communist sentiment was so strong that the supposedly independent and powerful Supreme Court justices had to retreat in the mid-1950s from their previous favorable decisions toward accused communists. According to Robert M. Lichman, the Supreme Court had also tweaked its decisions under political pressure shortly after World War One.[39] If the United States, a supposed exemplar of democracy, could not always uphold its cherished judicial independence in times of political repression,

33 Eugenia Belova and Paul Gregory, 2009: 464-465.

34 For Soviet law and judicial system see Peter H. Solomon, *Soviet Criminal Justice Under Stalin* (Cambridge: Cambridge University Press, 1996): 17.

35 Thurston, 1998: 16-58.

36 M.J. Heale, *McCarthy's Americans: Red Scare Politics in State and Nation, 1935-1965* (Georgia: University of Georgia Press, 1998): 3.

37 Ellen Schrecker, "McCarthyism: Political Repression and the Fear of Communism" in *Social Research*, Vol. 71, No. 4, Fear: Its Political Uses & Abuses (Winter, 2004), pp. 1041-1086: 1060-1068.

38 William M. Tuttle, Jr., "Red Summer, Red Scare" in William Graeber and Leonard Richards, eds., *The American Record: Images of the Nation's Past, Vol. II* (Boston: McGraw Hill, 2001), pp. 175-192.

39 Robert M. Lichtman, *The Supreme Court and McCarthy-Era Repression: One Hundred Decisions* (Urbana: University of Illinois Press, 2012): 3-8.

it would be less likely for other states, especially so-called authoritarian regimes, to do so. It should be noted that there is still a crucial difference between a Soviet judicial system and its counterpart in the US. In China, the judicial system was from the outset built as a state tool to defend the Party by all means necessary, including force, while the judicial system in the US was originally created as an independent body sharing authority with the legislative and executive branches and helping to maintain a balance of political power.

Legal Hodgepodge

W.E. Butler has argued that Soviet law and the Soviet legal system are "comprehensible only against the background of their past: what was rejected, what was transformed, what has endured."[40] This argument can be applied to the legal system in Communist China. In other words, it is impossible to have a better grasp of the PRC judicial system without knowing its rich and profound historical heritage. In February 1949, about six months before the founding of the PRC, CCP leaders declared that it would scrap all "reactionary" GMD laws and replace them with "people's" laws. For the CCP, the GMD along with its laws was emblematic of reaction, capitalism, and imperialism, which conflicted with both the goals and principles of a new China.[41] However solemn the pledge, throughout Mao's China, the law and judicial system of the PRC had failed to sever itself from either traditional laws or GMD laws. As this book will show, the PRC laws under Mao were at best a judicial hodgepodge carrying laws and legal traditions not just from dynastic China and the Soviet Union but also from the GMD and Western countries that the CCP had vehemently denounced.

In 1973, while China was experiencing the Cultural Revolution, radical Party leaders organized a group of scholars from Peking and Tsinghua universities, to compose articles against Confucius and Lin Biao. Lin was the former successor of Mao and an alleged advocate of Confucianism.[42] Some individual criminals in this hyper-political era learned to attribute their crimes to the "poisonous inculcation" of Confucianism to evade heavier

40 W.E. Butler, *Soviet Law* (London: Butterworths, 1983): 9.

41 For CCP's order see *Studying Documents for People's Judicial Construction* (*renmin sifa jianshe xuexi wenjian*人民司法建设学习文件) (Beijing: Zhongyang sifa jiguan sifa gaige bangongshi, 1952): 8-12.

42 Fan Daren, *The Rise and Fall of the Royal Pens in the Cultural Revolution: The History of Liangxiao* (Hong Kong: Mingbao chubanshe, 1999).

punishment.[43] Nevertheless, the CCP might not have been aware or willing to admit that the PRC judicial system had actually preserved certain key Confucian legal concepts. The most conspicuous one is "Reform through Labor (*laogai*)" that aims to reeducate criminals to become good men. As Frank Dikotter has remarked, prison in China was a "modern tool to pursue a more traditional vision of an ordered and cohesive social body governed by virtue."[44] The "traditional vision" is what Confucius once said: "If a [ruler] governs people with virtue and disciplines them with ritual, people will develop a sense of shame and refrain from transgressing the law."[45] While the idea of reforming prisoners started in the early Republic of China, the CCP added hard labor, another traditional punishment, to the reform that it believed would be both reformative and profitable.[46]

Mediation is arguably another legal practice that the CCP inherited from Confucianism. In the words of Randle Peerenboom, China's emphasis on mediation could be a "traditional cum Confucian preference for harmony and face-saving."[47] Moreover, like Confucius who tried in 513 BCE to dissuade a Jin minister from publicizing law, Mao's China also seemed to have a distrust of or hostility to crucial written laws.[48] Apart from a handful of laws such as a constitution, an organic law of the court, and some government regulations including an anti-counterrevolutionary one, the PRC had no criminal law, civil law, and many other crucial laws (e.g. criminal procedural law) until 1979. The main difference between Mao and Confucius might be that the former feared that written laws could restrict the CCP's arbitrary punishments, while the latter was afraid that people with more legal knowledge would disrespect elites and dodge laws. As Jennifer Altehenger has argued,

43 In 1971, one Meng Qinghe was sentenced to five years for theft. Before his prison term was over, Meng wrote a confession in which he blamed his crime on Confucianism. See "The Criminal Verdict of Meng Qinghe by the Zhangqiu County Military Control Commission" in the Archives of the Liangshan County, May 30, 1971. Y-8-15-1976.

44 Frank Dikotter, *Crime, Punishment and the Prison in Modern China* (New York: Columbia University Press, 2002): 7-8.

45 Zhu Xi朱熹, ed, *Collective Connotation of the Four Books* (*sishu zhangju jizhu*四书章句集注) (Liaoning: Liaoning jiaoyu chubanshe, 1998): 55.

46 For more information about PRC hard labor in prisons see Harry Wu, *Laogai: The Chinese Gulag* (Boulder: Westview Press, 1992)

47 Randle Peerenboom, *China's Long March toward Rule of Law* (Cambridge: Cambridge University Press, 2002): 288.

48 Creel, 1980, pp. 26-55: 51; Yang Bojun, ed., *The History of Zuo* (*zuozhuan*) (Beijing: Zhonghua shujü, 2018): 1314; for Mao's distrust of law see Daniel Leese and Puck Engman, *Victims, Perpetrators, and the Role of Law in Maoist China: A Case Study* (Berlin: Walter de Gruyter GmbH & Co KG, 2018): 10; Li Rui李锐, *Arguments of Li Rui* (*Lirui lunshuo wenxuan*李锐论说文选) (Beijing: Zhongguo shehui kexue chubanshe 1998): 178.

the history of law in the PRC is marked by "extremes." On the one hand, people were inundated with legal education on a few laws such as the 1950 Marriage Law and the 1954 constitution; on the other hand, state agents and ordinary people routinely "broke or circumvented laws."[49]

In contrast to Confucianism, legalism may have had a greater impact on the PRC's laws. Lord Shang (c. 395-338 BCE), a renowned legalist, stressed the importance of heavy punishments and light rewards. In his words, "[N]othing is better than heavy punishment in deterring evils and crimes [...]. If harsh penalty is applied, people will not dare to transgress the law."[50] This is what Lord Shang meant when he advocated using punishment to end punishment (*yixing quxing*) and why the great historian Sima Qian categorized legalism as a form of Daoism.[51] Han Feizi, the most erudite legalist, unswervingly backed Lord Shang's heavy punishment. "If a ruler loves his people, he will adopt heavy punishment and light reward," Han noted, "although heavy punishments are resented by people, they help a state to attain better government."[52] In political campaigns before and after the PRC was created, millions of people had reportedly been detained, imprisoned, tortured, or even executed. As this book will show, many people – especially those with "historical stains" – would be sentenced to years of incarceration for petty misconduct such as praying for rain, dropping Mao's books, or unintentionally chanting a false slogan. The CCP might believe that harsh punishments would, as Lord Shang had argued, generate fear and thus "end punishment."

Another similarity between the PRC judicial system and legalism is collective punishment (*lianzuo*). Lord Shang once said if any official violated state law he would be executed along with all the three-kinship of his family.[53] When Lord Shang ruled the Qin, he made people responsible for each other's crimes. People failing to expose their neighbors' treachery would be killed. The exposer/s would be rewarded in "the same [way] as [he/they would be for] killing an enemy in a battle."[54] Despite persisting criticism of legalism for its harsh penalties in succeeding dynasties, collective punishment was

49 Jennifer Altehenger, *Legal Lessons: Popularizing Laws in the People's Republic, 1949-1989* (Cambridge, Ma: Harvard East Asian Monograph, 2018): 3.

50 Lord Shang商鞅, *Book of Lord Shang* (*shangjunshu*商君书) (Shanghai: Shanghai sanlian shudian, 2018: 152; also see Mühlhahn, 2011: 21.

51 Sima Qian司马迁, *Historical Records* (*shiji*史记) (Beijing: Zhonghua shujü, 1959): Ch. 63.

52 Han Fei韩非, translated by Zhang Jue张觉, *Han Feizi* 韩非子(Guizhou: Guizhou renmin chubanshe, 1992): 189.

53 Lord Shang商鞅, 2018: 173. Three Kinship includes parents, brothers, and wife/children.

54 Sima Qian司马迁, 1959: Ch. 68.

largely retained in Mao's China. Children from black-category families would suffer punishment and discrimination because their relatives had been subjected to struggle sessions. For instance, after Liang Heng's mother was declared a rightist in 1957, his father immediately demanded a divorce to protect his children from being discriminated against in access to education. According to the Yunnan Provincial gazetteers, if CCP cadres in the Cultural Revolution found that some targeted landlords and rich peasants had died, they would struggle their children instead. Regardless of what they had done, the cadres would first beat them. If anyone expressed any "bad attitude" (i.e. resistance), he or she would be beaten to death.[55]

To be sure, early PRC's adoption of Confucian and legalist concepts was selective and not comprehensive. Unlike Confucius who demanded that punishment be exactly right, many judges in Mao's China and beyond exercised punishments based on their "common sense" rather than by law or reason.[56] By imposing heavy penalties on black-category people or counterrevolutionaries, Mao's China deviated from both legalism's principle of "one punishment for all (*yixing*)" and its own laws such as the constitution of 1954 and the Organic Law of the Courts.

In addition to Confucianism and legalism, remnants of some other traditional or "feudal" customs and practices could also be found in the aspirationally socialist PRC. As in the dynasties when death penalties were conducted in open markets (*qishi*), the PRC continued to struggle and execute alleged criminals in public meetings and venues.[57] While the PRC nominally attempted to reestablish the institution of lawyers in the early 1950s, most alleged political criminals, if not all, could not find lawyers who were willing to defend them. This is reminiscent of what litigation masters experienced in the dynasties. The biggest difference might be that lawyers or litigation tricksters were outside the law in the dynasties but were nominally "legal" in the PRC.[58]

55 *Yunnan Provincial Gazette Vol. 55. Gazetter of Trial* (*Yunnansheng shenpanzhi*云南省审判志) (Yunan: Yunnan renmin chubanshe, 1999): 256.

56 Mühlhahn, 2011: 18.

57 For Mao's China see Harold Tanner, *Strike Hard: Anti-Crime Campaigns and Chinese Criminal Justice, 1979-1985* (Cornell: Cornell University Press, 1999); for executions in the Qing see Brook, Bourgon, and Blue, 2008; for recent public trials and executions see "Do Not Perform the Drama of Public Exposition and Death Trials (*sixing xuanpan shizhongju biezai jixu shangyanle*)" in *Xinjinbao*, December 18, 2017.

58 See Melissa Macauley, *Social Power and Legal Culture: Litigation Masters in Late Imperial China* (Stanford: Stanford University Press, 1998); Max Weber, *Confucianism and Daoism* (*rujiao hedaojiao*) (Beijing: Shangwu yinshuguan, 1998): 157; Stanley Lubman, *Bird in a Cage: Legal Reform in China after Mao* (Stanford: Stanford University Press, 2000): 29; Sida Liu, "With or Without

Ever since the early PRC, court cadres were subject to the dual leadership of their peer local governments and higher-level courts.[59] After the 1952 legal reform, most new judges would be appointed by the Party for their loyalty to the Party and not for their professional competence in the law. We can see the precedence in dynasties when local officials versed in Confucian texts acted as both "people's parental officials" and as judges who had no legal training but had to deal with lawsuits.[60] Dynastic magistrates typically sought confessions as conclusive evidence of guilt, and cadres in the Communist base areas and the PRC continued the same practices.[61] For centuries, dynastic rulers had consecutively treated civil conflicts as minor cases and many rulers in the Ming and Qing forbade people to appeal civil cases in the capital.[62] In Mao's China, the CCP considered most civil cases as internal contradictions among the people that should be resolved via mediation. As some chapters of this book will indicate, most of the cases adjudicated by people's courts were counterrevolutionary or political cases. Only a small proportion of the cases was related to marriage, property, or debt.

Scholars such as Mark C. Elliott and Pär Cassel have discussed legal privileges of the Manchus in the Qing,[63] which apparently hark back to eight categories of legal privileges (*bayi*) in the Zhou.[64] There were also similar legal privileges in the PRC for certain special groups of people which have not been previously mentioned in scholarly works. In Chapter 5, we will find that the Shanghai government in 1954 explicitly excluded eight groups of

the Law: The Changing Meaning of Ordinary Legal Work in China, 1979-2003" in Margret Y.K. Woo and Mary E. Gallagher, eds., *Chinese Justice: Civil Dispute Resolution in Contemporary China* (Cambridge: Cambridge University Press, 2011), pp. 234-268: 234.

59 *Shaanxi Provincial Gazette – Judicial Gazette* (*Shanxishengzhi shenpanzhi*) (Shaanxi: Shanxi Renmin chubanshe, 1994): 202.

60 Lubman, 2000: 29.

61 For abusive confessions in the Qing dynasty see William Alford, 1984. "Of Arsenic and Old Laws: Looking Anew at Criminal Justice in Late Imperial China" in *California Law Review*, Vol. 72, No. 6 (Dec., 1984), pp. 1180-1256.

62 Qiang Fang, "Hot Potatoes: Chinese Complaint Systems from Early Times to 1898" in *The Journal of Asian Studies*, Vol. 68, No. 4 (November) 2009: 1105-35. For studies on judicial status of civil cases in the Qing see Philip Huang, "Codified Law and Magisterial Adjudication in the Qing" in Kathryn Bernhardt and Philip Huang, eds., *Civil Law in Qing and Republican China* (Stanford: Stanford University Press, 1994), pp. 142-186: 143.

63 Mark C. Elliott, *The Manchu Way: The Eight Banners and Ethnic Identity in Late Imperial China* (Stanford: Stanford University Press, 2001); Pär Cassel, "Excavating Extraterritoriality: The 'Judicial Sub-Prefect' as a Prototype for the Mixed Court in Shanghai" in *Late Imperial China*, Vol. 24, No. 2 (Dec., 2003), pp. 156-180.

64 Sun Yirang, annotates. *The Ritual of the Zhou Dynasty* (*zhouli zhengyi*) (Beijing: Zhonghua shujü, 2015): 3340.

"important people" from being punished without governmental approval. There is no little irony that the constitution in the same year pledged to recognize the equality of all citizens before the law. This contradiction reminds one of that between the phraseology of the American declaration of independence and the institution of slavery in the early decades of the United States. Even more discordant was the persistence of the traditional marriage custom of "seven outs and three exceptions (*qichu sanbuqu*)"[65] well into the Cultural Revolution when all old customs and laws were supposed to be smashed, let alone its violation of the highly promoted new marriage law in 1950 that purportedly accorded women the same rights as men in divorce and marriage proceedings (Chapter 7).

While the CCP swore to relinquish all of the GMD's capitalist laws and legal institutions, it nonetheless inherited some GMD laws. The most evident was its new marriage law in 1950, which, according to Susan L. Glosser, was "nearly identical" to a civil code issued by the GMD in 1931, almost twenty years earlier. "In fact," Glosser points out, "the CCP Marriage Law resembled the GMD code of 1931 in both its particulars and objectives."[66] Moreover, many provisions of the PRC's 1954 constitution and the Organizational Law of Courts. such as people's rights and judicial independence, were akin to laws of numerous Republican constitutions since 1912.

As a party owing much of its birth, development, and even conquest of mainland China to the Soviet Union, the CCP inevitably sought to duplicate Soviet models including its judicial systems. According to Jerome A. Cohen, "Many of the norms that continued to be enforced, such as the proscribed counterrevolutionary acts, are of obvious Soviet origin." Moreover, the PRC's application of the criminal law, its procuracy, and its labor camps also came from Soviet models.[67] Indeed, as early as the Jiangxi Soviet base areas, the Chinese Red Army had adopted Soviet "Cheka" or political police. In the same period, the CCP created the *laogai* system or labor camp, which were patterned after the Soviet *gulag*. More important, the CCP from its outset

65 The seven outs are the seven reasons for a husband to divorce his wife, such as barrenness, wanton conduct, neglect of parents-in-law, garrulousness, theft, jealousy, incurable disease; Three exceptions are that the wife has nowhere to go, within the three-year mourning period, or her husband was poor when married and is now rich. See Hugh D.R. Baker, *Chinese Family and Kinship* (London: The Macmillan Press, 2015): 45.

66 Susan L. Glosser, *Chinese Visions of Family and State, 1915-1953* (Berkeley: University of California Press, 2003): 170; also see Xiaoping Cong, *Marriage, Law and Gender in Revolutionary China* (Cambridge: Cambridge University Press, 2018): 246.

67 Jerome A. Cohen, *The Criminal Process in the People's Republic of China, 1949-1963: An Introduction* (Cambridge, Ma: Harvard University Press, 1968): 11-13.

had learned from Lenin's arguments about the legal system and its role in a Communist polity.[68] Like its Soviet "big brother," the CCP made law an instrument of state authority and went further than the Soviets by singling out class enemies such as, inter alia, counterrevolutionaries, landlords, rich peasants, former GMD agents and officials. They were all the main targets of law who should be "controlled by dictatorial means."[69]

Nevertheless, the CCP also copied some positive legal apparatuses from the Soviet Union. For example, one of them was people's jury that the Soviet inherited from Russia's 1864 legal reform.[70] The CCP adopted the system in the base areas and expanded it to the whole country shortly after it took control of the mainland.[71] The other was the institution of lawyers ushered in after the 1952 legal reform, notwithstanding that its power, impartiality, and function were compromised under Party rule. The 1954 constitution was also "influenced profoundly" by the 1936 Soviet Constitution.[72]

With regard to Soviet law, according to Cohen, CCP leaders "had never felt comfortable about the decision to import the Soviet judicial model."[73] Rather, the Party took a largely utilitarian approach by adopting what it deemed useful to strengthen its power and rejecting what it thought harmful to its rule. It was more forthright in its selectivity after Stalin's death and the elevation of the prestige of the newly established PRC which forced the United States to sign an armistice agreement in Korea. In late 1955, while a head of the Shanghai High Court praised the succinctness, explicitness, and logic of Soviet court verdicts, he warned Chinese judges not to blindly copy the Soviet model. Instead, they should learn the spirit of Soviet law and "maintain both flexibility and legality" in adjudication. In other words, Chinese judges did not have to stick to the codes of law as rigorously as their Soviet counterparts had done.[74]

For instance, at the behest of Lenin, the Bolsheviks promulgated a criminal code in 1922, one year after the inauguration of the New Economic Policy. However dysfunctional the Soviet criminal law was during Stalin's rule, it

68 Solomon, 1996: 17-19; Gong Tingtai 龚廷泰and Wang Jianguo 王建国, "Lenin's Judicial Thought and its Historical Value (*Lienin desifa sixiang jiqi shidai jiazhi*列宁的司法思想及其时代价值)" in *Falü kexue*法律科学, Vol. 6, 2008, pp. 9-16: 12; Butler, 1983: 27-28.

69 Altehenger, 2018: 8.

70 Butler, 1983: 25.

71 Gong and Wang, 2008: 15.

72 Shiping Hua, *Chinese Legal Culture and Constitutional Order* (Abingdon: Routledge, 2018): Ch. 6; also see Peerenboom, 2002: 44.

73 Cohen, 1968: 14.

74 "The Report of Deputy Head Gao Kelin at the Shanghai High Court (*Gao Kelin fuyuanzhang zai Shanghai gaoji fayuan debaogao*)" in the Shanghai Archives, B2-1-14-24. November 1, 1955.

provided certain protection to Soviet citizens. Yet the CCP consistently refused to promulgate a comparable law until 1979, 30 years after its establishment. In addition, the Soviet government generally prohibited local cadres from directly intervening in specific cases. In the PRC, however, the Party demanded that local officials review and approve court decisions before they were enforced. Other Soviet models that the PRC turned down or was unwilling to adopt were legal concepts such as judicial independence and nonretroactivity. They were dismissed by the CCP as Western capitalist principles.[75]

The Judicial Pendulum

Another striking feature of the Communist judicial system in Mao's China was its swing between "right" and "left" in compliance with central policies. There have been many studies of the politics, society, leaders, and economy of the PRC.[76] There have been many fewer studies of the law and legal history of the PRC. Even fewer studies have discussed the law in the Soviet base period (1927-1935) and the Yan'an or Border Region period (1936-1947). Western and Chinese scholars such as Randle Peerenboom, Stanley Lubman, Albert Chen, Hongyi Chen, Bin Liang, Xin Ren, and Yan Wang have both deepened and broadened our understandings of China's legal reform under Deng Xiaoping and his successors.[77] While their books are centered on contemporary legal reform in China, those scholars have traced Chinese law to its historical origins and tradition in the dynasties and the Republican periods. Peerenboom, Lubman, and Ren have also discussed Chinese law prior to 1978.

75 Cohen, 1968: 15-16.

76 Most of the studies have spilled over the general history under Mao and post-Mao reform leaders such as Deng Xiaoping and Jiang Zemin. Some have also focused on specific periods such as the Great Famine, the Cultural Revolution, the Anti-Rightist Movement, the Gang of Four, the student movements, and the like.

77 See Peerenboom, 2002; Lubman, 2000; Stanley Lubman, *The Evolution of Law Reform in China: An Uncertain Path* (New York: Edward Elgar, 2012); Stanley Lubman, ed., *China's Legal Reform* (Oxford: Oxford University Press, 1996); John Gillespie, Albert Chen, and Hongyi Chen, eds., *Legal Reforms in China and Vietnam: A Comparison of Asian Communist Regimes* (Abingdon: Routledge, 2010); Bin Liang, *The Changing Chinese Legal System, 1978-Present: Centralization of Power and Rationalization of the Legal System* (Abingdon: Routledge, 2008); Bin Liang and Hong Lu, eds., *The Death Penalty in China: Policy, Practice, and Reform* (New York: Columbia University Press, 2015); Xin Ren, *Tradition of the Law and Law of the Tradition: Law, State, and Social Control in China* (New York: Praeger, 1997) ; Yan Wang, *Chinese Legal Reform: The Case of Foreign Investment Law* (Abingdon: Routledge, 2004).

Among these studies, Jerome Cohen's book on the criminal process in the early PRC remains a classic. Based on a great number of interviews of Chinese exiles, Cohen paints a preliminary picture of the PRC criminal justice from the 1950s through the early 1960s.[78] In recent years, thanks to newly available primary materials, some historians have done excellent studies on specific topics of law in Communist China. For example, Klaus Mühlhahn has made an in-depth study of labor camps in the PRC.[79] Xiaoping Cong has examined the new marriage law in the Yan'an period with a focus on a case of Liu Qiaoer and a distinction between free marriage and self-determined marriage.[80] Jennifer Altehenger's book centers on legal education and CCP propaganda in the 1950s to propagate the 1950 Marriage Law and the 1954 constitution. She pinpoints a dilemma of the CCP's official promotion of mass legal education. Although the CCP has wanted to disseminate legal knowledge among the masses in order to persuade them to obey the law, the Party has also wanted to retain control of "how laws were interpreted and how laws would serve the state."[81]

In his study of Communist police, Michael Dutton discovers that the friend/enemy binary originated in the Jiangxi Soviet period when the CCP was besieged by the GMD army. Dutton argues that the binary "completely dominated" CCP thinking from 1927 to 1978.[82] Glenn Tiffert has done a comprehensive study on the Beijing Municipal People's Court, but his focus is mostly on the origin, organization, development, and practice of the local court from the CCP border period in Shaanxi to 1958. He argues that the PRC judicial system bore a "concealed and congenital Republican imprint" that ignores the "humanity and [Communist] principle" that many CCP judges had utilized since the Yan'an period when there was no law. Apart from a few chapters that discuss the judicial system in other parts of the PRC, Tiffert fails to notice the wide disparities among different provinces/cities in the PRC, let alone the huge differences between major cities such as Beijing and the countryside.

In a recent book edited by Daniel Leese and Puck Engman, scholars have used specific cases of victims of political campaigns to explore the role, process, and enforcement of law in Mao's China. Both Xu Lizhi and Jeremy Brown have challenged the conventional view that the Cultural Revolution

78 Cohen, 1968.

79 Mühlhahn, 2011.

80 Xiaoping Cong, 2018.

81 Altehenger, 2018: 3.

82 Michael Dutton, *Policing Chinese Politics: A History* (Duke: Duke University Press, 2005): 13-19.

was lawless.[83] Although the bulk of their studies is about the legal systems in the Republican periods, Frank Dikotter and Susan L. Glosser have briefly touched on the prison and marriage law in the early PRC.[84]

The biggest obstacle to research on the law and judicial system in Mao's China has long been the limited accessibility of archival court records.[85] For a long time, the CCP has tightly controlled the release of legal and political archives as well as official documents. Like their Western colleagues, Chinese scholars on Communist law generally face the same hostile situation. General studies on the history of Chinese law in China have had to skip the legal history of Mao's China.[86] Scholars who have covered the law in Mao's China including the turbulent periods in the late 1950s and the Cultural Revolution may be critical of its violations of law, but they would normally maintain positive views on the legal reform under Deng Xiaoping.[87] As a safe haven, many Chinese scholars intend to narrow their studies to a single legal case or a particular topic such as the 1952 legal reform or the Great Leap Forward (1958-1960) to avoid political consequences.[88] Consequently, much of the law in Mao's China has been understudied and our comprehension of the legal history in this crucial period remains limited and sometimes wrong.

83 Xu Lizhi, "Beyond 'Destruction' and 'Lawlessness': The Legal System during the Cultural Revolution" in Daniel Leese and Puck Engman, *Victims, Perpetrators, and the Role of Law in Maoist China*, pp. 25-51; Jeremy Brown, "A Policeman, His Gun, and an Alleged Rape: Competing Appeals for Justice in Tianjin" in Leese and Engman, 2018, pp. 127-149.

84 Dikotter, 2002; Glosser, 2003.

85 Leese and Engman, 2018: 6.

86 See Zeng Xianyi曾宪义, *History of Chinese Legal System* (*zhongguo fazhishi*中国法制史) (Beijing: Beijing daxue chubanshe, 2002); Ye Xiaoxin叶孝信, *History of Chinese Legal System* (*zhongguo fazhishi*中国法制史) (Shanghai: Fudan daxue chubanshe, 2002).

87 Gong Pixiang公丕祥, ed., *China's Current Legal Revolution* (*zhongguo dangdai defalü geming* 当代中国的法律革命) (Beijing: Falü chubanshe, 1999); Xin Chunying信春鹰, *Chinese Legal System and its Reform* (*Zhongguode falü zhidu jiqi gaige*中国的法律制度及其改革) (Beijing: Falü chubanshe, 1999).

88 See for example, Huang Wenzhi黄文治, "Conflict among Local Officials and Judicial Interference in the Great Leap Forward: Centering on the Case of Fang Shixin in Feixi County (*dayuejin shiqi jiceng ganbu chongtu jisifa jieru: yi Feixixian Fang Shixin anwei zhongxin*大跃进时期基层干部冲突及司法介入)" in *Anhui shixue*, Vol. 2, No. 22, 2016; Li Yusheng, "Legal Reform Movement (*sifa gaige yundong*)" in *Faxue yanjiu*, September 1999, pp. 49-54; Chen Guangzhong 陈光中 and Zeng Xinhua曾新华, "A Review of the Legal Reform Movement in the Early PRC (*jianguo chuqi sifa gaige yundong shuping*建国初期司法改革运动述评)" in *Faxuejia*, No. 6, 2009, pp. 1-8; Li Lu李露, "Rethinking the Situation and Policy of the 'Coordination of Repression and Magnanimity' (*zhenya yu kuanda xiangjiehe xingshi zhengce fansi*镇压与宽大相结合刑事政策反思)" in *Renmin luntan*, 2014. 3, pp. 33-38.

Due to the paucity or lack of primary sources, there has not yet been any serious and in-depth study of the complexities and dynamics of the Chinese Communist judicial system in such periods as the 1955 anti-counterrevolutionary campaigns, the Anti-Rightist Movement, the Great Leap Forward, and the Cultural Revolution. The lack of evidence and vivid legal cases has led to mistaken interpretations. For example, with few open archives of legal records of the PRC judicial system, some scholars in China and the West are inclined to argue that the period between 1953 and 1956 was a "golden age" or consider the PRC judicial system as an "heir" to Republican judicial modernization, ignoring the imbedded tradition of Chinese law dating back to the dynasties.[89] Similarly, most scholars dismiss the Cultural Revolution as a period of legal nihilism or even lawlessness which was worse than any other periods in the PRC. Building on both rare and newly available primary legal archives and official documents as well as on existing scholarship on PRC law, this book centers on the Communist judicial system from CCP's base areas to the end of the Cultural Revolution in 1976. Unlike studies focusing more on the normal judicial organization and operation on one city or one legal practice, this book, drawing numerous new court trials and litigation accounts, will probe deeply into the daily court files and functions, the contradictions and dilemmas faced by judges, the incongruity between central judicial policies and county court judgments, and the dynamic dichotomies between major cities like Shanghai and poorer or remote regions/counties.

As this book will show, the Communist judicial system originated in a period when the CCP was overwhelmed by a fundamental fear of its possible extinction at the hands of a superior nationalist military force. From its inception, therefore, the aim of the judicial system was to safeguard the Party and to crack down on its enemies. During the Yan'an period when the CCP acknowledged Chiang Kai-shek as the sole national leader so as to form a coalition against the Japanese, it had the opportunity to reconstruct its judicial system and develop its own legal mechanism. Unlike in the Jiangxi Soviet period which had few laws, Communist judges in the Border Region period began to adopt key Republican laws in dealing with cases. Emerging as a victor of the civil war in 1949, an assertive CCP denounced all

89 Julia Strauss has correctly argued that the early PRC was not a golden age. But her argument is based on PRC politics and not its law. The details of the "golden age" will be discussed in Chapter 5. For the argument about the "heir" see Tiffert, 2015: xxvi. For Strauss see Julia Strauss, "Morality, Coercion and State Building by Campaign in the Early PRC: Regime Consolidation and After, 1949-1956" in *The China Quarterly*, No. 188. The History of the PRC (1949-1976) (Dec., 2006), pp. 891-912: 894.

GMD laws and vowed to replace them with socialist codes. Yet, GMD laws and retained judges and lawyers still dominated PRC judicial system until the outbreak of the Korean War. As a result, counterrevolutionaries were initially treated magnanimously as normal criminals and their punishments were mostly fairly light. Then, suddenly facing both internal sabotage and an external war with the United States, the CCP abruptly reversed its erstwhile lenient polices and launched merciless anti-counterrevolutionary crackdowns. The military commissions as well as regular courts ordered arbitrary executions and imprisonments of alleged counterrevolutionaries. In 1952, as the war dragged on, the CCP moved forward to strengthen its power by purging former GMD judges and lawyers from its judicial system along with their "capitalist legal principles" such as judicial independence and the supremacy of law.

Shortly after the armistice in Korea, top CCP leaders tried to restore some common legal principles that they had denounced two years earlier. Both the first PRC constitution and an organic law of the court in 1954 reaffirmed judicial independence and the equality of persons before the law. However, the return to judicial "normalcy" did not last long. When another anti-counterrevolutionary campaign began in the spring of 1955, judicial negligence and infringement of law were unbridled and brazen. Some provincial governments rendered judges a minimum of five years imprisonment for most counterrevolutionary actions. With the exception of one year from early 1956 to the summer of 1957, the Communist judicial system was soon engaged in a new campaign – the Anti-Rightist Movement, which proved to be larger in scale and more terrible in effect than past campaigns. The new round of repression did not taper off until the end of the Great Famine in 1961 when central leaders and the Supreme Court stepped in to restore legal principles and began rehabilitating victims who were falsely charged and punished. Despite law violations like in the Four Cleanups (*siqing*), the restoration of law generally proceeded until the eve of the Cultural Revolution.

Up to the present, the role of the judicial system and the daily practice of law in the Cultural Revolution remain little known. New court archives and documents reveal that judicial cadres were actively involved in the first two years of the Cultural Revolution (1966-1968). After the military took over the judicial system in early 1968, the judicial system resumed their function, albeit almost all the cases were criminal. The harsh treatment of "counterrevolutionary" critics of central leaders (e.g. Mao, Lin Biao, and Jiang Qing) reached its peak in 1970 and then started to diminish in 1971. Lin Biao's unexpected death in September 1971 and the reinstitution of moderate leaders (e.g. Deng Xiaoping) opened the door for rehabilitating victims who had been punished for criticizing Lin Biao and backing former chairman Liu Shaoqi. This wave of legal and political rectification carried on to the spring of 1976, just months before Mao's death and the end of the Cultural Revolution.

From the Jiangxi Soviet period in the 1920s to 1976, two years before the CCP kicked off the current legal reform, the Communist judicial system had become a pendulum which had frequently swung from upholding universal legal principles to adopting utilitarian legal policies. During relatively peaceful years or whenever the threat was not imminent, such as 1950, 1954, 1956-1957, early 1960s, and 1971-1976, the Party would lean toward common legal principles by shifting to lenient policies and correcting false charges and punishments. Once the political situation turned hostile and the Party's survival became precarious (e.g. 1951, 1955, 1957-60, 1966-1970), the Party would become alarmed and would quickly direct its judicial system to severely and often arbitrarily punish alleged enemies/criminals without having tangible evidence or rational reasons for doing so. In addition, it is fair to argue that Communist judges were not all the stereotyped "knife hilt" of the CCP who blindly followed Party policies. As this book will show, even in the darkest periods of political campaigns many judges strived to hold on to "erroneous" legal principles and their legal professionalism and refused to make whimsical charges and impose irrational punishments.

Sources and Chapters

This book is based primarily on newly accessible archives and myriad official materials. In the Shanghai Archives, probably the most open and comprehensive in China, I collected numerous court documents from the 1950s, including, among other things, court verdicts, meeting memos, speeches of national and municipal court leaders, judicial plans, criminals' confessions, and the like. Boasting one of the largest collections of materials on the Cultural Revolution in the world, the Chinese University of Hong Kong houses numerous provincial and county judicial gazetteers and detailed court chronicles and statistics. The Department of History at the Shanghai Jiaotong University possesses a good collection of rarely seen judicial archives of several counties in Shandong and Henan that cover the period from the early PRC to the late 1970s.

This book includes seven chapters each of which focuses on the Chinese Communist judicial system in one specific period. The first traces the origin of the Communist judicial system in its Jiangxi Soviet base area (c. 1927-1935). Facing repeated GMD military attacks, the CCP formed its own army and mobilized its judicial system to counter its internal and external enemies. Born in blood and fear, the primitive Communist judicial system in CCP bases was from its outset designed as an integral mechanism of the Party based on Marxist and Leninist theories. Its principal objective was to eliminate counterrevolutionaries and protect the fledgling Soviet base (i.e. elected body that was different from the Soviet Union). Alarmed by mass killings and brutal torture by Red armies, the CCP took steps to create a more formal judicial system after 1931 that was expected to comply with certain legal procedures. Still, the Communist judicial system was not independent of the Party. Alleged criminals' confessions, often under pressure including torture, remained the main basis of adjudication.

Many scholars in China have applauded the legal system and practices such as the Ma Xiwu method of dealing with rural marriage cases in the Shaanxi Border Region as a main pillar of the PRC legal construction. Chapter 2 challenges this view with an argument that those scholars have ignored the enormous number of arbitrary transgressions of the law, such as torture and imprisonment. Nor do those scholars pay much attention to the CCP's "voluntary" acceptance of Republican laws during the anti-Japanese war. In stark contrast to CCP's previous and ensuing anti-GMD propaganda and policies, the period of the Border Area could be better called an aberration from the Communist judicial tradition rather than a cornerstone.

After the CCP conquered mainland China, the Party did not immediately abolish all GMD laws and legal mechanisms as it had once vowed to do. As Chapter 3 shows, the Party chose instead to try to make a smooth transition in the judicial system by retaining most former Republican judges and lawyers. As a result, many "counterrevolutionaries" were tried and punished more leniently in accordance with Republican laws. The mild legal policy underwent an abrupt shift shortly after the eruption of the Korean War. Facing a possible GMD effort to retake the mainland, the military commissions, police, procuracy, and courts launched fierce sanctions against counterrevolutionaries with more forced labor and executions. Furthermore, the court reversed its previous balanced handling of disputes between workers and capitalists by siding with labor against management.

Chapter 4 outlines the Party's growing distrust of the retained GMD judges and lawyers. Using excuses such as the high proportion of retained judges in people's court and the halfheartedness of retained judges in advocating Party's legal policies during the Three-Antis and Five-Antis Movements, the Party in 1952 overhauled its legal system and dismissed most retained GMD judges and lawyers. To replace such court personnel, the Party enlisted progressive workers, military veterans, and students as future judges. Their political allegiance might have been impeccable, but they had little or no legal knowledge and training. This chapter argues that CCP's purge of former GMD judges was an intentional program clearly aimed at making the judicial system a more submissive and faithful instrument of the Party in future campaigns.

As the Korean War neared its end, the Communist judicial system pendulum began swinging to the right (liberal side) and reached its apogee in the fall of 1954 with the promulgation of the first Constitution and the Organic Law of the Court. Many scholars in China and the West therefore claim that the years between 1953 to 1957 were a "golden age" of the PRC. In fact, Chapter 5 argues that, with the exception of a short period from spring 1956 to early summer of 1957, this period was not much different from others. The widespread abuses of law, the use of torture, and the meting out of excessive punishment in the second anti-counterrevolutionary campaign of 1955-1956 were almost as bad as in the first one of 1951. Even after the Party called for righting the wrongs in 1956, official infringement of the law persisted in remote counties.

The role of the judicial system in the period from the Anti-Rightist Movement to the eve of the Cultural Revolution has been studied the least. Most scholarship has centered on the Anti-Rightist Movement, the Great Leap Forward, the 7000-Person Meeting, and the Four Cleanups. Chapter 6 explores a leap forward of law in this period and how judicial cadres in the three principal law-enforcing agencies (i.e. police, procuracy, and court) coordinated and fulfilled their revolutionary missions. It also examines the Communist judicial system in the early 1960s after the Party scaled back its severity and unlawful activities. But the era after the Great Famine was highly volatile and the Party policies were inconsistent and sometimes contradictory. My argument in this chapter is that the Communist judicial system swung between being a loyal Party instrument and honoring legal principles such as judicial independence and legal procedures.

The last chapter focuses on the role of the judicial system in the Cultural Revolution, an era that is often reduced to political turmoil, lawlessness, Red Guard brutality, and mass killings. Little ink has been spilled on describing the day-to-day function and practice of the judicial system in this significant period. In the first two years, the Communist judicial system was clouded by inaction and revolutionary chaos as judicial cadres were involved in factional fights but stayed mostly free of street violence. Starting from early

1968, the military took over the judicial system. Unlike local gazetteers that tend to emphasize the harsh punishments of military-controlled courts, local archives offer a more moderate picture of courts that is consistent with the early years of the PRC. As had happened several times in the past, the judicial rehabilitation began as early as 1970 and it lasted until the spring of 1976. While judicial and official violations of the law were excessive, they were not as egregious as in some other periods of Mao's China.

Triggered by fear of being crushed by the GMD, the CCP had from its cradle state-building era built a judicial system that was both powerful and obedient. The primary purpose of the Communist judicial system was to severely punish internal class enemies and other criminals. During relatively safe and peaceful times, the Party would try to stress partial legal principles such as judicial independence and legal process. The instrumental role of the Communist judicial system and its frequent oscillation from harshness to lenience and back continued throughout Mao's China. From 1949 to 1976, CCP's judicial policies often shifted from one side to the other to adapt to domestic and foreign political situations. The fear of losing power and swings of the judicial pendulum did not end with Mao's death. In the era of Deng Xiaoping and beyond, China has been undergoing one of its largest legal reforms ever with a promise of embracing the rule of law. Its judicial system, however, has continued to ignore laws by imposing draconian punishments against any person even remotely threatening Party rule. In that regard, so long as the CCP rules China, it will be unlikely to feel free from fear and its judicial system confident enough to embrace the rule of law.

1 Born in Blood

Origin of the Communist Judicial System in China, 1927-1935

Abstract

This chapter traces the origin of the Communist judicial system in its Jiangxi Soviet base area (c. 1927-1935). Facing repeated GMD military attacks, the CCP formed its own army and mobilized its judicial system to counter its internal and external enemies. Born in blood and fear, the primitive Communist judicial system in CCP bases was from its outset designed as an integral mechanism of the Party based on Marxist and Leninist theories. Its principal objective was to eliminate counterrevolutionaries and protect the fledgling Soviet base (i.e. elected body that was different from the Soviet Union). Alarmed by mass killings and brutal torture by Red armies, the CCP took steps to create a more formal judicial system after 1931 that was expected to comply with certain legal procedures. Still, the Communist judicial system was not independent of the Party. Alleged criminals' confessions, often under pressure including torture, remained the main basis of adjudication.

Keywords: born in blood, Minxi Soviet government, Jiangxi Soviet base, wartime judicial system, GMD military campaign

On September 13, 1933, the Soviet Court of Huang County in the recently established Chinese Soviet Republic (1930-1935) was completing a trial of six alleged criminals. According to the court, they were Huang Yufa, Zhang Wenshun, Zhou Mingzhao, Ou Shangqiu, Wu Chunfen, and Tu Laoxi. Huang Yufa was a landlord, a member of the class which the Chinese Communist Party (CCP) regarded as antagonistic, but the rest were all poor peasants or tenants. Huang had joined the Nationalist Party (the Guomindang, or GMD) in 1932 and had allegedly participated in a battle that resulted in the capture and killing of around 80 revolutionary commoners and comrades. Like Huang, Zhang Wenshun had joined the GMD and was a private in

Fang, Qiang, *The Communist Judicial System in China, 1927-1976: Building on Fear.*
Taylor & Francis Group 2021
DOI: 10.5117/9789463729451_CH01

the Nationalist army. Zhang had joined Zhou Mingzhao and several other GMD soldiers in sneaking into a Communist base to spy on the Red Army. He had carried a handgun and dozens of bullets.

Unlike the three GMD soldiers, Ou Shangqiu was a 39-year-old poor peasant. On the evening of August 20, two Red Army soldiers had asked him to take them to join the GMD. According to the record, Ou had agreed to do so. Wu Chunfen was another poor peasant. In March 1932, he made 600 pennies in cash for transmitting two letters from a local security chief (*baozhang*) to local unit heads (*jiazhang*) in March 1932. He was thus regarded by the CCP as a "running dog" of the GMD.[1]

After describing the actions of each defendant, the Soviet court wrote that all "have betrayed their class and sabotaged revolution" and thus were the "deadly enemies" of the Soviet. To eradicate counterrevolutionary factions and consolidate Soviet power, the court sentenced Huang Yufa, Zhang Wenshun, and Zhou Mingzhao to execution. Ou Shangqiu was sentenced to three years in prison and Wu Chunfen was sentenced to two-months of hard labor.[2]

Capital punishment may have been a reasonable punishment for landlord Huang Yufa who had allegedly killed scores of revolutionaries, but the executions of Zhang Wenshun and Zhou Zhaoming were hardly justified. They were merely GMD soldiers who acted as spies in the Soviet base. Neither of them had injured or killed any revolutionaries. Even more unfortunate was Ou Shangqiu who was sentenced to three years in prison simply because he had agreed to take two Red Army deserters to the GMD. There was not even any evidence that he had had done so. Wu Chunfen was also sentenced to two months of hard labor simply for transmitting two letters from a local security chief and Wu apparently did not even know what the contents of the letters were.

When and why did the CCP judicial system impose such harsh punishments on spies and helpers of Red Army deserters? Under what political and military circumstances did the CCP create its judicial system? To what extent did CCP judges have the discretion in making judgments? What was the key role of the judicial system in the Soviet bases? To answer these questions, we must first understand the orthodox Communist views on law

1 For the *baojia* 保甲system see Thomas Heberer and Christian Gobel, *The Politics of Community Building in Urban China* (Abingdon: Routledge, 2011): 21.

2 Ruijinxian renmin fayuan瑞金县人民法院, ed., *Selected Trial Materials of the Chinese Soviet Republic* (*Zhonghua suweiai gongheguo shenpan ziliao xuanbian*中华苏维埃共和国审判资料选编) (Beijing: Renmin fayuan chubanshe, 1991): 208-210.

and violence, the historical backdrop and main threats to the very survival of the CCP bases, the influence of the Soviet Union legal model, the fledgling CCP legal apparatus and makeshift proceedings, the CCP judges who had used and practiced law, and the increasingly dire and hostile environment in which the Communist judicial system developed.

Most Western studies on the Communist base-area period (1931-1935) have focused on its laws and regulations, its crackdowns on counterrevolutionary actions, and its general concept of justice. They have paid less attention to the crucial formative period of the Communist judicial system prior to 1931 as well as to the extremely hostile and bloody conditions that shaped the nature of the judicial system.[3] Due to the political sensitivity of the topic, most Chinese scholars have shied away from doing profound and impartial studies of this period. Instead, they have opted to study prominent CCP judges such as He Shuhen and Liang Botai or individual laws such as the Labor Law, the Marriage Law, or the People's Jury. A few have turned their attention to the whole judicial system of the CCP Jiangxi base, but none has discussed the bloody inception of the Communist judicial system and the extent to which that had shaped the nature of the Communist judicial system in the Soviet base period, the Yan'an period, and the People's Republic of China (PRC).[4]

3 See William E. Butler, ed., *The Legal System of the Chinese Soviet Republic, 1931-1934* (New York: Transnational Press, 1983); Patricia Griffin, *The Chinese Communist Treatment of Counter-Revolutionaries, 1924-1949* (Princeton: Princeton University Press, 1976); Trygve Lötveit, *Chinese Communism 1931-1934: Experience in Civil Government* (Lund: Studentlitteratur, 1979).

4 For example, Yang Musheng杨木生, "The Judicial System in the Soviet Base (*lun suqude sifa zhidu*论苏区的司法制度)" in Qiushi, http://www.zhlzw.com/qx/fxlw/683882_5.html; Miao Tijun苗体君, "The Exploration and Contribution of He Shuheng to the Rule of Law Enterprise of the Central Soviet Base (*He Shuheng duizhongyang suqu fazhi shiyede tansuo yugongxian*何叔衡对中央苏区法制事业的探索) in *The Journal of Hunan First Normal University*, Apr. 2012, Vol. 2, No. 2, pp. 76-81; Shen Weiwei 沈玮玮and Han Wei韩伟, "An Overview of the Studies on the Legal Construction of the Central Soviet Base (*zhongyang suqu fazhi jianshe yanjiu zonglun*中央苏区法制建设研究综论)" in *The Journal of China Executive Leadership Academy Jinggangshan*, Vol. 5, No. 4, July 25, 2012; Liu Shouchu刘受初, "The Legal Construction of the Chinese Soviet Republic (*zhonghua suweiai gongheguo defazhi jianshe*中华苏维埃共和国的法制建设)" in *The Journal of Ji'an Teachers College*, Vol. 16, No. 4. Nov 1995; Shi Shui石水, "The Social Protection Law in the Central Soviet Base (*zhongyang suqude shehui baozhang lifa*中央苏区的社会保障立法)" in *The Circular of the Labor Protection*, Vol. 7, P19, 2001; Li Yixia李宜霞, "Liang Botai and the Construction of the Judicial System in the Chinese Soviet Republic (*Liang Botai yuzhonghua suweiai gongheguo sifa zhidu zhijianshe*梁柏台与中华苏维埃共和国司法制度之建设)" in *The Journal of the Central CCP Party School*, Vol. 3, 2004; Huang Dong黄东, "A Study on the Reform of the Marriage Law in the Red Soviet Base (*hongse suqu hunyin gaizao shulun*红色苏区婚姻改造述论)" in *The Journal of Capital Normal University*, Vol. 3, 2003; Zeng Shaodong曾绍东, "The Land Law System of the Central Soviet Base (*zhongyang suqu tudi falü zhidu*中央苏区土地法律制度)" in *Agricultural Archeology*, Vol. 3, 2010.

In this chapter, I will argue that, during the early building of a new Soviet state in China, the CCP was overwhelmingly afraid of being brutally attacked by the GMD. Most CCP policies, be they military or legal, were designed to ensure the very survival of the Party. Accordingly, the CCP and the Chinese Soviet bases, like the Soviet Union, treated law as a forceful and effective political tool, which could purge class enemies from the Soviet base, suppress GMD espionage, and attract commoners to the revolutionary cause.

Theoretical Foundations of Communist Law

From its inception in 1921, the CCP had owed its establishment to the vital assistance of the Communist International. The Party had thus been receptive to Karl Marx's theories of the state and law and to lessons learned from the Bolsheviks' experience under Lenin and Stalin.[5]

In laying the theoretical foundations of future Communist parties, Marx, the founding father of the modern Communist movement, made a number of important arguments on law and violence in his *Communist Manifesto* of 1848. In 1871, after the Paris Commune was crushed by Thiers's regular army, Marx argued in *The Civil War in France* that the commune had failed to destroy the old state apparatus. He warned that the Paris proletariat could not "simply lay hold on the existent State body and wield this ready-made agency for their own purpose."[6] In other words, the "power base" of the old order had to be smashed. Marx also pointed out the nature and function of law, which was and always would be a tool which the ruling class could use to strengthen its rule and suppress those of other classes.[7] This argument has been accepted and developed by almost all so-called Communist states to justify their destruction of the capitalist apparatus and their own extralegal arrests and killings.

Moreover, Marx strongly upheld the use of violence against enemies of the proletariat, especially as a reprisal against similar violence imposed on socialists by the bourgeoisie. Supporting the execution by the Paris Commune of the "sixty-four hostages, with the Archbishop of Paris at their

5 According to John N. Hazard, the CCP was selective in accepting Russian laws and a good example is its ambiguity in religious propaganda. For the influence of the Comintern upon the CCP see Stuart R. Schram, "The Chinese Soviet Republic: Some Introductory Reflections" in Butler, 1983, pp. 7-21: 8-11; for Hazard's view see John N. Hazard, "The Experience with Constitutionalism" in Butler, 1983, pp. 21-45: 34.

6 Karl Marx, *The Civil War in France*, Second Draft – No. 6. "The Commune," 1871-1872. https://www.marxists.org/archive/marx/works/1871/civil-war-france/drafts/ch02.htm#D2s1

7 Butler, 1983: 27-30.

head," Marx argued that the "brutal custom" of killing hostages was initiated by the bourgeoisie and its army during the 1848 Revolution when many defenseless prisoners were shot by the suppressors.[8]

To the young CCP, the Soviet Union was not only a big brother and patron but also an exemplar and source of imitation. As Elizabeth Perry has argued, the CCP from its early period in Anyuan had "in many respects replicated those [policies] of the Soviet Union." Liu Shaoqi, one of its leaders, was "a confirmed Leninist."[9] To demonstrate its loyalty or gratitude to the Soviet Union, the CCP took up "Soviet" as the name for its central base in Jiangxi. And, according to the late historian Gao Hua, most of the CCP political, economic, military motivation, and ideological control apparatuses in the Jiangxi central base were virtually a replica of the Soviet Union. "The central Soviet region was filled with a rich environment of Russianization," Gao wrote, "[the CCP] celebrated most important Soviet events such as Lenin's birthday, the anniversary of the Russian Revolution."[10] Moreover, after 1931, the returned students or the so-called 28 Bolsheviks who had received their education and training in the Soviet Union took control of the Jiangxi Soviet base. Their leaders such as Wang Ming and Bo Gu carried orders directly from the Comintern.[11]

Russian Bolshevik leader Vladimir Lenin, like Marx, also believed that the proletariat, upon winning its war against capitalism, should wipe out all state machine, including army and the police of the bourgeois. It should "substitute for them a more democratic state machine."[12] But Lenin also stressed the importance of the people's jury and saw it as a road to democratize the judicial system. In agreement with Marx, Lenin demanded the public election of judges and the creation of the procuracy to supervise

8 Marx, "The Fall of Paris" in *The Civil War in France*, May 1871. https://www.marxists.org/archive/marx/works/1871/civil-war-france/ch06.htm

9 Elizabeth J. Perry, *Anyuan: Mining China's Revolutionary Tradition* (Berkeley: University of California Press, 2012): 119.

10 Gao Hua高华, *How Did the Red Sun Rise: The Entire Course of the Yan'an Rectification Movement* (*Hongtaiyang shizenyang shengqide: Yan'an Zhengfeng yundong shimo*红太阳是怎样升起的：延安整风运动始末) (Hong Kong: Hong Kong Chinese University Press, 2000): 74-75; also see William B. Simons, "Reflections on State Administration in the Chinese Soviet Republic and the Soviet Union" in Butler, 1983, pp. 47-52: 48.

11 Guo Dehong郭德宏, ed., *Chronicle of Wang Ming* (*Wang Ming nianpu*王明年谱) (Beijing: Social Sciences Academic Press, 2014): 186-187.

12 Vladimir Lenin, *The State and Revolution* (Chicago: Haymarket Books, 2014): 138; also see Lü Shilun吕世伦, *History of Lenin's Legal Thought* (*Liening falü sixiangshi*列宁法律思想史) (Beijing: Falü chubanshe, 2000): 117; Qiu Xue, *The Declaration of China in the 21st Century: World Section* (Salt Lake City: American Academic Press, 2015): 152.

the court. Although Lenin ostensibly supported the rule of law and the separation of the Party and law, he viewed law as an instrument of politics, which was strengthened under Stalin in the 1930s to "suppress domestic and international enemies as well as to aid socialist construction."[13] As a revolutionary leader, Lenin himself may have been behind numerous violations of the law (i.e. criminal law) and the "red terror" during the civil war.[14] For Lenin, the red terror in 1918 was "immanent in the dialectics of revolution and counterrevolution."[15]

There is no doubt that both Marx's and Lenin's advocacy of using violence against class enemies had a profound impact on the CCP. Equally influential were Lenin's arguments on law and judicial reforms such as the people's jury system. In 1917, the Bolsheviks promulgated an order that the people's court would have one judge and two jurors. In addition, Lenin seemed to endorse the separation of his party and law in 1922 because he argued that the judicial system should be independent from political government. Lenin also urged the party to abide by law and said that the people's court should only comply with the law and safeguard justice.[16] The CCP in the Jiangxi Soviet later adopted Lenin's people's jury system but not his ostensible judicial independence.

In the Soviet Union under Lenin and especially under Stalin, the judicial system quickly turned into a tool of the Communist party and lost its residual independence.[17] After founding the Jiangxi Soviet republic in 1930, the CCP adopted not only Lenin's Party-state system but also the instrumental Soviet judicial system including its anti-counterrevolutionary concepts, statutes, and mechanisms.

The CCP's Early Views of Law

In late 1925, Mao Zedong, a leading Communist active in mobilizing the peasants, argued that all warlords, officials, compradors, and big landlords

13 Daniel Leese and Puck Engman, "Introduction" in Leese and Engman, 2018, pp. 1-24: 4; Gong Tingtai龚廷泰 and Wang Jianguo王建国, "Lenin's Thought on the Judicial Right and its Contemporary Value (*Leningde sifaquan sixiang jiqi shidaijiazhi*列宁的司法权思想及其时代价值)" in *Falü kexue*, Vol. 6, 2008, pp. 9-17.

14 Solomon, 1996: 19.

15 James Ryan, *Lenin's Terror: The Ideological Origins of Early Soviet State Violence* (Abingdon: Routledge, 2012): 106-110.

16 Gong Tingtai and Wang Jianguo, 2008: 9-17.

17 Peter H. Solomon, 1996: 17-18; W.E. Butler, *Soviet Law* (London: Butterworths, 1983): 34.

who collaborated with the imperialists were adversaries. The proletariat was the leading force of the revolution, and all semi-proletariat and petty bourgeoisie were close friends.[18] Mao's classification of China's classes, while unorthodox, helped single out the major enemies of the revolution who would later become the target of merciless violence in CCP controlled regions. In March 1927, about one month before Chiang Kai-shek (aka. Jiang Jieshi)'s "betrayal" of the revolution and repression of the CCP and its allies in Shanghai, Mao completed an empirical report on the Hunan peasant movements in which he defended the use of violence in the movements against landlords and rebuked accusations that peasant attacks were excessive.

Before Mao's extensive investigation in five Hunan counties in early 1927, many centrists and right-wing GMD members had reportedly blamed peasants for acting willfully and fomenting terror in the countryside. In some cases, peasants stormed the homes of landlords and other elites who were opposed to peasant societies. They also detained "bad" local bullies and corrupt gentry and paraded them on the streets. These lawless activities won Mao's applause because he had deep contempt for law and legal procedures.[19] For Mao, the excessive lawless violence of the peasants was nothing but a resistance to oppression by local strongmen and corrupt gentry. Places with the most violent resistance were where landlords and gentrymen had done the worst evil against peasants. To justify peasants' use of violence, Mao said that the violence was necessary because "revolution is an insurrection and violent actions of one class overthrowing another." If peasants did not use massive force, they would not be able to topple the deeply rooted power of landlords.

For Mao, "Revolution is not a dinner party" and peasants' using violence against evil landlords and gentrymen was in concert with revolution. Mao associated anyone opposing peasant movements with counterrevolution. He praised the main revolutionary cause of the peasant movements as "always correct" and argued that "if anyone tries to discredit peasants' violent activities, s/he will discredit revolution; if anyone tries to denounce peasants, s/he will attack revolution." In other words, the peasant violence, however unlawful, brutal, and humiliating it may

18 Mao Zedong毛泽东, "An Analysis of China's Social Classes (zhongguo shehui gejiejide fenxi中国社会各阶级的分析)," December 1, 1925. http://cpc.people.com.cn/GB/64184/64185/66615/4488901.html

19 For Mao's lawlessness see Yan Wang, 2004: 12; Tang Tsou, *The Cultural Revolution and Post-Mao Reforms: A Historical Perspective* (Chicago: University of Chicago Press, 1999): 315. Xin Ren, 1997: 57; Gong Pixiang, 1999: 287.

have been, was absolutely legitimate and a "necessity" of revolution that should be championed and not subdued.[20] This reflected the high status of revolution ever since the overthrow of the Qing in 1911. The GMD was distancing itself from revolution and embracing restoration in this period.[21]

Shortly after Chiang Kai-shek clamped down on the Communist and labor movements in Shanghai, the CCP responded by joining with peasant and labor uprisings in a number of places. Peng Pai and his cohorts established the Hailufeng Soviet in Guangdong province, arguably the first Soviet-style government in China.[22] As a method of retaliation and class struggle, peasants in Hailufeng launched a red terror against local landlords and gentrymen. As Klaus Mühlhahn has put it, the whole process of the Hailufeng peasant movement was a form of "terrorizing that was exercised in the name of class justice." During a typical mass trial, a speaker would first loudly read the crimes of an accused landlord or gentryman to the audience. Then the crowd would express their opinion by shouting and yelling. The final decision would be made by a simple popular vote and the punishment, usually corporal or capital, would be carried out on the spot. The heads of decapitated landlords or evil gentry would be hung and displayed in marketplaces for days. In some cases, the corporal punishment was cruel, reportedly including cannibalism to show the "full revenge of [criminals'] misdeeds." Aside from assembling the peasants and conveying a clear political message, the mass trials and bloody spectacles of revenge were also in accord with the cruel eating habits in rural Guangdong and peasants' traditional antipathy to human dignity and law.[23]

The violence exercised in peasant movements was not ephemeral or restricted to the early periods of the CCP. In fact, as the GMD violent repression of the CCP intensified after it solidified national power around 1930, the violence of and against peasant movements and the massive disregard of law and legal process on both sides would continue, expand, and become more serious in most CCP controlled rural Soviets as well as in society at large.

20 Mao Zedong毛泽东, *An Investigation Report on Hunan Peasant Movements* (*Hunan nongmin yundong kaocha baogao*湖南农民运动考察报告), March, 1927. http://cpc.people.com.cn/GB/64184/64185/66615/4488900.html See also Fanon's argument in the case of North Africa. Frantz Fanon, *Wretched of the Earth* (New York: Grove Press, 1963).

21 See Mary C. Wright, "The Heritage of the Restoration" in *The Last Stand of Chinese Conservatism: The Tung-Chih Restoration, 1862-1874* (Stanford: Stanford University Press, 1957).

22 John N. Hazard, 1983: 26.

23 Mühlhahn, 2011: 159-161.

Overwhelming Threats of GMD Campaigns

After the brief alliance between the GMD and the CCP ended with an abrupt and open rupture in the spring of 1927, the GMD rolled out massive and brutal campaigns against the Communists. In Jiangxi, local tyrants and GMD armies "detained and killed countless" numbers of workers and peasants. They also ordered every five households to establish a hoary collective protection system in order to ferret out Communists or other activists. Residents failing to join the system would be incarcerated or executed.[24] At Shantou, Guangdong, the GMD members threw Communist prisoners into the sea with weights attached to their bodies.[25]

To survive, many Communist leaders such as Mao Zedong, Zhu De, and Zhang Guotao decided to create a Red Army and establish military bases to resist the GMD onslaught. Thanks to Chiang's ongoing wars with powerful warlords before 1930,[26] the Communist bases had thrived and gained much territory and influence.[27] As Communist bases were expanding at an alarming rate, Chiang believed that the CCP was his primary adversary and a "disease in the heart."[28] On December 1, 1930, Chiang Kai-shek ordered the governors of Hunan and Hubei to recover territories lost to the Red Army. He also instructed Lu Diping, the governor of Jiangxi, to move forward to attack the CCP bases in Jiangxi.[29]

From 1930 to 1935, the GMD launched a series of large-scale and bloody military campaigns against the CCP's central bases in Jiangxi. Against this critical historical backdrop, the Communist judicial system was from the very outset intimately intertwined with the overwhelming life-and-death fight with the GMD. The bulk of the early CCP legal apparatus was designed as a main instrument for the Party to survive under desperate

24 *The Red China* (*hongse zhongguo*红色中国), June 28, 1930.

25 Jonathan Fenby, *Chiang Kai-shek: China's Generalissimo and the Nation He Lost* (Cambridge: Da Capo Press, 2009): 185.

26 For a detailed account on Chinese warlordism and Chiang's wars with warlords see James E. Sheridan, *Chinese Warlord: The Career of Feng Yu-hsiang* (Stanford: Stanford University Press, 1966): 1, 240-267.

27 For GMD's wars against other warlords see Original Archives of President Chiang Kai-shek's Biographical Account (*Jiang Zhongzheng zongtong dang'an shilue gaoben*蒋中正总统档案史略稿本) (Taibei: Guoshiguan yinxing, 2006): Vol. 6-8.

28 Lloyd E. Eastman, "Nationalist China during the Nanking Decade, 1927-1937" in John K. Fairbanks and Albert Feuerwerker, eds., *The Cambridge History of China, Vol. 13, Republican China 1912-1949, Part 2* (Cambridge: Cambridge University Press, 1986): 148.

29 *Jiang Zhongzheng zongtong dangan shilue gaoben*, 2006: 9. 177; also see Ilpyong J. Kim, *The Politics of Chinese Communism*, 1973: 37.

military and political situations. As Michael Dutton has argued, the siege and attack of the Nationalist army virtually forced the CCP in the Jiangxi base to initiate a "massive purge designed to eliminate this invisible enemy within, the Communists, quite literally, began to devour their own."[30] Under tremendously hazardous pressure, the CCP was pushed to the brink of total destruction. The biggest and most successful campaign of the GMD was the fifth extermination campaign, which lasted over a year from the summer of 1933 to late 1934. It managed to drive the Red Army out of its central base. *The Red China*, the official publication of the CCP in Jiangxi, immediately warned that the Soviet bases were at a very critical moment.[31]

Along with the military campaigns, the GMD also imposed strict economic sanctions on the Soviet bases in Jiangxi, Hubei, Anhui, and Fujian. Trade between the Jiangxi Soviets and outside had been banned since 1928 and all staple food or basic commodities such as grain, kerosene, and salt had been monopolized and rationed by the Communist government. Ordinary people were allowed to buy only very limited amounts. Due to the economic blockade, the Red Army's economic needs had relied exclusively on attacking local tyrants (*e'ba*; e.g. powerful landlords or local officials). According to one report in early 1929, the Red Army had for months not been able to pay soldiers any cash. In the winter of 1928, Red soldiers had almost no cotton-padded clothing. The grave monetary and living conditions had caused diminishing morale among soldiers and desertion was common.[32] In 1931, although people in the Soviet bases could buy daily necessities such as towels, salt, matches, and toothbrushes, they had to pay twice as much as was required in Shanghai. The GMD economic sanctions had made trade between the Soviets and outside almost impossible.[33]

As we have seen, sending spies or using local supporters to sabotage the Soviet bases from within was another scheme of the GMD, which compelled the CCP to meticulously differentiate between friends and enemies inside the bases.[34] According to CCP documents and reports, the internal enemies allegedly sent or led by the GMD were mostly the AB *tuan* (Anti-Bolshevik League), the Reorganization Faction, and the Trotskyist Faction who had

30 Michael Dutton, *Policing Chinese Politics: A History* (Duke: Duke University Press, 2005): 13.

31 *The Red China*, August 13, 1933.

32 Jiangxisheng danganguan江西省档案馆, 1982. *Selected Historical Sources of the Central Revolutionary Base* (*zhongyang geming genjudi shiliao xuanbian*中央革命根据地史料选编). Nanchang: Jiangxi renmin chubanshe, 1982): 1. 44-45.

33 Ouyang Qin欧阳钦, "A Report on the Central Soviet Region (*zhongyang suweiai quyu baogao* 关于中央苏维埃区域报告)" in Ibid., 1982: 1. 385.

34 Dutton, 2005: 31.

infiltrated the Soviet bases and even the CCP. Among them, the AB *tuan* was most deadly and threatening.[35] Many AB *tuan* members reportedly sneaked into the Communist bases and used intimidation, slander, murder, and monetary allurement to achieve their goals.[36]

As the GMD was increasing its military and economic pressures on the Soviet bases, the CCP was constantly obsessed by an intense fear of GMD attacks and sabotages. Since early 1933, the CCP had required local governments and judiciaries to take swift and resolute actions to arrest and execute all internal counterrevolutionaries and to expose their crimes to the people.[37] These pressures might have led to more legal action against counterrevolutionaries, but the cases with which we began this chapter suggest that they also led to the execution of suspected GMD agents or class enemies for minor offenses without going through legitimate legal processes. These cases were just the tip of the CCP's strike-hard iceberg in the midst of a bloody war.

Early Judicial System in Soviet Bases

As I have argued, the creation and development of the early Communist judicial system was consistently linked to the very survival of the CCP. Indeed, during the entire period of the Soviet bases, the predominant concern of the Communist judicial system was how to strengthen CCP control and suppress enemies within the bases.

Soon after the Autumn Harvest Uprising failed in the fall of 1927, Mao and his adherents fled to the Jinggang Mountains. Meanwhile, the Jiangxi Revolutionary Committee drafted its Action Platform (*xingdong zhenggang*) in which it announced that the authority of the revolution belonged to all revolutionary commoners and that all men and women had equal economic, legal, and educational rights. In particular, the committee took initial steps toward founding a Communist judicial system with a promise of promulgating a labor law and a labor insurance law to ameliorate workers' living and working conditions.[38]

In November, the CCP headquarters in mountainous Jiangxi planned the establishment of a Soviet government. In its Interim Soviet Organic Law, the Jiangxi CCP explained that the name "Soviet or a council" originated in

35 Jiangxisheng danganguan, 1982: 2. 649.
36 Ibid., 1982: 2. 651.
37 Ibid., 1982: 2. 683.
38 Ibid., 1982: 2. 1-3.

Russia and was a sort of "democratic" polity close to the majority of working people. Unlike capitalist polities that had a separation of powers, the Soviet would concentrate all political, legislative, and judicial powers. Therefore, the Communist judicial system from its inception was to be under the CCP's firm control. The CCP claimed that the advantages of a Soviet polity were its proximity to commoners, its nimble control over the state, and its freedom from the inefficiency of the mutual restraints of different powers. To counter internal GMD agents and other enemies, the law for the first time indicated the need to create Committees to Punish Counterrevolutionaries (*chengzhi fangeming weiyuanhui*). These semi-judicial committees were different from formal courts and were to be established at all provincial, district, and county levels of the government to attack counterrevolutionaries. The law did not specify the functions and procedures of the committee and whether it needed to be staffed by professional judges or only by Soviet-style assessors.[39] The reason might be that the Soviet base in Jiangxi did not have a stable civil government and the anti-counterrevolutionary committee was merely a stopgap measure to tackle immediate threats.

As the Soviet bases grew and expanded in the following two years, local elites and the GMD waged more attacks against them. GMD officials in Fujian reportedly dispatched agents to the Minxi Soviet base in western Fujian to foment chaos.[40] Facing soaring external and internal attacks, the increasingly powerful and confident CCP tried to intensify its repression of counterrevolutionaries.[41] In July 1929, the Minxi Soviet government stated that its missions were to mobilize the masses, expand the labor unions, purge counterrevolutionary forces, and confiscate the properties of reactionaries and landlords, etc.[42] One month later, the Soviet base modified the Interim Soviet Organizational Law and changed the name of the Committee for Purging Counterrevolutionaries (*sufan weiyuanhui*) at the district, county, and township levels into the Committee for Judging and Purging Counterrevolutionaries (*caipanjian sufan weiyuanhui*).[43] The name change is important as it suggests that the Soviets were forming a more mature government and were establishing a replica of a comparable institution in the Soviet Union.[44]

39 Ibid., 1982: 2. 4-14.

40 Ibid., 1982: 2. 162.

41 For CCP's execution of the local counterrevolutionaries prior to 1931 see Griffin, 1976: 12-25.

42 Jiangxisheng danganguan, 1982: 2. 15-20.

43 *Soviet Organizational Law* (*Suweiai zuzhifa*苏维埃组织法) in Ibid., 1982: 2. 20-28.

44 For the history of Cheka see George Leggett, *Lenin's Political Police: The All Russian Extraordinary Commission for Combating Counter-revolution and Sabotage* (Oxford: Clarendon Press, 1981).

In May 1930, a few months before Chiang Kai-shek's anti-Communist military campaigns, the Minxi Soviet drafted the CCP's first Adjudicating Regulations (*caipan tiaoli*) for its judicial system. The new law marked a milestone of the Soviet bases as it demonstrated that the CCP Soviets had attained a more sophisticated form of a state-like political entity. The law consisted of three parts: adjudicating organs, regulations regarding people's appeals, and methods of penalizing criminals. The first part noted that the township government would be an organ of first instance and the county government would be the appellate court. All important cases would be judged by the Minxi Soviet government. The judicial system with local Communist officials serving as judges was reminiscent of the local judicial institutions in dynastic China and colonial America.[45]

The biggest difference between the Soviet judicial system and the dynastic judiciaries lay in regard to capital punishment. A Soviet official at the county level had the authority to mete out death penalties, whereas in most periods of Chinese history only the ruler or the central government's Board of Punishment had the final say on capital punishment.[46] In special circumstances such as wartime, however, a township cadre of the Minxi Soviet government was able to execute a criminal before filing a report to the county government. During a revolt, local Soviet cadres could kill any alleged criminal at will. According to one Minxi government report, many CCP cadres were responsible for wantonly burning property and killing "enemies." The report ascribed the excessive violence to officials who adopted a "killing mindset" and believed that they had the right to "execute all reactionaries."[47] The new law also authorized officials to indict and convict counterrevolutionaries in mass meetings to deter crime and educate people. Owing probably to the paucity of qualified judges and the context of open warfare, the new law did not ban the use of confession as evidence of guilt. That was tantamount to giving local prosecutors a green light to employ corporal punishments and even torture to extract confessions from alleged criminals.[48]

Litigants in the Minxi Soviet area had to abide by certain procedural laws. As in most post-Tang polities, the Minxi government prohibited people

45 For colonial America see Lawrence M. Friedman, *A History of American Law* (Touchstone, 2005): 36.

46 Qianfan Zhang, *The Constitution of China: A Contextual Analysis* (Oxford: Hart Publishing, 2012): 210.

47 Jiangxisheng danganguan, 1982: 2. 165.

48 Ruijinxian renmin fayuan瑞金县人民法院, 1991: 135.

from skipping administrative levels in lodging complaints and appeals.[49] In other words, if a litigant wanted to appeal, s/he had to start at the lowest level – the township government. If not satisfied with the township government's decision, the litigant could go to the upper levels within a legal period ranging from three to seven days. Once the county government made a final ruling, no more appeals to higher levels would be accepted. To demonstrate the revolutionary nature of the Soviet government, the law permitted ordinary litigants to lodge either oral or written complaints. More important, litigants in the Soviet base area did not have to pay suing fees as their counterparts living in the GMD-controlled regions did.[50] The last part of the Minxi law listed acceptable punishments, including execution, confiscation of properties, deportation, imprisonment, deprivation of voting rights, forced labor, and pillory (*shizhong*). The law explicitly forbade cruel punishments such as decapitation, disembowelment, and torture. Burning houses and imposing collective punishment were also outlawed.[51]

In June 1930, four months after the Minxi Soviet government emphasized the need to clamp down on internal enemies, another law was announced specifically targeting counterrevolutionaries, a term both the CCP and the GMD learned from the Soviet Union.[52] The new law was titled Regulations on Punishing Counterrevolutionaries (*chengzhi fangeming tiaoli*; a similar but more detailed law was enacted in 1951. These laws were extremely tough on a list of counterrevolutionary activities. The death penalty would be applied to local tyrants who oppressed poor peasants, reactionary political and military leaders who harmed revolution, and people who collaborated with the GMD, concealed reactionaries and spies, resisted paying taxes, and/or destroyed revolutionary units and Soviets. For relatively minor crimes, such as illegally possessing weapon, making reactionary propaganda, spreading rumors, and purposely damaging revolutionary posters and transportation, the perpetrators would be "severely punished." The law did not specify what kind of severe punishments were to be applied to such offenses. The "deliberate" vagueness of the law provided the Red Army with unrestricted

49 For a complete study on the complaint proceedings in Chinese history see Qiang Fang, 2013.

50 For the suing fees in the Republic see Lin Jiaqi and Liu Junlin刘俊麟, *Civil Procedural Law* (*minshi susongfa*民事诉讼法) (Taiwan: Shuquan chubanshe, 2017): 153-210; for the early Republic see Qiang Fang, 2013a: 82.

51 Jiangxisheng danganguan, 1982: 2. 27.

52 Sun Guangyan 孙光妍and Yu Yisheng于逸生, "A Review of the Influence of the Soviet Law on the Development of the Chinese Legal System (*sulianfa yingxiang zhongguo fazhi jianshe Jincheng zhihuigu*苏联法影响中国法制建设进程之回顾)" in *faxue yanjiu*, Vol. 1, 2003: 139-151: 147.

discretion in dealing with counterrevolutionaries in the early state-building stage when the CCP was confronting dangerous and life-threatening situations. More often than not, the term "severe punishments" referred to the death penalty or hard labor in the Soviet bases. Whatever the real purpose of Minxi Soviet lawmakers, one thing was clear. The law indicated both the self-confidence of the revolutionaries in forming a Soviet government and their worry that a growing internal threat could kill the fledgling revolutionary government.[53]

Like Minxi and Jiangxi Soviet bases, some other Communist bases also began promulgating their own regulations on legal process and the penalizing of counterrevolutionaries. For instance, in September 1930, the Shanghang county government in west Fujian province, made its own adjudicating law and punishment that was modeled on the Minxi Soviet. Yet, unlike the Minxi Soviet that was more tacit on the use of torture to extract confessions, the Shanghang government boldly endorsed corporal punishments in dealing with certain criminals. "No beheading, disembowelment, and corporal punishment are allowed," the law wrote, "but to extract 'real' confessions from the criminals such as spies, corporal punishments can be adopted."[54] Given the lack of modern means (e.g. DNA testing) of criminal investigation and the overall lack of respect for suspects' human dignity or rights in contemporary China,[55] the use of torture in the Soviet bases was not surprising.[56]

At the beginning of 1931, due to increasing pressures from the GMD army, the CCP worried that many supposedly pro-GMD forces such as the Trotskyists, Reorganizationists, and AB *tuan* would step up their actions and sabotage inside the Jiangxi and Minxi bases. In some cases, GMD spies reportedly propagated deceitful rumors inside the Red Army and instigated Red soldiers to defect to the GMD. Facing a crescendo of counterrevolutionary sabotage and espionage, the CCP felt an urgency to clamp down on counterrevolutionaries. The Minxi Soviet government issued a notice denouncing pro-GMD spies as the "primary and most dangerous adversaries" of the CCP. The government called on all revolutionary toilers to discern the

53 Ruijinxian renmin fayuan, 1991: 138-139.

54 Ibid., 1991: 152-155.

55 The practice of torture was also common in GMD controlled areas in which GMD tormentors tortured Communist suspects to extract confessions or valuable information. See Wakeman Jr., 1995: 175.

56 Torture is also used in the US even today. See "USA and Torture: A History of Hypocrisy" in *Human Rights Watch*, December 9, 2014. https://www.hrw.org/news/2014/12/09/usa-and-torture-history-hypocrisy#

reactionary conspiracies of the pro-GMD groups and to actively participate in anti-counterrevolutionary movements.[57]

On February 21, the Minxi Soviet informed all adjudicating and purging committees that one of their principal missions was to protect and solidify the Soviet bases, particularly during periods when struggles between the CCP and the GMD were increasingly fierce. The government noted, "[I]f we cannot completely eliminate internal reactionary forces, [we] will not be able to consolidate the Soviet government [...] let alone make extraordinary outward expansion to liberate one or more provinces." In addition, the circular urged cadres to mobilize the masses to attack counterrevolutionaries. To educate the masses, Communist judges were ordered to thoroughly expose the "counterrevolutionary faces" of all reactionary political figures in public trials.[58]

Indeed, the threats of internal sabotage were not just imaginary but often real enough. About two weeks later, the Minxi Soviet claimed that one Red Army force (the 12th) had cracked down on several reactionary organizations and arrested their leaders. The reactionary units had challenged CCP policies on land reform and labor-capital disputes. In the Soviet's words, they had attempted to "disrupt the Soviets, oppose land distribution, and conduct assassination." The reactionaries were mainly leaders of the three anti-Soviet organizations, namely the AB *tuan*, Reorganizationists, and Trotskyists.[59]

As concerns about internal sabotage mounted, the Minxi Soviet government began rendering county governments the jurisdiction to kill potential reactionaries. While it was still required for county governments to bring criminals' confessions to the Minxi Soviet for approval before execution, some exceptions were allowed. County governments could now kill suspected reactionaries on their own and report their actions to upper-level governments later for retroactive approval. Indeed, upper-level governments might well not have any motivation to investigate the reports from below before approving them. Overwhelmed by brutal warfare, few cadres were willing to take serious interest in the fate of innocent people who were wronged by the process. In addition to exercising the new "authority" to execute counterrevolutionaries, county officials in this period, as later in the PRC (see Chapters 3-5), were responsible for educating and mobilizing the masses to join the anti-counterrevolutionary movement. The Minxi Soviet

57 Ruijinxian renmin fayuan, 1991: 143-144.

58 Jiangxisheng danganguan, 1982: 2. 133-134.

59 "Circular of the Minxi Soviet Government: Number 22 (*minxi suweiai zhengfu bugao: diershierhao*)" in Ruijinxian renmin fayuan瑞金县人民法院, 1991: 147-149.

ostensibly continued to oppose using torture in interrogating alleged political criminals, and it required local officials to use unspecified "persuasive and technical means" in their investigations. But as we have seen and will see again later, this government order was largely ceremonial and few, if any, county officials would heed it in handling political enemies. Making matters worse, unlike in the Yan'an period (1936-1947), there was no upper-level organ in the Jiangxi Soviet base that was interested in supervising the interrogation methods at the lower level and righting the wrongs discovered there.[60]

The first and only criminal law enacted by the CCP from the base period to 1979 in the People's Republic of China was drafted on May 19, 1931 by the northeast Jiangxi Soviet under CCP leader Fang Zhimin. According to the law, before the central CCP government promulgated a criminal law, the interim law in northeast Jiangxi would have "absolute force." In hindsight, the first Communist criminal law has been hailed to have had both a more scientific format and a more comprehensive content than the 1979 Criminal Law. Some of its statutes regarding obstructing justice, threatening hygiene, and coercing women to practice prostitution contain more details than the 1979 Criminal Law.[61]

This early criminal law included 22 main categories of crime or crime-related items and 149 articles but none of them dealt with counterrevolutionaries. The first part of the law discussed various offenses: such as non-crimes, unaccomplished crimes, recidivistic crimes, multiple crimes, and accomplice in crime. Then the law listed certain ways of dealing with criminals including categories of punishments, voluntary surrenders, probation, sentence period, and reduction or addition of punishment. The last part of the law entailed specific crimes such as perjury, arson, gambling, prostitution, injury, abortion, robbery, burglary, and opium use.[62]

Both the format and the content of the criminal law were drastically different from those of the Regulations on Punishing Counterrevolutionaries in the Minxi Soviet. Interestingly, this criminal law was in many aspects akin to the 1928 Criminal Law of the Republic of China, now the archenemy of the CCP. For Communist lawmakers, the criminal law did not so much target counterrevolutionaries as order society in general.[63] Because the law was designed to be used in a normal country with a fully legitimate central

60 Ibid., 1991: 150-151.

61 *The New Legal Daily*, May 20, 2015.

62 Interim Soviet Criminal Law in the Northeast Jiangxi Special Zon (*gandongbei tequ suweiai zanxing xinglu*) in Ruijinxian renmin fayuan, 1991: 112-129.

63 Lai Chengzuo, *A Tiny Complete Book of Chinese Six Laws* (*xiuzhen zhonghua liufa quanshu*) (Beijing: Zhonghua shujü, 1936).

government, it was less influential and less practical than the Minxi law, which was more suited to the intense and bloody wars of the time.

Before any central law could be promulgated for all Soviet bases, a handful of Soviet bases in Minxi and other counties of northeast Jiangxi had drafted regional laws on adjudication, counterrevolutionaries, or general crimes. To counter growing internal sabotage and the infiltration of GMD agents, the Minxi Soviet allowed local governments to use torture and carry out arbitrary executions. While other Soviet bases failed to enact public and explicit laws dealing with enemies as Minxi did, they might actually have exercised similarly broad judicial discretion in applying all possible means, including torture and summary execution, in punishing political enemies. These methods might well have been justified by the "Red terror" acknowledged by the orthodox revolutionary theories of Marx and Lenin, in the context of an ongoing civil war, the GMD's brutal repression of Communists, and the extralegal methods of the pre-1927 Hunan peasant movements endorsed by Mao. Whether openly or covertly, the green light given by local Communist governments to use torture and to disregard human life and legal process could easily have led to untold cruel torture and serious grievances. Among them, the most notorious and merciless case to be recorded was the campaign against the AB *tuan* despite claims by CCP officials that torture and perjury of witnesses were strictly forbidden by judiciaries in the Soviet bases.[64]

One of the most effective counterrevolutionary units, the AB *tuan* had reportedly infiltrated Soviet bases and attempted to entice Red soldiers and civilians to desert. During a bloody war, soldiers were obviously vital to the CCP's survival. The AB *tuan* was blamed for plotting to attack peasant societies, murder CCP members, and torpedo the labor-peasant coalitions. Its ultimate goal was to "guide the reactionary army to arrest and kill revolutionaries." The first warning exposing the crimes of AB *tuan* and Reorganizationists was made on June 25, 1930 when the CCP noticed that the AB *tuan* was collaborating with a Hunan warlord to kill Jiangxi workers and peasants. The CCP believed that if it wanted to solidify the Soviet bases, the party had to purge AB *tuan* from within.[65]

In September, the CCP seemed to have made some progress in clamping down on the AB *tuan*. A CCP committee in Jiangxi claimed that the government had recently destroyed AB *tuan* units in southwest Jiangxi and executed many of their leaders. The committee tried to assure the

64 Ruijinxian renmin fayuan, 1991: 231-239.
65 Jiangxisheng danganguan, 1982: 2. 631-636.

local people that the Red Army killed only AB *tuan* leaders. It promised that revolutionary people who had been misled should not worry so long as they could "correct their mistakes and actively join in the revolutionary struggle."[66]

Notwithstanding the claim of victory in destroying a local AB *tuan*, the Jiangxi Soviet government admitted in an "Emergency Circular" at the time that the AB *tuan* was still a key enemy of the revolutionary people and a colossal obstacle to the CCP effort to take major cities. To root out the AB *tuan* completely, the circular allowed the CCP and revolutionary people to use "both tough and soft means," including the "most brutal torture," to break AB *tuan* members. The reason was that AB *tuan* members were "very sinister, treacherous, and crafty."[67] With this permission from the top, local political and judicial cadres in the central Jiangxi base could disregard basic legal procedures and inflict virtually all kinds of cruel torture against suspected AB *tuan* members.

Shortly after the Red Army took Ji'an, CCP cadres in security departments (acting as both police and judges) in Jiangxi Soviet bases began to launch a massive and merciless crackdown on AB *tuan*. As a result, numerous AB *tuan* members, real or false, had been detained, tormented, and executed. According to CCP reports, the attacks on AB *tuan* were based primarily on suspects' confessions and the CCP torturers had no "patience to investigate the confessions and search for circumstantial evidence." The sole technology applied throughout the interrogatory process was gruesome torture such as hanging suspects by their hands, beating them with an oxtail, or burning with incense or oil. In extreme cases, CCP executioners disemboweled AB *tuan* members and took out their hearts. During the campaign against the AB *tuan*, local CCP security departments had absolute authority to kill any alleged AB *tuan* members without the need to report to their superiors or to get their permission. Some CCP officials even announced publicly that they would rather kill 100 innocent people than let one guilty AB *tuan* member escape.[68]

According to the recollection of Xiao Ke who was then a division commander in the Jiangxi Soviet, around 1300 or 1400 out of 7000 men in the revolutionary Fourth Army were struck down in this purge of the ranks. In the First Army, among 4400 officers and soldiers who had confessed to have certain links with the AB *tuan*, more than 2000 of them were summarily

66 Ibid., 1982: 2. 637-638.
67 Ibid., 1982: 2. 639-651.
68 Ibid., 1982: 1. 425-498.

shot.[69] The unchecked use of torture in extracting confessions and the utter neglect of legal process and human life doubtlessly caused countless grievances and erroneous killings in this campaign.

In his detailed account of the movement against the AB *tuan* in the Soviet bases, historian Gao Hua centers on the incident of Futian in Jiangxi in late 1930. He accuses Mao Zedong, the head of the Jiangxi Soviet, of being behind the inhuman tortures and subsequent extralegal executions of thousands of alleged AB *tuan* members. The largely lawless massacre forced most CCP officials and commoners to remain reticent as any private talk between two persons could draw suspicion that they were AB *tuan* members.[70] Official CCP documents used to ascribe the anti-AB *tuan* movement to the left-leaning line of Wang Ming, a Russia-educated Communist leader. But the zenith of the movement and especially the Futian incident took place in late 1930 when Wang Ming spent most of his time in Shanghai and Jiangsu and should have had little role in the movement.[71]

Creating a Wartime Communist Judicial System

After the Chinese Soviet Republic was founded in November 1931, the CCP tried to institutionalize its judicial system and make it more fit for a Communist state. Aside from promulgating more laws such as a constitution, a labor law, and a marriage law that not only demonstrated the existence of a formal Soviet republic but also echoed its revolutionary nature, the CCP took steps to curb the excessive lawlessness or abnormal practices such as the ruthless and somewhat barbaric crackdown of the AB *tuan*. On December 13, the central committee of the Soviet republic issued an order calling for a review of the past anti-counterrevolutionary mistakes and killings. To begin with, the order stated that an urgent task of the CCP was to create a revolutionary order and safeguard people's rights now that the interim central Soviet government was being consolidated. The primary concern of the central order was to distance itself from the erroneous attacks on the counterrevolutionaries in the past years. In its words, "As we all know, the anti-counterrevolutionary work has not been faultless," and "the interim central government prudently tells all Soviet governments that

69 Philip Short, *Mao: A Life* (New York: Henry Holt Co., 2000): 270-271.

70 Gao Hua, 2000: 22-61.

71 Zhang Hongmou, "Yifeng Judicial System in the Democratic Revolutionary Period (*Minzhu geming shiqi yifeng renmin sifa zhidu*)" in *Yifeng wenshi ziliao*, 1988: 86-97.

the anti-counterrevolutionary work in the past has made many mistakes." The mistakes included arrests based on confessions, torture during interrogations, and punishments irrespective of the suspect's social class and role. Consequently, the order said that many criminals who should have been treated lightly suffered severe punishments. To speedily establish a revolutionary order and protect the life and legal rights of revolutionary people, the central order decided to draft temporary legal procedures for judges to follow.[72]

From now on, the State Political Security Bureau (*guojia zhengzhi baoweiju,* hereinafter SPSB), a political security unit patterned after the *cheka* or "political police" of the Soviet Union, would make arrests and preliminary interrogations in all counterrevolutionary cases.[73] The SPSB would act as a plaintiff that would lodge an appeal to the state judicial organ (court or judging department). Barring special circumstances, county-level judicial organs would no longer have the power to decide death sentence. Only judicial departments in the central district and surrounding provinces could made decisions on death penalty. Once a defender was sentenced to death, he or she was now able to appeal to the central judicial department within fourteen days. In the future, local Soviet governments would have no power to arrest or interrogate counterrevolutionaries and they should submit the report to the local SPSB. In Soviet bases that had no SPSB units, local governments had at first to seek permission from the provincial SPSB before conducting arrests. Unless there were particular circumstances such as an imminent counterrevolutionary revolt or no connection with the provincial Soviet government, local district or county governments could not apprehend any suspect.

Moreover, the central order demanded that all counterrevolutionary members be classified in accordance with their classes. If a counterrevolutionary member was a leader or a local tyrant, landlord, rich peasant, or a bourgeois, the punishment should be harsher, whereas a follower or a working-class counterrevolutionary would receive a more lenient penalty. The legal principle of punishment based on class status illustrated in this central order was crucial because the Communist judicial system being established in the Soviet bases would quickly apply it in targeting counterrevolutionaries. And after the CCP established the PRC, the Communist judicial system would continue to take up the legal principle regarding class throughout Mao's China.

72 Jiangxisheng danganguan, 1982: 2. 656-659.

73 Solomon, 1996: 19.

In the wake of the widespread use of torture in numerous Soviet bases, the central order unequivocally banned torture and replaced it with the independent collection of evidence and other "effective methods." More important, the order helped pave the way for formal judicial systems as it asked all provincial, district, and county Soviet governments to create Adjudicating Departments (*caipanbu*) as interim judicial organs whose mission was to tackle all criminal and civil cases. In a stern warning consistent with the emphasis on law, the central order noted that any violation of this order would be severely punished.[74]

The central order of December 1931 symbolized CCP's first solid step toward founding a Communist judicial system in the Soviet bases. Before long, some local Soviet governments such as Tongling, Anhui had built Adjudicating Departments. In February 1932, the Soviet republic founded the Provisional Supreme Court and appointed He Shuheng, a veteran Communist, as the head. As Trygve Lötveit has argued, the status of the supreme court was "rather ambiguous" because its "supremacy" was "subordinated to the Central Executive Committee."[75] In the meantime, the CCP enacted the Provisional Organic Laws of the Military Court in the republic. During wartime, it is understandable that a military court would be established before a civil court. The military court aimed to resolve cases involving Red Army soldiers who had violated laws such as the criminal law and the military law. There were four levels of military courts: elementary, battleground, high, and supreme. The Supreme Military Court would have a final say on a case. At an elementary military court, there would be one judge and two jurors, a system introduced from the Soviet Union. To ensure power sharing, the jurors had to be elected from the soldiers every week. The law did not say whether the elementary military court had the power to sentence a criminal to death.[76]

In June, the Communist republic publicized its first Provisional Law Regarding the Organization and Judgment of the adjudicating departments proposed in the previous central order. Article 1 said that the adjudicating departments would temporarily handle all civil and criminal cases before the establishment of a formal court. Unlike in Western judicial systems, the upper-level adjudicating department in the Soviet republic had the power to appoint and dismiss employees in lower-level departments. Like

74 Jiangxisheng danganguan, 1982: 2. 656-659; also see *The Red China*, December 28, 1931.

75 Trygve Lötveit, *Chinese Communism 1931-1934: Experience in Civil Government* (Lund: Studentlitteratur, 1979): 107.

76 Ruijinxian renmin fayuan瑞金县人民法院, 1991: 41-49.

their counterparts in the Soviet Union, the adjudicating departments in the Jiangxi Soviet base were subject to the leadership of the same-level Soviet governments, a typical judicial form in a party state that would surely undermine judicial independence.

All adjudicating departments were able to organize their own civil or criminal courts and each of them would comprise one judge and two jurors, which was the same as in a military court. Jurors would be elected by the societies of workers, tenants, poor peasants, and other mass organizations. When a judge and the two jurors were making decisions, the minority had to obey the opinion of the majority. All cases were required to be openly tried unless a case entailed confidentiality. The law also ushered in a principle of avoidance that proscribed any judge or juror who had a private relationship with the defendant from participating in the trial. All defendants had the right to appeal to an appellate court but they had to do so within two weeks after the first verdict. In cases involving a potential death penalty, even though the defendant chose not to appeal, the adjudicating department, as an ostensible way to honor human life, had to report the case to the upper-level department (i.e. provincial adjudicating department) for approval. The law also granted judges such powers as admonition, fine, confiscation of property, forced labor, imprisonment, and execution by a bullet.

Unlike previous regulations, this law, in particular, discussed the task and mission of the procuracy, a system that also came from the Soviet Union. Its theoretical function was to prosecute a suspect on behalf of the state and to oversee the adjudicating department. Both provincial and county governments needed to appoint one or two procurators. Before any case entered a court, it first had to undergo a preliminary investigation by a procurator.[77] The procurator possessed the jurisdiction to arrest and interrogate suspects. In so doing, the procurator in the Soviet republic combined the functions of procuracy and police. With enough evidence, procurators could represent the state and lodge charges at the court. If a procurator disagreed with a court decision, he could request the adjudicating department to conduct a second trial.[78] But according to Hiroshi Oda, there were some fundamental differences between the USSR and the Chinese Soviet Republic in the relations between chief procurators and investigators.[79]

77 "Provisional Organization and Judging Law of the Judging Departments (*caipanbude zanxing zuzhi jicaipan tiaoli*)" in Ruijinxian renmin fayuan, 1991: 51-56.

78 Zhang Hongmou, 1988: 89.

79 Hiroshi Oda, "Criminal Law and Procedure in the Chinese Soviet Republic" in Butler, 1983, pp. 53-70: 57.

While the CCP in Jiangxi was on track to create the adjudicating departments, it was also drafting the regulations and working outline of the revolutionary court. The person in charge of those laws was Liang Botai, a Soviet-trained legal official who planned to incorporate the Russian Soviet judicial model into the Chinese Jiangxi Soviet base. The draft of the Regulations Regarding Revolutionary Courts (*geming fating tiaoli*) in 1932 was meant to orchestrate the internal organizations of the court. Article 1 of the regulations stated that the court would manage the trials and issue the verdicts of all lawsuits. Any decisions of a county court were subject to the approval of a provincial court. Like their counterparts in the Soviet Union and the PRC, the revolutionary courts in the Jiangxi Soviet base had no independence from the central administration as leaders of provincial courts were to be appointed and dismissed by the Soviet executive committee. The provincial courts were empowered to decide the fate of county court leaders, further compromising judicial independence at the lower levels. In addition, each court would have three to five committee members with the court leader as the chairman, though the head of the SPSB, a Soviet form of secret police, should be a committee member that would represent the state and act as the public prosecutor. All committee members in a court would discuss every case and the chairman would report to the same-level government standing committee. The involvement of the SPSB and the requirement of court leaders to report to the same-level governments were actually making the judicial system a loyal tool of the CCP.

To confirm its revolutionary nature, Article 9 gave alleged criminals from different social classes different treatment. For instance, if a suspect was a laborer, he or she would enjoy a period in which to lodge an appeal. A suspect from a predatory class (e.g. a landlord or a capitalist), on the other hand, could not appeal to an appellate court. For the first time, the regulations said that the revolutionary court would establish a Labor Penitentiary (*laodong ganhuayuan*). In theory, the jail was meant to educate criminals, but in reality it was a forced-labor camp aimed to provide support to the Red Army in wartime.[80]

The Working Outline of the Revolutionary Courts (*geming fatingde gongzuo dagang*) was another effort of the CCP to dictate the purpose and nature of its courts. In the "General Principles," the outline stated that the revolutionary court would help the Soviet republic consolidate its anti-Japanese bases and "severely punish" all traitors and counterrevolutionary activities. The court would also protect the "vital interests" of all working

80 Ruijinxian renmin fayuan, 1991: 30-31.

people such as workers, tenants, poor peasants, and middle peasants. While the outline seemed to mainly target traitors who collaborated with the Japanese, the CCP had no interest at the moment to oppose the Japanese when its principal foe was the GMD. The wording of the outline was rhetorical and misleading because it tried to create the impression among the people that the GMD was a collaborator of the Japanese and thus a traitor. The outline also made clear that the revolutionary court had the right to publicly try and judge all traitors and counterrevolutionary cases charged by the SPSB as well as all other civil and criminal cases in the Soviet republic.

Additionally, the working outline included more details on trials, court decisions, and appeals than the Regulations Regarding Revolutionary Courts. First, the outline outlawed torture in preliminary court trials; second, all trials had to be public and all citizens of the Soviet republic could attend. The minimum number of jurors would be five, a number that exceeded other laws and regulations. The outline also laid down specific procedures. After the chief judge announced a case, the state plaintiff/prosecutor (SPSB or procuracy) would file charges. The chief judge would then start the trial and let both plaintiff and defender deliver statements. Later, the chief judge would ask the jurors for opinions and all participants could comment on the case. The court would have a five-minute recess before arriving at a final verdict.

Like the Regulations Regarding Revolutionary Courts, the working outline allowed other citizens but not traitors and counterrevolutionaries to appeal to an upper court within seven days. People from predatory classes such as factory bosses, rich peasants, and businessmen who were dissatisfied with court rulings were allowed to appeal. But they had only three days in which to do so, four days less than ordinary Soviet citizens. The discrepancies served to strengthen the revolutionary nature of the CCP and the Soviet governments.

The outline further specified the roles of the procuracy, which would have two main functions. It would: 1) implement all Soviet laws and regulations, safeguard people's interests, and supervise the judicial system on behalf of the Soviet government; and 2) inspect all criminal cases and publicly prosecute on behalf of the state. However, before arresting any suspect, the procuracy had to seek approval from the court leader, a legal process that differed significantly from that of the later judicial system in the PRC.[81]

81 In the PRC, the police would take charge of initial interrogation and arrest. The Procuracy would bring charges at the court on the basis of police reports. Neither of the judicial organs

Despite the passage of a series of laws and regulations regarding the establishment and operation of the adjudicating departments and courts since late 1931, many counties in the Jiangxi Soviet base did not begin creating their adjudicating departments until March 1932. By June, all counties had founded one such department. Within a few months, the adjudicating departments had drawn much public attention as many people were said to have heard about them and even to have filed appeals there. The biggest obstacle to founding the departments was the shortage of qualified judges. Mostly because of that problem, many districts had yet to have their adjudicating departments in the summer of 1932. To solve that problem, the CCP had to send judges who worked in the county adjudicating departments to provincial courts for legal training. After a short period of training, the judges would go back to their original departments.[82]

According to a 1932 annual report of the People's Committee Department of Judicial system (*sifa renmin weiyuanbu*), the central mission of the adjudicating departments was to serve the people in the ongoing wars against internal enemies. Therefore, the departments were supposed to ramp up its repression of counterrevolutionaries and solidify the Soviet bases. From July to September 1932, 271 criminals had been shot dead and 349 incarcerated in the Soviet republic. The number of executions was relatively high and no one knew exactly how many victims had received correct and impartial trials under largely unqualified Communist judges.

Criminals who had committed minor crimes often found themselves sentenced to forced labor. To assist the Red Army in the war, adjudicating departments were asked to coerce all prisoners sentenced up to two years to do hard labor in factories. In 1932, over 900 prisoners in the Jiangxi Soviet base were reported to do hard labor. Prisoners during hard labor had to make envelopes, paper, ink, straw shoes, chalks, and so forth.[83] According to Hongda H. Wu, a former victim of China's labor camp, the labor camp persisted after the CCP took power in China in 1949, by which time it had become an "economic enterprise" and an "indispensable component of the national economy."[84] Moreover, judges were ordered to accelerate the investigation and ruling processes in order to reduce the number of prisoners under trial and the need to feed them. From 1932 on, it was stipulated that

has to ask the court for permission. See *The PRC Criminal Procedural Law* (Beijing: Zhongguo fazhi chubanshe, 2006); for the working outline see Ruijinxian renmin fayuan, 1991: 33-35.

82 *The Red China*, November 7, 1932; also see Lotveit, 1979: 108.

83 Ibid., November 7, 1932.

84 Wu, 1992: 5.

all cases, no matter how complex, should be decided within fifteen days. Undoubtedly, the new order would force judges to make swift but cursory decisions that might leave behind numerous grievances of one party or another.

As I have mentioned, the CCP tried to realize its revolutionary principles through its judiciaries. Making punishments fit the criminals' social classes was one of them. Taking account of criminals' roles (i.e. primary or secondary) in perpetrating crimes was another.[85] The continuous ban of torture, though sometimes honored in the breach, seemed to encourage judges to rely on evidence rather than confessions to establish guilt.

One year after establishing the adjudicating departments, the People's Committee Department of Judicial system discovered some problems inside the Communist judicial system. Firstly, lower-level judges often could not quickly and correctly implement the orders and instructions from their superiors. Secondly, many judges with little judicial experience and common legal sense made many mistakes. Thirdly, numerous lower-ranking cadres were not familiar with government laws and often unwittingly violated them.[86]

The Communist Judicial System as Revealed in Cases

To better grasp the nature, role, mission, and practice of the Communist judicial system in the Soviet bases, we need to look into some of the cases in this period. In one case, on February 25, 1932, the Provisional Supreme Court of the Soviet republic tried its first case on AB *tuan*. The leading judge was He Shuheng, the Party's "first chief justice."[87] The trial started with a state prosecutor charging three AB *tuan* members, Cao Shuxiang, Kong Fanshu, and Chen Zongjun, with sabotaging the Soviet government, murdering wounded Red soldiers, and collaborating with the GMD. According to available records, the three defendants "quickly confessed their crimes." In the afternoon, Judge He Shuheng announced that Cao and Chen would be jailed for two years and three years respectively. Since Kong, the third defendant, had previously joined the Red Army and done much "revolutionary work," the court reduced his incarceration from three years to eighteen months. However, after the CCP Central Executive Committee reviewed the court verdicts, it questioned the punishments of both Cao

85 Lotveit, 1979: 129.

86 *The Red China*, November 7, 1932; for the hard labor see also Griffin, 1976: 37-38.

87 Miao Tijun, 2012.

and Kong as too "lenient." The committee argued that Cao's decision to "publicly join the AB *tuan* and sabotage the Soviet republic and Red Army" had betrayed the trust of the Soviet republic and the CCP. For that reason, the committee suggested that Cao's imprisonment be increased by fifteen months. For Kong, though the committee understood the rationale behind the reduction of his punishment, it pointed out that Kong had served as a leading officer in the AB *tuan* and therefore his imprisonment should be augmented by three months.[88]

In this case, while lower-level courts were still under construction, the newly founded Interim Supreme Court had to directly deal with cases. None of the defendants had any lawyer to help him. And while the court's expeditious judgment might be appropriate in a period of warring parties, hasty adjudication by the high-level court could set up a dangerous precedent lower courts might be tempted to follow in the future. Additionally, the Supreme Court decision was partly based on the social status of the defendants and their contributions to the Red Army. The revision of the punishments by the central committee shows that the Supreme Court had no independence as the central committee held the ultimate power to question, modify, or reject court decisions on counterrevolutionary cases. To be sure, this case also testifies to certain positive developments of the judicial system in the Soviet republic. In stark contrast to the massive and ruthless treatments of suspected AB *tuan* members just two years earlier, even the augmented penalties of the three counterrevolutionaries were quite "magnanimous."

In another trial on April 3, 1932, the Jiangxi Provincial Adjudicating Department ruled on a case in which three men, Zhu Xidong, Lu Jibin, and Yang Renrui, were charged with being AB *tuan* members. Coming from a rich peasant family, Zhu was a 32-year-old man and a former CCP member. In 1927, Zhu joined the AB *tuan* and later became a local head. In August 1930, Zhu allegedly colluded with the GMD and plotted to destroy the Red Army. In order to provoke people's dissatisfaction with the CCP, Zhu purposely forced people to join the Red Army. During the trial, Zhu tried to retract his previous confessions (probably under torture).

Unlike Zhu Xidong, Lu Jibin was a carpenter belonging to the working class, the theoretical leadership of the revolution. Lu participated in the AB *tuan* in June 1930 and served as a committee member in Xingguo County. After becoming the chairman of the anti-counterrevolutionary committee in the Soviet base, Lu allegedly persecuted revolutionary comrades and "brutally killed members of the masses." Although the provincial Soviet

88 *The Red China*, March 2, 1932.

government had allowed Lu to "make a fresh start" due to his working-class background, he had no remorse and continued his "counterrevolutionary instigations and activities." Yang Renrui was the youngest of the three at only age 25. He was a middle peasant, a member of a class which the CCP was trying to win over to the revolution. Yang became a member of the AB *tuan* in the anti-counterrevolutionary committee of Xinguo county in early 1931 and served as a secretary. In the army, Yang had collaborated with a "white bandit" called Ma Kun and attempted to exterminate the CCP organizations, the masses, and the army in southern Jiangxi.

According to the court verdict, all three criminals had done "factual" counterrevolutionary work and had confessed their crimes. The court sentenced all three on the basis of their "classes," the seriousness of their crimes, and their attitudes. Thus, it sentenced Zhu Xidong to death not only because he was an important AB *tuan* member but also because he had refused to admit his crimes and had recanted his former confession. Zhu's penalty was more severe because of his rich peasant status. While Lu Jibing had been accused of "betraying his [working] class and remaining unaware [of his crimes]," he, most likely due to his worker background, received a light sentence of only three years imprisonment and was allowed to "make a fresh start." Yang Renrui, the youngest AB *tuan* member whose offense was the least, would be behind bars for three years, the same as Lu. Yang's relatively severe punishment might have been caused by his class status as a middle peasant, higher than Lu's working class.[89]

This case tells us that the provincial judges in the Jiangxi base were rather unprofessional, biased, and careless in their judgments. With no jury present, the judges leveled many ambiguous charges against the defendants, such as "plotted," "attempted," "chicanery," "refused to admit crimes" and the so-called "factual crimes" that actually lacked sufficient testimony and evidence. More alarming was the court's report that all three defendants had confessed their crimes and its accusation that Zhu had recanted his previous confession. While "confession" per se has been a "bad but long" tradition in Chinese legal history,[90] the court apparently accepted confessions as evidence of guilt and did not explain what kind of

89 Ibid., April 12, 1932.

90 Confession, often interconnected with torture, has been used widely throughout Chinese history, be it imperial, republican, or the PRC. See Alford, 1984; Wang, Celai, *The Case of Yang Naiwu and Xiao Baicai* (*Yangnaiwu yu xiaobaicaian*) (Beijing: Zhongguo jiancha chubanshe, 2002); Fang, 2013; Amnesty International Report, "China: Torture and Forced Confessions Rampant amid Systematic Trampling of Lawyers" in https://www.amnesty.org/en/latest/news/2015/11/china-torture-forced-confession/

confessions the criminals had made and the circumstances under which they made them. The class-based decision, while perhaps appropriate to a time of social revolution and civil war, also violated legal principles such as justice and "equality before the law." In short, the case further exposes the poor quality of the politically charged Communist judges who based their sentences on problematic confessions and vague crimes. As in Stalin's Russia, the judicial system in the Jiangxi Soviet areas served more as a Party tool than a just arbiter.[91]

Trygve Lötveit attributes the judicial lenience in 1932 to Mao's moderate policy and the severity in 1934 to the 28 Bolsheviks.[92] But a more important reason behind the 1932 lenience might be that judges at the Supreme Court with better legal training were more likely to be lenient than judges at lower-level courts whose legal education and training were limited. In May 1932, for instance, the Ruijin County Adjudicating Department sentenced one Zhu Duoshen to death. Zhu, a 72-year-old "evil gentryman (*lieshen*)," was charged with five crimes he had committed in the past: 1) bullying and oppressing poor people; 2) refusing to distribute his land to others; 3) embezzling public funds and fines; 4) claiming to be the inspector of three counties; 5) stealing public bullets and selling them for profit. None of the above crimes seemed to warrant a death penalty because Zhu had committed neither murder nor robbery. Nor did the court verdict contain details or evidence of the alleged crimes. But it allowed Zhu to appeal to an upper-level court within one week. Since this case involved a potential death sentence, the Provisional Supreme Court reviewed the case. Justice He Shuheng immediately rejected the death penalty on grounds that Zhu was merely a corrupt and selfish person and Zhu's claim that he had been a county inspector was an "ordinary" criminal case. Moreover, He Shuheng remarked that Zhu had joined the revolution in the past and was also an old man. Therefore, He Shuheng noted that Zhu should instead be sentenced to two years in prison.[93]

The above case illustrates that many county judges who had little legal training and were indifferent to people's lives would haphazardly sentence a person to death for obscure crimes. Communist judges in Ruijin County did not even bother to cite Zhu's confession but only used alleged uncorroborated accusations. Had the final decision to execute Zhu not been reviewed by the Supreme Court, Zhu would have lost his life due

91 *The Red China*, April 12, 1932.

92 Lotveit, 1979: 144.

93 *The Red China*, June 2, 1932.

to unqualified and careless county judges. Yet, as we will see later, the CCP again granted county judges the jurisdiction to kill criminals when its wars with the GMD intensified after 1932. Many more unfortunate suspects with relatively minor or ambiguous crimes similar to that of Zhu Duoshen would have been executed without an upper-level court coming to their aid.

In the above cases, a major concern of the Soviet courts that had drawn criticism from the Supreme Court justice was the lack of legal professionalism and the poor quality of many CCP judges. But in cases involving counterrevolutionaries, judges were chastised for their legalistic and just rulings. For instance, on October 15 and 16, 1932, Supreme Court justice He Shuheng sharply lambasted judges in the Xunwu County adjudicating department for their "right opportunism" because they failed to base their rulings on criminals' social classes. For instance, one Lan Changxu had allegedly organized an assassination squad, talked in meetings about killing government officials and CCP members, and dissuaded people from fighting the GMD. Lan was sentenced to six months of hard labor. According to He Shuheng, any of the three counterrevolutionary crimes would have merited a death penalty. The lenience toward counterrevolutionaries would certainly be detrimental in a period of intense class warfare. He ordered the county judges to execute Lan. Questioning the limited number of counterrevolutionaries in Xunwu County, He Shuheng argued that there should be more reactionaries inside the county who were trying to take advantage of the ongoing wars. Invoking Lenin's words, He Shuheng warned the judges, "The looseness/lenience toward counterrevolutionaries is tantamount to disloyalty to the revolution." Therefore, even in 1932, the Supreme Court could be very harsh if a case entailed counterrevolutionaries who would threaten the survival of the CCP.[94]

Here, He Shuheng who himself was criticized for being too lenient to counterrevolutionaries in early 1932, now placed social class and the CCP's bloody wars with the GMD above legal principles and the law. As the aforementioned cases show, there was often a paucity of tangible evidence for many alleged crimes which, in a more sophisticated and professional court, would either be dismissed entirely or sent back for more evidence. In tackling political criminal cases, judges in Xunwu County may have just tried to be professional and unbiased and they forgot that they were Communist judges who should punish counterrevolutionaries more harshly.

94 Ruijinxian renmin fayuan, 1991: 200-201.

Final Years of the Jiangxi Soviet Judicial System

Right after the founding of the formal judicial system in the central Soviet base in Jiangxi, the treatment of counterrevolutionaries and other class enemies appeared to be uneven. Some local judges seemed to be haphazard in employing death penalties, while other judges at local courts treated counterrevolutionaries or political enemies with some lenience according to the relevant laws. For instance, judges in the case of Lan Changxu punished him to only six months of hard labor, while justice He Shuheng claimed that any one of Lan's alleged crimes would be sufficient for execution. The Supreme Court was also generally lenient in handling regular criminal cases except when the counterrevolutionary crimes were serious.

The irregular ephemeral merciful treatment of counterrevolutionaries soon vanished, however, as Chiang Kai-shek and the GMD stepped up military pressure on the Soviet bases. The GMD's fourth military campaign began in late 1932 and ended in spring 1933. Six months later, Chiang launched the fifth and by far the largest campaign against the Soviet base. Over one million troops had been deployed to encircle and attack the Jiangxi central Soviet base in October 1933. The fifth military campaign lasted about one year and succeeded in driving the CCP and the Red Army out of the central base they had occupied for almost seven years. In addition to the GMD's military attacks from outside, GMD allies and spies inside the Soviet bases reportedly increased their sabotage. In the face of both external and internal enemies, the CCP was in a desperate and nearly hopeless situation and survival became the top concern of the Party.

To stamp out the threats from within, the CCP initiated a massive crackdown against counterrevolutionaries in the Soviet bases. On December 5, 1932, the provincial Soviet government in Fujian province issued a report censuring judges who were not being tough on counterrevolutionaries in a critical time. "As the class struggle becomes increasingly violent, counterrevolutionary factions such as local tyrants, landlords, and rich peasants will definitely speed up their activities." The report noted, "Yet [we] still do not have a generally intensified repression of the counterrevolutionaries, which is our biggest mistake."[95]

Being a loyal instrument of the CCP, the Soviet judicial system quickly became much harsher and more relentless in dealing with counterrevolutionary cases. As attested in the counterrevolutionary case of Huang Yufa at the beginning of this chapter, many alleged political adversaries of the CCP were

95 *The Red China*, December 5, 1933.

summarily executed for minor crimes in the military campaigns. When the war became more intense in 1933, the judicial system was slow to respond, so the Red Army and the SPSB moved to bypass the courts and to charge and execute alleged counterrevolutionaries themselves. Some executions were reportedly made at the request of the masses.[96]

On April 26, 1933, the Central Unit of Youth Pioneers (*shaoxiandui zhongyang zongdui*) publicly tried four criminals who had allegedly sabotaged the revolution and instigated Red soldiers to defect. Two of them were members of the Social Revolutionary Party, a counterrevolutionary party, who had spread rumors among the people and secretly organized counterrevolutionary units. The other two had merely complained about the poor conditions of the Red Army and encouraged other soldiers to defect. The trial began with slogans against sabotage and defection. Then the SPSB publicly prosecuted the alleged criminals. After all the criminals had "confessed," delegates from various Soviet areas denounced their crimes and demanded harsh punishment. At the reportedly "unanimous" request from the audience, the "quasi-court" ruled that the two counterrevolutionary party members would be executed and the other two would do hard labor.[97]

While the SPSB was supposed to be only the public prosecutor who charged suspects on behalf of the Soviet government, it took over the entire court duty when the war situation turned graver and CCP's survival hung by a thread. In early 1934, the Red Army had fought several months resisting the GMD's fifth campaign and the war became increasingly hopeless for the besieged Red Army. On February 20, the SPSB arrested four counterrevolutionaries in Ruijin County. Among them, Hu Xiazhou was charged with disturbing the economy by buying cheap commodities and selling them dearly. Lai Dakui, a former landlord, had "dared" to "exploit workers and peasants" in the Soviet capital. Two other defendants had committed more minor crimes such as instigating people to leave the Soviet area and "purposely" lowering the value of the Soviet currency. Upon announcing the crimes of the four counterrevolutionaries, the SPSB paraded them through the streets wearing paper hats.[98] Although most of the crimes seemed insignificant or even legal in the Republic of China, the SPSB decided to execute both Hu and Lai. The penalty imposed on the other two was

96 Griffin, 1976: 63; for the deaths pressed by the mass see Lotveil, 1979: 137-138.

97 *The Red China*, May 5, 1933.

98 In Mao's 1927 report on the Hunan peasant movement, he claimed that peasants paraded landlords and local tyrants through the streets. In the PRC, parading criminals continues to be a common scene. For the PRC see Tanner, 1999.

unknown, but a likely fate would have been hard labor desperately needed in a war.[99]

The fierce war prompted CCP leaders to make laws more suitable to wartime and to empower local governments to handle counterrevolutionaries. On March 1, 1934, *Red China* published an article of Supreme Court justice Liang Botai in which Liang stated that in a critical time, repressing counterrevolutionaries would be the principal mission of the Communist judicial system. "In the face of a decisive war to destroy the GMD's fifth military campaign and in a period when class struggle is becoming extremely acute," Liang wrote, "the central mission of the judicial system will be to strike the rising number of counterrevolutionaries in the Soviets, suppress their activities, and to help the Red Army speedily and successfully smash the fifth military campaign." Liang criticized judges who had been unwilling to resolutely punish counterrevolutionaries. These judges tended to rigidly abide by the law, Liang observed, and did not understand that law should be practiced in tune with revolutionary needs. Liang also said that in the present time, "Whatever is conducive to the revolution will be legal. If the revolution needs something, law should be adjusted to provide it. The legal process should not hinder revolutionary interests."

To make the Communist judicial system more attuned to the grave wartime situation, Liang ordered all Soviet judges to repress counterrevolutionaries. Once a court discovered that class enemies such as landlords, local tyrants, or rich peasants had done any "factual" counterrevolutionary action, the court should execute them, no matter how small their actions. In addition, Liang told Soviet courts to resolve all cases except special ones within three days so as to accelerate the legal process. It is comprehensible that judges would not be given ample time to deal with cases in wartime, but the Supreme Court order for a hasty resolution of most cases would undoubtedly cause numerous deaths and grievances. As the war turned uglier and more brutal, Soviet courts would have had its remaining legality and professionalism further eroded.[100] Given the new "authority" from the Supreme Court, Communist judges or officials might capitalize on it to avenge whomever they had a grudge against or disliked, using torture or even execution. They knew that no one would bother to supervise or inspect their actions so long as they branded the victim as a "class enemy."

Obviously, Liang Botai could not issue orders without approval from his superior, the Jiangxi Soviet government. Two weeks after Liang's article,

99 *The Red China*, February 20, 1934.
100 Ibid., March 1, 1934.

Mao, as chairman of the Soviet Republic, ordered that during emergency times local Soviet governments could execute any criminals who had committed "factual" counterrevolutionary crimes even before reporting to their superiors. For landlords and rich peasants who had committed no "factual" counterrevolutionary crimes, local Soviet governments should mobilize people to supervise them but not arrest them.[101] The precedence set by the CCP leaders to officially allow local governments to execute political enemies without waiting for the endorsements of the Supreme Court would continue to be practiced during later political movements in the PRC.

To prevent some "rightist" judges from hindering the ongoing anti-counterrevolutionary movement, the central Soviet government decided in April 1934 to purge judges who had been "too lenient" toward political criminals. For example, Li Shisen, head of the Guangdong and Jiangxi Provincial Adjudicating Department, was accused of being lax and soft in penalizing counterrevolutionaries. Another judge named Wang Fadian was head of the Gonglu County Adjudicating Department. The Soviet government dismissed him for "stubbornly" applying state laws in dealing with class enemies. In one case, Wang reportedly ignored the people's call to execute an army deserter, claiming insufficient evidence for the alleged crime.[102]

In May 1934, as the Red Army was on the verge of losing the war in Jiangxi, the CCP leader Bo Gu called on the people to "use their hot blood and heads" to join the Red Army and defend the republic.[103] Meanwhile, the CCP ordered that "public will" would suffice to execute a counterrevolutionary and there was no need for a trial. In other words, if the people demanded an execution, the court would have to agree to it.[104] Moreover, in Shengli County, people were encouraged to kill alleged counterrevolutionaries without public trials. Judges who had refused to bow to the "public will" to punish counterrevolutionaries harshly were themselves condemned and purged. Some worker and peasant cadres who had little legal knowledge but possessed firm "class-consciousness" were appointed as new judges.[105] Both the purge of "rightist" judges and their replacement by worker and farmer cadres were precursors of the 1952 legal reform in the PRC.

On December 20, 1934, after the bulk of the Red Army abandoned the Jiangxi Soviet base and fled to the west, the interim government office of

101 Jiangxisheng danganguan, 1982: 2. 672.
102 *The Red China*, April 12, 1934.
103 Bo Gu博古, "Editorial" in *The Red China*, May 16, 1934.
104 Ibid., May 23, 1934.
105 Ibid.

the Soviet Republic that stayed to fight guerrilla warfare against the GMD ascribed the failure of the revolution in Jiangxi to traitors who had guided the GMD army into the Soviet bases, done propaganda work at the behest of the GMD, or killed revolutionary workers and peasants. The government issued an emergency order to allow revolutionary people to kill any traitor at will. Meanwhile, the Soviet Republic had largely ceased to exist and there was no formal Communist judicial system. Thus, the order may have been ineffective as the interim government quickly moved underground and Liang Botai, its deputy head, would soon be captured and executed by the GMD.[106]

The speedy shift of the Jiangxi Soviet judicial system toward a more bloody, lawless, and hasty campaign against alleged counterrevolutionaries after late 1932 can be understood as a relatively legitimate reciprocation to the equally relentless and treacherous tactics of the GMD. Before the CCP adopted a repressive means to deal with class enemies and GMD spies in the Soviet areas, the GMD had already suppressed the CCP and killed numerous Communists in its domain. When the CCP failed to defeat the GMD's fifth military campaign and escaped, the GMD tracked and killed surviving CCP members including more than 200 judges.[107]

Born in Blood

For the CCP in its early history, Marxist and Leninist theories of class struggle and survival from enemy attacks were the two crucial and driving factors behind the creation and changing policies of the Communist judicial system. From its outset, the CCP judicial system had been closely interconnected with blood and violence due to a fundamental fear and insecurity. Long before the CCP created a judicial system, some leaders such as Mao Zedong had praised the bloody movements in the Hunan rural areas against landlords. After the GMD "betrayed" the revolution and relentlessly attacked the CCP, the CCP responded by founding its own army and Soviet bases in several provinces. The Purging Counterrevolutionary Committee, arguably the earliest form of the Communist judicial system, aimed exclusively to protect the Soviet bases by suppressing internal counterrevolutionaries and GMD agents. The informal but powerful committees had adopted cruel methods against alleged class enemies, especially the AB *tuan*. The enormous and unbridled lawless crackdowns in the Soviet bases culminated in the

106 Ruijin renmin fayuan, 1991: 90-92.
107 Ibid., 1991: 279-300; for detailed GMD's brutality against the CCP see Wakeman, 1995.

notorious Futian Incident in 1930 which resulted in the deaths of thousands of CCP cadres and soldiers.

The mass killing and brutal torture against the AB *tuan* prompted the CCP to proceed to establish a more formal and disciplined judicial system in late 1931. Soviet bases at provincial, district, and county levels were asked to create adjudicating departments. Communist judges had to abide by certain legal procedures such as public trials and juries, and torture was prohibited. The class line persisted as a principle for Communist judges. Suspects from predatory classes would be punished more severely than workers and peasants. However, due to unqualified judges and lack of modern interrogating methods (i.e. the SPSB), confessions that were often associated with torture continued to be used as bases for judicial verdicts. Adding to its imperfection were scanty judicial independence and judges' inferiority to upper-level courts and peer governments. Despite their instrumental role of the CCP, many Communist judges had defied the class line and tried to treat suspects equally and somewhat leniently.

The problems of the Communist judicial system were aggravated amid the GMD's fourth and fifth military campaigns during which the CCP encountered unprecedented challenges to its very survival. As a result, the transient practice of "mercy" disappeared and was replaced by more severe, ruthless, and indiscriminate punishments of alleged counterrevolutionaries. Infractions as minor as a rumor or selling goods at higher prices could be enough for an execution. The powerful SPSB intervened to make its own trials and punishments. Some judges who had refused to implement rigorous penalties were accused and removed. The so-called "public will" of the people weighed more than Soviet laws and court judges. In its final days, the supreme court virtually gave the judicial system "a free hand" to conduct executions. The life-and-death war quickly compelled the Communist judicial system to morph from an ostensible law defender to a naked political mechanism and even a "legal violator" of law.

Unfortunately, as I will discuss in the following chapters, the lawlessness in the final stage of the Soviet Republic did not disappear after the CCP moved to Yan'an, its new base until 1947, and founded the PRC. As palpably evidenced in the 1942 Rectification Campaign, the counterrevolutionary movements in the 1950s, the Cultural Revolution, the bloody and violent origin of the Communist judicial system and above all the CCP's inherent fear of extinction, enemy subversion, and losing power have remained overwhelming and have continued to haunt the CCP to this day.

2 Cornerstone or Aberration?

The Communist Judicial System during Wars with Japan and the GMD, 1936-1949

Abstract
Many scholars in China have applauded the legal system and practices such as the Ma Xiwu method of dealing with rural marriage cases in the Shaanxi Border Region as a main pillar of the PRC legal construction. This chapter challenges this view with an argument that those scholars have ignored the enormous number of arbitrary transgressions of the law, such as torture and imprisonment. Nor do those scholars pay much attention to the CCP's "voluntary" acceptance of Republican laws during the anti-Japanese war. In stark contrast to CCP's previous and ensuing anti-GMD propaganda and policies, the period of the Border Area could be better called an aberration from the Communist judicial tradition rather than a cornerstone.

Keywords: Shanganning Border Area High Court, Li Mu'an, Lei Jingtian, human sentiment, rectification campaign

The year of 1936 was a turning point for the Chinese Communist Party (CCP). On the one hand, the main force of the Red Army had completed its heroic long march in early 1936 and joined a local Communist force in the region of northern Shaanxi; on the other hand, Zhang Xueliang, the "Young Marshall" who was prodded by Chiang Kai-shek to fight the Red Army, decided to kidnap Chiang on December 12 and to force him to turn his guns against the Japanese rather than the Red Army. These dramatic developments offered CCP leader Mao Zedong a prime opportunity to consolidate the fragile Communist control in the Shanganning Border Area (hereinafter the Border Area). Together they transformed the Party from being a "marginal force on the periphery of Chinese society" into being

Fang, Qiang, *The Communist Judicial System in China, 1927-1976: Building on Fear.*
Taylor & Francis Group 2021
DOI: 10.5117/9789463729451_CH02

the "major contender for national power" after the war.[1] According to Zhang Guotao, one of CCP's founders and a contender with Mao for power inside the Party, a negotiation with Chiang Kai-shek was critical to the survival of the CCP. Mao therefore "concealed" his animosity toward Chiang and "pretended" to make resistance to the Japanese a primary goal of the CCP.[2] The CCP publicly announced that it was willing to make significant compromises such as declaring the Border Area a regional government under the Nationalist Party (the Guomindang, or GMD) and recognizing Chiang Kai-shek as China's sole leader.

Soon after Japan launched a sweeping attack on China in July 1937, the CCP proclaimed that resisting Japan should be the top priority of the nation and the Red Army would fight under the GMD.[3] Wang Ming, a young CCP leader who had recently returned from Russia, stressed the importance of a united front against Japan. He argued that the CCP should "follow GMD leadership in all times, all matters, and all areas."[4] On July 8, 1937, the CCP stated that it would strive to realize GMD's Three People's Principles, modify its class struggles, and renounce any actions against the GMD. Despite the CCP's ostensible public submission to the GMD, Mao and his followers may actually have wished to prod the GMD to fight the Japanese so as to save and develop the Border Area.[5]

Throughout the Second Sino-Japanese War (1937-1945), the CCP, in name or actuality, governed its autonomous region in the northwest and fought the Japanese as a local government of the Republic of China under leader

1 David S.G. Goodman, *Social and Political Change in Revolutionary China: The Taihang Base Area in the War of Resistance to Japan, 1937-1945* (New York: Rowman & Littlefield, 2000): vi.

2 Zhang Guotao张国焘, *My Memoir* (*Wode huiyi*我的回忆), (Hong Kong: Minbao yuekan, 1966): 350.

3 Zhang Guotao, 1966: 378; also see Guo Dehong郭德宏, *A Chronicle of Wang Ming* (*Wang Ming nianpu*王明年谱) (Beijing: Shehui kexue wenxian chubanshe, 2014): 351; Lei Jingtian雷经天, "The Judicial System of the Shanganning Border Area (*Shanganning bianqu desifa zhidu* 陕甘宁边区的司法制度)" in Zhang Shibin张世斌, ed., *The Historical Traces of the High Court in the Shanganning Border Area* (*Shanganning bianqu gaodeng fayuan shiji*陕甘宁边区高等法院史迹) (Shaanxi: Shaanxi renmin chubanshe, 2004): 73.

4 Guo Dehong, 2014: 388.

5 See Zhang Guotao, 1966: 380. Zhang Guotao's view may be justified by some other accounts. For example, Mao himself expressed his gratitude to the visiting Japanese prime minister Tanaka Kakue in 1972 that the Japanese invasion helped the CCP in taking power in China. See Zheng Wang, *Never Forget National Humiliation: Historical Memory in Chinese Politics and Foreign Relations* (New York: Columbia University Press, 2014): 89; Peter Vladimirov, a Russian journalist who stayed in Yan'an during the war criticized the Red Army for not fighting the Japanese, see Peter Vladimirov, *Yan'an Diary* (*Yan'an riji*延安日记) (Beijing: Dongfang chubanshe, 2004): 38.

Chiang Kai-shek. In the Border Area, while the CCP exerted a full control over its judicial system and promulgated many local laws, it nonetheless introduced a number of modified GMD laws such as the Criminal Law, the Criminal Procedural Law, the Civil Law, and the Civil Procedural Law to show its respect for GMD leadership and private property, both anathema to Communist ideology. To make its judicial system more "modern" and "formal," the CCP also adopted Republican judicial forms such as the format of court verdict.[6] Yet, the CCP maintained a two-tier trial system (local and high courts) instead of the GMD's tertiary trial system. The biggest reason is that people living in the autonomous Border Area could not appeal to the Republican Supreme Court if dissatisfied with the decisions of the Communist high court.[7]

In both China and the West, many scholars have studied the judicial system in the Border Area during the Sino-Japanese War and a few of them have touched on the subsequent civil war (1945-1949). These scholarly contributions can be roughly classified into three general categories: the judicial system in the Border Area;[8] certain parts of the judicial system such as marriage law and labor camp;[9] and renowned judges such as Ma Xiwu, Xie Juezai, and Lei Jingtian in the high court.[10]

6 The typical format of an ROC court usually contained four parts: Litigants, Main Body, Reason, and Fact.

7 Yang Yonghua 杨永华and Fang Keqin方克勤, *Historical Materials of the Shanganning Border Area* (*Shanganning bianqu fazhi shigao*陕甘宁边区法制史稿) (Beijing: Law Press, 1987): 112.

8 Ibid., 1987; also Wang Shirong汪世荣, ed., *The Cornerstone of the New China Judicial System* (*Xinzhongguo sifa zhidude jishi*新中国司法制度的基石) (Beijing: Shangwu yinshuguan, 2011); also Wang Shirong汪世荣, "The Accomplishments of the Shanganning High Court (*Shanganning bianqu gaodeng fayuande chengjiu*陕甘宁边区高等法院的成就)" in *The Journal of Southwest University of Politics and Law*, December 2010, Vol. 12, No. 6, pp. 10-17.

9 For the marriage law see Xiaoping Cong, *Marriage, Law and Gender in Revolutionary China, 1940-1960* (Cambridge University Press, 2016) and "Zuo Run suing Wang Yinsuo: Women, Marriage, and State Building in the 1940s Shanganning Border Area (*Zuorunsu Wang Yinsuo: ershi shiji sishi niandai Shanganning bianqude funu hunyinyu guojia jiangou*左润诉王银锁：二十世纪四十年代陕甘宁边区妇女婚姻与国家建构)" in *Kaifang shidai*, Vol. 10, 2009; for the labor camp and prison see Klaus Mühlhahn, *Criminal Justice in China: A History* (Cambridge, Ma: Harvard University Press, 2009): 147-165.

10 See Zhang Bo张波, "An Analysis of the Argument of 'Discourse Milieu' in the Shanganning Border Area (*Shanganning bainqu sifa zhidude 'yujinglun' fenxi*陕甘宁边区司法制度的语境论)" in *Lilun daokan*, Vol. 9, 2016; Xiao Zhoulu肖周录, "A Study on the Compiled Book of Legal Cases in the Shanganning Border Area (*Shanganning bianqu panli huibian kaolue*陕甘宁边区判例汇编考略)" in *Faxue yanjiu*, Vol. 1, 2014, pp. 190-208; He Bing何兵, "Lei Jingtian, the Person who Founded the Red Judicial System but had no Legal Values (*Meiyou Falü guandiande hongse sifa dianjiren Lei Jingtian*没有法律观点的红色司法奠基人雷经天)" in *Nanfang dushibao*, July 20, 2014; Feng Jie冯杰, "A Brief Study on Xie Juezai's Thought on Legal Development (*Qianxi Xie*

Each of these researches has helped us understand more about the role, nature, principles, and practice of the judicial system in the Border Area. This chapter is based on those studies but also differs from them in several key aspects. First, none of these scholars has paid attention as I have to the massive unlawful activities conducted by the CCP in the Border Area in which thousands of people, mostly Party members or sympathizers, were detained, tortured, and forced to kill themselves. Second, none compares, as I will, crucial Communist Border Area criminal and civil laws with their GMD counterparts. Third, the chapter will look for the first time into the changes and continuities between the laws in the Jiangxi Soviet Base and those in the later Border Area. Finally, most existing studies have centered on the period of the Sino-Japanese War and largely ignored the developments and reforms in the second civil war. This study will fill that gap with a section devoted to conditions in the second civil war, which to some extent may have had a more significant impact than the war of Resistance against Japan on the judicial system in the early People's Republic of China (PRC).

War-Time Compromises of the CCP

Before the CCP and the Red Army fled to the Border Area, the CCP had adopted a radical revolutionary policy against the GMD and such class enemies as landlords, rich peasants, and capitalists. According to the 1934 constitution of the Jiangxi Soviet, the ultimate objectives of the CCP were to overthrow the rule of imperialism and the GMD and to found a Soviet Republic in China. In a Soviet Republic, only workers, peasants, and Red soldiers would have the right to elect their members to the government. Exploiters and counterrevolutionaries would have no political rights.[11]

However, as the specter of a Japanese aggression was looming large, CCP leaders, with their adroit flexibility and adjustment or successful "Cultural Positioning" to survive,[12] quickly reversed their former hostility toward the GMD, Chiang Kai-shek, and the so-called exploitive classes (i.e. landlords

*Juezai fazhi jianshe sixiang*浅析谢觉哉法制建设思想)," April 3, 2015, http://www.npxfy.gov.cn/dcyj/125.html

11 "The Constitutional Outline of the Chinese Soviet Republic (*Zhonghua suweiai gongheguo xianfa dagang*中华苏维埃共和国宪法大纲)" in Ruijinxian renmin fayuan瑞金县人民法院, ed., 1991: 12-16.

12 Elizabeth Perry argues that educated CCP leaders including Mao brought to their organizing efforts substantial cultural capital and creativity. See Perry, 2012: 3-5; for CCP's flexibility see also Cong, 2016: 19.

and capitalists) in order to form a wartime alliance with the GMD. On May 15, 1938, ten months after the war began, the Border Government and the Eighth Route Army publicly announced that Chiang Kai-shek would be the national leader and the GMD would be the central government. "Since the Marco Polo Bridge incident, our Chinese people have determined to resist [the Japanese] under the leadership of the central government and president Chiang Kai-shek," the announcement stated. It added "the Shanganning Border Area is a part of the Republic of China and it follows the orders of the central government." To prevent "certain people" from taking advantage of the CCP's fresh stance by forcing peasants to return their land to former landlords, forcing debtors to pay their previously abolished debts, or forcing ordinary people to abandon the established democratic system, the CCP charged these people with sabotaging the united front and damaging the authority of the Border Government.[13] This note reveals that the CCP overtly recognized GMD leadership and policies but covertly wanted to limit its submission so that it would be more nominal than real.

In the early stage of the Sino-Japanese War, certain important laws of the Border Area mirrored CCP's recognition of GMD leadership. On April 4, 1939, the preamble of the Wartime Administrative Program of the Border Area remarked that the Border Area would adopt Sun Yat-sen's Three People's Principles and follow the rule of the national government and president Chiang Kai-shek. The CCP vowed to unite with its former enemies such as landlords and capitalists in the ongoing war against the Japanese. The CCP also reiterated its earlier promise that it would protect private property and merchants' freedom to manage business, compromises appropriate to wartime.[14]

In early 1941, the Wan'nan incident exposed the fundamental rift and distrust between the two parties.[15] But the CCP was not ready to openly split with the GMD. In the wake of growing tensions between the two parties, the CCP revised its previous administrative program in May. Unlike the former program, the new one no longer mentioned Sun Yat-sen's Three

13 Ai Shaorun艾邵润, ed., *A Collection of Laws and Regulations of the Shanganning Border Area* (*Shanganning bianqu Falü fagui huibian*陕甘宁边区法律法规汇编) (Shaanxi: Shaanxi renmin chubanshe, 2007a): 85.

14 Ibid., 2007a: 3-4.

15 The Wannan Incident was a military clash between CCP's New Fourth Army and the GMD in January 1941 during which about a third of the 9000 Communist soldiers were killed. This incident sparked a fear that the domestic conflict between the two parties would derail China's war against the Japanese. See Xiaobing Li, ed., *China at War: An Encyclopedia* (Santa Barbara: ABC-CLIO, 2012): 319-320.

People's Principles. Instead, it expressed the CCP's willingness to cooperate with all mass groups and parties in the Border Area. It voluntarily reduced the number of Communist delegates in local governments to one third. In Article 6, the CCP reaffirmed its pledge of safeguarding the human, political, and financial rights of all anti-Japanese people including landlords, capitalists, peasants, and workers.[16]

Rebuilding a Wartime Communist Judicial System

Judicial reform was one of the most important missions of the CCP under the policy of a united front. As a "regional" government of the Republic of China, the CCP felt it imperative to comply with Republican laws by jettisoning or at least revising many of its old laws and judicial mechanisms.

On April 4, 1939, the Border Government promulgated an Organic Regulation of the High Court. The regulation first noted that the enactment was in accordance with the Republican Organic Law of Court. The high court at the Border Area would be subject to the jurisdiction of the Republican Supreme Court, a further recognition of the central power of the GMD. While the regulation asserted that the high court would exert its independent power, it contradicted itself by placing the high court under the supervision of the Border Area senate and the leadership of the Border Government. This, of course, was consistent with the longstanding instrumental role of the Communist judicial system. The regulation contained several chapters such as the organization, supervisory department, court, secretary unit, and detention center. In the chapter on "organization," the regulation stipulated the authority of the chief judge, legal cases with which the court should deal, and internal departments.[17] With the birth of this organic regulation, the Border Area could boast a more "modern" and "formal" judicial system than in the Jiangxi Soviet base.

The 1941 administrative program promised for the first time to revamp the judicial system in the Border Area. That included, among other things, abolishing corporal punishment, limiting the power to arrest and interrogate to the judicial system and the police, providing people with the right to charge government employees with misconduct, and emphasizing evidence rather than confession. In addition, the program also ushered in a milder treatment of traitors and anti-Communists (aka. counterrevolutionaries

16 Ai Shaorun, 2007a: 4-6.

17 Ibid., 2007a: 25-28.

in other times). For example, the program said that traitors, except those unrepentant, should be treated magnanimously and offered a new way of living no matter what they had done in the past. The government should not execute, humiliate, or force them to confess. These new policies, if strictly implemented, would have been a major deviation from the extralegal methods and cruel laws in the Jiangxi Soviet base during which summary execution, corporal punishment or torture, and forced hard labor were common.[18]

While the 1941 administrative program failed to provide details of the proposed judicial reform, another law made in late 1941 was more specific. The law entitled Statutes in Safeguarding Human and Financial Rights in the Shanganning Border Area contained several articles on the judicial reform. Article 7 noted that, apart from active criminals (*xianxingfan* or people committing new crimes), all other suspects had to be arrested and interrogated only by judicial or police departments. If any public employee violated people's rights, people could use all means to accuse the public employee. Article 8 required the judicial system and police to have sufficient evidence and follow legal procedures in arrests. If a non-judicial department arrested any active criminal, the department should surrender the criminal along with evidence to the procuracy or police within 24 hours. Like the 1941 administrative program, Article 10 banned torture and stressed evidence. More details of the judicial reform included: 1) investigation and decision of civil cases should not exceed 30 days; 2) people in civil cases who had not resisted court decisions should not be detained; 3) the property of arrested criminals should not be confiscated before court rulings; 4) governments below the district level could only investigate and mediate cases. They could not interrogate, detain, or punish.

To differentiate this law from GMD laws, Article 14 stated that the court in the Border Area would not charge any litigation fee. But like GMD laws, this law also asked appealers to follow the judicial hierarchy in their appeals.[19] Moreover, the CCP was aware of the important relations between the military and civilians during wartime. On December 9, 1942, the Border Government enacted a tentative method to deal with military-civilian relations. The law required local people to respect the rights of anti-Japanese soldiers suspected of committing crimes. Law-violating soldiers would be tried and punished by the military department rather than a civilian government. Local governments or citizens should not arrest or abuse soldiers accused

18 See Ruijinxian renmin fayuan, 1991: 28-30, 152-154.

19 Ai Shaorun, 2007a: 7-8.

of committing crimes. The law also required military personnel to respect people's rights and rigorously prohibit any unlawful arrest, fine, beating, or torture.[20]

From the outset, the judicial system in the Border Area adopted a three-level court system, including county, high, and supreme court, similar to that of the GMD.[21] Yet, such a tertiary system existed only in theory because the GMD did not recognize the Communist judicial system and there was no cooperation between the two judiciaries.[22] Therefore, any decision of the high court in the Border Area actually became final. If a plaintiff or defendant was dissatisfied with the high court decision, he or she would have to appeal to the Government Committee in the Border Area and not the GMD Supreme Court.

In practice, the judicial system in the Border Area was quite messy. Many appealers paid no attention to the judicial levels and continued the imbedded and informal tradition of lodging complaints to wherever they deemed fit.[23] In 1942, to clean up the mess, the Border Government revised the law and made the Government Adjudicating Committee its highest court (above the high court). With the exception of special and grave cases, all other lawsuits that had not gone through county judicial departments/local courts would not be accepted by the high court. Two years later, the judicial system again experienced another major change as the Government Adjudicating Committee was abolished and the tertiary system became a binary system: county/local court and the high court.[24] After 1944, the high court in the Border Area played a dual role as both an appellate court and a de facto supreme court.

Before its termination in 1944, the Government Adjudicating Committee in the Border Area had functioned for two years as the "Supreme Court." On August 22, 1942, Lin Boqu, a veteran Communist and the chairman of the Border Government, issued an order to create the adjudicating committee. The proposed committee would have five committee members. The chairman and deputy chairman of the Border Government would simultaneously serve as the head and deputy head of the committee, reminiscent of the

20 Ibid., 2007a: 8.

21 For the GMD judicial grade system see Nie Xin聂鑫, "The Transition of the Judicial Grade System in Modern China: Concept and Reality (*Jindai zhongguo shenji zhidude bianqian: linianyu xianshi*近代中国审极制度的变迁：理念与现实)" in *Peking University Law Journal*, Vol. 22, No. 2 (2010), pp. 246-261: 252-253.

22 Yang Yonghua and Fang Keqin, 1987: 112.

23 For the informal tradition of complaint system see Qiang Fang, 2013a.

24 Yang Yonghua and Fang Keqin, 1987: 113.

imperial judicial system in which the emperor acted as the supreme justice. The committee was designed to accept criminal cases that had gone through the high court. Other cases or issues such as administrative lawsuits, marriage cases, review of death penalty, and law interpretation could also be decided by the committee.[25]

In the Border Area, county courts or magistrates acted as the first-instance court. From the Jiangxi Soviet base to late 1942, the county court consisted of county Party secretary, magistrate, judge, head of security department whose primary mission was to safeguard the Communist government and assail its enemies. After the CCP recognized GMD's leadership in the Sino-Japanese War, the old form of "county court" seemed no longer suitable to the new situation. Accordingly, the high court of the Border Government dictated in November 1942 that county adjudicating committees be dissolved and that all important and complicated cases be decided by the county government committee.[26]

In March 1943, to substitute for the county adjudicating committees, the Border Government asked counties that did not have local courts to establish judicial departments/units to deal with first-instance criminal and civil cases. Like GMD controlled regions where most of the county magistrates continued to act as judges, many magistrates in the Border Area also served as heads of the judicial departments who would monitor judges in the departments.[27] In counties with a limited number of lawsuits, the heads of the judicial department would be judges. For civil cases involving bids over 10,000 *yuan* or those related to government policies, serious criminal cases, and important cases of military and civilian relations, the county judicial departments should hand them over to the county government committees for discussion. For the first time, the Border Government required the county judicial departments to abide by the new criminal and civil procedural laws in handling cases. If facing questions regarding legal procedures, law, and administrative decisions, a judicial department should report to the regional branches of the high court.[28]

By law, litigants in the Border Area had to appeal first to the county judicial departments or local courts. If dissatisfied, they could then appeal

25 Ai Shaorun, 2007a: 37.

26 Ibid., 2007a: 39.

27 In 1936, magistrates in over 1400 republican counties still functioned as judges owing to a paucity of funding and professional judges. See Pan Zhenqiu 潘振球ed., *A Draft of Historical Compendium of the Republican China Town* (*Zhonghua minguo shishi jiyao-chugao*中华民国史实纪要初稿) (Nanjing: Guoshiguan, January 1936): 17.

28 Ai Shaorun, 2007a: 41.

to the high court. With only one high court, it would be highly difficult or inconvenient for appellants living in remote counties to lodge suits or wait for a long time for the decision. To reduce the burden of both the high court and the appellants, the Border Government in March 1943 decided to create some high court branches. Each branch would have one head, one judge, and one or two clerks. The branch head would be appointed by the high court with the approval of the Border Government. These high court branches were supposed to be the second-instance court for most light criminal cases. But for prison sentences of more than three years, the branch should submit all documents to the high court for review. People dissatisfied with a branch decision could appeal to the high court.[29]

Aside from the major reforms and changes at all levels of the Border Area judicial system, the Border Government also made efforts to formalize court discipline and verdicts so as to be in concert with that of the Republican judicial system.[30] For instance, a 1942 regulation on court trials stipulated that litigants should stay in the waiting room and not walk around after they arrived in a court. Once a trial began, all parties should stay in their seats and not leave unless granted permission. People irrelevant to the trial should not enter the court and listen. Any troublemaker in the court would be punished. In a civil trial, the court could allow people to listen, but the audience should not disrupt court order or help the litigant with hints or other behavior. After the judge made a decision, litigants should not engage in irrational entanglement (*wuli jiuchan*) or refuse to leave the court. Violators would be taken out by force.[31] This regulation is a far cry from the court in both the Jiangxi Soviet base and the pre-1941 Border Area when most trials were casual and there were no restrictions on litigants and audience. After 1942, police would maintain court order and discipline and both the layout and decoration of the court were to be more like a Republican court.[32]

The informal and cursory verdicts made by untrained judges mentioned in Chapter 1 also caught the attention of the high court. Many untrained

29 Ibid., 2007a: 40.

30 The Republican judicial system also experienced a particization under the GMD. See Xiaoqun Xu, *Trial of Modernity: Judicial Reform in Early Twentieth-Century China, 1901-1937* (Stanford: Stanford University Press, 2008).

31 "Tentative Regulations Regarding High Court and Local Court in the Shanganning Border Area (*Shanganning bianqu gaodeng fayuan fating defang fayuan fating shenxun zanxing guize*)" in Ai Shaorun, 2007a: 49.

32 Yang Yonghua and Fang Keqin, 1987: 119.

judges had forgotten to tell litigants when and where to appeal if they were not content, which resulted in lots of trouble. On October 17, 1942, Li Mu'an, head of the high court, ordered all judges to add the time limits and venues onto their verdicts so that dissatisfied litigants could appeal if they wished to.[33]

Defending a Communist Judicial System

Throughout the Sino-Japanese War, the debate on the nature and role of the judicial system did not die down. Generally speaking, there were two contentious views among judicial and governmental officials in the Border Area. The first view envisioned the Communist judicial system as an independent organ administered by professional judges that could adopt useful GMD laws. The other view argued that the Communist judicial system should revoke all GMD laws and preserve its "red color" by serving only the goals of the CCP and the masses. Unlike opponents of judicial independence, officials championing the first view normally had a formal legal education. For example, Li Mu'an, the interim head of the high court from June 1942 to late 1943, graduated from the prestigious Capital Institute of Law and Politics in 1905, a time when the late Qing dynasty proposed a comprehensive duplication of Western law and legal system. Later Li became a lawyer in Beijing and Tianjin. After leading the high court in the Border Area, Li embarked on a major reform of the legal system and endeavored to turn the informal and unprofessional legal system into a modern and formal one. Li stressed the importance of judicial independence and process. In late 1942, it was Li Mu'an who ordered judges to tell dissatisfied litigants when and where to appeal. In the words of Glenn Tiffert, Li's "most far-reaching contribution" was his support of mediation that accounted for more than 30% of all civil cases.[34]

Another advocator of modern Western judicial principles was Zhu Ying, who, like Li Mu'an, held a law degree. After he reached Yan'an in 1938, Zhu was first appointed as the head of the legal training unit in the Border Area and later a high court secretary. According to Wang Shirong, Zhu sided with Li Mu'an in supporting a Western-style tertiary judicial system to give people more legal remedies. When high court head Lei Jingtian,

33 Ai Shaorun, 2007a: 50.

34 Glenn Tiffert, *Judging Revolution: Beijing and the Birth of the PRC Judicial System, 1906-1958* (unpublished dissertation, University of California Berkeley, 2015): 52.

an orthodox Communist official, asked Zhu to lead a county court, Zhu demanded judicial independence and no official meddling.[35]

The more prominent but inconsistent supporter of judicial independence was Xie Juezai, a veteran Communist official who once served as the head of both the justice department and the high court in the Border Area. In one case that took place in 1941, Xie was dealing with an "important" official who had violated the law. Many officials had reportedly pressed Xie not to punish him. But Xie insisted on punishing the official and he reported the case to Mao Zedong. Mao backed Xie and praised him for defending the law. In 1942, Xie argued that most violators of the law were officials, and he said that "[judges] should resist all kinds of pressure and threats and should punish them."[36] In 1943 when the internal purge reached its peak, Xie Juezai changed his stance on judicial independence.[37] On December 4, 1943, he criticized the principle of judicial independence in his diary as "harmful" in a new society, namely the Communist Border Area.[38] In early 1945, political tensions in the Border Area eased after Mao successfully defeated his key enemies and consolidated his power in the CCP. Xie Juezai then seems to have returned to his earlier stance on judicial independence. On January 22, 1945, he wrote about the terms regarding judicial independence in the Soviet constitution under Joseph Stalin (1936) and mocked CCP officials who had opposed judicial independence.

> Stalin Constitution:
> Article 112: All judges are independent and should only follow the law.
> Article 117: All members of the procuracy should exert their power independently and obey the chief of the Soviet procuracy without being influenced by any local government.
>
> It seems rather difficult to find any evidence against judicial independence [in Stalin Constitution]. It should be said that it would be an "invention" for us (i.e. CCP officials) to argue against judicial independence.

35 Wang Shirong, 2011: 271-277; Xie Xiangjing谢祥京, "Li Mu'an: CCP's First Constitutional Advocator (*Li Mu'an: zhonggong xianzheng diyiren*李木庵：中共宪政第一人)," February 5, 2015, in http://www.mingjingnews.com/MIB/News/news.aspx?ID=N000075073&Page=2

36 Yang Yonghua and Fang Keqin, 1987: 95.

37 For a complete historical account on the political purge or so-called "Rectification Campaign" in Yan'an see Gao Hua高华, *How Did the Red Sun Rise: The Entire Course of the Yan'an Rectification Movement* (*Hongtaiyang shizenyang shengqide: Yan'an Zhengfeng yundong shimo*红太阳是怎样升起的：延安整风运动始末) (Hong Kong: Hong Kong Chinese University Press, 2000).

38 Xie Juezai谢觉哉, *Diary of Xie Juezai* (*Xie Juezai Riji*谢觉哉日记) (Beijing: Renmin chubanshe, 1984): 411, 533-557.

In July 1945, Xie denounced some CCP leaders who in a meeting argued against judicial independence and in favor of subordinating the judicial system to the political government.[39]

For most of the time, Lei Jingtian, a loyal Communist and longtime head of the high court, stood firmly against judicial independence. Unlike Li Mu'an and Zhu Ying, Lei had no law degree or training before he joined the CCP and the Red Army. After completing the Long March, he arrived in Yan'an and soon became the head of the high court in spite of his minimal legal education. In August 1938, Lei set the principles of the Communist judicial system that included: basing court verdicts on both GMD laws and local revolutionary tradition and documents; adopting simple legal procedures intelligible to the working class; abolishing the litigation fee; and using casual persuasion to achieve convictions.[40]

According to one observer, Lei's lack of legal training and his colleagues' dismissal of him led him to be biased against legal specialists. In the debate over judicial independence, Lei vehemently opposed Li and Zhu and demanded that the judicial system be under administrative control. In Lei's view, the judicial system was a crucial part of political authority and not a unit independent of the rest of the government. The primary requirement of a legal official was his loyalty to the revolution; his legal knowledge and capability were only secondary. Lei also looked down upon judicial procedures. Judges under his leadership adopted simple procedures and imposed no restrictions on the behavior of litigants. After trials were completed, judges only gave litigants a hand-written piece of paper. In 1943, during the height of the Rectification Campaign, Lei launched an official check inside the judicial system. Among the 26 judicial officials in the high court, seventeen were accused of being "GMD agents" and three were "suspects." One of them was Zhu Ying who was denounced as a GMD agent and forced to do menial secretarial work in the high court.[41]

Lei Jingtian's revolutionary rhetoric and stance on the judicial system won the support of some high-ranking CCP officials. On November 5, 1944, Xi Zhongxun, the Party secretary of the Suide District, delivered a speech on the direction of the Communist judicial system. First, Xi backed Lei's view that the judicial system was not independent and was an important component of the people's regime. Unlike the GMD judicial system that only served the interest of the rich and powerful, the Communist judicial system strived to

39 Ibid., 1984: 754, 822.

40 Cong, 2016: 113; also Zhang Shibin, 2004: 73.

41 He Bing, 2014; Wang Shirong荣, 2011: 276-278.

unite, educate, and protect ordinary people. Xi also criticized some judges in the Border Area for having infringed people's interests by using GMD laws. Second, Xi stated that judges should stand among and with people and not above them as "masters or officials." "If a judge continues to simply make decisions, sit in a court, put on a solemn face [...] and let people know that he is an official or master," Xi said, "that will be very bad." Third, Xi called on all judges to walk out of the courts and go to the remote countryside. "If a judge could only write 'beautiful' verdicts in court," Xi said, "he would be an unsuccessful judge because, without building close relationships with the people, the judge could not determine the truth of a case." Therefore, Xi encouraged judges to rely on the masses for the resolution of their cases.[42] In late 1944, the Japanese army was crumbling and the CCP was gaining more confidence in its growing military might. It was ready for a wholesale split with its wartime ally, the GMD. CCP officials like Xi Zhongxun no longer felt it was necessary to disguise their fundamental animosity toward the GMD to sustain an improbable united front.

After supporters of judicial independence such as Li Mu'an and Zhu Ying were attacked in the turbulent purge in 1943, the high court adopted a safe and neutral stance by invoking China's traditional Confucian legal principles. On December 20, it sent a letter to all local courts and judicial departments in which it argued that Communist judges should tackle cases with patience and use reason to persuade litigants to reconcile. If an attempt failed, judges should wait and let both parties have time to soften their positions. "Humans are not grass or trees [without sentiment] and there should be times when they change their minds," the letter said. It continued "only a few litigants would insist on irrational demands [...] if judges can make reasonable rulings in time that will prevent much litigation, which will be in tune with the judicial policies of the New Democracy."[43] New Democracy was Mao's idea that the Chinese Communist Party could play the roles played by the bourgeoisie in more developed societies.

The inclusion of human sentiments in the legal process was congruent with the views of some leading legal cadres in the Border Area. As Xiaoping Cong has pointed out, both Xie Juezai and Lei Jingtian argued that a good law should be a balance between "humanity (*renqing*) and principles (*daoli*)."[44] This opinion also seems to be consistent with China's post-Tang legal principle that reflected Confucius' favoring of virtue and

42 *Jiefang daily*, November 5, 1944.

43 Ai Shaorun, 2007a: 343.

44 Similar views could also found in Xie Juezai. Cong, 2016: 132-133.

Mencius' emphasis on good human nature over legalist punishment.[45] At the beginning of the influential Tang Code, with Commentaries drafted in 651, it read "Virtue and rites are the roots of politics, while punishments are the application of politics."[46] Indeed, if we can look into the Communist policies such as the complaint system and Mao's prescriptions for resolving people's internal contradictions in the early PRC, the legacy of Confucian law remained evident.[47]

A Comparison of GMD and CCP Criminal Laws

In hindsight, between 1921, the birth of the CCP, and 1979, the beginning of PRC's latest reform era, the Communist government in the Border Area (1936-1947) was the only period that had both criminal law and criminal procedure law. In the Jiangxi Soviet base, the CCP only enacted several regulations to punish counterrevolutionaries and none of them was dealing with regular criminal activities such as theft, robbery, and rape.[48] The biggest reason is that the Border Area was, unlike the Jiangxi Soviet base, no longer an independent Communist base during the Sino-Japanese War. By recognizing Chiang Kai-shek as the sole leader of the Chinese state, the Border Area was in theory reduced to a regional government and the Red Army became a part of the Republican army. Therefore, it was reasonable for the autonomous CCP to accept the existing "national laws" including Republican Criminal Law, Criminal Procedural Law, and some other laws as a token sign of submission. Willingly or unwillingly, the Border Government adopted many GMD laws. But the CCP refused to accept wholesale Republican laws as some Communist cadres have claimed.[49] In fact, CCP legal specialists modified GMD laws more or less to suit the aim of the Party and the Border Area. If necessary, the CCP would add its own terms or statutes.

45 For a detailed account on the Legalist and Confucian principles see Lubman, 1999: also see Yonglin Jiang, "In the Name of 'Taizu': The Construction of Zhu Yuanzhang's Legal Philosophy and Chinese Cultural Identity in the 'Varitable Records of Taizu'" in *T'oung Pao*, Second Series, Vol. 96, Fasc. 4/5 (2010), pp. 408-70; Qiang Fang and Roger Des Forges, 2007.

46 Zhangsun Wuji长孙无忌, *Tang code with commentaries* (*Tanglu shuyi*唐律疏议) (Beijing: Falü chubanshe, 1999): 1.

47 See Qiang Fang, 2013a: Ch. 5.

48 The only exception was the 1931 Criminal Law under the late Communist regional leader Fang Zhimin that, like the criminal law in the Border Area, was also a replica of the GMD law. See Chapter 1.

49 For the claim that the CCP adopted GMD laws see Yang Yonghua and Fang Keqin, 1987: 7.

If we compare the Republican Criminal Law and Criminal Procedural Law and their Communist counterparts in the wartime, we will find distinct similarities and differences. For example, although the 1942 Communist Criminal Procedural Law and the 1935 Republican Criminal Procedural Law have similar formats, the total number of provisions of the Communist law was merely a small fraction of that in the Republican law. Specifically, the Communist criminal law had 76 articles, about merely one-seventh of the Republican law totaling 516 articles. The Communist criminal procedural law contained six chapters: 1) General Principles; 2) Procedures of the First Instance; 3) Appellate Procedures; 4) Procedures of the Third Trial; 5) Procedures of Enforcement; 6) Attached Civil Litigation. In contrast, the Republican law had nine chapters: 1) General Principles; 2) The First Instance; 3) Appellate Procedures; 4) Counter-appeal (*kanggao*); 5) The Third Trial; 6) Special Appeal; 7) Simple Procedures; 8) Enforcement; 9) Attached Civil Litigation.

While the Communist law had fewer chapters, it retained the basic provisions of the Republican law. For the Communists, the three missing chapters – the "counter-appeal," "special appeal," and "simple procedures" – may not have been that important, as they would only give litigants more options in seeking legal remedies. In each chapter, the Communist law was significantly succinct in contents. As far as the "General Principles" are concerned, the CCP law had only 21 terms, while the GMD law had 206 terms, almost ten times more. Yet, whatever the law's true intention or the Party's willingness to implement it, the Communist law preserved the spirit of the GMD law, such as the prohibition of unwarranted arrest, the protection of the rights of defendants, the avoidance of judges familiar with the litigants, the limits of detention to 24 hours, and defendants' rights to seek a lawyer.[50]

Along with the Criminal Procedural Law, the CCP in the Border Area also made its Criminal Law, which resembled the 1935 Republican Criminal Law. In the "General Principles," while the CCP law consisted of sixteen provisions, four more than its Republican counterpart, almost eleven of them or 68% were identical to the Republican law. In particular, eight out of the nine sub-provisions of Article 8 were the same. In the "Specific Provisions (*fenze*)," the CCP law had a total of 37 crimes, three more than that of the Republican law. Among the 37 crimes, at least 21, or about 56%, were the same as those in the Republican law

50 For the Communist Criminal Procedure Law see Ai Shaorun, 2007a: 61-66; for the GMD law see https://zh.wikisource.org/zh/中華民國刑事訴訟法_(民國23年立法24年公布).

Indeed, there were also some explicit differences and emphases between the two criminal laws. The "General Principles" of the Republican Criminal Law tended to stress the specific interpretation and the range of its application of the law, while the focal point of the CCP Criminal Law was how to strengthen the CCP's authority, a reflection of its fundamental fear of losing power. The second article of the "General Principles" of the CCP law stated that the purpose of the law was to solidify the democratic government and maintain legal order. To further emphasize the gravity of crimes committed in opposition to the CCP/Border Government, the top three articles of the "Specific Provisions" included more details of such crimes. Article 1 stated that any action attempting to "overthrow or weaken the people's united democratic government or its economy and politics, national interest, and foreign credit" would constitute the crime of destroying the democratic government. Article 2 wrote that, people "harboring purposes unfavorable to the democratic government and using violence or political schemes" against the union of all nationalities and all classes, or trying to wrest power from the Communist government, would be sentenced to five years of forced education (i.e. hard labor). For more serious crimes, the criminals would be sentenced to death.

The divergences between the Republican and CCP criminal laws reveal the different needs, priorities, and contexts of the two parties. In 1935 the GMD sought to promulgate its Criminal Law and Criminal Procedural Law for a state that had just emerged with the prospect of vanquishing the Communist revolt. In contrast, the CCP in 1942, a year of more precarious political and military situation in the face of both Japanese and GMD hostilities, enacted the two laws prioritizing its security and very survival.[51]

Table 2.1 shows a snapshot of the criminal cases resolved by Communist courts in the Border Area between 1938 and 1943.

This table clearly demonstrates that political security was the priority of the CCP. Six political and economic crimes – "Traitor," "Sabotaging Border Area," "Bandits," "Damaging Finance," "Violating Law," and "Damaging Public Service" – were only one fourth of the 24 kinds of reported crimes committed, but they included 3579, cases or 50% of all the crimes committed. Similar ratios will reappear in the PRC whenever the CCP was obsessed with perceived threats to its security and authority.

51 For the Communist Criminal Law see Ai Shaorun, 2007a: 104-126; for the GMD law see https://zh.wikisource.org/zh/中華民國刑法_(民國23年立法24年公布).

Table 2.1 Criminal cases in the border area (1938-1943)[52]

	1938	1939	1940	1941	1942	1943	Total	Percentage
Traitor	48	16		2			66	0.9
Sabotaging Border Area	88	144	381	824	96	164	1697	23.8
Bandits	143	61	64	44	51	73	436	6.1
Murder	17	11	42	38	31	35	174	2.4
Escape	71	63	93	53	71	27	378	5.3
Corruption	53	72	101	69	80	68	443	6.2
Damaging Finance		18	18	26	83	95	240	3.3
Drug	88	120	198	126	88	124	744	10.5
Theft	36	35	64	108	129	84	456	6.3
Gambling	48	60	92	236	80	76	592	8
Violating Law	11	80	88	181	76	102	538	7.5
Mayhem	48	60	49	192	177	105	631	8.8
Damaging Morality	3	24	37	58	36	42	200	2.8
Damaging Marriage	33	35	53	86	96	30	333	4.6
Kidnapping					2	88	90	1.1
Damaging Freedom	92	81	68	64	31	81	417	5.8
Fraud	13	98	31	38	34	33	247	3.4
Damaging Public Service	5	4	10	19	41	14	93	1.2
False Charge	15	14	18	32	28	17	124	1.7
Trespass	80	18	14	19	30	17	178	2.4
Dereliction of Duty	2	19	23	32	16		92	1.2
Other	130	37	40	32	92	38	369	5.1
Total	1024	868	1477	1516	1304	1186	7131	100

Criminal Cases in the Border Area

Before the CCP made its Criminal Law and Criminal Procedural Law in 1942, judges in the Border Area had largely adjudicated cases without citing specific laws. But after the CCP had its own "new" laws, Communist judges preferred Republican Criminal Law and Criminal Procedural Law to their new laws in justifying their decisions. In addition, the format of verdicts was the same as that in a Republican court. In 1945, some high court judges made straight verdicts without invoking any laws.

In one case that took place in the early border period, the protagonist Huang Kegong was a 26-year-old Red Army veteran who had served as a division head of the Resisting Japan Military and Political University. In August 1937, Liu Qian, a sixteen-year-old girl from Shaanxi, came to Yan'an

52 Zhang Shibin, 2004: 76.

hoping to join the Communist army and resist Japan. She was first assigned to the university where Huang was a division head. Huang quickly fell in love with Liu. Unfortunately, after Liu was transferred to another cadre school in September, the physical separation distanced the relationship between the two young people. As Liu repeatedly refused to marry him and began loving another man in the school, Huang lost his head and shot Liu to death on October 5.

The university administration arrested Huang who quickly admitted his crime. According to the high court decision on October 11, only six days later, Huang was denounced as "frenzied" for killing a revolutionary comrade who had come to the Border Area to resist Japan. As a Communist cadre, Huang attempted to force Liu to marry him regardless of the fact that Liu was only sixteen and was prohibited to marry by the Marriage Law. Moreover, marriage had by law to be voluntary. If Liu refused to marry Huang, Huang should not have tried to force her to do so. The court also accused Huang of having tried to cover up his crime by generating false evidence. In conclusion, the court suggested that Huang should be sentenced to death.[53]

Before the court made its final decision, judge Lei Jingtian asked Mao for guidance because Huang was a high-ranking military officer. Mao quickly approved the court decision and said that Huang's previous revolutionary glory could not warrant his being pardoned. As a Red Army cadre, Huang had committed a "despicable and ruthless crime." If Huang were not punished, it would be difficult to educate the Party, the Red Army, and the revolutionaries about just implementation of the law. "Precisely because Huang is a longtime Communist and a red soldier," Mao wrote, "the Party has to [punish him]. The Party and the Red Army must enforce more stringent discipline of Party members and red soldiers than of ordinary people."[54]

In this case, citing no criminal law, but only the civil marriage law, judge Lei Jingtian had to use several "reasonable" facts, such as Huang's deliberate intent to murder, his killing of a revolutionary comrade, and his cover-up of his crime to justify Huang's punishment. As I have discussed above, Lei had no formal legal training. But his verdict was based on the idea that the values of "humanity and principle" continued to be regarded by many as logical and reasonable. Similarly, Mao, the CCP leader, perceived the significance of the case to be its educational, not legal, value.

53 Ibid., 2004: 102-106; Ai Shaorun, ed., *Selected Cases of the Precedent Cases of the Shanganning Border Area* (*Shanganning bianqu panlian lixuan*陕甘宁边区判例案例选) (Shaanxi: Shaanxi remin chubanshe, 2007b): 9-13.

54 Zhang Shibin, 2004: 105-106.

In another case, the Border Area High Court on March 11, 1942 charged Liu Wenyi with being a traitor and imprisoned him for two years. The alleged crimes of Liu included his one month of training by a Japanese agent, his collection of Red Army information, and his attempt to poison a local well. While Liu rejected all these charges, the court still blamed him for other, more ambiguous crimes, such as "extreme faltering (*yichang zhiwu*)," quibbling (*jiaobian*), and his refusal to repent. These vague accusations are synonymous to those made in the Jiangxi Soviet base that neither invoked any law nor followed any legal process, albeit the penalty made in the Border Area was more lenient than the one in the Jiangxi Soviet base. One reason might be that the new Criminal Law and Criminal Procedural Law had not been in use or the judges had not been familiar with the new laws.[55]

Since the summer of 1942, judges had begun to quote the new Criminal Law and the Criminal Procedural Law in their verdicts. For instance, the Government Adjudicating Committee, the acting "Supreme Court" in the Border Area, ruled on December 1, 1942 to sentence Li Senjie to five years in prison for crimes of theft, false accusation, and forgery.

Li had been a department chief in Qingyang county. In August 1941, while staying together with his brother Li Hecai, a government secretary, Li Senjie absconded with 6000 *yuan* from the county government. The Qingyang government managed to capture him soon afterward, but Li Senjie forged evidence and falsely accused his brother Li Hecai of collaborating with counterrevolutionaries and stealing the money. Without verifying Li's accusation and evidence, the county magistrate immediately detained and tortured Li Hecai who died three months later. After Li Juncai, a relative of Li Hecai, brought the case to a local court, the judge found out that it was Li Senjie who had stolen the money. The judge therefore sentenced Li Senjie to two years for theft but not for his false accusation that had resulted in the death of Li Hecai. To redress the grievance of Li Hecai, Li Juncai appealed to the high court, which only added ten months to Li Senjie's imprisonment.

Still dissatisfied, the plaintiff filed a suit to the Government Adjudicating Committee. The committee led by Lin Boqu dismissed the punishment of the high court as too light because Li Senjie, a government official, had committed not only theft but also a false charge causing the death of Li Hecai. Thus, the committee increased the sentence of Li Senjie to five years. The increase, according to the verdict, was based on both "Articles 370 and 389 of the Criminal Procedural Law." Interestingly, the law that the committee cited was actually the Republican law and not the Communist

55 Ai Shaorun, 2007b: 133-134.

law. The committee also decided to punish the county magistrate who had tortured Li Hecai with no hard evidence of his alleged crime.[56]

The Communist use of Republican laws was common in the Border Area. In another case, the Yan'an local court in August 1943 also invoked the Republican Criminal Law to sentence Xiao Jijin, a corrupt official who had allegedly embezzled 60,000 *yuan* of public funds, to four years in prison.[57] Why did Communist judges in the Border Area like to cite Republican laws when they had their own comparable laws? There could be two reasons: 1) the CCP recognized the GMD as the central government during the Sino-Japanese War and therefore all Republican laws were national laws that judges in the Border Area were supposed to adopt and observe; 2) new CCP laws were still considerably simpler than their Republican analogues and Communist judges found Republican laws more detailed and specific in dealing with particular cases.

In the spring of 1945, as the war against Japan was nearing its end, high court judges became increasingly unwilling to cite any law, be it Criminal Law or Criminal Procedural Law, in their verdicts. The poor quality and training of the judges after the 1943 purge and the CCP's growing self-confidence and assertiveness might be the explanation. To cite only one case, when Hao Qinglong in Yanchuan county tried to use traditional Chinese medicine to treat the abdominal pain of a woman, she died. The county government arrested Hao and subjected him to criticism. The high court believed that Hao Qinglong's unscientific treatment was responsible for the death of his patient. But, without mentioning any law, the high court ordered the county to sentence Hao to only three years in jail.[58]

Civil Cases in the Border Area

Like the CCP's Criminal Law and Criminal Procedural Law, its Civil Law and Civil Procedural Law drew much of their contents from the Republican counterparts but also differed from them. For example, four out of the five chapters of the Communist Civil Procedural Law promulgated in 1942 bore the same titles as those of the Republican law, which had twelve chapters. The articles in the Communist law however totaled only 50, which were greatly exceeded by the 636 articles in the Republican law. One distinctive

56 Ibid., 2007b: 3-8.
57 Ibid., 2007b: 135-136.
58 Ibid., 2007a: 128.

feature of the Communist law was its abolition of the litigation fee that would help poor litigants.[59] The similarities between the Communist and Republican marriage laws were more explicit.

Since its first Marriage Law in 1934 in the Jiangxi Soviet base, the CCP arguably replicated or incorporated some of the spirit and provisions of the Republican law such as the abolition of arranged marriage, the ban on polygamy, the prohibition of people with certain diseases from getting married, and the outlawing of forced marriage. Major differences between the 1934 Communist Marriage Law and the 1931 Republican Civil Law[60] included: 1) the Communist law had older marriage ages with men at twenty and women at eighteen in comparison to the Republican's seventeen and fifteen; 2) the wife of a Red Army soldier had to have her husband's permission to divorce unless she had not heard from him for at least two years.[61]

After the CCP moved to northwest China in 1936, its marriage law underwent minor revisions in 1939, 1942, and 1944. The first article of the 1939 marriage law stated that the law was based on the fundamental spirit of Sun Yat-sen's Three People's Principles and the real circumstances in the Border Area. Three years later, the newly revised marriage law had a more detailed explanation of the generations of lineal relatives to marry and lower ages for men and women to marry (men at eighteen, women at sixteen), which were closer to that in the Republican law.[62]

Despite consecutive laws against arranged marriage in the Border Area, the traditional practice died hard. In December 1942, the Border Government outlawed all utilitarian betrothal gifts as part of arranged marriage but allowed regular gifts. To end arranged marriage, the Border Government ordered all engaged couples to register. Once the government discovered an arranged marriage, it would confiscate 20-60% of the value of the betrothal gifts, devote it to public welfare, and return the rest to the payer. Regarding existing concubines and child brides, the government did not want to interfere but it tolerated no new cases of either one.[63]

59 For the Communist civil procedural law see Ai Shaorun, 2007: 66-70; for the GMD law see https:// zh.wikisource.org/zh/中華民國民事訴訟法_(民國23年立法24年公布).

60 Unlike the Communist Marriage Law, the statutes regarding marriage were merely a part of the GMD civil law.

61 For the Communist marriage law see *Hongse zhonghua* (*The Red China*), April 26, 1934; for the GMD law see the 1931 Republican Civil Law, http://www.6law.idv.tw/6law/law/%E6%B0%91%E6%B3%95.htm

62 The marriage age here refers to the minimum age of men and women to engage. Ai Shaorun, 2007a: 218-224.

63 Ibid., 2007a: 224.

On January 17, 1943, to stabilize the morale of its soldiers, the Border Government issued instructions on divorces involving soldiers who were fighting the Japanese. Unlike the Marriage Law in the Jiangxi Soviet base that required only two years of missing information for soldiers' wives to file for divorce, the new government order stipulated at least five years of no information before a wife could divorce her military husband.[64]

To explain more about the marriage laws and their effects in the Border Area, I discuss a couple of representative cases. In the first case, Tian Lanfang was a 21-year-old woman who married Huo Rufa in early 1939. Shortly after the marriage, Huo joined the army and since then there had been no information from him. In late 1942, Tian, having waited for almost four years, filed a divorce suit in a local court. The local court rejected her request because a 1939 regulation had dropped a clause regarding soldiers' marriages in the 1934 Marriage Law. As Xiaoping Cong has correctly argued, one of the reasons might be that the government wanted no divorces during a national crisis.[65] Dissatisfied, Tian appealed to the high court. On January 21, 1943, Ren Fuzhong, a high court judge, ruled that, because Huo was a soldier fighting for the state, his marriage should be protected by the government to maintain the morale of soldiers. Invoking the new government order, the judge told Tian that she should wait one more year before filing a divorce suit. Hence, the judge believed that the former court decision was correct and turned down Tian's appeal. In this case, the judge in the high court cited the latest government order to justify his decision.[66]

In another case, Hou Zhangshi, a sixteen-year-old woman, married Hou Dingmao who was two years older in 1933. Hou Zhangshi soon discovered that her husband was mentally handicapped and epileptic. At first, she wished her husband could find a treatment, but after nine years, she had lost hope and decided to file for divorce in a local court. Having tolerated an unfortunate and bizarre marriage for such a long time, Hou was more like a "traditional" woman than a modern one.[67] The local court's decision supported the poor woman. Discontented, Hou Dingmao, with the help of his father Hou Xianru, appealed to the high court. In his lawsuit, Hou Xianru argued that his son was still young and had no incurable disease. The high court judge summoned Hou Dingmao twice and confirmed that

64 Ibid., 2007a: 225.

65 Cong, 2016: 89-90.

66 Ai Shaorun, 2007b: 24-26.

67 For the modern women in the Border Area who had been shaped by the May Fourth Movement see Cong Xiaoping, 2009.

he was indeed mentally disabled and could neither count numbers over five, recall his own age, or understand sexual intercourse. It also confirmed that Hou Dingmao had epilepsy. The court remarked that it was human nature for Hou Zhangshi to request a divorce. Quoting both Article 11 of the marriage regulations of the Border Area and human "sentiment (*qing*)" advocated by high-ranking judges like Lei Jingtian, the court endorsed the divorce request of Hou Zhangshi.[68] With both law and human sentiment in the decision, the high court judge seemed to have been influenced by a longtime practice in Chinese legal history.[69]

The most prominent civil practice in the Border Area was the Ma Xiwu adjudicating method. Due to long distances and poor road conditions, many people in remote counties had much difficulty lodging lawsuits at local courts, much less the high court in Yan'an. To help those people settle disputes, Ma Xiwu, head of a high court branch and later head of the high court and deputy president of the PRC Supreme Court, created a simple and convenient method by going down to the remote villages, conducting empirical investigations, and making on-site judgments rather than sitting in the court and waiting for litigants to come. Most of the cases that Ma resolved involved petty marriage disputes. Ma Xiwu's method, which was similar to the English circuit courts in the thirteenth century,[70] was highly acclaimed in the Border Area for its convenience and consistency with the Party's mass line (*qunzhong luxian*). Its biggest limitation was that it could not deal with serious and complicated cases in urban areas.[71] Philip Huang also notes that Ma Xiwu's method/style was not practical even for a county magistrate in the Qing dynasty who "very rarely indeed undertook mediation in the manner of official representations."[72]

68 Ai Shaorun, 2007b: 15-16.

69 For the equal importance of state law and human sentiment see Jiang Yonglin and Wu Yanhong, "Satisfying Both Sentiment and Law: Fairness-Centered Judicial Reasoning as Seen in Late Ming Casebooks" in Charlotte Furth, Judith Zeitlin, and Ping-chen Hsiung, eds., *Thinking with Cases: Specialist Knowledge in Chinese Cultural History* (Seattle: University of Washington Press, 2007): 31-61.

70 Yu Ming于明, *Ruling a State in Accordance with Law: Political History of English tribunals, 1154-1701* (*sifa zhiguo: yingguo fatingde zhengzhishi, 1154-1701*司法治国：英国法庭的政治史，1154-1701) (Beijing: Falü chubanshe, 2015): 144-145.

71 "The Adjudicating Method of Comrade Ma Xiwu (*Ma Xiwu tongzhide shenpan fangshi*马锡五同志的审判方式)" in *Jiefang Daily*, March 13, 1944; also see Wang Shirong荣, 2011: 217-239; Yang Yonghua and Fang Keqin, 1987: 131-144.

72 Philip C. Huang, *Chinese Civil Justice, Past and Present* (Lanham: Roman & Littlefield Publisher, 2010): 4.

Legal Violations in the Border Area

Most scholars studying the judicial system in the Border Area tend to focus on its general legal system or specific laws, institutions, and judges. Few of them have heeded the massive abuse of power, resort to torture, and other violations of the law in the Border Area. As shown in the abovementioned criminal cases (Li Senjie and Hao Qinglong), the use of torture, forced confessions, and false judgments remained major problems in the Border Area despite repeated government laws and regulations to interdict them.

One of the main reasons behind this judicial misconduct was, of course, the incompetence of judges or judicial officials. In many parts of Republican China including the Border Area, many magistrates and local officials concurrently acted as judges due to a serious shortage of professional judges. On May 21, 1939, a report of the border government complained that the biggest problem in the judicial system was the lack of qualified Party officials. Most counties had asked the Border Government to solve the problem, but the Border Government had no proper persons to send. As a makeshift plan, the report told county governments to let the Military Law Unit (*junfachu*) deal with critical criminals such as traitors, bandits, and organizers of assassinations who would threaten CCP rule. County governments should handle only ordinary criminals such as thieves and rapists as well as civil cases. Other minor civil and criminal cases such as debts, marriage, and drugs should seek people's mediation.[73]

As a result of the shortage of qualified legal specialists, posts in many local courts and judicial departments were filled with cadres with little or no legal training. Lei Jingtian, the head of the high court, did not have any formal legal education, let alone many other judges in the Border Area. On February 1943, Xie Juezai, former head of the high court, admitted that law was one of the backward elements of the Border Government because few officials had legal knowledge.[74] This problem did not see much improvement in 1944. As disclosed in a high court report that year, some counties' judicial reports were "too simple and too intangible." For instance, in the case of an alleged bandit named Yang Deqing, the report of Dingbian County simply read: "the criminal (Yang Deqing) does nothing right. After Shang Wanhai,

73 Shaanxisheng danganguan and Shaanxisheng shehui kexueyuan陕西省档案馆和陕西省社会科学院, eds., *Selected Documents of the Shanganning Border Government* (*Shanganning bianqu zhengfu wenjian xuanbian*陕甘宁边区政府文件选编) (Dangan chubanshe, 1987): 1. 259; also see Wang Shirong荣, 2011: 41.

74 Xie Juezai, 1984: 411.

his accomplice, was arrested, Yang fled to Dingbian [county] where he was detained [by the county government]." In the column of "punishment," the report put "five months' hard labor." Nothing in the report indicated the specific time, venue, number of people involved, the use of guns, or the value of goods they had robbed. Furthermore, in some county court reports, there was no mention of any plaintiffs or defendants. In others, the titles of crimes were not standardized. In one case, an old woman in Zizhou County had abused her daughter-in-law and forced her to commit suicide. The crime should have been classified as "Mayhem (*shanhaizui*)," but the county put it into a category titled "Abuse that Causes Death (*nuedai zhirenming*)."[75]

While torture had been banned by many border laws such as the 1941 Administrative Program, the 1942 Regulations on Protecting Human Rights and Property Rights, and the 1942 Criminal Procedural Law, it continued to be used widely throughout the Border Area and beyond, further evidencing the poor quality of judicial cadres.[76]

On May 22, 1945, due to rampant torture in the counties, the Border Government once again ordered an "authentic" prohibition of torture. "Although for several years the judicial system has seen phenomenal progress [since the 1941 Administrative Program]," the order proclaimed, "it is still very common for many county governments to employ such tortures as to tie and beat people. The infringements of the administrative program and government policies is truly a grave mistake in our democratic politics." The order mentioned one recent case in Qingjian County. After one Liu Guobin had stolen two bundles of cloth with Wang Liuer, he felt guilty and turned himself in to the local police. When the police asked him where he had concealed the cloth, Liu suddenly changed his mind and falsely accused four innocent men as his accomplices. Without looking into hard evidence, the police arrested the four men and tortured them. Before the stolen cloth was finally found, one of the four men had one of his hands mutilated.[77]

In his diary on May 11, 1944, veteran judge Xie Juezai also conceded that torture, random arrest, and heavy punishment remained serious in the Border Area. In late 1945, Xie warned that, even in dealing with counterrevolutionaries, corporal punishment should be absolutely forbidden. That was because torture was inhumane and ineffective: torturers rarely got what they wanted.[78]

75 Ai Shaorun, 2007a: 131.
76 See Yang Yonghua and Fang Keqin, 1987: 85.
77 Ai Shaorun, 2007a: 133.
78 Xie Juezai, 1984: 621, 870.

However critical were this use of torture and false arrest by many local officials in the Border Area, they were by no means comparable to the state-organized and widespread transgressions of the law during the Rectification Campaign in 1942 and 1943. According to Gao Hua, the campaign was initially launched by Mao to destroy challengers such as Wang Ming, a Soviet-educated cadre, who had been a primary foe of Mao's since 1937.[79] The campaign began in 1942 after some writers such as Wang Shiwei and Ding Ling criticized the social hierarchy and privileges of high-ranking cadres in Yan'an. Authorized by Mao, officials launched public denunciations against Wang Shiwei and labeled him a Trotskyist. Wang was subsequently arrested and taken into custody where he remained until he was beheaded in 1947.[80] To wipe out all hidden Trotskyists and GMD agents in the Border Area, Mao and Kang Sheng, the head of the Information Department, unleashed a relentless campaign nicknamed "Movement to Rescue the People," which was akin to what the Red Army had done in the Jiangxi Soviet base in 1931. Thousands of Communist cadres and ordinary people were detained and tortured. The four main methods of torture were: driving to exhaustion, physical damage, starvation, and bogus executions. Having suffered those physical and psychological tortures, many victims suffered chronic pain the rest of their lives. Victims who were unable to bear the humiliation and torture often chose to end their lives.[81]

From April to July 1943, Soviet diplomat and journalist Peter Vladimirov recorded the fiendish and relentless campaign in his diary. "The campaign and capturing of [GMD] agents have created more tension in Yan'an" (April 23). "[The CCP] is arresting GMD agents, how many [GMD] agents does Yan'an have?" "Who has given Mao Zedong the right to suspect every Communist of treason?" (June 24). "The situation is very grave as a large group of GMD agents have been exposed and arrested" (July 15).[82]

Some departments in the Border Area took a heavy toll in the campaign. For example, about 70 percent of the employees of the *Jiefang Daily*,

79 For the personal feud between Wang Ming and Mao see Guo Dehong, 2011: 346-491.

80 For a detailed study of Wang Shiwei see Jonathan Spence, *The Gate of Heavenly Peace: The Chinese and Their Revolution* (London: Penguin Books, 1982): 327-352.

81 Gao Hua, 2000: 253-419. In his study on the Rectification Campaign, Hao Zaijin argues that there were 24 kinds of torture in one county; more commonly used tortures were persistent interrogation or fake death penalties because physical abuse was not allowed. See Hao Zaijin郝在今, *The Precedent History of the Cultural Revolution: A True Record of the Rescuing Movement in Yan'an* (*"Wenge" qianshi: Yan'an qiangjiu yundong jishi*文革前史：延安抢救运动纪实) (Hong Kong: Liwen chubanshe, 2006): 121-123.

82 Peter Vladimirov, 2004: 63-71.

a key voice of the CCP with Bo Gu, Mao's earlier political foe, as the leader, were identified as "GMD agents" who needed to be "rescued." The Resist-Japan University, a major military academy in the Border Area with Lin Biao, Mao's protégé, as the president, was not exempted. Among the 1052 platoon leaders in the university, 602 or 57.2% had been charged with being GMD agents or suspects. In the Cadre Training Unit, 373 out of 496, or 75.2%, were suspects. One account estimated later that the total number of detained "GMD agents" between 1943 and 1944 was about 15,000 in Yan'an alone. Unable to put up with the torture and brutal interrogations, many suspects lost their minds or took their own lives, others were simply missing. In 1947, around 100 GMD "agents" including the young scholar Wang Shiwei were executed by the order of Kang Sheng.[83]

In this political campaign, independent-leaning judges such as Zhu Ying and Li Mu'an became targets of the "rescue," and Lei Jingtian who stood up for a judicial system under CCP control won. When top CCP leaders launched the "rescue" movement, the high court had no reason or stamina to challenge its superiors, much less to defend any legal process.

Legal Reform during the Second Civil War, 1945-1949

Benefiting from its remote location and a largely passive strategy of resistance, the CCP and the Red Army grew quickly to become a formidable force during the Sino-Japanese War. After Japan surrendered in August 1945, the CCP was poised to challenge GMD's national power and sought to capitalize on the GMD's growing "popular discontent" and "unprecedented corruption."[84] Always seeing the CCP as the "disease in the heart," Chiang Kai-shek wasted little time before he launched a full-scale war against the Communists in 1946. Soon after the US mediation failed in early 1946, the GMD began to attack Communist regions.[85] The civil war lasted about four years, which ended in a fiasco for Chiang Kai-shek and his Party.

83 Gao Hua, 2000: 423-496.

84 Suzanne Pepper argues that the fundamental reason for the GMD's loss in the civil war was not so much its military incompetence as its political problems. See Suzanne Pepper, *Civil War in China: The Political Struggle, 1945-1949* (Lanham: Roman & Littlefield, 1999): 8; for the corruption of the GMD after 1945 also see Lloyd E. Eastman, *Seeds of Destruction: Nationalist China and Revolution, 1937-1949* (Stanford: Stanford University Press, 2002).

85 For a good study on General Marshall's failed mediation see Tsou Tang, *America's Failure in China, 1941-1950* (Chicago: University of Chicago Press, 1963).

While fighting a civil war with the GMD, the CCP took steps to enact new laws and improve its judicial system. The Border Area continued to be the Communist center until spring 1947. Even after 1947, the Border Area remained one of the most important bases of the CCP. Its judicial system actively served the CCP cause in the land reform and anti-counterrevolutionary campaign. But most studies of the law in the Border Area have spilled little ink on the Communist judicial system after 1945.[86]

Among the most important new laws were the constitutions in the Border Area. On April 23, 1946, two months before the civil war erupted, the Border Government implemented the Constitutional Principles of the Shanganning Border Area, the first Communist constitution since the 1931 Constitutional Outline of the Chinese Soviet Republic under Mao Zedong. Aside from reiterating the basic political and economic rights stated in the 1939 wartime administrative program, the new law did not forget to repeat the clichéd and largely non-existent judicial independence. The law also allowed people to sue any official for his or her misconduct and required a lenient attitude toward alleged criminals.[87]

Six months later, a more formal constitution was enacted in the Border Area. Still regarding itself as a region of the Republic of China, the law was titled The Revised Autonomous Constitutional Draft of the Shanganning Border Area in the Republic of China. It pledged that the Border Government aimed to protect the democratic rights of the people and minorities as well as judicial principles such as judicial independence and a people's jury. The crucial point of the law was an emphasis on CCP's loyalty to the GMD because the Border Government, one of the "highest autonomies" in the Republic, had enforced all "people's rights and responsibilities that were to be included in future constitutions of the Republic of China."[88] Why was the CCP so eager to declare the Border Area autonomous inside the Republic amid a civil war with the Republican army? One practical explanation might be that the law was a tactical good gesture made by the CCP that it had no intention of antagonizing the GMD and hoped Chiang Kai-shek would call off the ongoing military attacks.

In the meantime, Communist cadres in charge of the judicial system acted again to revamp the court discipline. On August 21, 1946, the high court

86 One of the scholars who have touched on this period is Xiaoping Cong whose study mostly focuses on the marriage law throughout the 1940s. See Cong, 2016. Yong Yonghua and Fang Keqin have only briefly mentioned this period. See Yang Yonghua and Fang Keqin, 1987; Klaus Mühlhahn's research centers on the Communist labor camp and prison. See Mühlhahn, 2009.

87 Ai Shaorun, 2007a: 9-10.

88 Ibid., 2007a: 10-17; also see Xie Xie Juezai, 1984: 999-1009.

created administrative rules on court discipline. The new rules restricted litigants' activities in the court including expressing views and waiting. The court police had the right to punish violators. The rules also standardized the template of formal court verdicts that had to include litigants' personal information, main facts and reasons of cases, judges' names and dates. The template was almost the same as that being used by Republican judges.[89]

During the latter part of the civil war, one of the biggest reforms of the Communist judicial system was the change in its name from a regional high court of the Republic to the people's court, a term coined by the Russian Bolsheviks in 1918. The significance of the change of nomenclature echoed the growing confidence of the CCP in the prospect of winning the civil war. It abandoned its previous submissive attitude and shifted to a more assertive stance. In this period, the Border Government had also promulgated several laws or regulations regarding the public trial, court organization, and working rules of the "people's court" between 1947 and 1948.[90]

In 1947, to draw more rural support to its revolutionary cause, the CCP resumed the land reform in its occupied areas that had been suspended during the Sino-Japanese War. On October 28, 1947, Ma Xiwu, the head of the high court, sent a directive letter to all judicial officials encouraging them to assist with the land reform. At the beginning, ignoring the fact of massive torture in the Border Area, the letter acclaimed the accomplishments of the revolutionary judicial system including, inter alia, the abolition of torture, no litigation fee, simple procedure, circuit courts, and reforming criminals through labor. However, the letter quickly shifted to the so-called main problems inside the judicial system, one of which was the missing "class line." In other words, the letter said, the judicial system as a whole failed to know who was the target of law and whose interests the law should protect. For instance, in March 1947, among the 346 prisoners in the high court prison, only 23 of them were landlords or rich peasants. Most prisoners were poor peasants. "Only a few of those landlords and local tyrants who have repressed and exploited peasants [...] are jailed," the letter claimed, "Some cadres even seek profits through shielding landlords [...]. The [cause of the problem] is the ambiguous class and mass line of our judicial system."

Therefore, the letter ordered all judicial officials to back poor peasants and tenants and to struggle against landlords. In that regard, the Communist judicial system would forfeit the judicial independence pledged in the 1946 Constitution Draft. It would continue to be a faithful instrument of the

89 Ai Shaorun, 2007a: 50; also see Yang Yonghua and Fang Keqin, 1987: 121.

90 Ai Shaorun, 2007a: 50-55.

CCP. In addition, to further revolutionize the judicial system, the letter asked cadres to follow whatever most poor peasants wanted (i.e. punishing landlords). The judges should only be assistants to the masses. "[Some judges] must overcome their misconceptions that the masses do not know law and thus will make mistakes," the letter warned, "we must correct the false views that [judges] can sit on the top of GMD laws and serve the toilers."

The letter also called on all judicial departments to scrutinize the class, status, and thought of each judicial official, a practice inherited from the Jiangxi Soviet base. "Besides the aforementioned reasons that have caused [our] mistakes," the letter continued, "the impurity of class and thought of judicial workers is the most important reason [...] all class dissenters (*jieji yiji fenzi*), speculators, and recalcitrants must be purged."[91] This new policy to eliminate all politically unqualified and unreliable judicial officials was an ominous predecessor of the 1952 legal reform in which thousands of "retained judicial personnel" were expelled from the people's courts.[92]

After 1948, the Border Area was no longer the center of the Communist movement because Party leaders had moved to Hebei province, which was closer to the center of the war and the economy. Under the Huabei People's government, Liu Shaoqi ordered to implement the Republican criminal and civil laws, as the PRC courts did in 1949 and 1950, partly because the Party did not have its own laws to replace the "old laws."[93]

As the former "red capital," however, the Border Area remained a major Communist region whose political, economic, and judicial rules continued to reflect the national policies of the CCP. One good example was the enforcement of the Organic Regulation of the People's Court in the Border Area. The goal of the new regulation was to assist the ongoing national land reform. The proposed special and temporary people's tribunals were empowered to deal with any first-instance criminal and civil cases involving alleged sabotage or resistance to land reform, violation of people's democratic rights, damage to production or the war effort, or harming of people's lives or property. All judges should be upright and loyal and would be elected through peasants' meetings during the land reform. Although the people's court could make decisions on death, incarceration, hard labor, fines, and confiscation, the Border Government reserved the final say on the death penalty. The precedence of creating special people's tribunals for political

91 Ibid., 2007a: 205-207.

92 The 1952 legal reform will be discussed in another study.

93 For a more detailed study on the judicial system in the Huabei People's Government see Tiffert, 2015: 71.

purposes would reappear in the Three-Antis and Five-Antis Movements in the early PRC.

In the late 1940s, as the CCP emerged as the victor of the civil war, the Communist judicial system sped up its departure from its legal practice in the Sino-Japanese War and Republican laws. The following case shows the extent to which judges differed from many of their fellow Communist judges during the Sino-Japanese War and judges in the Republic of China. On the evening of August 29, 1948, one An Junjie stole some money and cloth from the home of Wang Hongbin, the victim and plaintiff. Later Wang found his lost goods in the hands of a merchant who told Wang that those goods came from An. But An refused to admit his crime and lied that he had bought the goods from Sun Yunshan and Yue Peijie. Instead of conducting any serious investigation, the county court detained An, Sun, and Yue and interrogated them. With no hard evidence, the court released An. An quickly absconded and that caught the attention of the county court. As soon as the Yan'an county court recaptured An, he admitted his crime and said that his wife Liu Yuezeng had concealed his booty and his friend Sun Jiwu had helped him sell them. In October 1949, the court accused An of having not only stolen goods but also framed innocent people (Sun Yunshan and Yue Peijie). An was sentenced to four years of prison and his accomplices received several months. Although the judge said that the decision was made in accordance with the law, the verdict did not cite any Communist or Republican law.[94]

The above case reflects a clear departure of Communist judges in the late civil war from their earlier practice after 1942 that usually invoked current Communist laws and regulations or Republican laws in making decisions. Due mostly to a rejection of Republican laws and an emphasis on judges' loyalty to the Party and not legal education, Communist judges in the Border Area were inclined to use more "sentiment" or "common sense" than actual laws in judgments.

Cornerstone or Aberration?

The entire period of the Border Area was battered by two major wars: the Second Sino-Japanese War and the second civil war between the Communists and the nationalists. Adopting a pragmatic strategy to build a united front against the Japanese, the CCP recognized the GMD as the

94 Ai Shaorun, 2007b: 142-145.

central government and Chiang-Kai-shek as the sole national leader. Besides political and military concessions, the CCP in the Border Area also reformed its judicial system in line with its status as a regional government within the Republic. The CCP adopted important Republican laws such as its Criminal Law and the Criminal Procedural Law and made certain important revisions to suit its own political and ideological purposes. Although the Republican Supreme Court was the titular highest court in the Border Area, it had no actual jurisdiction over the Communist region. During the latter part of the Sino-Japanese War, many Communist judges, especially those in the high court, could cite specific laws to justify their verdicts. But many local officials functioning as judges invariably abused their power and violated laws. Some professional Communist judges such as Li Mu'an and Zhu Ying had attempted to introduce modern Western judicial principles into the Border Area, but Communist and judicial leaders, as they had done in the Jiangxi Soviet base, continued to regard the judicial system as an instrument of the Party. During the painful years of the Rectification Campaign, both Li and Zhu had suffered relatively more lenient attacks in comparison with thousands of other Communist officials and scholars who had been denounced, interrogated, tortured, executed or forced to commit suicide for being alleged GMD agents or spies.

Shortly after Japan surrendered in 1945, the CCP and the GMD engaged in a civil war. With growing confidence in winning the war, the CCP began to change its court name and stress the loyalty and purity of its judges. To seek support from the peasants, Communist judges were ordered to stick to the right class line and punish landlords and rich peasants. By abolishing Republican laws and purging disloyal Communist judges, many new Communist judges no longer found it necessary to cite laws or regulations in their judgments. In so doing, the Communist judicial system had resumed its previous role as a loyal CCP instrument as before in the Jiangxi Soviet base.

Some China scholars have hailed the judicial experiment and practice in the Border Area as a "cornerstone" for the future PRC judicial system.[95] They argue that the high court in the Border Area contributed three far-reaching features: 1) the role of the judicial system as a CCP instrument; 2) a "creative and pragmatic judicial system" including the people's jury, circuit courts, and the adjudicating method of Ma Xiwu in this period; 3) a "remedial judicial system" including mediation and transforming prisoners into normal people through hard labor. While their arguments have some merit in terms of the newly implemented institutions such as the circuit court and mediation,

95 See authors in the book edited by Wang Shirong荣, 2011.

they have not been aware that the instrumental role of the Communist judicial system originated in the Jiangxi Soviet base. Additionally, these scholars have purposely or inadvertently neglected that the massive violations of law and the use of torture in both the Jiangxi Soviet base and the Rectification Campaign could be considered to be another "cornerstone" or "model" for the future judicial system in the PRC.[96] If we focus on the Border Government's brief adoption and citation of some contemporary Republican laws including its Criminal Law and the Criminal Procedural Law, template, and formality, this period of the Sino-Japanese and civil war could be considered as an "aberration" rather than as a "cornerstone" of the PRC before 1979. Only in that year did that formation become a "cornerstone" on which the PRC established its first Criminal Law and Criminal Procedure Law, three decades after its establishment in 1949.[97]

96 As shown in the following chapters, the CCP from 1950 to 1976 or beyond launched numerous political campaigns against class enemies or criminals during which violations of law were arguably more widespread and severe than in the Border Area or the Jiangxi Soviet base.
97 In the first few months of the PRC, many retained judges in Shanghai still used the template of Republican verdicts but did not explicitly cite Republican laws due to the ostensible abolition of all Republican laws in the PRC. See Chapter 3.

3 From "Excessive Lenience" to Harshness

The Communist Judicial System in the Early PRC, 1949-1952

Abstract
After the CCP and its army conquered mainland China, the Party did not immediately abolish all GMD laws and legal mechanisms as it had once vowed to do. This chapter shows that the Party chose instead to try to make a smooth transition in the judicial system by retaining most former Republican judges and lawyers. As a result, many "counterrevolutionaries" were tried and punished more leniently in accordance with Republican laws. The mild legal policy underwent an abrupt shift shortly after the eruption of the Korean War. Facing a possible GMD effort to retake the mainland, the military commissions, police, procuracy, and courts launched fierce sanctions against counterrevolutionaries with more forced labor and executions. Furthermore, the court reversed its previous balanced handling of disputes between workers and capitalists by siding with labor against management.

Keywords: abolition of GMD laws, "excessive" lenience, SPC guidelines for handling cases, self-reform, anti-counterrevolutionary campaign

The legal system in the early People's Republic of China (PRC) was nothing but a natural and logical extension of its precursor in the revolutionary war period (i.e. 1927-1949). Both were consistently based on the Party ideology, goals, class line, and, above all, the Party's fundamental insecurity and its fear of the loss of power. The major difference is that the early PRC was no longer just a regional and fledgling political power, it now controlled almost all of mainland China. Yet, as in previous periods, the Chinese Communist Party (CCP) continued to fear sabotage from within and threats from without.

Fang, Qiang, *The Communist Judicial System in China, 1927-1976: Building on Fear.*
Taylor & Francis Group 2021
DOI: 10.5117/9789463729451_CH03

From the outset, the CCP had learned from Marx and Lenin that a socialist government and public ownership of the principal means of production was incompatible with capitalism and private ownership.[1] Therefore, in an aspirational Communist China, all of the capitalist state apparatus, including its army, police, and judicial system, had to be scrapped. In January 1949, as the People's Liberation Army (PLA) was poised to take over China, Mao declared that the CCP would abolish all the Nationalist Party (Guomindang, or GMD) laws and legal institutions. "Any legal institution, constitution, and law can only be created by a certain class in the midst of a class struggle," the CCP proclaimed in a statement, "the nature of the constitution and legal institution [in a country] is determined solely by the nature of the polity." In other words, a Communist China should establish a constitution and all other legal institutions in accordance with its nature: proletarian dictatorship. The Party demanded that all Communist judicial cadres use people's laws instead of GMD laws to make judgments in governing the country. Once former GMD judges were willing to reform themselves by learning Communist theories, policies, and laws, the Party would welcome them to work for the PRC.[2] In late September 1949, when the CCP was nearing its final victory, Article 17 of the Common Program, a provisional constitution, called again for the repeal of all GMD repressive laws and judicial systems and their replacement by laws and a judicial system designed to protect the people.[3]

This chapter will look into the formation of the PRC judicial system. It will address some questions that have been largely overlooked such as: How did the CCP create a revolutionary judicial system after it abolished all GMD laws? What kinds of roles did the judicial system play in the early PRC? How did Communist judges adjudicate cases in the absence of criminal and civil laws? How did the Korean War transform the Communist judicial system? To what extent did the early Communist judicial system depart from that of the GMD? Up to now, most conventional scholarship has centered on the prisons, labor camps, the marriage law, and legal education in the early PRC or has made general arguments. Very few scholars have paid close attention to the PRC judicial system in this transitional and important period.[4]

1 "The First and Second Congresses of the Chinese Communist Party" in http://www.gov.cn/test/2007-08/28/content_729220.htm; November 7, 2019.

2 *Studying Documents of Constructing People's Judicial system* (*renmin sifa jianshe xuexi wenjian* 人民司法建设学习文件) (Beijing: Zhongyang zhengfa jiguan sifa gaige bangognshi, 1952): 8.

3 *Common Program*, September 29, 1949.

4 For those scholars who have briefly touched on this important period see Altehenger, 2018: 33-35; Mühlhahn, 2011: 176-179; Klaus Mühlhahn, "Repaying Blood Debt: State Violence and

Based on new archival sources, this chapter will first examine the origin, organization, and practice of the Communist judicial system. Then it will look at case studies to find out how judges actually dealt with criminal and civil cases. In addition, the chapter will attempt to ascertain how successful the Communist judicial system was in serving as a revolutionary court in building the new state. Finally, the chapter will discuss the impact of the Korean War on the PRC judicial system.

A Communist Court without Laws

According to orthodox Marxist and Leninist theories, laws are tools used by the ruling class to monopolize violence, which means that a socialist country should have a socialist judicial system that represents the working class.[5] From its origins, the CCP believed that the judicial system is a crucial instrument for it to maintain power and assault its enemies. As Dong Biwu, a senior CCP leader and the head of PRC Supreme Court, clearly remarked in the early PRC, the key reason for the CCP to abolish all GMD laws was that those laws only protected the rule of predatory classes such as feudal landlords, compradors, and bureaucratic capitalists. In other words, they were used to suppress people's resistance to oppression. The law that the CCP planned to make was to safeguard people's governing and clamp down on the resistance of reactionaries. Due to the differences in class interests, the nature of laws will be different.[6]

The importance of law to the survival and safety of the CCP prompted some newly liberated city and provincial governments to create their judiciaries months before the founding of the PRC. The lingering shortage of qualified Communist judges, however, compelled the CCP to retain Republican judges and legal officers so long as they could shift their allegiance to the Party.

Mass Crimes During the 1950s in China" in Mechthild Leutner, *Rethinking China in the 1950s* (Berlin: Lit, 2007): 35-48; Pitman B. Potter, *From Leninist Discipline to Socialist Legalism: Peng Zhen on Law and Political Authority* (Stanford: Stanford University Press, 2003); Short, 2000: 434-435; Meisner, 1999: 67-68; Peerenboom, 2002; Frank Dikotter, "Crime and Punishment in Post-Liberation China: The Prisoners of a Beijing Gaol in the 1950s" in *The China Quarterly*, No. 149 (Mar., 1997), pp. 147-159; Shaochuan Leng, *Criminal Justice in Post-Mao China: Analysis and Documents* (Albany: State University of New York Press, 1985): 11; Jerome Cohen, *Criminal Process in the PRC, 1949-1963: An Introduction* (Cambridge, Ma: Harvard University Press, 1969): 9; Ren, 1997: 53; for a "generous" account, see Strauss, 2006: 904.

5 See Chapter 1.

6 Dong Biwu董必武, *Collected Law Articles of Dong Biwu* (*Dong Biwu faxue wenji*董必武法学文集) (Beijing: Falü chubanshe, 2001): 14.

For example, after the CCP liberated Baoji, Shaanxi, on July 14, 1949, the Communist military commission wasted no time in taking over its local court and allowing former Republican judges, court police, and other officers to continue their service for the time being. Xi'an, the capital of the province, had started a Communist judicial system in May, two months before Baoji.[7]

In Shanghai, the largest and most prosperous modern city, the new Shanghai People's Government issued an order on July 9, 1949 to build the Shanghai People's Court (hereinafter SPC). Tang Yong, a veteran cadre, was appointed as the head of the court. The SPC was formally established on August 11, 1949.[8] Soon after the founding of the PRC, the fledgling SPC drafted the SPC Organizational Procedure on October 20. Article 1 of the draft made it explicit that the court was affiliated with the Shanghai People's Government, whose mission was to adjudicate or mediate all civil and criminal disputes in compliance with the policies, resolutions, laws, and regulations of the people's government. In addition, the SPC should become a judicial organ safeguarding all political policies of the people's government and defending state security. The SPC would comprise subdivisions such as an Adjudicating Committee, a Mediating Committee, a Secretariat (*mishushi*), and the like. The number of judges in each committee would be 60.[9]

Smaller regions built their courts later than bigger cities. The Jinhua regional court was not created until December 1949 when the Zhejiang provincial government appointed Yang Yuanshi as the head of the court. There were only three units in the court: adjudication, general, and labor education. Among the twelve court cadres, seven were army veterans and five were retained GMD judges. In the spring of 1950, the court was renamed the Jinhua Branch of the Zhejiang Provincial Court. By the end of 1950, the court contained 36 cadres and it was responsible for all cases of nine counties and two cities.[10]

After the CCP abolished all Republican laws, the Party asked judicial cadres to use existing CCP laws including the Common Program, albeit it as yet had no specific laws regarding civil or criminal cases.[11] For Communist judges and especially retained GMD judges, their largest obstacle and dilemma in the early PRC, as Jerome Cohen notes, is that there were few laws by which they could justify their judgments in major criminal

7 *Shaanxi Provincial Gazette – Judicial Gazette*陕西省志-审判志, 1994: 201-202.

8 Shanghai Archives, July 9, 1949. B1-1-009-996.

9 Ibid., October 20, 1949. B1-1-009-996.

10 *Jinhua Court Gazette* (*Jinhua fayuanzhi*金华法院志) (Beijing: Fangzhi chubanshe, 1999): 161.

11 *Studying Documents of Constructing People's Judicial System*, 1952: 8.

cases.[12] As a result, Communist judges had to make rulings based on their "common sense" or revolutionary principles, a "tradition" inherited from the Border Area and the Civil War. In his study on the new Beijing courts in the early PRC, Glenn Tiffert notes that CCP policymakers faced the shortage of "concrete laws and resources."[13] While studying a rape case, Jeremy Brown has noted that the lack of law in the PRC meant that law enforcers "had latitude in dealing with" criminal cases.[14]

To cite just one case, on December 15, 1949, the Shanghai Huangpu District Police Bureau accused one 24-year-old Wei Zhenghan of armed robbery to the SPC. The police alleged that Wei had since 1948 robbed several times. The latest was on June 14, the day Wei allegedly had tied his victim into one room before robbery. After the police came, Wei fired shots at the police three times. The judges (one head judge and two assistant judges) ruled that Wei's actions had jeopardized society and accordingly a long incarceration (seven years) was necessary to educate him. Citing no laws to justify the punishment, the judges apparently utilized their common sense or human sentiment, a tradition of the Communist judicial system since the Yan'an period (1936-1947), that robberies harmed social security. But Wei's emphasis on the need to educate/reform was largely in line with both the CCP's advocacy of reform through labor and Confucius' legal concept.[15] The court allowed Wei to appeal to the same court within ten days.

Considering the seven-year imprisonment as too long, Wei filed an appeal imploring the court to reduce his penalty on the grounds that he had been forced to rob after GMD soldiers seized all the chickens and ducks that he planned to sell for a living. By blaming the GMD for his crime, Wei hoped that the court would lessen his punishment. Unfortunately, the Shanghai Military Commission, the tentative "appellate court," rejected Wei's request. The decision of the commission was understandable. According to Frederic Wakeman Jr., armed robbery and other "serious crimes" were the "second priority" of the CCP to create a new order in the early PRC.[16]

12 Cohen, 1968: 22.

13 Tiffert, 2015: 116.

14 Jeremy Brown, "A Policeman, His Gun, and an Alleged Rape: Competing Appeals for Justice in Tianjin, 1966-1979" in Leese and Engman, 2018: 131.

15 For the labor camps and education see Mühlhahn, 2009; for Confucius' legal concept see Zhu Xi朱熹, ed, *Collective Connotation of the Four Books* (*sishu zhangju jizhu*四书章句集注) (Liaoning: Liaoning jiaoyu chubanshe, 1998): 55.

16 Frederic Wakeman Jr. "'Cleanup': The New Order in Shanghai" in Jeremy Brown and Paul G. Pickowicz, eds., *Dilemmas of Victory: The Early Years of the People's Republic of China* (Cambridge, Ma: The Harvard University Press, 2007), pp. 21-58: 49.

The commission noted that Wei's crime was "tremendously detrimental to society" because he had not only robbed three times but also had dared to shoot at the police. Thus, the seven-year sentence was proper to "educate" him and "protect innocent people." However, the commission left room for Wei to reduce his punishment in the future. The commission hoped that Wei would obtain good education in prison and eliminate the root of his crime thinking If he could really reform fast and behave well, "[the government] will shorten [Wei's] prison time."[17] In this case, it is worth noting that the format of the court verdict was completely identical to that in a Republican court. As Pitman B. Potter has pointed out, in the early PRC many GMD laws continued to be relied on.[18] Daniel Leese and Puck Engman have also argued that "both in theory and practice, the [PRC's] break with the past was less clear."[19] We can extrapolate from this case that many of the judges were retained former GMD judges whose "common sense" may have been based on the "abolished" Republican Criminal Law.[20]

"Reviving" GMD Criminal Laws and Procedures

Indeed, many central and local officials had perceived the problem and potential consequences of no necessary laws and regulations for judges and they tried different ways to tackle it. On November 10, 1949, Li Xiannian, the governor of Hubei, prescribed a directive on law and legal procedure for judicial officials to follow. The directive first admitted a serious shortage of judicial cadres after the provincial government was founded. Most of the 70 local governments in the province had yet to create judicial departments/courts, which resulted in a tremendous pileup of unresolved cases. More severe problems were the untold number of arbitrary arrests, beatings, and killings in many localities. "Such actions that damage the revolutionary cause," the directive stated, "would alienate [the Party] from the masses, isolate ourselves, and end up with turbulence in the social order." To solve the judicial problems, the directive pinpointed three key issues: the nature and aim of law, the division and collaboration between court and police, and adjudicating procedure.[21]

17 Shanghai Archives, December 15, 1949-January 31, 1950. B1-2-945.

18 Potter, 2003: 63.

19 Leese and Engman, 2018: 3.

20 As they had no law to cite, judges had to use common sense. As shown in following cases, the clement punishment of Wei Zhenghan was in line with Republican laws.

21 *Hubei Political Documents* (*Hubei zhengbao*湖北政报), November 10, 1949: 45.

As the Party had always emphasized, the nature of law was pertinent to class struggle. The PRC law was a major mechanism of the people's democratic dictatorship whose missions were to protect all revolutionary classes and suppress the resistance of imperialists, class enemies, and all counterrevolutionary agents. Owing to the abolition of all Republican laws and the lack of new PRC laws, the directive required courts to base their future decisions on the Common Program and other Party polices and regulations. Judges were encouraged to study the spirit of Mao Zedong thought and develop new laws in practice. The directive drew a distinct line between court and police. With no procuracy in existence, the early police were supposed to investigate, interrogate, and prosecute criminals who had infringed people's interests. The court would conduct trials and make judgments. All criminal cases involving GMD agents, saboteurs, and war criminals would be managed by the police. If the police deemed a case to be chargeable, they needed to transfer it to the court. All civil cases and ordinary criminal cases would be decided by the court.

The legal procedure would be a two-instance system with county courts as the first instance and the provincial court as the second. In all cases, judicial units should undergo formal investigative process before they could arrive at any decision. The investigation had to entail both on-site and verbal interrogation. On-site investigations should be conducted by judges only, while verbal investigations should first obtain personal information from the litigants including their class status. Torture, corporal punishment, and forced confession were to be "absolutely" prohibited. Court verdicts should comprise the following items: 1) judicial unit; 2) category of the case; 3) names, genders, ages, and birth places of both plaintiff and defendant; 4) main body; 5) content; 6) reason; 7) appeal date and appeal organ; 8) title and name of the judge; 9) official seal and sending of the verdicts to both litigants. Once litigants received court verdicts, they could appeal to the same court within twenty days if it was a civil case or fifteen days if it was a criminal case. As soon as a court received a case, it should try and make judgment within two months for a civil case and one month for a criminal case to prevent people from waiting too long.

Additionally, the directive made clear provisions for applying the death penalty. All death penalties should be decided by the provincial government. Only the police and court had the right to arrest suspects. Other organs and organizations could only charge but not arrest a suspect. Sentenced criminals would be transferred by courts to prisons. If a prisoner was repentant and asked for reduction of penalty, he or she was allowed to appeal to the original court for a review. For both special (i.e. counterrevolutionaries) and ordinary criminals, their death verdicts should be sent to defendants who were to be given a last chance to appeal. Executions of criminals should be carried out in a mass meeting in order to deter potential criminals. All executions had to be made by guns and not by any other means. Major regions were required to build "self-reform (*zixin*)" buildings to house prisoners and counties needed to have prisons. Abuse of prisoners was to be strictly outlawed.[22]

Although the provincial order in Hubei did not mention judicial independence, it was highly specific and detailed in stressing both the importance of legal procedure and the divisions between police and court. The format of the court verdicts was, like the Shanghai court and the high court in the Border Area (see Chapter 2), the same as what appeared in a Republican court. The ban of torture, the time period for litigants to appeal, and particularly the right for death row criminals to appeal demonstrated that many Communist cadres still craved a formal legal procedure that respected criminals' human dignity and continued the legacy of the Westernized legal reform since the late Qing.[23]

As the largest city, financial center, and economic engine in both the Republican period and the PRC, Shanghai's position and situation were more complicated than those of most other cities. The new Shanghai court had from the beginning attempted to enact laws to handle both civil and criminal cases. On November 25, 1949, in a report to the Shanghai Military Commission, Tang Yong, the head of the SPC, argued that it was imperative for judges to have a standard measurement of penalty. "While dealing with criminal cases, we have discovered a great disparity in penalty measurement due to a missing criminal law," the report admitted, "although the severity of some criminal cases is highly divergent, their punishments could differ from several months to several years. This has caused widespread dissatisfaction among criminals." As a result, more criminals had recently filed appeals to the court for review, which had put the court in strained circumstances.

In December 1949, the SPC drafted the SPC's Guidelines for Handling Cases. According to the guidelines, there would be five major punishments: death penalty, sentences from two months to fifteen years or lifetime, fines from one *yuan* and up, detainments from one day to up to two months, and discipline. Article 3 said that all adjudications should be made in accordance with the seriousness of crimes. Because national security was the overriding

22 Ibid.

23 For the human dignity first evinced in the late Qing see Shen Jiaben沈家本, *Factual Study of the Past Criminal Laws* (*lidai xingfakao*历代刑法考) (Beijing: Zhonghua shujü1976): 1.20; also see Fang, 2013: Ch. 2.

concern for the budding regime, most serious crimes were against the people's government, state and public properties, or trying to obstruct the ongoing liberation war. Light crimes included, inter alia, first-time law violation, crimes caused by criminals' stupidity or lack of education, or a property crime (e.g. theft, robbery) triggered by hunger or family burdens.

Article 9 stipulated the specific punishment of grave crimes: 1) Anyone not just plotting but also taking actions to block revolution, sabotage the people's democratic dictatorship, or to overthrow the PRC would be jailed from three to seven years. Anyone conniving with the enemies [of the PRC] would be sentenced from seven to fifteen years in prison. If the circumstances of the crime were very grave, the person would be sentenced to life in prison. People committing treason, including collaborating with imperialist military forces against the PRC, would be executed. Other traitors would receive a seven-year incarceration. Serious treason could end up with life sentences or death penalties. Article 16 stated that anyone who tried to block or resist orders of the people's government or who used violence against government employees would be punished with up to one year of imprisonment. Compared with similar laws in the PRC today, the articles of law proposed in Shanghai in the early PRC were fairly lenient, and they were very lenient when compared with laws during political campaigns in the 1950s.

Aside from political crimes, the guidelines also stipulated punishments for ordinary crimes, such as robbery, arson, counterfeit money, rape, and homicide. Arsonists who destroyed public buildings would be imprisoned from three to seven years. Criminals who counterfeited currency would stay in custody from five to ten years, a more serious punishment than that for arson. While rapists would generally be imprisoned for from three to seven years, criminals raping underaged girls would have their punishment increased by 50%. Murderers would be jailed for at least ten years. But criminals who had committed the following murders would be sentenced to death or lifetime: 1) killing a direct relative or parent; 2) murdering by using cruel means; 3) heading a group of murderers; 4) killing twice. Robbers would be sentenced to from three to seven years in prison. If a robber also committed rape or murder, the punishment would be death or a life sentence.[24]

The guidelines drafted by the SPC for dealing with crimes were in many respects reminiscent of dynastic laws and especially the Republican laws. For example, the more severe punishment on murder of parent/s in both the SPC

24 Shanghai Archives, December 1949. B1-2-308.

Guidelines and the Republican Criminal Law (Article 272) resembled the Ten Abominations since the Southern and Northern dynasties (420-589 CE).[25]

Moreover, in terms of its categories and punishments, the guidelines were synonymous with the 1935 Criminal Law under the GMD, one of the six laws that the CCP vowed to renounce. For instance, in Article 9 of the SPC Guidelines, the sentencing of any criminal who plotted to overthrow the legitimate government to seven years was almost identical to Article 100 of the Republican Criminal Law, which stated that criminals "harboring intention and acting to damage the polity, seize territory, or to adopt illegal methods to change constitution and overthrow the [legitimate] government will receive seven years imprisonment." The leaders would be "sentenced to life in prison" and "plotters of the aforementioned crimes would be sentenced to from six months to five years in prison."

The only difference was that the SPC Guidelines did not mention the penalty for the leading criminals. The criminals in this article were tantamount to counterrevolutionaries in the PRC, but their punishments were extremely mild if compared to similar crimes in the ensuing anti-counterrevolutionary campaigns. In Article 11, the SPC Guidelines imposed the death penalty on criminals who had collaborated with or relied on the imperialist military to oppose the PRC, which was in line with Article 105 of the Republican Criminal Law, which would sentence any criminal to life imprisonment or death who had fought for enemy troops or colluded with enemy states against the Republic and its allies. In the early PRC the imperialist enemy, of course, was no longer Japan but the United States.

Similar categories or punishments could also be found in ordinary crimes. Chapter 5 of the SPC Guidelines entitled "Public Danger Crime (*gonggong weixianzui*)" was the same as Chapter 11 of the Republican Criminal Law. Other articles were close in contents. Article 33 of the SPC Guidelines, for example, said that arsonists destroying other people's buildings and causing public danger would be jailed for up to three to seven years. Article 174 of the Republican Criminal Law was essentially the same crime except that it added more public facilities and venues (e.g. train, trolleybus, mine, ship, etc.) than the SPC Guidelines. Another difference was that the range of incarceration in the Republican law was three to ten years, three years more than the SPC Guidelines. In addition, several chapters in the Republican Criminal Law such as "Damaging Freedom, Damaging Reputation, and Homicides" were combined into one chapter entitled "Damaging Life, Health, and Reputation" in the SPC guidelines. The law and guidelines differed insofar

25 Xue Yunsheng薛允升, 1999: 2-3.

as the highest penalty in the Republican law for these crimes was death whereas the highest penalty in the SPC guidelines was only a life sentence.[26]

The SPC submitted the guidelines to the Shanghai government. The government, which ostensibly knew little about the judicial system, passed the guidelines to the Supreme Court. Five months later, on April 20, 1950, Shen Junru, the Supreme Court Justice and a famous jurist and political activist aligning with the CCP in the Republican period, responded to the SPC Guidelines with his comments. To begin with, Shen praised the intent of the SPC Guidelines that would help provide SPC judges with a standard in handling cases. However, Shen questioned the guidelines' "insufficient" embodiment of the standpoint of the people's democratic dictatorship and the need to consolidate revolutionary order. Shen then pointed out a number of specific examples of the "extreme lenience" in the guidelines. The first was Article 9 that sentenced only up to seven years to prison anyone attempting to obstruct revolution, sabotage the people's democratic dictatorship, or overthrow the PRC no matter how severe their crimes were. Criminals who had connived with enemies (i.e. the GMD) would only be punished with a jail time up to fifteen years. Even more inappropriate was that the highest punishment in this category was merely a life sentence. In addition, Article 12 stated that the highest grade of penalty for any person who had leaked, spied out, transmitted, or handed in military intelligence to enemies was a life sentence. In Article 36, Shen questioned the light ten-year imprisonment for the most sinister crime of counterfeiting the currency of the people's bank. Shen argued that none of the above criminals need fear the prospect of capital punishment, which was not congruous with the current policies of the people's government to suppress reactionaries and solidify the revolutionary order.

Besides political crimes, Shen indicated that penalties for some non-political crimes were also too mild. One of them was Article 74, which stated that in principle the punishment of robberies was up to seven years in custody. Only cases involving death, arson, rape, or homicide would carry a death penalty. In Article 52, whatever the circumstances of the crime, all criminals charged with homicide would be incarcerated from ten years to lifetime. In contrast to other highly lenient laws, Article 53 seemed to Shen

26 For the SPC Guideline see Shanghai People's Court, "The Guidelines for Dealing with Cases (*Shanghaishi renmin fayuan chuxing biaozhun*上海市人民法院处刑标准" in Shanghai Archives, December 1949. B1-2-308; for the GMD Criminal Law see "The Criminal Law of the Republic of China (*Zhonghua minguo xingfa*中华民国宪法)", 1935. https://zh.wikisource.org/zh/中华民国刑法_(民国23年立法24年公布).

too harsh or dumb for certain cases. As the article stated, of all the four listed homicides (killing direct relatives, killing by cruel means, killing many people, and committing more than two homicides), regardless of the intent of the criminals, the punishment would contain death or lifetime sentence. Shen wrote: "If a person has committed more than two killings but did so to advance the revolutionary cause, that person should be differentiated from other criminals."[27]

No sooner had Tang Yong, the head of the SPC, received the comments from the Supreme Court than he reported to Chen Yi, the mayor of Shanghai, with a self-criticism about the errors and imperfections of the SPC Guidelines. Tang conceded that the guidelines had failed to emphasize the platform of the people's democratic dictatorship and the necessity of strengthening revolutionary order. The biggest mistake of the guidelines was, in Tang's words, that the SPC rashly tried to draft a stopgap standard for SPC judges to tackle cases but failed to ponder whether the guidelines contained any political faults. Tang blamed himself for insufficient "class-consciousness," failure to fully understand the spirit and nature of CCP policies, and his "grave" style of utilitarianism.

Moreover, Tang Yong acknowledged to the Shanghai government that the guidelines had been drafted by a former inspector of the Republican Supreme Court. Now it is clear that, although the CCP had promised to repeal all Republican laws and institutions, many former judicial specialists of the GMD continued to work for the PRC judicial system and the SPC was just one of them.[28] According to the *Compendium of Judicial Investigation Report*, which was published in 1952, more than 50% of the employees in some people's courts such as the Central-China Branch of the Supreme Court and the Wuhan Court were former GMD judicial officials. In East China, about 24% of judicial employees were former GMD officials. That was because some CCP judicial leaders believed that those former GMD judicial officials had legal knowledge and experience and wanted to retain them.[29] Tang criticized himself and the SPC leadership for having failed to pay attention to the intention of the former GMD inspector and "unknowingly" approved the guidelines. In conclusion, Tang believed that the comments of the Supreme Court Justice were absolutely correct and had immense

27 Shanghai Archives, April 20, 1950. B1-2-308-20.

28 Ibid., May 4, 1950. B1-2-308-23.

29 The Joint Inspection Group of the Central Political and Legal Organs (*zhongyang sifa jiguan lianhe shenjiz*中央司法机关联合审计组), edited, *Compendium of Judicial Investigation Report* (*sifa diaocha baogao huibian*司法调查报告汇编), June 1952 (An Internal Edition).

educational significance for him. Tang promised that he would in the future reform his thought and enhance his class-consciousness.[30]

From the standpoint of today's Chinese judicial system, the SPC guidelines had nothing wrong. They simply mirrored some of the universal legal principles and laws largely adopted by most countries today including the Republic and the post-1978 PRC.[31] Yet, for a confident CCP that had just founded the PRC, the judicial system should be, as both Marx and Lenin had stressed, one of the instruments of the political authority against its class enemies.[32] As a self-claimed representative of the workers and peasants, the CCP deemed its enemies to be exploitive classes such as landlords and capitalists whom the Communist judicial system should target. In early 1950, the new PRC was barely a year old and the CCP was fearing imminent and tangible threats from remaining GMD agents and other saboteurs, potential military invasion from the GMD in Taiwan, and from the GMD's longtime ally, the United States. To strengthen its new rule and eliminate hostile forces, the CCP had little inclination to implement judicial fairness and lenience toward its enemies. It was against this historical backdrop that the Supreme Court Justice questioned and censured the guidelines of the SPC and demanded harsher penalties on PRC's enemies.

Continued Leniency Toward Enemies

Despite the Supreme Court criticism of the SPC Guidelines as being too lenient and lacking class-consciousness, many SPC judges, if not all, continued to follow the guidelines in dealing with political crimes. In some cases, SPC judges remained quite "lenient" toward counterrevolutionaries. With no criminal law to invoke, judges (who were mostly retained from the Republic and/or the GMD) had to base their decisions on their "Republican" common sense.

On May 2, 1950, about two weeks after the Supreme Court justice chastised SPC's "extreme lenience" toward counterrevolutionaries, the SPC adjudicated a case involving three counterrevolutionaries: Ni Rongchang, Wang Da, and Li Jin'gen. According to the court verdict, Ni was originally a businessman.

30 Shanghai Archives, May 4, 1950. B1-2-308-23.
31 Article 105 of the PRC Criminal Law states that a subverter of the PRC will be sentenced from three to ten years in prison and the leader will be imprisoned from ten years to life sentence. http://www.npc.gov.cn/wxzl/wxzl/2000-12/17/content_4680.htm
32 Potter, 2003: 80.

In 1945, he had joined the GMD Intelligence Service and had become a security guard. Shortly after the CCP liberated Shanghai in late May 1949, Ni and Wang Da, a GMD agent, plotted to form a counterrevolutionary organization in Shanghai, which was later named "The Shanghai Youth Corps of the GMD Central Executive Committee." Ni recruited Li Jin'gen and Wang Da as underground agents. The main aim of this organization was to collect information on the Communist army in Shanghai and cable it to the Taiwan-based GMD. In August 1949, Ni also planned to murder a CCP official.

There should be no doubt that Ni and his followers were counterrevolutionaries who posed a grave and imminent threat to the newborn Communist regime. All of them had "confessed" their crimes. The SPC, however, sentenced Ni Rongchang, a former GMD party member and head of a counterrevolutionary organization who had tried to murder a Communist cadre, to only five years in prison, two years less than the sentence stipulated in the SPC Guidelines. Wang Da and Li Jin'gen for their part, were sentenced to only three years of imprisonment each. The highly lenient penalty of Ni was, according to the judge, not based on any existing law but was justified by the vague "good remorse" and cooperation Ni demonstrated after his arrest.[33]

In another case on June 30, 1950, more than two months after SPC president Tang Yong made his self-criticism to the Shanghai government, the SPC publicly sentenced one Jin Yinchang to three years in prison. Jin was a follower of a GMD military unit headed by Huang Bamei. Not long after the CCP took Shanghai in May 1949, Jin fled to Daishan island, Zhejiang, where Huang formed a counterrevolutionary guerrilla force against the PRC. Jin served as a sergeant in the force. In October 1949, Jin sneaked back to Shanghai and maintained regular contacts with covert GMD agents. Jin also attempted to rejoin the Daishan guerrilla. Unfortunately for him, the police arrested Jin before he could accomplish his plan.

Using "common sense" rather than any existing law to justify his decision, an SPC judge argued that Jin should be punished because of his "reactionary thoughts and determination to become an enemy of the people." Jin was sentenced to three years of imprisonment. Dissatisfied nonetheless, Jin Yinchang appealed to the Shanghai Military Commission in hopes of a reduction of his already "light" penalty. Jin ascribed his crimes to his illiteracy and stupidity and claimed that he had been coerced to join the GMD guerrillas in Daishan. Noting Jin's anti-people mindset and dismissing his claim of being forced to join the GMD guerrillas, the military commission

33 Shanghai Archives, May 2, 1950. B1-2-945.

under Chen Yi turned down Jin's appeal. The commission noted that Jin should accept the three-year imprisonment and transform himself into a new person. In this case, the SPC judge who had adjudicated Jin might have not paid attention to the Supreme Court's criticism of the SPC guidelines. It is also clear that the "lenient" punishment of Jin, a counterrevolutionary, won the support of the military commission.[34]

The clemency of PRC judges was further exemplified by a prison report in June 1950. In its report, the Shanghai People's Court suggested that many of the inmates have their sentences reduced. 500 of them had been convicted and imprisoned by the GMD. Aside from traitors and murderers, most of the rest were major robbers or drug addicts. Their sentences were more than ten years, including life and death sentences. Some prisoners were victims of the harsh laws imposed by the GMD either to protect its booty or in response to a losing war with the CCP. For instance, a first-time seller of narcotics would be executed, which was a far cry from comparable crimes today that average one year of imprisonment. "In light of the generous educational policy of the people's government," the prison report wrote, "it is necessary to mitigate the penalties of those prisoners." The report went on to suggest that the punishments of robbers be reduced by 50%, cases involving narcotics be cut by five years, life sentences be lowered to four years in prison, and all the others (except traitors and murderers) be lessened by one fourth. Still, the reduction of penalty would be contingent on the actual performance of a prisoner. The prison report did nothing but echo the overall contemporary lenience of the CCP, which could be evidenced by the endorsement of it by the Shanghai government. On June 17, mayor Chen Yi "approved in principle" the prison's suggestions and deemed them "feasible." The mayor only cast doubt on the rigid uniformity in decreasing penalties of most cases without taking the "real circumstances" of each individual prisoner into account. In particular, the government highlighted the disparate backgrounds and habitual criminality in each robbery case that needed further investigation and study before any reduction was approved.[35]

As shown in the above three cases, many SPC judges in the early PRC demonstrated a strong sense of lenience toward both ordinary criminals and counterrevolutionaries. If the lenience toward ordinary criminals was somewhat hard to comprehend, the judicial clemency to "class enemies" or "major" counterrevolutionaries in a critical period would be more incredible. More important, some of SPC's highly tolerant decisions on

34 Ibid., June 30, 1950. B1-2-012-028-935.

35 Ibid., June 1950. B1-2-003-312.

counterrevolutionaries were made after Supreme Court Justice Shen Junru's criticism of the "unprincipled lenience" in the SPC Guidelines. In these cases, SPC judges, many of them were former Republican judges, obviously did not care much about Shen's questions and continued to adjudicate on the basis of their professional training or the "hidden laws" (i.e. Republican laws) in their minds. Probably the most crucial was the Shanghai government's backing of the court's guidelines and the sentence reductions.

Tang Yong, the head of the SPC, noted in November 1949 that the lack of a legal standard had caused a wide disparity among court penalties on similar crimes. After the Supreme Court struck down the SPC Guidelines, judges would have to make decisions in accordance with their "common sense" and not any laws. As a result, penalties for analogous crimes decided by different judges would continue to manifest enormous discrepancies. In the case of Ni Rongchang, a diehard GMD agent and counterrevolutionary opponent of the PRC, the punishment was five years, which was phenomenally light. Around the same time in the same court, a counterrevolutionary named Jiang Keqiang whose crimes was similar to that of Ni Rongchang was sentenced to death and quickly executed despite appeals by his wife and a dozen neighbors.

On April 29, 1950, three days before Ni Rongchang's generous treatment, the Shanghai police accused Jiang Keqiang, a young man in his early twenties, along with 23 other criminals of conspiring to overthrow the PRC, organizing a reactionary military force, and conducting killings. According to the court verdict, Jiang had joined the GMD and was appointed as the head of the Shanghai Youth Service Unit in the late 1940s. Shortly before the CCP took over Shanghai, Hui Gui, a GMD official, attempted to create the Great Alliance of the Chinese People, an anti-CCP organization. Hu contacted some former GMD agents including Jiang Keqiang and Zhang Jianmin. The Great Alliance had four subdivisions and Jiang was assigned to lead one of them. Jiang and other GMD agents allegedly had colluded to make terrorist attacks, spread rumors, and conduct sabotages. Although no evidence was adduced to prove that Jiang and his collaborators had committed any real crimes or terrorist attacks, the judge, most likely a Communist cadre, sentenced Jiang and five other counterrevolutionary defendants to the death penalty. In contrast to Ni Rongchang who had personally founded a counterrevolutionary organization and plotted to murder a Communist cadre, Jiang was at most a lower-ranking counterrevolutionary who was merely the head of a subdivision of a counterrevolutionary organization. Moreover, no evidence showed that Jiang had committed any actual crimes. Yet, due to the lack of any legal standard to follow, judges in the same court imposed drastically different punishments. Jiang's death sentence was far more drastic than Ni's five-year imprisonment.

Dissatisfied, Jiang appealed to the Shanghai Military Commission for a review of his case. He claimed that he was just a junior member in the organization and had only become the head of the second subdivision of the Great Alliance for several days before his arrest. Jiang blamed Zhang Jianmin for luring him to join the organization. While Jiang admitted the "fundamental error of his thought," he asserted that he had been controlled by Zhang Jianmin and another member of the Alliance. Meanwhile, Jiang's wife and neighbors also appealed to the court imploring mercy for Jiang. On May 9, Jiang's wife begged the military commission to consider the fact that Jiang was an inveterate coward on the one hand, and the main bread-earner for the family on the other. Without Jiang, the whole family would lose its livelihood. Jiang seems to have had a good relationship with his neighbors as 28 of them filed a collective appeal asking the military commission to reduce Jiang's punishment. They claimed that Jiang had always been a lawful person. "The cause of Jiang's serious crimes," the neighbors pleaded, "was his immaturity or carelessness in making friends." In a final plea, the neighbors asked the military commission to pardon Jiang based on the government's ongoing magnanimous policy, and to provide him, the pillar of his family, a chance to atone for his crimes by good deeds.

On June 2, obviously unmoved by the appeals on behalf of Jiang Keqiang, the Shanghai Military Commission endorsed his execution along with four other counterrevolutionaries proposed by the SPC. The only exception was given to Zhang Jianming for his speedy confession and assistance to the police in detaining key criminals.[36]

If the dearth of legal standards in bigger and wealthier cities like Shanghai could lead to widely divergent penalties for similar crimes among different judges, conditions would be much more dire and bloody in rural areas. In the bigger cities, many court judges were retained GMD legal specialists who had some formal legal training. But many, if not most, judges in small towns or the countryside were CCP cadres or military veterans who had little or no legal knowledge. In February 1950, an order of the Hubei provincial government chastised the massive violations of law and legal procedures in many rural areas. Several months before, the provincial government had already warned some rural cadres to stop unbridled arrests, tortures, and forced killings, a likely revival of the grisly political campaigns in the Jiangxi Soviet base and the Yan'an period. Recently, complaints and accusations from

36 Ibid., May 2, 1950. B1-2-945.

some regions showed that infringements of law by rural cadres persisted. In one complaint, for instance, one woman from Macheng charged Hu Lihong and Xu Weizheng, two district cadres who had squandered public money in gambling, with beating and hanging her husband to vent their anger. They also tortured a peasant Nie Yijia, who later committed suicide. The provincial government demanded that local cadres obey the legal procedures and renounce torture and any corporal punishments because they were antagonistic to the Party's mass-line policy (i.e. its effort to win broad popular support).[37] However harsh the tone of the provincial government, its criticism did not include any punitive actions against official torturers and therefore probably did little to rein in rural lawbreakers.

Balance in Labor Disputes

In Chinese history, the emphasis was on criminal law and other kinds of laws were regarded as "minor or relatively insignificant. Before the late Qing dynasty (1644-1911) drafted its Civil Law, based on the German Civil Law, Chinese codes of law did not have express categories for civil law and civil cases.[38] For that reason, Joseph Needham described Chinese law as penal because there was no explicit space for civil law.[39] Although scholars such as William Alford and Philip C. Huang have convincingly argued that China did have laws and cases that were effectively civil both within and outside of penal law codes, nonetheless, it is still true that official codes of law seldom mentioned civil laws or cases. As Huang has pointed out, civil cases in the Qing dynasty were largely solved through mediation, and if necessary, magistrates would be involved and exercise pressure on both parties.[40]

In the late Republican period (1928-1949), courts could judge civil cases in compliance with the 1929 Civil Law. In the Shaanxi Border/Yan'an period, the primary means to tackle civil cases was mediation. After the CCP denounced almost all Republican laws, it took the Party many years to promulgate a

37 Hubei Provincial Government, *Hubei Political Report* (*hubei zhengbao*湖北政报), February 16, 1950. Vol. 6, pp. 29-30.

38 For the late Qing civil law see Jerome Bourgon, "Rights, Freedoms, and Customs in the Making of Chinese Civil Law, 1900-1936" in William C. Kirby, ed, *Realms of Freedom in Modern China* (Stanford: Stanford University Press, 2004), pp. 84-112: 94; Qiang Fang, 2013a: Ch. 2.

39 Joseph Needham, *Science and Civilization in China*, Vol. 2, "History of Scientific Thought" (Cambridge: Cambridge University Press, 1975): 2. 258.

40 Philip C. Huang, *Civil Justice in China: Representation and Practice in the Qing* (Stanford: Stanford University Press, 1998).

complete and formal civil law. As in the Border Area, the CCP in the early PRC continued to mediate civil cases. In March 1950, the Shanghai People's Court drafted the Tentative Methods in Resolving Civil and Criminal Cases. Article 8 of the methods said that civil or light criminal cases should all first go through the process of mediation. Only after exhausting all mediation efforts could the court accept and adjudicate those cases.[41]

Why did the CCP require civil cases to be addressed first by mediation? A likely reason is that the CCP claimed from the beginning that it represented Chinese workers and peasants. Unlike criminal cases that normally impaired people's personal lives and threatened Communist rule and social order, civil cases were regarded as internal contradictions among the people and thus should be settled via mediation. Additionally, being an ideologically charged revolutionary party, the CCP intended to stand up for workers' rights in disputes between employees and employers.[42]

To cite only one case, one Zhang Yuqi and his family had run a factory called Shanghai Daxin Silk Factory for a dozen years. In August 1949, however, the factory was in big trouble: sales of its products decreased and prices fell below the actual costs of production. To mitigate the cost, Zhang decided to run the factory only every other day. On January 9, 1950, owing to continuous sluggish sales, Zhang was forced to shut down the factory and lay off all workers. On March 20, Zhang and the Shanghai Labor Bureau reached an agreement in which Zhang promised to pay each worker two months of wages as a parting gift. Zhang was to provide half of the gift by April 3, 1950, and the rest by April 15. At the end of March, however, Zhang suddenly absconded due probably to his inability to pay the compensation. Outraged, the workers sued Zhang and the factory to the SPC.

The trial was held in the absence of Zhang. The court demanded that Zhang's family fulfill Zhang's commitments in his agreement with the Shanghai Labor Bureau. Interestingly, the court requested Zhang's family to pay the worker plaintiffs only from one to one-and-a-half months of severance pay, 25% or even 50% less than the erstwhile agreed amount. Why did the court reduce the family's agreed fee to the workers? Why did the court express sympathy to the employer? Was it not true that the Party pledged to safeguard workers' rights and oppose capitalists' privileges? In the section of "Reason" in the court verdict, a typical Republican-style legal format, the judge, most likely one retained from the previous period,

41 See Shanghai Archives, March 1, 1950. B1-2-311-8.

42 For the view that civil disputes were internal struggles among the people see Mao Zedong, *Articles of Mao Zedong* (*Maozedong wenji*) (Beijing: Renmin chubanshe, 2001): 7. 205-206.

based the compensation on the starting date of the workers in the factory. For example, workers entering the factory in 1946 would take the most compensation: one-and-a-half months' wage, but they would still lose half a month's wage. Those coming to the factory after 1947 would get only one month's wage as severance pay. The judge also stated that the reduction of the compensation was in light of the request of the defendant, who was very probably facing financial difficulties.

In this case, while the judge was supposed to stand with the workers and require the factory owner to pay severance payments, the court tried to maintain a delicate balance between the capitalist defendant and worker plaintiffs. Supporting defendant's request, the SPC significantly cut the compensations for each worker and allowed the factory to renege on its earlier promise. In that regard, while the court's decision could not be seen as "revolutionary," it was likely to be deemed both lawful and reasonable in the early 1950s.

On March 7, 1950, the *Shanghai Commerce and Industry* published an article entitled "How to Accurately Enforce the Policy of 'Mutual Benefit between Capital and Labor'." Chen Minshan, the author, argued that the mutual benefit between capitalists and workers was one of the key principles of the economic policy in the stage of New Democracy. After the establishment of the PRC, workers became the masters of the new country and accordingly they were prejudiced against capitalists. The author encouraged workers to follow CCP polices and solve their disputes with the capitalists through negotiation before the promulgation of any central laws.[43]

Some Western scholars have also taken note of the moderate policy in the early PRC. As Lowell Dittmer has argued, in the beginning of the PRC, the CCP tended to discourage workers from demanding higher wages. Workers were instead informed that "it was in the interest of the working class to cooperate with the bourgeoisie until production recovered."[44] According to Pitman Potter, Peng Zhen, an army veteran and the deputy leader in the powerful Political and Legal Commission, remarked in August 1950 that laws "should apply not just to counterrevolutionaries but also to workers, peasants, cadres, and others who have violated the law, no matter how good they might be."[45] With the tone of a balance between capitalists and

43 Chen Minshan陈敏山, "How to Accurately Enforce the Policy of 'Mutual Benefit between Capitalist and Labor' (*zenyang laizhunquede zhixing Laozi liangli zhengce*怎样来准确地执行劳资两利政策)" in *Shanghai Commerce and Industry*, March 7, 1950: 6.

44 Lowell Dittmer, *China's Continuous Revolution: The Post-Liberation Epoch 1949-1981* (Berkeley: University of California, 1989): 14-15.

45 Potter, 2003: 64.

workers set at the top, it was no wonder that court judges demonstrated sympathy for capitalist defendants.

The Judicial System in an Anti-counterrevolutionary Campaign

Starting from the early summer of 1950, top judicial leaders such as Peng Zhen who viewed law as "a vehicle for political repression" and a crucial advocate in "crafting the attack on counterrevolutionaries," became increasingly rattled by what they called the "boundless lenience" in dealing with counterrevolutionaries.[46] In some courts, like the one in Shanghai, some "heinous counterrevolutionaries" did not get the death penalty. Even though some local courts meted out death sentences, they would often be reversed by the appellate courts. Because the current judicial "boundless lenience" had emboldened counterrevolutionaries and alienated the CCP from the mass, Peng suggested that the Party make great efforts to correct the erroneous policy.[47]

In late June, the Korean War broke out. The North Korean army moved quickly south and the US and its allies speedily intervened. Mao denounced US meddling and accordingly made military preparations to assist North Korea.[48] All of a sudden, the young PRC that was still consolidating its authority was overwhelmed by a fundamental fear of both a threat from the US and a likely attack or soaring sabotage from the GMD in Taiwan. Luo Ruiqing, the Minister of Public Security, called on the police to impose the death penalty or at least life sentences against leading counterrevolutionaries who, among other crimes, initiated arms riots, robbed warehouses, sabotaged factories, railroads, and ships, or murdered revolutionary cadres.[49]

On July 23, 1950, about one month after the eruption of the war, the State Council and the Supreme Court publicized a joint directive to roll out the first anti-counterrevolutionary campaign in the PRC. The primary mission of the judicial system in the campaign, as Vice Premier and judicial leader Dong Biwu remarked later, was not so much to safeguard the law as

46 For Peng Zhen see Potter, 2002: 64; Altehenger, 2018: 34.

47 Central Legal System Committee (Zhongyang fazhiweiyuanhui中央法制委员会), ed., *Repressing Counterrevolutionaries* (*zhenya fangeming*镇压反革命), October 26, 1950: 19.

48 Chen Jian, *China's Road to the Korean War* (Columbia: Columbia University Press, 1994): 129-131.

49 Luo Ruiqing罗瑞卿, *Luo Ruiqing's Comments on People's Public Security Work* (*Luo Ruiqing lunrenmin gongan gongzuo*罗瑞卿论人民公安工作) (Beijing: Qunzhong chubanshe, 1994): 22-23.

to "directly consolidate the people's democratic dictatorship."[50] The joint directive asserted that, although the people's government had controlled most parts of the PRC, many remaining GMD forces with the assistance of the imperialists (i.e. the US) continued to attack the people's government using armed riots and hidden assassinations. As the CCP had done in the final days of the Jiangxi Soviet base, the directive demanded harsher punishment on counterrevolutionaries to strengthen the revolutionary order and to protect people's democratic rights and myriad social reforms. Long-term sentences or death penalties would be adopted in the following cases: 1) Bandit leaders holding arms and plotting rebellions; 2) Counterrevolutionaries who had killed public employees and people, destroyed factories, mines, and storehouses, looted state and people's properties, stole state secrets or instigated backward people to oppose the people's government; 3) All intransigent GMD agents and habitual bandits; 4) Anyone who had collaborated with or covered up these counterrevolutionaries.[51]

Some studies have found that the Korean War prompted the CCP to reverse its earlier "excessive lenience" and to "exhort local cadres to enact a harsh policy" against enemies.[52] On October 10, 1950, the CCP stepped up its suppression of counterrevolutionaries by issuing an order entitled "A Directive Regarding Repressing Counterrevolutionaries" under Mao that would call off all "lenience" toward counterrevolutionaries and enforce a novel Party policy of "combining lenience and suppression."[53]

Although the central government had unleashed the anti-counterrevolutionary campaign, the efforts of the Party and some judicial cadres to enact laws and improve judicial procedures seemed not to have been immediately stymied. On August 15, about three weeks after the campaign began, Premier Zhou Enlai, with the approval of Mao, ordered the publicizing of the General

50 Dong, 2001: 89.

51 State Council and Supreme People's Court (zhengwuyuan政务院, zuigao renmin fayuan最高人民法院), "*Directives Regarding Counterrevolutionary Actions* (*guanyu zhenya fangeming huodong dezhishi*关于镇压反革命活动的指示)," July 23, 1950. See zh.wikisource.org/wiki/政务院、最高人民法院关于镇压反革命活动的指示(October 22, 2020); *Sichuan Provincial Trial Gazette* (*Sichuan shengzhi*四川审判志) (Beijing: Dianzi keji saxue chubanshe, 2003): 315.

52 Strauss, 2006: 904; also see Nara Dillion, "New Democracy and the Demise of Private Charity in Shanghai" in Jeremy Brown and Paul G. Pickowicz, 2007, pp. 80-102: 88.

53 State Council and Supreme People's Court (zhengwuyuan政务院, zuigao renmin fayuan最高人民法院), "*Directives Regarding Counterrevolutionary Actions* (*guanyu zhenya fangeming huodong dezhishi*关于镇压反革命活动的指示)," October 10, 1950. http://cpc.people.com.cn/GB/64162/64165/70486/70496/4844076.html; also *Guangdong Provincial Trial Gazette* (Guangdongshengzhi shenpanzhi广东省志审判志) (Guangzhou: Guangdong renmin chubanshe, 1999): 71.

Organizational Regulations of People's Tribunals (*renmin fating zuzhi tongze*) for local courts to follow certain legal procedures. Article 1 allowed provincial governments to create county and city courts to guarantee revolutionary order and implement policies related to land reform. The mission of the tribunals was to "use legal procedures" to punish criminals harming state interests, plotting rebellions, and impairing social orders. Article 5 strictly prohibited torture and demanded judges to conduct serious and detailed investigations. Judges should also permit the audience to speak. Defendants had the right to seek lawyers' help, albeit the lawyers had to be approved by the tribunal. County and city tribunals had the power to arrest, detain, and punish defendants with imprisonment, confiscation of property, hard labor and death. The death penalty decided by tribunals had to be approved by provincial governors. Imprisonments under five years or innocence could be decided by county and city governments.

Unlike the Hubei provincial order in November 1949 that provided counterrevolutionaries sentenced to death with the right to appeal, Article 8 of the "General Organizational Regulations" stated that counterrevolutionaries who had received death sentences could not appeal.[54] This new policy indicated that the central government sought a tougher line toward enemies in a political campaign. Yet, the central government, regardless of the efficacy of its new regulations, appeared to remain in theory committed to its ban of torture, defending rights, and legal procedures.

More discordant with the ongoing political campaign was a letter of request made by the SPC on November 25, 1950, four months after the CCP launched the anti-counterrevolutionary campaign, for more judicial power in dealing with major or complex cases. According to the letter, the Government Review System (*fuhe zhidu*) began in wartime, which required county courts to report first-instance cases to both magistrates and upper-level courts for approvals. While the review system was necessary in wartime when many institutions were inadequate, it was no longer practical in the PRC after the adjudicating level system (*shenji zhidu*) of the judicial system had clearly been established. The old system not only conflicted with the current system but also caused more trouble to the court.

In one case, after a man (A) left his girlfriend and went to another city, his girlfriend quickly fell in love with another man (B). Months later, A came back and resumed his love affair with his former girlfriend. But A soon discovered that his girlfriend had lost her chastity. Under pressure, the woman confessed her affair with B. Infuriated, A and the woman murdered

54 *Hubei Political Documents*, August 15, 1950, pp. 34-35.

B together. Charging A with raping the woman (no marriage) and murdering B, the Hangzhou Municipal Court sentenced A to death and reported the case to the Zhejiang provincial government for approval. The government transferred the case to the provincial high court for review, which endorsed the punishment in the name of the government. But A and his relatives disputed the penalty that forced the Hangzhou Municipal Court to allow them to appeal to the provincial court. In its second review, the provincial court reversed its previous decision and opposed a death sentence. In so doing, not merely the authority of the provincial government's order was undercut, but also the municipal court was pushed to an awkward status.

Due to the problem of the old system, the SPC suggested that in the future, ordinary first-instance death sentences or grave crimes (e.g. damaging government, economic development, or state properties) adjudicated first at county courts that had either missed the deadlines of appeal or the litigants had no plan to appeal should be sent to provincial courts for review. First-instance cases judged by a provincial court would be transferred to a regional branch of the Supreme Court.[55] In its request, the SPC explicitly pointed out the significance of legal process and the detrimental consequences of the makeshift judicial system in wartime. Once a high court and not a government had the power to review cases first judged by a local court, it would help PRC legal system move one step closer to a modern legal system that various Chinese polities had tried to model since the late Qing.

In the midst of a political campaign, any sober calls for legal procedures would be out of step. Before long, a widespread, decisive, and relentless political campaign engulfed the PRC. In December 1950, Mao dictated that the campaign against counterrevolutionaries should be rigorous, accurate, and harsh. In January 1951, Mao further remarked that the campaign should execute all counterrevolutionaries who deserved death. But he also cautioned in several directives that cadres should not kill innocent people. He stressed the importance of investigation and evidence and opposed haphazard arrests and executions. Probably because the campaign had caused unchecked arrests and deaths at the local level, Mao in the spring of 1951 tried to curb the excesses of the campaign.[56] On April 2, he wanted the repression to be "strictly" confined to bandit leaders, habitual bandits,

55 Shanghai Archives, November 25, 1950. B1-2-003-310.

56 According to Nara Dillon, in Shanghai alone, 8359 alleged counterrevolutionaries were arrested in raids on April 27, 1951. On April 29, nine of them were tried publicly in a mass meeting of over 10,000 and subsequently executed. On April 30, 285 were publicly executed. See Dillon, 2007: 88; Mühlhahn argues that 4 million arrests were made by the police, the army, and party organs in this campaign, see Mühlhahn, 2011: 183.

GMD agents, and the like. Thieves, drug addicts, ordinary landlords, and former GMD members and military officers should not be punished. Only "serious criminals" would be executed.[57]

As in the Jiangxi Soviet base, Mao suggested in the Third National Public Security Meeting on May 15, 1951 that the labor force of incarcerated counterrevolutionaries should not be wasted. "To reform them, to solve the problem of the prisons, and to prevent counterrevolutionaries from sponging off the government," Mao noted, "we must speedily begin the reform through labor." Moreover, with the exception of counterrevolutionaries whose crimes were grave enough for immediate executions, Mao ordered the killing of around 10-20% of the counterrevolutionaries whose crimes deserved death penalties but were not most serious. The rest of them should have death sentences with two years of probation followed by hard labor. The benefits of the policy were, in Mao's words, "to gain social sympathy [for the campaign], to avoid unwarranted executions, to divide our enemies [...] and to have lots of labor for the construction of state projects."[58]

To provide specific guidelines for local judiciaries and for military commissions to subdue counterrevolutionaries, the central government promulgated the Regulations on Punishing Counterrevolutionaries on February 22, 1951. Article 1 confirmed that the principal purpose of the regulations was to "punish counterrevolutionaries, repress counterrevolutionary actions, and consolidate the people's democratic dictatorship." Articles 3-13 were related to counterrevolutionaries who would be convicted to life or death sentences. Most of the crimes were similar to those mentioned in the joint directive of the State Council and the Supreme Court in July 1950. New crimes warranting capital punishment included, inter alia, instigating the masses to resist or sabotage government policies, spreading counterrevolutionary propaganda, illegally crossing the border, and covering up the activities of counterrevolutionary criminals. Unlike former regulations or guidelines, the new regulations against counterrevolutionaries did not mention any legal procedures for judiciaries or military commissions to follow. Nor did it prohibit the use of torture in dealing with counterrevolutionaries. It seemed to give Communist judiciaries and military commissions a green light to do whatever they deemed necessary to attack real or alleged enemies.[59]

57 Mao Zedong毛泽东, "Notes on the Work of Suppressing and Purging Counterrevolutionaries" in *Studying Materials* (*Xuexi ziliao*学习资料), 1949-1956, p. 69. Modern China Institute, Academia Sinica, Taiwan.

58 *Unofficially Published Works of Mao Zedong*, Vol. 8, May 15, 1951, 1991: 4-5.

59 Regulations on Punishing Counterrevolutionaries (*chengzhi fangeming tiaoli*), in *The People's Daily*, February 22, 1951; also see Potter, 2002: 64.

Harsher Penalties Amid the Campaign

Although Mao had harped on "accurate and limited" suppression of counterrevolutionaries, the campaign in many regions became very severe and unrestricted. In the end, hundreds of thousands of people were summarily killed or at least imprisoned as counterrevolutionaries. As Klaus Mühlhahn has argued, many suspected class enemies or criminals accused of political crimes were punished "without any real involvement of the regular courts."[60] There is no doubt that many of the dead might well have been innocent and/or belonged to categories that Mao had said should not be killed. Vice premier Dong Biwu remarked on September 11, 1951, that the "goal of the judicial system" in this political campaign was to "directly solidify the people's democratic dictatorship." In other words, the primary mission of the judicial system was not to safeguard the law but to protect the regime.[61]

Since early 1951, the campaign had become increasingly merciless toward counterrevolutionaries and many government organs took part in the campaign. Not just the people's court, but also the police, procuracy, and the military commissions could punish counterrevolutionaries or interfere in court decisions. For example, in March 1951, after the SPC tried an anti-Communist organization, the court sentenced its leaders Zhou Zhixiang and Jia Zubo to fifteen years and eight years respectively. Zhou was a former GMD street policeman who joined the organization and helped find secret meeting places for the "bandits." Zhou also allegedly colluded with one Ma Zongrong to counterfeit PRC currency and participated in several meetings with GMD agents. Like Zhou, Jia had also been a GMD policeman for many years. In the PRC, Jia collaborated with a GMD agent and illegally concealed two of his handguns. After Jia joined a counterrevolutionary organization, he attempted to rent a boat and join a guerrilla force on Lake Tai to plot against the Communist government. When he was arrested, the police found three handguns in his boat.

It is clear that neither man had committed serious "counterrevolutionary" crimes such as assassinating CCP cadres, robbing public properties, or harming ordinary people. Their alleged crimes were being former GMD policemen, and, at most, being accomplices in a counterrevolutionary organization. In light of their crimes, the long-term imprisonments should have been harsh enough. However, upon reviewing the court rulings, the Shanghai

60 Mühlhahn, 2009: 183; also see Frank Dikotter, 1997: 149.

61 Dong, 2001: 89.

Municipal Procuracy cast doubt on the punishments and recommended death penalties to the Shanghai Military Commission. While the commission had approved many of the SPC lenient penalties prior to the campaign, Pan Hannian, current head of the commission, chose to approve the increase in the penalty without further investigations.[62] At the peak of a political campaign, the commission might have had neither the patience nor the reason to care about the lives and grievances of counterrevolutionaries.

Not only did the procuracy pressure the court to impose more severe penalties on counterrevolutionaries, but it also reviewed counterrevolutionary cases before the campaign. Once the procuracy discovered a case that it thought had been handled with "excessive lenience," it asked the military commission to replace previous lenience with harshness. On April 11, 1951, in a commentary to the Shanghai Military Commission, the Shanghai Procuracy called into question the SPC's 1950 decision on Ni Rongchang, head of a counterrevolutionary organization who had been sentenced to five years of imprisonment. The commentary argued that Ni was an intransigent former GMD agent who had carried on counterrevolutionary activities in the PRC but had been sentenced too lightly. Why did the procuracy question the court decision one year later? It is clear that the ongoing campaign against counterrevolutionaries played a key role. Shortly after it received the commentary from the procuracy, the military commission reviewed Ni's case and overturned the court's previous decision. Totally agreeing with the procuracy, the military commission now ruled that Ni should be executed. Because the military commission was the highest government of Shanghai, Ni had nowhere to seek exoneration.[63]

During the anti-counterrevolutionary campaign, the military commissions/committees played a crucial role in charging and penalizing criminals. The commissions restored the practice in the Jiangxi Soviet base of weighing both historical and current crimes of counterrevolutionaries or other criminals when determining their punishments. In one case occurring in October 1951, the Shanghai Military Commission decided to execute Yang Wenfu with a two-year reprieve. According to the commission decision note, which was different from a court verdict, on May 29, 1948, Yang and his accomplices had beaten and injured Dai Shaonong, a store manager, who had died shortly thereafter. A Republican court had arrested Yang and had imprisoned him for about a year. In March 1950, Yang allegedly conspired with bandits (i.e. the GMD) and tried to join a GMD guerrilla

62 Shanghai Archives, March 16, 1951. B1-2-1002.

63 Ibid., April 1951. B1-2-945.

force, but apparently committed no other crimes. The military committee nonetheless traced Yang's crimes back to the Republican period and punished him heavily.[64] In this case, the decision was arguably irrational but the military commission cited Article 16 of the recent Regulations on Punishing Counterrevolutionaries, to give its decision a tint of legality in the course of a political campaign. Because the military commission was both the de jure local political leader and the superior of people's courts, court judges had neither the power nor the audacity to challenge the rationale behind commission punishments, let alone the legitimacy of regulations against counterrevolutionaries that had omitted any mention of legal procedures.

If a defendant had not joined a rebellious organization to oppose the PRC, the punishment would normally be lighter. Wang Changchun, a member of the GMD guerrilla forces against the Japanese during the Sino-Japanese War, allegedly established roadblocks after the war and forced local people to pay fees. While he was serving as a local village head in the Republican period, Wang had extorted and beaten people. In the early PRC, he did not correct his bad behavior and therefore was "hated by the masses." Despite the rather vague and unsubstantiated charges that Wang had committed crimes, the Shanghai Military Commission invoked Article 16 of the Regulations on Punishing Counterrevolutionaries to sentence Wang to fifteen years in prison. The relatively "light" penalty was mostly because Wang had never joined any GMD organizations. All his crimes were thuggery in the PRC plus his earlier connections with the GMD.[65]

In the political campaign, the severity of many court decisions against alleged counterrevolutionaries was in line with those made by military commissions. In October 1951, the Gaoqiao District Division of the SPC adjudicated a counterrevolutionary case. In this case, Zhu Fujin was regarded as a local despot. According to the court judgment, during the Sino-Japanese War (1937-1945), Zhu had served as the township head in Gaoqiao and had beaten a local resident to death. After the Japanese surrendered, Zhu became a district representative under the GMD. In the early PRC, Zhu allegedly disseminated rumors against the land reform and threatened village cadres. In stark contrast to the formal and detailed Republican-period verdicts before the campaign, the Gaoqiao District Court announced a very terse verdict on Zhu, although the format of the verdict was virtually the same as that of the military commission. With no solid evidence that Zhu had

64 Ibid., October 1951. B1-2-30.

65 Ibid.

violated the law, the court, like the military commission, still combined both vague historical and contemporary crimes and sentenced Zhu to life imprisonment. Again, the Gaoqiao District Court cited Article 16 of the Regulations on Punishing Counterrevolutionaries in its ruling. Yet, as the judge said, the purpose of severely punishing Zhu was to repress counterrevolutionaries in general.[66] One has the impression that the court was less interested in achieving justice in Zhu's particular case than in deterring others from committing similar crimes.

Like their counterparts in major cities, judges in county courts also showed no mercy to defendants who had had connections with the GMD. For example, in February 1952, the Jiaxing County Court sentenced Zhou Baochang to seven years of incarceration for raping and abusing a child bride (*tongyangxi*) named Zhao Xiaomei. Coming from a poor family, Zhao had been sold by her father as a child bride to Zhou Baochang's son. Zhou was a former member of a GMD guerrilla force during the Sino-Japanese War. From 1943 to the eve of the PRC, Zhou had been a local head who allegedly had "bullied people." In the early PRC, Zhou assisted local GMD agents with logistics. Zhou and his wife had frequently beaten Zhao and the abuse lasted to the early PRC in spite of the 1950 Marriage Law that outlawed child brides.[67] Since March 1951, Zhou had secretly raped Zhao three times and threatened to kill her if she dared to expose the rape. It was not until November 1951 when Zhao had an abortion that finally exposed the domestic abuse and rape. After Zhou received his punishment from the court, the local government freed Zhao Xiaomei of her child bride relationship with Zhou's son. As Susan L. Glosser has argued, in the PRC, the CCP and not the parents took control of marriage.[68] Had Zhou not had connections with the GMD, his penalty could have been lighter because all the abuses and rapes took place inside Zhou's home and there was no witness. But Zhou was also fortunate that his crimes were adjudicated by a county court and not a military commission, which otherwise would have imposed more severe punishment in a political campaign.[69]

In late 1951, partly to deter counterrevolutionary activities and partly to show off its accomplishments against counterrevolutionaries, the SPC announced in a poster that it had investigated many criminals who had been

66 Ibid.

67 For detailed studies on the 1950 Marriage Law see Xiaoping Cong, 2018.

68 Glosser, 2003: 171; also see Xiaoping Cong, 2018: 247.

69 Jiaxing County Archives, February 5, 1952. 94-1-273.

arrested and charged by the Shanghai police and the people's government. After lawful interrogations of the defendants and assistance, accusations, and witness testimony from the masses, the court had based its decision on the severity of each crime. Criminals committing the following crimes were executed: 1) heavy blood debts (e.g. killing Communists); 2) other serious crimes; 3) crimes too outrageous to be tolerated; 4) crimes causing the most serious damage to state interests. Criminals with no blood debts, whose crimes had not caused big public anger, or who had not impaired state interests to the most serious degree but still deserved death would be sentenced to the death penalty with a two-year reprieve, a punishment dictated by Mao in early 1951. These criminals would be forced to work for the betterment of the state during their incarcerations and under close watch. All other criminals should receive punishments ranging from life to limited term imprisonments in concert with their crimes [...][70]

Equally important but understudied is the shift of the Communist judicial system in dealing with civil cases in the political campaign. As I have discussed above, before the political campaign, the Communist judicial system had carefully maintained a delicate balance between the capitalists and the workers and had tried not to favor the workers. After the campaign began, the judicial system swiftly turned more "revolutionary" and dealt more harshly with alleged counterrevolutionaries. Its previous impartial policies on labor disputes were now superseded by leaning to one side – the "working class."

On October 11, 1952, for instance, the SPC adjudicated a labor dispute. The plaintiff Huang Jishan was a worker who represented all the workers of the Shenhe Rubber Factory; the defendant was Xie Hequan, the owner of the factory. Since January 1952, the factory had stopped running. In June, both employees and employers began negotiating layoffs. Through government mediation, both sides agreed that the factory could dismiss all workers, but each worker would receive a three-month severance pay. The agreement also noted that the factory should pay the back pay and part of the severance pay before July 5. Yet, when the deadline arrived, the factory failed to make the payments. While the court was investigating, Xie pleaded for the court's permission to cut the severance payments for his workers by half. Had the case occurred prior to the anti-counterrevolutionary campaign, the court would very likely have taken the factory bankruptcy into account and approved Xie's request. But in the context of a political campaign, the court chose not to sympathize with Xie and asked him to pay all of the

70 Shanghai Archives, 1951. B1-2-566-8.

severance payments. The court noted that the agreement between the factory employer and the employees had been signed long before. It was the employer who had delayed making the required payments, resulting in the extreme hardship of the workers. Thus, the court decided that the employer "must fulfill his promise in the agreement and Xie's request of reducing payment by half will not be accepted."[71] In this verdict, the Shanghai court was no longer sympathetic with capitalists under financial troubles and it chose to palpably side with the workers and enforce the original agreement.

In another case that took place around the same time, the Guohua Tobacco Company, with 579 workers, was much bigger than the Shenhe Rubber Factory. Due to longtime mismanagement, the company owed a huge debt. In 1952, to keep the company running, the board of the company planned to borrow one billion *yuan* from the members of the board. But when the deadline for the deal arrived, most board members refused to lend the money. In despair, the company filed for bankruptcy and began to lay off its employees. The employer rejected the workers' demand for a severance payment. The labor bureau mediated with a plan that the employer should pay each employee a severance payment of two-and-half-months' wages. The employer disagreed and appealed to the SPC. The court believed that it was the company that first proposed layoffs and later it emphasized its difficulties and refused to pay the workers severance payments. The workers had to endure the hardship of living with no job and compensation. Therefore, the court vehemently condemned the company's lack of commitment to production and its irresponsibility for the workers. The court verdict was that, because most board members of the company were in good financial condition and the workers had high spirits in production, the company employer should immediately resume production and not dismiss any workers.[72]

This civil case further testifies that the court took a firm stand on the side of the workers and did not want to see the layoffs occur. The court disregarded not just the financial difficulties of the company but also the reluctance of most board members to support the resumption of production. The court decision simply assumed that most board members were financially strong and should be able to reopen the production of the company. Although the ongoing economic woes were one of the court's concerns, the anti-counterrevolutionary campaign might also have played a critical role in prodding the court to become more revolutionary and less impartial.

71 Ibid., B128-2-1206-199.

72 Ibid., B128-2-928-81.

The swift change of the Communist judicial system's stance during the political campaign is understandable. As the key suppressing mechanism of the CCP, the Communist judicial system had to lean toward the so-called ruling working class rather than toward the capitalists many of whom had now been labeled counterrevolutionaries or class foes of the proletarian state. In the words of Klaus Mühlhahn, the violent campaign against so-called class enemies was a "particular politico-legal discourse which shaped and justified the use of force." Law, for the CCP, was merely an instrument of government that was neither "a value in itself" nor "tied to ideas of justice (or fairness)."[73]

In September 1951, the draconian and rampant punishments made by military commissions and police rather than by regular judicial system organs might have galvanized the central government to issue a regulation emphasizing legal process. which was similar to what Hubei province had done in November 1949. The regulation entitled The Interim Organizational Regulations of the People's Court, a precursor of The Organic Law of the Court in 1954, not only reiterated the nature of the people's courts but also prescribed courts at all levels to follow certain organizational rules and legal processes.

Like previous government directives and laws, Article 3 of the latest regulation stated that the people's court was created to strengthen the people's democratic dictatorship and to protect both social order and revolutionary fruits. Its missions were to handle both criminal and civil cases and to educate litigants and other people to abide by state laws and rules. To help people participate in trials, the people's court had to adopt the system of people's jury. Jurors could help investigate cases, join trials, and make suggestions to judges. Article 7 wanted courts to conduct on-site investigation, trials, and circuit trials (*xunhui shenpan*). Unless the law prohibited it, all trials should be conducted in public. The regulations, like the Common Program but not the 1954 Organic Law of the Court, did not mention judicial independence. Instead, Article 10 clearly noted that all lower-level courts would be supervised and led by a dual leadership: upper-level courts and peer local governments. The regulations also distinguished the people's procuracy from the courts. The people's procuracy would mainly serve as the prosecutor and could take part in court investigation. If a court found the prosecution from the procuracy was insufficient, the court could ask the procuracy for additional information. Similarly, if a procuracy deemed the verdict of a court illegal or improper, it could question the court verdict

73 Mühlhahn, 2007: 36.

and send the files to an upper-level court for review.[74] In the case of Ni Rongchang, the Shanghai procuracy raised questions on the light penalty and suggested to the Shanghai government impose a death sentence on Ni. While the regulation, like other CCP rules and regulations, opposed judicial independence, its biggest contribution was its reemphasis on legal procedure and mutual oversight, two necessary legal principles that had often been missing in PRC campaigns.

Conclusion

From the outset, the CCP accused Republican laws of serving imperialism and bureaucratic capitalism and swore to abolish them. However, due to the paucity of laws that could be used to handle daily criminal and civil cases and the fact that a good proportion of judicial cadres in the early PRC were retained GMD judges and lawyers, many judges in big cities like Shanghai had no choice but to use Republican laws with which they had long been familiar. In Hubei, provincial leaders issued directives to local courts to follow legal procedures and allow counterrevolutionaries to appeal. Accordingly, the punishments of counterrevolutionaries were rather lenient, which irritated top CCP leaders such as Peng Zhen and Luo Ruiqing. Shortly after the outbreak of the Korean War, the fledging PRC, fearing imminent threats from the United States army and potentially more sabotage by GMD agents, launched a campaign against counterrevolutionaries to consolidate its power on the mainland. In a major policy change, a harsher crackdown against alleged counterrevolutionaries was kicked off by the Party and led by military commissions. As loyal mechanisms of the Party, the people's courts, procuracy, and police were all involved in the campaign. Not only had previously clement punishments been reversed, but many new class enemies and criminals who had historical associations with the GMD were severely penalized. Even civil cases such as disputes between employers and labors were deeply affected by the campaign. The previously more balanced stands of SPC judges between employer defendants and employee plaintiffs were now replaced by positions favoring the working class and being less impartial. Yet, at the height of the campaign, the central government including Mao still tried to stress the importance of legal procedures and restrained use of violence. With its residual independence eroding in

74 Studying Documents of the People's Judicial Construction (Beijing: Zhongyang sifa jiguan sifa gaige bangongshi, 1952): 29-40.

late 1951 and 1952, the Communist judicial system had gradually rolled out its transformation from its fleeting quasi-independent and professional organ to a faithful political weapon of the CCP. And this transformation was to be solidified in the 1952 legal reform.

4 A Deliberate Purge

Legal Reform in the Early PRC, 1952-1953

Abstract
This chapter outlines the Party's growing distrust of the retained GMD judges and lawyers. Using excuses such as the high proportion of retained judges in people's court and the halfheartedness of retained judges in advocating Party's legal policies during the Three-Antis and Five-Antis Movements, the Party in 1952 overhauled its legal system and dismissed most retained GMD judges and lawyers. To replace such court personnel, the Party enlisted progressive workers, military veterans, and students as future judges. Their political allegiance might have been impeccable, but they had little or no legal knowledge and training. This chapter argues that CCP's purge of former GMD judges was an intentional program clearly aimed at making the judicial system a more submissive and faithful instrument of the Party in future campaigns.

Keywords: 1952 Legal Reform Movement, Shi Liang, Retain GMD Judges, new judges and old problems, deliberate purge

If the legal reform initiated in the late Qing (1901-1911) that went through the Republican period was the first in 20th-century China, then the 1952 Legal Reform Movement, less than three years after the establishment of the People's Republic of China (PRC), was the second major reform in mainland China. Not only did this reform condemn and jettison many long-held orthodox legal principles such as the "rule of law," "judicial independence," and "equality before the law;" it also officially set the model and rhetoric of the legal systems in the Mao Zedong era (1949-1976) in spite of several efforts of the Chinese Communist Party (CCP) to restore basic legal principles after the reform.

Given the great significance of the 1952 legal reform, it is quite surprising that the topic has been understudied by scholars. Most Western scholars

Fang, Qiang, *The Communist Judicial System in China, 1927-1976: Building on Fear.*
Taylor & Francis Group 2021
DOI: 10.5117/9789463729451_CH04

have barely mentioned it.[1] Chinese scholars have paid more attention to it, but, apart from minor differences in their writing styles and presentations, all of their arguments are very similar and fraught with tension. On the one hand, they all reference CCP's official accounts to justify the legal reform. On the other hand, they voice almost identical criticisms of its adverse consequences.[2] For instance, Li Yusheng praises the 1952 legal reform that "exterminated the influence of the old legal system." But he also acknowledges that the legal reform inevitably contained some flaws such as lowering the quality of judges and denouncing some principles of the rule of law.[3] Like Li Yuesheng, Gong Pixiang examines the causes and shortcomings of the reform. But he goes farther than Li in arguing that the legal reform "completely wiped out the residual influence of the old legal system" and paved the way for the "new" PRC legal system to be transformed from new democracy to socialism.[4]

In this chapter, I explore the origins, development, and consequences of legal reform with a focus on the two years 1952 and 1953. I address

1 See for example, Lubman, 1999: 73; Mühlhahn, 2009: 178-186; like Mühlhahn, Aminda M. Smith also studies the reeducation through labor in the early PRC, but Smith also does not talk much about the 1952 legal reform. See Aminda M. Smith, "The . of Thought Education: Beijing Reformatories and the Origins of Reeducation Through Labor, 1949-1957" in *Modern China*, 39 (2): 203-234; Alison W. Conner, "Training China's Lawyers: Enduring Influences and Disconnects" in Albert Chen and John Gillespie, eds., *Legal Development in East Asia: China and Vietnam Compared* (Abingdon: Routledge, 2010), pp. 276-298: 278; Frank Dikotter, *Crime, Punishment, and the Prison in Modern China* (New York: Columbia University Press, 2002): 366; Peerenboom, 2000: 44; Cong, 2016; for Jerome Cohen's argument see Jerome Cohen, *Criminal Process in the PRC, 1949-1963: An Introduction* (Cambridge, Ma: Harvard University Press, 1968): 10, 47, 51; Pitman B. Potter, *From Leninist Discipline to Socialist Legalism: Peng Zhen on Law and Political Authority* (Stanford: Stanford University Press, 2003): 63-65.

2 See Gong Pixiang, 1999: 115-124; Li Yusheng李玉生, "Comments on the Legal Reform Movement (*sifa gaige yundong shuping*司法改革运动述评)" in *Nanjing shehui kexue*, 1999/9, pp. 49-54; Zhang Min张慜, "A Tentative Study on the 1952 Legal Reform Movement (*shilun 1952 sifa gaige yundong*试论1952年司法改革运动)" in *Falü shiyong yuekan*, 2004/8, pp. 55-58; Hou Songtao侯松涛, "Legal Reform Movement in the Early PRC: Retrospect and Thinking (*jianguo chuqide sifa gaige yundong: huigu yusikao*建国初期的司法改革运动：回顾与思考)" in *Zhidu jianshe*, 2008/1, pp. 93-96; Liu Fengjing刘风景, "Ringing out the Old and Ringing the New in Legal Concepts: Using the Criticisms of the 1952 Legal Reform against Old Legal Concepts (*sifa liniande chujiu buxin: yi 1952nian sifa gaige duijiufaguandian depipan weisucai*司法理念的除旧布新：以1952年司法改革对旧法观点的批判为素材)" in *Beifang faxue* (Northern Jurisprudence), 2009/1, pp. 96-105; Chen Guangzhong 陈光中and Zeng Xinhua曾新华, "Comments on the Legal Reform in the Early PRC (*jianguo chuqi sifa gaige yundong shuping*建国初期司法改革运动述评)" in *Faxuejia* (Legalists), June, 2009, pp. 56-84; He Qinghua何清华, *A History of Chinese Jurisprudence* (*Zhongguo faxue shigang*中国法学史纲) (Beijing: Shangwu yinshuguan, 2012): 371-373.

3 Li Yusheng, 1999: 52.

4 Gong, 1999: 121-122; also see Liu Fengjing, 2009: 99.

such questions as: what were the historical and contemporary contexts of the legal reform movement in 1952? What were the motives of those who launched it? Why did retained GMD judges and lawyers become a primary target? How did the CCP conduct the legal reform and what were its consequences? In the process of answering these questions, I shall look into some typical civil and criminal cases that illustrate the nature and political dynamic of the reform. I shall challenge the official rhetoric blaming former GMD judges for numerous unresolved cases of torture, corruption, and other "bad" habits in the judicial system. I shall argue that the reform was a purge designed to tighten CCP control over untrusted elements or classes in a time when the PRC was under attack both internally and externally.

Initiating the Legal Reform Movement

The official start of the legal reform was August 13, 1952, the day when Shi Liang, the Minister of Justice and a renowned pro-Communist lawyer in the Republican period, made a report titled "Thoroughly Reforming and Reorganizing All Levels of People's Courts."[5]

In fact, long before Shi Liang formally initiated the legal reform, Party leaders and media had already cast doubt on retained Nationalist Party (the Guomindang, or GMD) judges and called for them to be subject to thought reform. In early 1950, Dong Biwu, a vice premier and the head of the powerful Political and Legal Affairs Commission (*Zhengfawei*), warned former Republican judges, lawyers, and legal scholars that they needed a thought reform in a new China whose social life and nature differed from those in the Republican period.[6] In Chapter 3, I have mentioned that Party leaders such as Peng Zhen and Luo Ruiqing in mid-1950 sharply voiced their discontent with the "excessive lenience" of the Communist judicial system in which many judges were retained Republican judges.[7] In May 1951, an editorial of the *People's Daily*, which often reflected the Party's view, accused some "old revolutionary cadres" of becoming "captives of reactionary legal theories and of promoting

5 Peitian Zhang and Hua Zhang, eds., *China Southwest Archives: The Material of Judicial Reform (1950-1952)* (Australia: International Culture Press, 2007): 1-4.

6 Dong, 2001: 30.

7 See Chapter 3.

GMD laws.[8] On June 24, 1952, Dong Biwu moved forward to set the tone of the upcoming legal reform. He remarked that "Former [GMD] judges cannot take charge of adjudicating duty" and "those [former judges] whose crimes have been exposed during the Three-Antis Movement should be either purged or punished. The rest of them should also not be judges again." Dong ordered that retained judges should be replaced with proper persons and they [the retained judges] should be allowed to pursue other careers.[9]

In her report, Shi Liang essentially echoed what Dong had noted. She pointed out that the ongoing Three-Antis and Five-Antis Movements had raised fear in the Party of the grave problems of "imperfect organization and thought" inside the people's courts.[10] "Among the 28,000 judicial cadres in the country," Shi Liang estimated, "around 6000 of them are 'old/retained' judicial personnel, making up almost 22% of the total." In some big cities like Shanghai, the problem was even worse. For example, among the 104 judges in Shanghai courts, 80 of them were retained judges. In Tianjin, 97 out of the 201 judges were retained judges. According to Shi, a more serious fact was that about 64% of the retained judges were GMD agents and members of the GMD or the Youth League of the Three People's Principles Corps (*Sanqingtuan*), a GMD-sponsored organization comparable to the CCP's Communist Youth League. Another problem, Shi claimed, was the disproportionally high number of corrupt cadres among retained judges. In the courts of Shanghai, Nanjing, and Hangzhou, almost 60% of retained judges were reportedly corrupt.[11] Therefore, Shi

8 Editorial, "Further Strengthening and Developing People's Democratic Dictatorship (*jinyibu gonggu yufazhan renmin minzhu zhuanzheng*进一步巩固与发展人民民主专政)" in *The People's Daily*, May 29, 1951.

9 Dong, 2001: 119-128. For the aim and function of the Political and Legal Affairs Commission see Peerenboom, 2002: 302-303.

10 To support the Chinese army in the ongoing Korean War, the CCP kicked off the Three-Antis movement (Anti-corruption, Anti-waste, Anti-bureaucracy) in late 1951 and the Five-Antis movement (Anti-bribery, Anti-theft of state property, Anti-tax evasion, Anti-cheating on government contracts, and Anti-stealing state economic information) in early 1952. Both movements established their own people's tribunals. For details about the two movements see Wang Chaobin 王朝彬, *An Authentic Record of the Three-Antis Movement* (*sanfan shilu*三反实录) (Beijing: Jingguan jiaoyu chubanshe, 1992): 48; Wu Jue吴珏, *A Veritable Record of the Three-Antis and Five-Antis Movements* (*sanfan wufan yundong jishi*三反五反运动纪实) (Beijing: Dongfang chubanshe, 2014); Dillon, 2007: 80-102.

11 The charge that many retained judges were corrupt is largely baseless and there is no evidence offered by Shi Liang.

called for a sweeping and thorough legal reform to allow people and not the retained GMD judges to control the judicial system, a crucial weapon of the CCP.[12]

Four days after Shi Liang's report, the *People's Daily* published another editorial highlighting the key points made by Shi and stressing the urgency and importance of the legal reform. The purpose of the reform was to "purify the politics, organization, and thought of the courts." The editorial also argued that retained judges and cadres believing in Republican laws did not understand that the people's courts were one of the pivotal apparatuses of the people's democratic dictatorship. Nor did they know whom the judicial system served and on whom the judicial system depended. Furthermore, the editorial foresaw the insufficiency of one reform to eliminate the detrimental influence of GMD law. "To guarantee the success of the legal reform," the editorial argued, there was a need for "a strengthened leadership of the Party in the judicial system."[13]

In various sites and speeches, Party officials and newspapers tried to identify the "main crimes" of retained judges so as to justify purging them. On September 2, the *Xinhua Daily*, a local Party newspaper based in Chongqing, made a short list of the "crimes" of retained judges: sitting in the court to listen to cases (*zuotang wenan*); stressing legal procedures and judicial solemnity; and using "not being intentional, insufficient evidence, or inchoate crimes" to exonerate counterrevolutionaries or unlawful landlords.[14]

In September 1952, Zhang Shuguang, head of the southwest branch of the Supreme Court, made a more detailed attack on Republican legal concepts and retained judges. Zhang first highlighted several cases in which some retained judges and seasoned old cadres who had been deeply influenced by "old" legal concepts turned out to be corrupt or undercover counterrevolutionaries. Then he warned that the old legal concepts would pardon counterrevolutionaries. Like the *Xinhua Daily*, Zhang listed a variety of modes of Republican laws and retained judges. Apart from the "crimes" of retained judges criticized by the *Xinhua Daily*, Zhang added more "crimes" of retained judges such as: no response until a lawsuit is filed (*bugao buli*);

12 Peitian Zhang and Hua Zhang, 2007: 1-4; also see *Sifa gongzuo shouce* (A Judicial Handbook), No. 3, 1952, pp. 1-4: 1.

13 Editorial, "Must Thoroughly Reform Judicial system (*bixu chedi gaige sifa gongzuo*必须彻底改革司法工作)" in *The People's Daily*, August 17, 1952.

14 Editorial of the *Xiahua Daily*, September 2, 1952, in Peitian Zhang and Hua Zhang, 2007: 7-8.

no response to litigants' lawsuits; corruption, careless judgments; inducing confessions and torture;[15] and raping or insulting female litigants. In addition, Zhang admonished that some law school professors who had not reformed themselves were still disseminating "old" legal concepts in colleges. As an important weapon of the people's democratic dictatorship, the court, Zhang noted, "must be grasped firmly by the people."[16]

A leader of the Fujian Provincial Court summarized people's criticism of retained judges into "Four Helps" and "Five Nos." The Four Helps were: Help counterrevolutionaries to harm people, Help landlords to exploit peasants, Help unlawful capitalists to suppress workers, and Help outlaws to reduce their punishments. The Five Nos were: No response [to people's charges], No issuance [of subpoenas even after long delay], No questioning [of defendants], No judgment [after long interrogation], and No enforcement [of judgments].[17] But, like other CCP leaders and newspapers, the court leader did not provide any sources and evidence for the people's views. Thus, the credibility of the summary was problematic.

Probably the most authoritative and comprehensive report on the problems of retained judges and their old legal concepts was the "Compendium of Judicial Investigation Report" published by the Investigation Unit of the Central Political and Judicial Organs shortly before the legal reform. The "Compendium" first focused on judicial units in East China, which included the most prosperous part of China and the former political, economic, and financial center of the GMD. It asserted that the organizational, stylistic, and intellectual problems in East China judiciaries were grave. For instance, among all 8284 judicial personnel in the region, 24.65% of them had worked for the GMD.[18] More important, most judges were retained because court leaders believed that retained judges had more legal experience and education.

15 In fact, CCP's policy on torture was not consistent. On July 21, 1950, in the directive jointly made by the State Council and the Supreme Court against counterrevolutionaries, it noted that torture was forbidden. But in the Regulations Punishing Counterrevolutionaries promulgated by the State Council in February 1951, at the height of the Korean War, there was no restriction of torture, which provided a leeway for Communist prosecutors to use torture to extract confessions. For the directive see The Directive of the State Council and the Supreme Court Regarding Suppressing Counterrevolutionaries (*zhengwuyuan zuigao fayuan guanyu zhenya fangeming dezhishi*), July 21, 1950 http://www.law-lib.com/law/law_view.asp?id=639; for the regulations see PRC Regulations Punishing Counterrevolutionaries (*Zhonghua renmin gongheguo chengzhi fangeming tiaoli*), February 9, 1951.

16 Peitian Zhang and Hua Zhang, 2007: 9-12.

17 Fujian Provincial People's Court, 1952: 3. 5-11: 6.

18 Here the judicial personnel does not mean only judges, but also men and women who were working in the courts including judges, clerks, and police.

During the anti-counterrevolutionary movement in late 1950 and 1951, the CCP discovered that many retained judges were former GMD members. In the Fujian Provincial Court, 42% of the retained judges had joined the GMD. The percentage in Zhejiang was even higher at almost 70%. Moreover, the proportion of corrupt cadres among retained judges was reportedly also very high. In Shanghai, Hangzhou, Nanjing, Zhejiang, and South-Jiangsu courts, 882 cadres had been punished for corruption. Among them, 525, or almost 60%, were retained judges. Many retained judges had allegedly committed crimes such as shielding counterrevolutionaries and raping female litigants.

The "Compendium" also blamed retained judges for the pileup or accumulation of unresolved cases. It argued that the courts in East China "cannot fulfill their duties." Invoking several unsubstantiated people's comments, the report claimed that people in the city of Nantong said, "[A] lthough the people's government is led by the CCP, its courts are not so different from those under the GMD."[19]

Among East China cities, Shanghai's problem was representative. Not only was the percentage of retained cadres high (48.76%) but the percentage of retained judges was much higher (76.92%) than those in many other cities. The report accused retained judges in Shanghai who "are wearing people's judge uniforms" of having enormous power in doing what they wanted. "No one can effectively rein them due to the 'old' legal concept of judicial independence," the report lamented. Even worse was that 30% of them were former GMD members and most corrupt judges were said to be retained cadres (70%). All the biggest corruption offenses (over 100 million) were allegedly committed by retained judges. The problem in Shanghai courts was rooted in court leaders' focus on the "[legal] education standard and technique" of retained judges but not their political quality or reliability, albeit most old Communist cadres, workers, peasants, and youth could not conduct trials.[20]

In addition to their reactionary standpoints and defective judicial organization and leadership, the "Compendium" further blamed retained judges for their dereliction and laxity that resulted in human tragedies. In one case, after the wife of a Shanghai tailor had fornicated and eloped with her lover, the poor tailor immediately reported to the local police and purchased a newspaper notice begging his wife to come home. With

19 The Investigation Unit of the Central Political and Judicial Organs (*zhongyang zhengfa jiguan lianhe shichazu*中央政法机关联合视察组), *Compendium of Judicial Investigation Report* (*sifa diaocha baogao huibian*司法调查报告汇编), June 1952. (Classified Internal Report).

20 Ibid., 1952: 9-10.

all efforts in vain, the tailor married a local woman and tried to register at the local government. Local government officials accused the tailor of bigamy and sent him to the court. A retained judge jailed the tailor for five months on grounds that the tailor and his escaped wife had not divorced and refused to heed the police reports and newspaper notice made by the tailor. Deeply humiliated, the "bride," a local innocent woman, committed suicide. If the case was true, it would be quite inappropriate for the judge to make such a decision because the tailor had tried all legal means before he married another woman.[21]

To be sure, not all courts attributed all judicial problems to retained judges. A report of the Xuzhou Court in northern Jiangsu province did not single out any retained judge to be blamed. For example, when the report argued that corruption was rather serious in the court, it did not say what percentage of those 52 corrupt judges were retained judges. Also, when criticizing cadres for violating laws, the report did not say whether those violators were retained or Communist judges. In one case, in 1950, after one female prisoner sang songs, Liu Xijiu, the vice head of the court, immediately issued an order to have all 36 prisoners in the same cell tied with wire for a whole night. Apparently, Liu was not a retained judge because the report would have said so if he had been.

Unlike major cities in East China, the percentage of retained judges in relatively rural and poor Central China and Northeast China was quite low. In the northeast, because the region was liberated earlier, retained judges constituted only 6% of the total number of judges. In Central China, only 10% of judges were retained ones. A report of the judicial system in Central China denounced retained judges for harboring "profound and reactionary" "old" legal concepts (e.g. judicial independence and legal process). In one case, Jiang Haonan, a retained judge and the head of a criminal tribunal in a Changsha court, Hunan, was so upset by the massive executions of so-called counterrevolutionaries that he cursed his Communist colleagues, saying "[I]f you sentence so many counterrevolutionaries to death, your children will be born without assholes (*piguyan*)." Another retained judge even demanded that Chairman Mao apologize to all the people for his harsh crackdown during the Three-Antis Movement.[22]

As the legal reform deepened, it went to an extreme level. Everything to do with the GMD law was wrong including even its professional writing style and the template of court verdicts. One of the primary reasons for retained

21 Ibid., 1952: 98.

22 Ibid., 1952: 21-42.

judges to keep their leading role in PRC courts was their professional training in law and their experience in writing verdicts. In the legal reform, the Party blamed judicial cadres for allowing retained judges to deal with important trials simply because they "could write verdicts," a task that was beyond the capacity of the working class. In the Liaoning Provincial Court, before a tribunal head left for Beijing, he told cadres to learn from a retained judge and let him handle all important cases." As part of the "old legal concepts," old template and style of verdicts were abolished in the legal reform.[23]

The overarching objective of the legal reform was to purge all politically unreliable retained judges as well as old cadres who had "capitulated to old legal concepts and styles." To replace them and properly resettle purged judges, the central government issued a circular in August 1952 that in principle all courts should try to retain former GMD judges. Retained judges should do technical work instead of presiding over trials. For retained judges who could not remain in courts, local governments should investigate and assign other jobs to them. The circular also required college law professors to engage in the legal reform movement so that they could reform their old thoughts. Some of the professors had to quit their teaching positions, were required to teach courses other than law, become middle-school teachers, or change their careers. Meanwhile, colleges needed to recruit proper (i.e. politically reliable) teachers to strengthen legal and political education.[24]

If retained judges were the main target of the movement, who would replace them and how? Prior to the legal reform, the State Council had already offered some preliminary opinions. In early June, after the State Council accused retained judges of being the villains inside people's courts and old cadres of caving in to "old "legal concepts and becoming corrupt, it decided to dismiss those corrupt old cadres and to purge all "bad" retained judges. Specifically, the State Council discussed the appointment of "new" judicial cadres to fill the positions left by purged judges. Local Party committees would be responsible for the replacement. "New" cadres should be: "old" cadres with staunch belief in communism, correct opinions, and much knowledge about policies; cadres chosen from other courts; army veterans; and outstanding people from unions or associations of labor, peasants, youth, and women. Finally, the people's courts had to undergo a complete transformation by opposing" old "legal concepts and reform all judicial systems. The "new" courts would use

23 Ibid., 1952: 49-62.
24 Peitian Zhang and Hua Zhang, 2007: 19-20.

Marxism, Leninism, and Mao's political and legal thought to educate and train judicial cadres.[25]

It is evident that, months before the legal reform movement, Party leaders had decided that retained judges and legal professionals posed a real threat to the new Communist regime. Many retained judges were arguably potential class enemies. They were corrupt, or politically unreliable, and should be purged from the people's courts, one of the Party's key weapons. Old cadres who had trusted retained judges and yielded to old legal concepts such as judicial independence and equality before the law should also be purged. Their substitutes would be chosen not for their legal knowledge but for their loyalty and reliability to the Party and the cause of the revolution.

Implementing the Legal Reform

Once the goal of the legal reform was set, local governments and judiciaries began taking largely similar steps and adopting similar methods to carry out the movement. In general, most courts were to hold meetings identifying old legal concepts and denouncing them. They also encouraged the masses to report "erroneous" verdicts and then forced judges (mostly retained judges) to apologize in public gatherings.

On September 15, roughly one month after the Ministry of Justice officially kicked off the legal reform, the provincial court of Xikang, a province west of Sichuan that was annexed to Tibet in 1955, launched its legal reform. According to a court report, most judicial cadres supported the reform with the exception of a few retained judges and cadres with historical mistakes whose "attitudes are still not correct." After a meeting on the legal reform, most cadres reportedly had "obtained basic comprehension of the reform, found their own problems, or clarified their muddled thoughts". For many retained judges, however, the reform was a nightmare if not a disaster. Some of them felt gloomy and worried about being punished; others either were dissatisfied with the movement or attempted to stay outside the reform. Wang Hanpin, a retained lawyer and former GMD military officer, feared that the Party would not trust him and braced for his bad fortune.[26]

The acute apprehension among retained judges was real and profound as they had reason to fear that they would be the target of the storm. In

25 Ibid., 2007: 20-22.
26 Ibid., 2007: 139-140.

October, minutes of another meeting of the court showed that some retained judges were so worried that they turned silent or inactive during discussions. For instance, when asked to speak at a discussion, former GMD magistrate and retained judge Chen Zhirong said, "[A]fter the round of inspection, all you have are merely mistakes, but what I have are all evils." Even some Communist cadres felt uncomfortable about the reform. Assistant judge Qin Chengxun complained that judicial work was quite difficult to do because it was closely intertwined with policies and concepts. Judge Ying Bowen simply wanted to stay in the court for a short period and then requested a transfer to work in other departments.[27]

In late October, the Xikang Provincial Court reported how it had conducted the legal reform. According to the report, the legal reform had lasted 46 days and involved 169 judicial cadres. The court first identified a number of "old" legal concepts or activities, many of which have been mentioned before. But it added a few "new crimes" of retained judges such as "trying to rescue counterrevolutionaries, refusing to obey the orders of upper-level officials, and arbitrarily changing punishments." The report accused judges who had been influenced by "old" judicial styles of "violating human rights," a term coming from the West but adopted by the Communists in the 1940s.[28] The report also chastised old judicial styles for delaying judgments, extracting confessions through torture and inducement, evading responsibilities, or harassing female litigants. While those "crimes" were not different from what I have mentioned in other official reports, the Xikang Provincial Court opted not to blame retained judges for all the "evils." Part of the reason might be that many old or new judicial cadres had also committed one or more of those old-style mistakes.

After the exposure of the "errors" of retained judges, most cadres reportedly learned that law was not above class and the notion of "equality before the law" was wrong and reactionary. One cadre noted that the Republican Civil Law stated that one man should only have one wife, but one counterrevolutionary was said to have 36 wives. Therefore, the cadre claimed that the Republican law was just fraudulent and social practice should supersede the law at least in the case of elites.

In the second phase of the movement, the court convened mass meetings to publicly correct false decisions about judgments, and, as Altehenger

27 Ibid., 2007: 141-142.

28 Xiao Shu笑蜀, *Precursor of History: Solemn Pledges Made a Half Century Ago* (*lishi dexiansheng: bange shiji qiande zhuangyan chengnuo*历史的先声：半个世纪前的的庄严承诺) (Shantou: Shantou daxue chubanshe, 1999): 94-95.

has remarked, to educate the masses about state laws.[29] In a typical mass meeting, a government leader was slated to speak first. The victims were then invited to denounce false judgments. Finally, the head of the provincial court made an open apology, expressed sympathy to the victims, and promised to correct the judgments as soon as possible. At the end of the meeting, the masses chanted slogans in support of court corrections. One ordinary member of the audience named Huang Shuxiu reportedly said that she had never heard that judges would apologize to people for their mistakes. She thought it happened only in the people's government led by Chairman Mao and the CCP.[30]

When the legal reform was completed in early 1953, Huang Xinyuan, a court official of the Xikang Provincial Court, wrote a summary of the legal reform. He argued that the movement had undergone three phases: 1) studying government documents, 2) exposing and criticizing false judgments, 3) reforming thought, organization, and institutions. After the movement was over, judicial cadres drew the boundaries between new and old legal systems. One of the key results of the movement was internal reorganization. Among 169 cadres, 49 or 29% were eliminated from the court roster through punishment, transferred to new posts, or demoted. To fill the vacancies, Huang Xinyuan asked the provincial Party committee and human resource departments to send outstanding activists from the labor, peasant, women, and youth organizations. Moreover, Huang stressed the importance of "dual leadership (court and Party)" and continued to oppose "judicial independence" and other so-called "old" legal concepts and modes. Unlike the old legal styles, the new judicial system would establish mass-line institutions such as on-the-spot or circuit trials (*xunhui jiushen*), covert trials (*anshen*), and public trials. The circuit trials are what Philip C. Huang calls "practical moralism," a traditional legal thought in the Qing that was "evident even in the Maoist period."[31] On-the-spot trials should be conducted every week or at least every month to help people. Also, the court should create a mediation system to tackle minor criminal or civil disputes.[32]

The Legal Reform Movement occurred in many other parts of Southwest China as it did in Xikang province. In Dechang County, Sichuan, the county court took three successive steps in promoting the movement: remedial

29 Altehenger, 2018: 9.

30 Peitian Zhang and Hua Zhang, 2007: 131-139.

31 Huang, 2010: 10.

32 Peitian Zhang and Hua Zhang, 2007: 148-162.

learning (*buke*), mobilizing the masses, and reporting possible offenses. In the first step, all judicial cadres studied central documents related to the legal reform and abolition of GMD laws. The remedial learning helped cadres understand the differences between old and new laws and recognize the importance of "abolishing all GMD laws." The second step required court cadres to assist the police departments in mobilizing the masses during land reform and legal reform movements.

At the inception, court cadres found that many local people knew little about the role of courts in society. One policeman even said that he did not know what the word "court" meant. After attending several mass meetings cosponsored by the police department and court cadres, many policemen could differentiate the old laws from the new laws. Peasant Liu Tongshi stated that it was wrong for a retained judge to punish counterrevolutionaries lightly because it would make the people's court the same as the GMD courts. The mass mobilization seemed quite successful. According to a local poll, only three out of 278 people in a village still did not understand – or at least admitted they did not understand – the meaning of the legal reform.

The third step was to encourage the masses to report cases that had been falsely judged. From early December of 1952 through January 17, 1953, the court had received 205 reports of problematic cases. Among them, 73 were discovered to have certain problems: six were improperly judged, 24 involved false corruption charges, and 43 were excessively lenient punishments designed to shield counterrevolutionaries. Adding to the legal reform were new mass-line legal methods such as collective mediation and on-the-spot-trials to deal with minor disputes among local residents.[33]

In the city of Ya'an, Sichuan, the city court received a total of 175 reports of false judgments. In one report, a woman accused judge Luo Lianhui of ordering her to stand up, lower her head, and not move, a form of torture. For such reports, the city court conducted investigations and modified the verdicts if they were proved wrong. Judges criticized for their bad attitudes or refusal to accept cases had to publicly apologize to the people in a mass meeting of over 3000 spectators. After the legal reform, the city court believed that most people's reports were right and any mistake in the judgments had to be seriously corrected. If so, people would become the real masters of the PRC and would treat the court as their own.[34]

33 Ibid., 2007: 177-181.

34 Ibid., 2007: 183-185.

In addition to following the general process of the legal reform, some counties in Sichuan published reports to share their experience with the legal reform, including the problems which they had faced. The court of Hanyuan county issued a detailed report highlighting past misconceptions among court cadres. The first one was that many cadres assumed that the court was just a venue to resolve people's disputes and maintain social order. They did not know that courts should assist national campaigns such as the anti-counterrevolutionary movement and land reform. Second, many judicial cadres tended to be too magnanimous in dealing with counterrevolutionaries in general. Third, cadres were unclear about the mission of state economic development. In one case, a businessman named Wang Xinfa was accused of amassing much fortune through a fraudulent provincial construction project. But the court only punished him lightly due to his carpenter origin and ignored the huge loss of state property. Fourth, cadres failed to comprehend the spirit of the new marriage law and its support of women against feudal forces. Accordingly, some cadres refused to deal with marriage cases unless a lawsuit was filed. Fifth, court verdicts continued to use obscure language, format, and jargon. Many cadres had no intention of connecting with people and make public trials.

The root of those misconceptions, as the court report argued, "was the lack of recognition of the mass line." Many cadres were accustomed to sit in the court to resolve disputes and were unwilling to travel around the county to conduct on-the-spot trials. The court promised to rely on people and to make trials convenient to the people in the future.[35]

During the legal reform, some courts took measures to single out one retained judge as a primary target of criticism in hopes of warning others not to harbor similar erroneous non-Communist legal thoughts. For example, the Southern Sichuan People's Court specifically denounced one Chen Yuanguang, a retained judge, for his allegedly false "capitalist thoughts." According to the court documents, judge Chen's first capitalist thought was his effort to be like a "basketball referee," or a third party who should be impartial in a dispute. Whenever he made a decision on a punishment, he always stressed generosity and education and "never stood on the basis of vindicating people's interest". He publicly stated that the "heavenly duty of judges is to try their best to lessen defendants' evil [...]. until they [judges] cannot find any excuse to diminish the punishment" any further.

35 Ibid., 2007: 185-191.

Judge Chen's second "mistake" was his working style. He only stayed in the court and believed that he could solve all problems from behind his desk. Having worked in the court for two years, he still refused to directly visit people in the country to solve their disputes. When court leaders asked him to go out and meet the masses, he said, "I would like to go to the countryside, but who is going to take care of my family?"

Judge Chen's erroneous attitudes during the Three-Antis Movement were another target. During a group discussion about Liu Qingshan and Zhang Zishan, two Communist veterans who had been executed for their serious corruption,[36] judge Chen argued that all men were selfish and both Liu and Zhang were no exception. He said many of his friends had joined the CCP in the 1920s. But after the GMD cracked down on the CCP in 1927, all his friends betrayed the CCP. "The reason was the selfish thought," Judge Chen remarked, "thus I believe the idea that the working class is unselfish is an exaggeration. There will not be such kind of people." This kind of thought, if true, would certainly place judge Chen at odds with orthodox Communist propaganda. His beliefs were reminiscent of the arguments of early Chinese philosopher Yang Zhu that everyone is selfish and pursues only his or her own interest.[37]

Moreover, when he was asked why he did not take graft, judge Chen replied that he was influenced by "old morality (*jiudaode*)," one that was dismissed by the official report as feudal and capitalist. Finally, the court report denounced judge Chen's capitalist thoughts and deemed them adverse. While the report still referred to judge Chen as "comrade" and did not say what punishment he would get, his career in the court would certainly be terminated just like those of thousands of other retained judges in the legal reform.[38]

In Yunnan, a province that shares borders with both Burma and Laos, the judicial system experienced a similar process in implementing the legal reform.[39] At the beginning of 1953, about five months after the legal reform started, the provincial court announced that most courts in the province had completed the legal reform. The legal reform in Yunnan experienced two phases: 1) Opposing old thoughts, old concepts, and old styles; 2) Constructing

36 For the case of Liu Qingshan and Zhang Zishan see Jeremy Brown, *City Versus Countryside in Mao's China: Negotiating the Divide* (Cambridge: Cambridge University Press, 2014): 24.

37 For the philosophy of Yang Zhu see Jiao Guocheng焦国成, "An Evaluation of Yang Zhu School's 'Egoism' (*Yang Zhu xuepai 'weiwo zhuyi' bianxi*杨朱学派唯我主义辨析)" in *The Journal of China People's University*, 1989, Vol. 6, pp. 88-95.

38 Peitian Zhang and Hua Zhang, 2007: 174-177.

39 Ibid., 2007: 214-218.

new courts by "commending outstanding judges and establishing a new direction of the people's judicial system."

Like their counterparts in Sichuan, the Yunnan Provincial Court urged all courts to step up denunciation of old concepts and thoughts and to beef up cadres' training to enhance their political standard, which, in other words, meant that the law was a knife hilt of the Party.[40] The provincial court also ordered court leaders at all levels to reinforce the adjudicating committees and make them primary units in the court. To deal with cases in a correct and timely fashion, all courts had to develop on-the-spot trials, public trials, collective mediation, street interrogations, people's juries, and the like.

In addition, probably alarmed by numerous indiscriminate arrests and punishments during the legal reform, the provincial court demanded that local courts strictly enforce the detention system regulation that most detentions should be approved by the leaders of county or city courts, and any arrest should be endorsed by magistrates or mayors. County and city courts could decide prison sentences of criminal cases up to ten years, while branches of provincial courts could decide prison sentences up to fifteen years. Life sentences and death penalties had to be approved by the provincial court.

To help poor and illiterate people to file lawsuits, the provincial court ordered all courts to simplify the legal process, abolish litigation fees, set up suing boxes, and build up temporary oral suing sites when judges did on-the-spot trials.[41] The suing box could hark back to the Han dynasty when the first petition box was established by a general, but it became more popular in the Tang dynasty under Empress Wu Zetian (r. 690-705).[42]

The enforcement of the movement was rather uneven across the PRC. Some remote and less developed regions did not start the movement until 1953. According to a report of the Xichang Provincial Court in the spring of 1953, mountainous counties such as Ningnan, Miyi, and Huidong had yet to begin their legal reform movement in early 1953, when Yunnan province had already wrapped up its reform. The court ascribed the tardiness to the lack of attention from the leadership, busy schedules, and a shortage of cadres. In some counties, court cadres were delinquent in dealing with people's lawsuits and disputes. In the county of Mianning, people had

40 The CCP called its judicial system its Knife Hilt to deal with its political enemies. See Qiang Fang and Xiaobing Li, 2017: Ch. 1.

41 Ibid., 2007: 210-214.

42 For a complete history of the petition box in China see Qiang Fang, 2013a.

filed 97 reports on legal problems, but none of them had been taken care of. People thus complained, saying "why should we report? It is useless to report because no [cadre] will take care of that."[43]

Some counties in Sichuan witnessed a similar problem. For example, Renshou county admitted in 1953 that the legal reform was far from satisfactory. While 10,672 local people had been "educated" through attending the county court's public trials, the number constituted less than 1% of the county population. The number of people's reports totaled 111 cases, which was merely 4.2% of all the 2686 cases the court had received. The county court argued that the main cause of the low participation was insufficient mass mobilization and decided to solve the problem.[44]

As we will see in the following sections, the process of and methods taken in implementing the legal reform in other regions of China were similar to those in Southwest China.

Fallout of Legal Reform

By the spring of 1953, the nationwide legal reform was nearing its end. As I have argued, the overriding objective of the movement was to purge unreliable retained judges who had joined the GMD and worked in Republican courts or who had a firm belief in the GMD's Six Laws and legal principles. Also being purged were old cadres and young judges who had become "captives" of retained judges and/or Republican laws and legal principles. In the movement, thousands of retained judges were forced to leave the positions where they had learned, trained, and worked during much of their careers. According to Yang Zhaolong, chief procurator of the Supreme Court and a former GMD central judicial officer, many purged retained judges in 1952 had been sent to hospitals to do registry, crematories to do sundry duties, or elementary schools to teach children. The fate of retained law school professors was no better. In the 1952 reorganization of colleges, the number of law schools was drastically reduced. Many retained law professors lost their teaching positions to young teaching assistants who were mostly CCP and Communist Youth League members. To many people including Yang, it was utterly "preposterous."[45]

43 Peitian Zhang and Hua Zhang, 2007: 165-171.

44 Ibid., 2007: 181-183.

45 Yang Zhaolong杨兆龙, "Between Party and Non-Party (*dangyu feidang zhijian*党与非党之间)" in *Wenhuibao*文汇报, May 8, 1957.

Table 4.1 "Purged, recruited, and current cadres during national legal reform"

	Cadre Numbers before Legal Reform	Purged Numbers	Percentage of Purged Cadres	Newly Recruited Cadres	Percentage of New Recruits of Original Court Cadres	Percentage of New recruiters of Current Court Cadres	Number of Current Court Cadres	Percentage of Current Court Cadres to Original Cadres	Increase or Decrease Percentage
Total No.	22492	5557	24.71	6505	28.92	28.07	23178	103.1	+3.1
Judges	15532	4111	26.47	5075	32.67	31.08	16331	105.1	+5.1
Administrators	6960	1446	20.78	1430	20.55	20.89	6847	98.4	-1.6
Old Cadres	4557	531	11.65	1608	35.29	29.06	5534	121.4	+21.4
New Cadres	12491	1659	14.88	4763	38.13	31.18	15275	122.3	+22.3
Retained Judges	**2720**	**1885**	**69.30**	**16**	**0.59**	**1.96**	**819**	**30.1**	**-69.9**
Other Retained Judicial Cadres	7224	1282	47.06	118	4.33	7.61	1550	56.9	-43.1
Female Cadres	2943	466	15.83	1707	58	42.93	3976	135.1	+35.1
CCP Members	N/A			2508		31.97	7844		
Youth League Members	N/A			1893		27.72	6829		

After the top-down purge of retained judges and other old cadres, the people's courts in the PRC enrolled politically progressive and loyal cadres to fill the vacancies. As aforementioned, many, if not most, new judicial cadres were not noted for their legal education and training. Table 4.1 can best attest to the extent of the purge of retained judges in Communist judiciaries.

In this table, the number of retained judges suffered the biggest loss as 69.3% of the pre-legal-reform retained judges were purged. Only sixteen retained judges were added during the reform. In comparison, old cadres and young cadres lost 11.65% and 14.88% respectively, far less than that of retained judges. The biggest beneficiaries of the legal reform were new CCP and Youth League members, reflecting the emphasis of the Party Central to "regain" the control of the courts and make them a faithful and reliable tool of the Party. Another group that greatly benefited was female cadres whose number saw a 135% increase.[46]

The change of judicial cadres in different regions is mirrored in two more tables below.

Table 4.2 shows that the percentages of retained judges in major regions and Inner Mongolia before the legal reform ranged between 12.62 and 37.73. Inner Mongolia should be an outlier because of its special status. Apart from Inner Mongolia, the northeast region had the smallest proportion of retained judges. The reason is simple as the northeast was the first major region taken over by the CCP. Similarly, the highest percentages of retained judges in northwest and southwest regions resulted from their late "liberation."

While I do not have the percentage of both retained judges and cadres of each major region in the post-legal-reform era, we can find detailed changes of retained judges and cadres in Table 4.3. More important, we will see the changes of the number, percentage, political status, and occupations of the newly recruited judicial cadres.

For example, even though the loss of all retained cadres was 43.1%, the number of retained judges before the reform was 2720 and it was down to 819 after the reform, a loss of 69.9%. This further demonstrated that the CCP's primary goal of the reform was to purge most retained judges and firmly control the judicial system. To cover the big loss of retained judges, new blood was instilled. Among the new judges was an increase of both old and new cadres. Old cadres increased about 21% because of their rich revolutionary experience and longtime loyalty to the Party. The number of young cadres was up 3784, an increase of 22.3%. The biggest jump was in

46 Peitian Zhang and Hua Zhang, 2007: 219.

Table 4.2 National judicial cadres before legal reform[47]

	Courts	Total No. of Cadres	Old Cadres	Old Cadres	New Cadres	New Cadres	All Retained Cadres	All Retained Cadres	Retained Judges	Retained Judges
			Number	%	Number	%	Number	%	**Number**	%
Total No.	2438	26089	5199	19.93	14454	55.4	6436	24.67	**3395**	13.01
North Region	345	3355	1265	27.7	1451	43.25	639	19.05	**254**	7.57
Northeast Region	198	2642	551	20.86	1657	62.72	434	16.43	**107**	4.05
Northwest Region	323	2852	519	18.20	1257	44.07	1076	37.73	**584**	20.48
Southwest Region	429	4034	325	8.06	2571	63.73	1138	28.21	**653**	16.19
South Central Region	606	6378	886	13.89	4055	63.58	1437	22.53	**737**	11.56
East Region	502	6519	1625	24.93	3221	49.41	1673	25.66	**1053**	16.15
Inner Mongolia Region	35	309	28	9.06	242	78.32	39	12.62	**7**	2.27

Remarks:

a The total number did not include retained judges and cadres purged in the Land Reform, Anti-counterrevolutionary, Three-Antis and Five-Antis Movements.

b Northwest Xinjiang cadres' 555 was an old number and incomplete.

c South Central region missed eleven units in Hunan and fourteen units in Guangxi.

d In East region, Shanghai was one unit, 38 district courts established after the legal reform were not included, Shandong missed eleven courts.

e The numbers in this table in most provinces and cities were made in accordance with their legal reform report, a few provinces used the numbers of their report due to no report or incomplete report units.

47 Ibid., 2007: 219-20.

Table 4.3 National judicial cadres' conditions before and after legal reform[48]

		Before Legal Reform	Before Legal Reform	After Legal Reform	After Legal Reform	Increase or Decrease of Numbers After Legal Reform	Increase or Decrease Percentage
		Number	%	Number	%		
Total No. of Cadres	Total No.	22492	100	23178	100	+686	+3.1
	Judges	15532	69.1	16331	70.5	+799	+5.1
	Administrators	6960	30.9	6847	29.5	-113	-1.6
Old Cadres	No.	4557	20.3	5534	23.9	+977	+21.4
New Cadres	No.	12491	55.5	15275	65.9	+3784	+22.3
	Young Intellectuals	9502	42.3	10460	45.1	+958	+10.1
	Worker Activist	480	2.1	1394	6	+91.4	+190.4
	Peasant Activist	1357	6	2026	8.8	+669	+49.3
	Others	1152	5.1	1395	6	+243	+21.1
Retained Cadres (Origin)	**No.**	**5444**	**24.2**	**2369**	**10.2**	**-3075**	**-56.5**
	Old Judges	**2720**	**12.1**	**819**	**3.5**	**-1901**	**-69.9**
	Common Old Cadres	2724	12.1	1550	6.7	-1174	-43.1
Female Cadres		2943	13.1	3976	17.2	+1033	+35.1

Remarks:

a After legal reform, CCP members were 7844, making up 33.84% of all cadres; Youth League members were 6892, making up 29.46% of all cadres. The combination of both made up 63.3%.

b After legal reform, retained judges and retained cadres lost 56.5% (not including purged cadres in the Land Reform, Anti-counterrevolutionary, Three-Antis and Five-Antis Movements)

c The combined number of old cadres was different, because the Jiangsu table did not have breakdown, other tables were the same.

48 Peitian Zhang and Hua Zhang, 2007: 221.

worker activists whose numbers were almost doubled. This was consistent with orthodox Marxism as well as the CCP's claim that the proletariat would be the leaders of a Communist state. The number of peasant judges also rose sharply by 49%. Unlike Republican courts, PRC courts before and during the legal reform greatly augmented the number of female cadres. A 35% increase of female judicial cadres no doubt substantiated the CCP's advocacy of women's rights, which was first embodied in the 1950 marriage law.[4748]

New Cadres and Old Problems

With retained judges purged and the coming of new politically reliable and obedient cadres, would the "new" people's courts better comply with PRC laws, justice, and judicial procedures and get rid of all the "crimes" or "evils" of retained judges alleged by central and judicial leaders? Unfortunately, many, if not most, of the newly recruited judges proved to be worse than retained judges. Not only did torture continue to be used but pileup cases and false detainments, arrests, and verdicts also became so serious that the Ministry of Justice ordered the conducting of a polity-wide inspection.

On May 6, 1953, several months after the end of the legal reform, the Shanghai People's Court hammered out a draft to enforce the resolution of the Second National Judicial Meeting. The draft lauded itself for having settled over 90,000 pileup cases since the legal reform. But the court quickly admitted that it still had 38,604 unresolved cases, most of which were civil cases involving largely marriage, property, and housing disputes. This was rather embarrassing as Party leaders often had blamed retained judges for the large number of unresolved cases prior to the legal reform. In fact, the problem continued to exist after the legal reform. Lacking an ideal scapegoat, the Shanghai court had to attribute the problem to judicial leaders' bureaucratism, an administrative negligence of people's plight criticized by Mao in May 1951.[49] The draft also conceded that, despite the dismissal of many retained judges during the legal reform, the court had discovered dozens of false arrests, detainments, and judgments. The main causes were the low standards and inexperience of most current cadres, even though they were politically "infallible."[50]

49 Zhonggong zhongyang wenxian yanjiushi中共中央文献研究室, ed. *Selected Works of Mao* (*Mao Zedong wenji*毛泽东文集) (Beijing: Renmin chubanshe, 2001): 6. 164-165.

50 Shanghai Archives, May 6, 1953. A6-2-109.

In late June, the problems generated by inexperienced new cadres seemed to persist. Therefore, in a letter to the Ministry of Justice and the Supreme Court, the Shanghai court formally summoned more qualified judicial cadres to the court to assist new judicial cadres, most of whom were workers, shop assistants, and students. "Although they have high working enthusiasm, a clear standpoint, and good political [attitudes]," the letter stated, "they know little about the judicial system, have low policy and educational standards, and lack social experience. Hence, their case-solving efficiency is quite low and cannot be improved in a short period of time."[51]

The problems of incompetent new cadres faced by Shanghai court leaders was anything but rare among other courts in the wake of the legal reform. In the fall of 1953, the Southwest Branch of the Supreme Court discerned certain problems in the region. The first was that judicial cadres no longer wanted to investigate cases of false charges after the reform. The reason was that many cadres believed that fallacious cases had been corrected during or after the legal reform and most cases had gone through the process of mass line, group evaluation, and leaders' approval. Accordingly, the reinvestigation would be useless. Second, some courts tried to resolve pileup cases before they righted wrongly judged cases, while other courts deemed correcting false cases an obstacle to resolving pileup cases. The last problem was judicial cadres. As in Shanghai, after purging retained judges, cadres in many southwest courts were largely insufficient in number and inexperienced in practice. In particular, the region had a shortage of court leaders and qualified cadres. One province was said to have recruited judges with little education and the head of one county court could read only a few words.

Owing mostly to the poor quality of new cadres, arbitrary arrests and judgments, especially torture and forced confessions, remained serious. According to a report issued by the Chongqing People's Court, by August the city had found hundreds of wronged cases among which marriage cases had the highest number. In one case, a peasant-activist named Gan Xingyun was elected as a member of his village evaluation committee and production committee member. This drew the animosity of former GMD agent Yang Zhongwen. After a worker in a local military warehouse was killed, Yang allegedly instigated several "backward people (*luohou fenzi*)" to fabricate evidence accusing Gan of killing the worker while he was having an affair with Gan's wife. Without conducting any investigation, a city court judge (a new cadre) relied on the forced charge and confession from the police to sentence Gan to life in prison. While the case had recently been corrected,

51 Ibid., June 25, 1953. B24-2-21-66.

Gan had been imprisoned for many months during which his wife had divorced him and his son had died.

In this traumatic case, the judge certainly was not a retained judge and the police who had tortured Gan were not retained cadres. Thus, the Chongqing court could no longer blame retained judges for the torture and serious false judgment. The court report said nothing but criticized the incompetence of new cadres.[52]

Using force to extract needed confessions was quite common in rural areas in Xikang Province where township cadres employed torture and more positive inducements to extract confessions from alleged criminals. After confessed "criminals" were sent to the county courts, judges were more likely to choose to trust "confessions" than to go down to the countryside to reinvestigate. The result was a rising number of local random arrests and detainments.

The Xikang Provincial Court was stunned by the high number of incarcerated criminals. One of its reports remarked that in the first half of 1953, a period roughly after the legal reform ended, 1817 criminals had been punished. The ratio of criminals to the provincial population (3.33 million) was rather high. "If this trend of indiscreet punishment continues [in the rest of 1953]," the court report warned, "it will hurt some people's sentiments toward the Party and government and it could be capitalized on by enemy agents." The court attributed the widespread meting out of punishments to three causes. First, judges' lack of understanding of the class boundaries in each case. Second, some judges' use of anti-enemy methods (i.e. torture) to deal with internal disputes among the people (which should be handled by mediation). The problems of torture, induced confessions, and indiscriminate detainments remained serious and prevalent. Local cadres liked to use hanging and beating, forced kneeling, tying, and other forms of torture to extract confessions. The worst scenario was that many judges refused to investigate when suspects retracted their confessions in court. Some judges used illegal enticements, such as offering release if defendants confessed.

The third cause of false punishments was that some judges scrambled to solve cases in order to complete their assignments as early as possible. But they were unwilling to conduct meticulous investigations which often led to numerous false detainments.[53]

All the problems in post-legal reform Shanghai and Xikang could also be found in Yunnan province. On August 18, 1953, the Political and Legal

52 Peitian Zhang and Hua Zhang, 2007: 55-60.

53 Ibid., 2007: 67-71.

Committee of the Yunnan provincial government published a review on the province's judicial problems after the legal reform. Unlike Shanghai and Xikang, which blamed the low quality of new cadres for the pileup of cases, the committee review stated that the summer locust plague was one of the main causes because many judges had spent most of their time fighting locusts. Another cause was the huge number of unresolved cases. The entire province had 12,630 cases and Kunming, the capital, alone had 4891 cases. Additionally, the correction of cases was not easy as many cases had been judged not only falsely but also senselessly. In one case, a judge mistakenly deemed some people's squabble to be a counterrevolutionary case.

The committee review believed that two erroneous thoughts and sentiments of judges had severely hampered the case-solving work in the courts. One was judges' complacency because they assumed that all false cases had been corrected in the legal reform; the other was judges' worry that they could be disciplined or publicly condemned like some of their colleagues had been in the reform.[54]

The Yunnan Provincial Court found that false judgments were particularly serious in some counties. For example, of all 415 marriage cases in the Xunwei County Court, 95 of them or 34.8% were adjudicated wrongly. Unlike the provincial political and legal committee, the provincial court ascribed the problems to judges' bureaucratism, a similar conviction to that of the Shanghai court, and the "low policy standard," a polite term referring to the insufficient education of some new cadres.[55] To borrow a popular saying, the courts were simply putting old wine into new bottles. Like the Shanghai court, the Yunnan Provincial Court dared not publicly criticize the CCP or the legal reform for those persistent problems.

A Deliberate Purge

As I have shown, the direct and foremost cause of the legal reform in 1952 was the CCP's accusations that retained cadres, and especially retained judges, were the main source of major problems inside the judicial system. The problems included insensitivity to workers, the use of torture, the pileup of cases, obscure verdicts, persistent corruption, false arrests, uninformed verdicts, and inappropriate punishments. However, after purging most retained judges and replacing them with politically reliable cadres drawn

54 Ibid., 2007: 201-204.

55 Ibid., 2007: 83-88.

from worker and peasant activists, young and female cadres, and army veterans, most of the old judicial problems failed to abate and, according to some documents, lingered or even worsened. Then some questions arise: Why did those problems persist after the legal reform? To what extent were the CCP's charges against retained judges true or false? What were the fundamental reasons behind the CCP's launch of the legal reform in 1952?

To answer these questions, I will try to make in-depth analyses of the rationale for several key charges of the CCP against retained judges.

1 A Premeditated Legal Reform

When Minister of Justice Shi Liang rolled out the legal reform movement in the summer of 1952, she asserted that the "serious organizational and thought impurity" inside the judicial system was exposed during the Three-Antis Movement. Many Chinese scholars in China today have accepted Shi Liang's justification of the legal reform.[56]

In fact, if we look back to the judicial history of the CCP, we will find that its scheme to remove retained/GMD judges had started long before the 1952 movement. Pace Shi Liang, the so-called problems exposed in the Three-Antis Movement were nothing more than a pretext.

In Chapter 2, I have mentioned that as early as October 1947, the CCP had realized that the Party could not count on Republican judges in its courts and sooner or later those politically unreliable judges should be removed. Ma Xiwu, the head of the Shanganning Border Area High Court, stated in a letter to Communist judicial cadres that it was imperative to eradicate all reactionary judges.[57] In early 1949, the CCP declared that it would relinquish all GMD laws, foreboding an omen for GMD judges.[58] Shortly after the establishment of the PRC, the CCP started the training of higher-ranking Communist judges. On May 15, 1950, the Ministry of Justice issued a guideline for judicial training in order to enhance the standard of their theory, policy, and service. To be qualified as a judge, a trainee had to be either a high-ranking cadre in a provincial court or the head of a county court, a civilian cadre who had worked in liberated regions for three years, or a military cadre with the ranking of regiment head who had worked for three years. The ministry planned to first train a total of about

56 For Shi Liang 史良see Fujian Provincial People's Court, 1952: 3. 1; for Chinese scholars see endnote 300.

57 Ai Shaorun, ed., 2007a: 205-207.

58 *Studying Documents of Constructing People's Judicial System*, 1952.

110 such judges nationally and the training would continue. It did not rule out female cadres as the guideline said that only pregnant cadres or cadres with children would not be trained.[59]

In November 1950, one month after the anti-counterrevolutionary movement began, Shi Liang ordered the creation of a long-term educational program to train old judicial cadres in the base periods (Jiangxi Soviet and Yan'an) whose education and experience were no longer sufficient for the new situation. The main curricula included the importance of the judicial system, the class nature of law, and the current missions of the judicial system. The textbooks included the Common Program, Mao's articles on people's dictatorship, and speeches and directives of Party leaders, the State Council, and the Supreme Court on issues such as the judicial system and the anti-counterrevolutionary movement.[60]

In June 1951, roughly one year before the legal reform, the State Council, the Supreme Court, and the Supreme Procuracy jointly ordered the establishment of the political and legal committee at the provincial level whose mission was to strengthen the CCP's control over court and police in order to ensure the success of political movements.[61] Ever since its inception, the political and legal committee had been a formidable force in the PRC, which had effectively uprooted the foundation of the rule of law, a notion that many retained judges believed to be holy.

The recruitment of progressive workers to be judges did not begin in the 1952 legal reform. In actuality, it started in the Yan'an Border period when many Communist judges such as Lei Jingtian in the early 1940s had little formal legal training. On December 19, 1951, the Southwest Military and Political Committee, the de facto government in the region, planned to buttress people's tribunals with ongoing movements. In the face of a dearth of judicial cadres, the committee allowed local governments to select worker and peasant activists to become judges.[62]

In East China around the same time, several provincial governments had denounced old legal concepts and purged retained judges prior to the legal reform. For example, Shandong in 1951 kicked off "struggles" against old legal concepts and cleansed some "bad [retained judicial cadres]." During the Three-Antis Movement that began in late 1951, the East China Branch of the Supreme Court penalized and dismissed unqualified

59 Peitian Zhang and Hua Zhang, 2007: 28-30.
60 Ibid., 2007: 26.
61 Ibid., 2007: 37-38.
62 Ibid.

and corrupt cadres. The vice heads of the Subei and Fuzhou courts were punished for their corruption; the heads of the Zhejiang Provincial Court, the Sunan Court, and the Nanjing Court were demoted for their "ambiguous class views (*jieji guandian mohu*) or grave bureaucratism and rightist thoughts."[63]

If the CCP had planned to eliminate unreliable judges as early as 1947, trained court leaders at the beginning of the PRC, created a committee to tighten its control over the judicial system, and appointed worker and peasant activists to be judges before 1952, it is rather far-fetched for Shi Liang and other CCP leaders and mouthpieces to claim that the 1952 legal reform was triggered by serious problems among retained judges in the Three-Antis and Five-Antis Movements. In other words, the CCP had premeditated the purge long before the legal reform.

2 Assisting Political Movements

According to Shi Liang, one of the big "evils" or "crimes" of retained judges was their refusal to uphold central missions (i.e. political movements) and reluctance to harshly punish counterrevolutionaries.[64]

Again, both archives and this chapter have clearly shown that this "evil" or "crime" was largely unsubstantiated. The cases that Shi Liang and other government documents used were at most misrepresentative, incomplete, or partial. In Chapter 3, I have discussed many civil and criminal cases from the Shanghai archives. As soon as the CCP embarked on the anti-counterrevolutionary campaign in October 1950, many, if not most, Shanghai judges (most were retained judges) quickly aligned themselves with the central policy by reversing previous "magnanimity" toward class enemies and adopting severe penalties. Furthermore, the dual oversight of the procuracy and the military commissions would make any residual judicial lenience impossible and dangerous in a political campaign. In civil cases, judges in Shanghai had since early 1951 steadfastly sided with the working class and opposed the management. As the anti-counterrevolutionary movement intensified in 1951, thousands of counterrevolutionaries including former GMD officials, agents, bandits, landlords, and even hoodlums had been either executed or sentenced to life imprisonment by the people's courts.

63 The Investigation Unit of the Central Political and Judicial Organs, 1952: 6.

64 See Fujian Provincial People's Court, 1952: 3 .3; The Investigation Unit of the Central Political and Judicial Organs, 1952: 37-8; and Chen Guangzhong陈光中 and Zeng Xinhua曾新华, 2009: 1-8.

To cite one more case about the severity of the judges in Shanghai, in October 1951, the Gaoqiao Branch of the Shanghai People's Tribunal sentenced a "counterrevolutionary" to life in prison. Zhu Jinfu, a 57-year-old man, was accused of being a former local tyrant, a township head under the Japanese aggressor, and a district representative under the GMD. After the liberation of Shanghai, Zhu continued to make rumors threatening village cadres. Most of Zhu's alleged crimes had been committed before 1949 and there was no tangible evidence to verify them. His new crimes were his rumor and threats. In a short and vaguely worded verdict, the court sentenced Zhu to life incarceration because he "has always bullied the masses and harmed people. After the liberation, he continues to threaten village cadres and sabotage the land reform."[65]

Therefore, CCP accusations that retained judges had tried to cover up counterrevolutionaries and capitalists and failed to adhere to central missions during political campaigns such as the Three-Antis and Five-Antis are not substantiated. At least the many cases in the Shanghai archives do not vindicate the CCP's assertions.

3 The Proportion of Retained Judges

When Shi Liang and other judicial leaders talked about the national legal reform, they expressed deep worries that most judges were retained judges and posed a potentially serious threat to the CCP's rule. In Shi Liang's words, about 22% of the 28,000 judicial cadres nationwide were retained cadres. Yet the percentage of retained cadres who took charge of trials was much higher especially in some big cities. Shi Liang used Shanghai and Tianjin as examples where the proportions of retained judges were 76.92% and 48% respectively. It seemed scarier for the CCP that most retained judges had joined the GMD or other Republican groups and the specter of a return of the GMD could not be averted without a potent control over the judicial system, one of the CCP's forceful tools.[66]

Indeed, the proportion of retained judges in big cities or regions close to the GMD's power centers such as Shanghai, Tianjin, and southern Jiangsu province might be correct. But if we look at the proportion of retained judges elsewhere, the problem may not be as serious as Shi Liang had worried about its being.

65 Shanghai Archives, October 1951. B1-2-30.

66 Peitian Zhang and Hua Zhang, 2007: 1, also see The Investigation Unit of the Central Political and Judicial Organs, 1952: 4-10.

Table 4.4 Current judicial cadres in Central China provinces and cities[67]

Provinces/Cities	Old Cadres	New Cadres	Retained Cadres	Total	Source of Materials
Central China Branch of Supreme Court	12	29	31	72	From the Inspection Unit
Wuhan City Court	20	85	89	194	From the Inspection Unit
Guangzhou City Court	7	32	58	97	Source of June 10, 1952
Henan Province		642 (Both Old and New Cadres)	55	697	According to Court Head Tian
Hunan Province	149	473	539	1161	Source of June 9, 1952
Jiangxi Province	126	674	242	1042	Source of December 1951
Hubei Province	112	628	222	962	Source of May 1952
Guangdong Province	170	665	229	1064	Source of February 1952
Guangxi Province	322	467	187	976	Source of June 1952
Total		4613 (Both Old and New Cadres)	1652	6265	
Percentage		73.7%	26.3%	100%	

According to Table 4.4, prior to the legal reform, retained cadres in provincial capitals such as Wuhan and Guangzhou had a high proportion of retained cadres, albeit their proportions in relatively interior or distant provinces such as Henan, Jiangxi, and Guangxi were very low. In Guangdong, while the percentage of retained cadres in its capital Guangzhou was almost 60%, the province in general had only 21% retained cadres. Henan had the lowest proportion of retained judges, less than 8%.

The proportions of retained cadres, let alone retained judges, in many county courts were even lower. For instance, in the Feicheng County Court, Fujian, among all nine cadres, only one was retained.[68] On July 26, 1952, the Fujian Provincial Court remarked that most retained cadres worked in provincial and major city courts and thus those courts were less politically "pure." The biggest problem in court branches and county courts was not "impurity" but the "weakness" and "poor quality" of cadres. Many cadres were simply incompetent.[69] This report coupled with other reports on the problems in interior provinces or counties showed much smaller proportions of retained cadres.

67 The Investigation Unit of the Central Political and Judicial Organs, 1952: 24.

68 Fujian Provincial People's Court, 1952: 3. 63-65: 64.

69 Ibid.: 2. 1-4: 1.

4 Torture

In the 1952 legal reform, torture became a key charge against retained cadres/judges. The CCP accused retained judges of "beating and hanging" workers and "believing in confessions under torture" that had resulted in the "miscarriage of justice."[70] These charges were fallacious if we can recollect the CCP's own history of extensive use of torture in both the Jiangxi Soviet Base and the Shanganning Border Area. As discussed in Chapters 1 and 2, CCP officials had inflicted cruel torture on comrades and associates inside and outside the Party. In addition to the 1930 Futian Incident, the CCP in Yan'an had launched a so-called "Rescue Movement" in 1942 in which numerous alleged GMD agents or spies had suffered brutal torture and many were driven to insanity or suicide. Furthermore, torture as a legal practice can be dated back to as early as the Zhou dynasty (c. 1100-256 BCE) when most of the Five Punishments (branding the body, cutting off the nose, mutilating the leg/s, and castration) millennia before anesthesia could well be considered forms of torture.[71] Under the rule of empress Wu Zetian, notorious torturers such as Zhou Xing and Lai Junchen reportedly used dozens of horrendous tortures against alleged traitors.[72] In the late Qing, torture had caused many injustices. One of them was the notorious case of Yang Naiwu and Xiao Baicai. Both defendants had been forced to confess their supposed adultery and murder under intolerable torture.[73] There is no denying that torture continued to be practiced in the Republic and in the Soviet bases. Torture was especially common in cases against political enemies and in counties without judges.[74]

The handful of cases in which central CCP officials charged that retained judges had used torture cannot be confirmed or disconfirmed by independent sources. However, many official documents and archival records from this period provide a different picture. According to them, many local party cadres frequently tortured class enemies such as landlords and ordinary people who did not support the government. According to an official report of the Eastern Sichuan District Party Department, landlords were more

70 See Fujian Provincial People's Court, 1952: 2. 13-8: 15; ibid.: 3. 74-81: 78; The Investigation Unit of the Central Political and Judicial Organs, 1952: 108.

71 For the five punishments in the Zhou and Qin dynasties see Zeng Xianyi, 2002.

72 See Qiang Fang, 2013a: Ch. 3.

73 Alford, 1984; Wang Celai, 2002.

74 For the abuse of power and torture in the Republican periods see Frederic Wakeman Jr., *Spymaster: Dai Li and the Chinese Secret Service* (Berkeley: University of California Press, 2003): 148; Qiang Fang, 2013a: Ch. 4.

afraid of the peasant association than of the tribunal. In early 1951, some peasant associations created their own tribunals and arbitrarily tortured and executed landlords. The report also revealed that "hangings, beatings, corporal punishments," and even executions were common in this period. Cadres in the tribunals of peasants' associations were certainly not retained judges.[75]

Another official report of a Fuling court branch noted that torture was common in that region. Over 40 people had been tortured to death by cadres in local peasant associations in Fengdu County alone. In one case, after a landlord alleged that a female tenant, Bai Zhimei, stole his clothes. Peasant association cadres immediately hanged Bai and tortured her. The cadres reportedly used pig hair to pierce into her nipple, which caused her to lose consciousness. To escape the inhuman torture, Bai asked her tormentors to let her go home and grab the clothes. She then hanged herself at home. In another case, Xiang Huaxing, a court inspector, reminded a township head that the Party policy was to ban torture. The township head retorted that he knew the policy, but landlords had cruelly exploited peasants in the past and now was the time for peasants to "retaliate [with torture]." The court inspector warned the township head not to be the "tail" of the masses (i.e. not to follow the peasants). The head replied, "You come from the court and speak about the law; I do not care about [the law]."[76]

In December 1955, a classified book edited and printed by the Judicial Work News Agency (*sifa gongzuo tongxunshe*) exposed more horrifying tortures and false executions that had been perpetrated before the legal reform. Most of the perpetrators were local officials and police, not retained judges. For example, after a tax officer and two militiamen of Ningyang County, Shandong, were killed on their way to Maoyi village, the Ningyang police detained Pan Lizhen and seven other suspects who had tried to evade taxes on their illegally brewed wine. Three of the suspects including Pan were Communists. To extract confessions, the local police tortured them with extremely cruel devices. Unable to bear the pain, Pan "confessed" that he and the others had killed the tax officer and militiamen. But he quickly retracted as soon as the police loosened his handcuffs. None of the other seven suspects confessed. With only the "confession" of Pan, a local judge in 1951 sentenced to death Pan and three of his "accomplices" (later reduced to two) and the remaining four were imprisoned for various lengths of time. The Shandong Provincial Court did not question the credibility of

75 Peitian Zhang and Hua Zhang, 2007: 92-95.

76 Ibid., pp. 120-129: 125.

the "confession" and approved the death sentence in November 1951. Shortly after Pan's execution, the local police interrogated a bandit who admitted that he was the real killer. While the police finally realized Pan's innocence, it was too late to save him.[77]

Without doubt, torture had a long history in China, and was widely used by CCP cadres in the Jiangxi Soviet base and Yan'an period. It is improper to blame only retained judges for using torture. The cases in official publications further demonstrate that Communist cadres in local governments, courts, and police bureaus had often inflicted torture to extract confessions. Most, if not all, of them were Communist cadres and not retained judges or cadres. That could sufficiently help to answer the question why torture turned worse after the legal reform and the purge of retained judges.

In addition to its exaggerated or false charges against retained judges,[78] Party officials had also claimed that retained judges should be responsible for the large number of accumulating cases. This accusation was also incorrect as the same problem remained serious after the purge of most retained judges. As this chapter has shown, two Shanghai court reports in 1953 had ascribed the recurring pileup of cases to the poor quality of new progressive judges. The official charges against retained judges ignored the fact that it was the successive political movements such as the anti-counterrevolutionary, Three-Antis, and Five-Antis Movements that had deprived judges of the time to deal with cases.[79] As more cases accumulated after the legal reform, some local courts hastened to tackle the problem, resulting in widespread and severe violations of law and even death. One county court in Sichuan rashly decided 167 civil cases, among which only three had been investigated. In Jiang'an County, a peasant named Yang Songchen committed suicide after a local court's misjudgment.[80]

The Ministry of Justice and the CCP's criticism of the retained judges' formats of verdicts and their belief in the rule of law, equality before the law, and legal procedures violated both fundamental and modern legal professionalism and principles. Not only did many rulers in Chinese history

77 The Judicial Work News Agency (*sifa gongzuo tongxunshe*司法工作通讯社), *Opposing Objectivism in Judging Work* (*fandui shenpan gongzuozhong dezhuguan zhuyi*反对审判工作中的主观主义) (Beijing: Judicial Work News Agency, 1955): 21-28.

78 The Investigation Unit of the Central Political and Judicial Organs, 1952: 5.

79 "Directives of the Yunnan Provincial People's Court (*Yunnansheng renmin fayuan zhishi*云南省人民法院指示)" in Peitian Zhang and Hua Zhang, 2007: 78-80.

80 "Circular of Sichuan Provincial People's Court (*Sichuansheng renmin fayuan tongbao*四川省人民法院通报)" in Peitian Zhang and Hua Zhang, 2007: 59-60.

do better than the CCP in recognizing the supremacy of the law,[81] but judges in the Soviet Union, a patron of the CCP, also, in theory at least, needed to follow law and legal procedures.[82] If the CCP had successfully forced retained judges to abandon essential legal norms, many of them would have found it impossible to escape the purge and to keep their jobs.

Conclusion

To initiate and justify a nationwide legal reform movement, officials in the Ministry of Justice and the Central Political and Legal Committee accused retained judicial cadres, and especially retained judges, of many "crimes or mistakes," including sabotaging political movements, aligning with class enemies, employing torture, allowing the pileup of cases, and adhering to GMD laws and old practices. As a result, most retained cadres/judges and law professors were purged or transferred to positions unrelated to law. The vacancies left in the courts were filled by progressive workers, peasants, students, female cadres, and military veterans chosen for their political loyalty rather than their legal training and education. While some of the restored revolutionary methods such as mass line, field investigation, and on-site tribunals had benefited people living in remote and less developed regions, the lack of professional training and legal experience among new judges actually worsened the legal situation and practice with more accumulated cases, use of torture, and leveling of false charges. Indeed, as I have argued, many of the CCP's alleged charges against retained judges were either false or unverified. It is very likely that the CCP simply used those allegations and false charges as pretexts to eliminate retained judges and tighten its control of the judicial system, one of its principal instruments of rule in a precarious period of internal (e.g. GMD agents and loyalists) and external (e.g. the Korea War) crises. In that regard, the 1952 legal reform was a deliberate purge whose primary target was the unreliable members in the judicial system. The purge may have been partially successful in consolidating CCP control of the PRC. However, the legal reform and its condemnations of legal professionalism and widely respected legal principles

81 For a history of the idea of the rule of law in China, see Qiang Fang and Roger Des Forges, 2007.

82 H. Sudalikefu, "Denouncing the Reactionary Nature of the Capitalist Jurisprudence (*duizichan jieji faxue fandong benzhi depipan*对资产阶级法学反动本质的批判)" in Fujian Provincial People's Court, 1952: 2. 169-202: 200.

had long-term harmful consequences. As Randle Peerenboom has pointed out, "The stress on political criteria ('red') at the expense of legal expertise was undermining the legitimacy of the legal system."[83] The 1952 legal reform marked a major retreat to an old CCP tradition of anti-law and anti-legal professionalism that began in the bloodbath of the Jiangxi Soviet base and revived sporadically throughout the Sino-Japanese War, the second Civil War, and the 1950-1951 anti-counterrevolutionary campaign. The historical legacy of the legal reform movement is long-lasting and significant. Since the legal reform, law has generally become a faithful and reliable instrument of the Party except in a few short periods in Mao's era. Even after the Party launched a sweeping legal reform in 1978, the instrumental nature of the judicial system has persisted, and it seems likely to linger as long as the Party rules.

83 Peerenboom, 2002: 45.

5 A Golden Age?

The Communist Judicial System in China, 1953-May 1957

Abstract

As the Korean War neared its end, the Communist judicial system pendulum began swinging to the right (liberal side) and reached its apogee in the fall of 1954 with the promulgation of the first Constitution and the Organic Law of the Court. Many scholars in China and the West therefore claim that the years between 1953 to 1957 were a "golden age" of the PRC. In fact, this chapter argues that, with the exception of a short period from spring 1956 to early summer of 1957, this period was not much different from others. The widespread abuses of law, the use of torture, and the meting out of excessive punishment in the second anti-counterrevolutionary campaign of 1955-1956 was almost as bad as the first one of 1951. Even after the Party called for righting the wrongs in 1956, official infringement of the law persisted in remote counties.

Keywords: limited golden age, 1954 constitution, Organic Law of the People's Court, Gao Gang, Hu Feng incident, lenience in Spring of 1956

While many scholars have expressed an interest in the legal system and its development in the early PRC, most have provided only fleeting and tangential coverage of the period between the Legal Reform Movement (1952-1953) and the Anti-Rightist Movement (1957).[1] For example, Chen Shouyi simply mentions the achievements of the 1954 constitution and the revival of jurisprudence around 1956. Other scholars have mostly centered their research on the political campaigns, abuses of law, and labor camps in this period, and they do not heed the Party's shift of policy toward lenience

1 With the exception of the 1954 constitution, He Qinghua and Gong Pixiang do not mention the legal development and practice from 1954 to early 1957 at all. See He Qinghua何清华, *A History of Chinese Jurisprudence* (*Zhongguo faxue shigang*中国法学史纲) (Beijing: Shangwu yinshuguan, 2012): 378-379; Gong Pixiang, 1999: 125-186.

Fang, Qiang, *The Communist Judicial System in China, 1927-1976: Building on Fear.* Taylor & Francis Group 2021
DOI: 10.5117/9789463729451_CH05

and legal professionalism in 1956 and 1957.[2] There are some scholars who tend to regard the legal developments between 1953 and 1957 as consistent and smooth without treating the dynamic policy changes during and after the 1955 anti-counterrevolutionary movement. But they hail the period 1953-1957 as a "Golden Age" during which the Chinese legal system was arguably at its best before 1976.

Hou Songtao wrote in 2008 that the three to four years after the 1952 legal reform were a "Golden Age" in legal construction, which had previously been mainly "propelled" by the "needs" of the Chinese Communist Party (CCP) to consolidate its political power and social reform.[3] In 1999, Xin Chunying asserted that the period from 1954, the promulgation of the PRC (People's Republic of China)'s first constitution and many other laws, to 1957, before the Anti-Rightist Movement, was a short but "golden age in the history of China's construction of its legal system."[4] Like their Chinese colleagues, some Western scholars have implicitly or explicitly praised the period between 1954 and 1957 as a golden age. For instance, as early as 1968, Jerome Cohen argued that the period between the first Five-Year Plan in 1953 and the Anti-Rightist Movement in mid-1957 "may be called with some exaggeration the 'golden age' of law" and a "constitutional era."[5] Jennifer Altehenger, in her recent book on PRC legal propaganda, also points out that in the 1980s the CCP generally believed that its rule including its legal system in the 1950s was "officially the golden age."[6]

In Chapter 4, I have analyzed the 1952-1953 legal reform movement and its political as well as legal ramifications. Unlike what the CCP claimed, the main motive behind the legal reform was to purge and replace most former Nationalist Party (Guomindang, or GMD) judges whose loyalty to the Party was questionable. With new and politically reliable judges who had little legal training presiding in people's courts, case pileup, torture, forced confession, and false trials were exacerbated in many parts of the country. To add several more evidences, in 1953 for instance, prisons in Xikang Province were filled

2 Chen Shouyi陈守一, *A Review of the Thirty-Year Jurisprudance in New China* (*xinzhongguo faxue sanshinian huigu*新中国法学三十年回顾) in *Faxue yanjiu*, 1980, No. 1, pp. 1-10; also see Stanley Lubman, *Bird in a Cage*, 2000: 75-78; Mühlhahn, 2007: 35-48; Dikotter, 1997.

3 Hou Songtao侯松涛, "Retrospect and Thinking of the Legal Reform Movement in the Early PRC (*jianguo chuqide sifa gaige yundong: huigu hesikao*建国初期的司法改革运动)" in *Zhidu jianshe*, Vol. 1, 2009, pp. 93-97: 97.

4 Xin Chunying信春鹰, *Chinese Legal System and its Reform* (*zhongguode falü zhidu jiqi gaige* 中国的法律制度及其改革) (Beijing: Falü chubanshe, 1999): 13-14.

5 Cohen, 1969: 10, 18; also see Lubman, 2000: 76; Peerenboom, 2002: 44.

6 Altehenger, 2018: 227.

with criminals. The Chongqing City Court blamed enormous torture and false punishments on the low quality of new judges. In Yunnan, there were over 10,000 unresolved cases and, in some counties, false judgments were so serious that more than a third of the marriage cases had been wrongly adjudicated. Judges in Shanghai, the largest and most modern city, were no better than those in other provinces. In one case, a capitalist defendant was detained and penalized in late 1953 simply because of his failure to pay workers' wages on time.[7] Those evidences should suffice to prove that in 1953, the year after the legal reform, the legal system had not improved or even deteriorated under newly appointed loyal but unprofessional judges.

Some recent studies have already questioned the idea of a general golden age in the early 1950s, but none of them has done so with a focus on the legal system.[8] In this chapter, I examine the legal practice between 1954 and 1957, a period not only marking a crucial and violent transition of the PRC legal system after the legal reform but also containing a short but tolerant period that could arguably be called a "golden age." First, I explore important laws such as the PRC's first Constitution and the Organic Law of the People's Court (hereinafter OLC) promulgated in 1954. Next, I shall focus on the law and people's courts during the second anti-counterrevolutionary movement initiated in the middle of 1955. Third, I shall examine the remaining months of 1956 and prior to the Anti-Rightist Movement in May 1957. In this period, the failed political reforms in both Poland and Hungary had compelled the CCP to loosen its grip on public criticism. As a result, the judicial system experienced a moderate era from the spring of 1956 to May 1957, which was reminiscent of the period from late 1949 to the summer of 1950.

Constructing Legal Professionalism, 1954-July 1955

1 First Constitution and OLC

For the CCP, 1953 was an important and promising year. Early in the year, the legal reform was almost concluded with Party members, army veterans, and progressive workers and women replacing retained GMD judges who were politically unreliable. In April, vice chairman Chen Yun drafted a plan of the Soviet-style strategic Five-Year Plan, albeit, as Ezra Vogel argues, the official

7 See Chapter 4 for information about the people's court in post-legal-reform China.
8 See Brown and Pickowicz, 2007.

content of the first Five-Year Plan was not revealed until 1955.[9] In July, both sides of the Korean War signed an armistice as a first step toward ending a prolonged and bloody war. Thanks to a relatively peaceful political situation and growing self-confidence after the war, the CCP began enacting several crucial laws in 1954 such as a constitution and the OLC to embrace law.

The most notable accomplishment of this period was PRC's first constitution passed by the National People's Congress (NPC) on September 20, 1954. On September 17, Peng Zhen, head of the *Zheng-fa* system at the Politburo, in the words of Pitman Potter, announced a plan to transform the PRC from Leninist discipline to socialist legalism[10] He accordingly emphasized the supremacy of law and the importance of equality before law of all citizens, including commoners and big officials who had served the Party in the past. Both principles – of the supremacy of law and the equality before the law – were later incorporated into the constitution and the OLC.[11]

The 1954 constitution claimed that the polity of the PRC was led by the proletariat and based on a coalition of workers and peasants. The legislative power belonged to the NPC, which could not only pass and interpret laws but also supervise the routine work of the State Council, the Supreme Court, and the Supreme Procuracy. More important, the constitution embraced key and universal notions of the rule of law. Article 78, for example, noted that the people's court should make judgments independently and follow nothing but the law. Article 85 recognized that all citizens were equal before the law. Other important provisions of the constitution required the people's court to adopt legal systems and institutions such as the people's jury, public trials, and lawyers. Without approval from the court and procuracy, no citizen could be arrested and citizens' personal freedom was inviolable.[12]

Many scholars agree that the 1954 constitution was patterned after the 1936 Soviet constitution. Gong Pixiang remarks that many parts of the General Principles, State Organs, and People's Rights and Duties were clearly copied from the Soviet constitution.[13] Altehenger argues that the PRC constitution was adapted from the 1936 Soviet constitution and other Eastern European constitutions. No sooner did the draft of the constitution

9 Ezra F. Vogel, *Canton under Communism: Programs and Politics in a Provincial Capital, 1949-1968* (Cambridge, Ma: Harvard University Press, 1980): 134.

10 Potter, 2003: 6-7.

11 Peng Zhen彭真, *Selected Works of Peng Zhen* (*Peng Zhen wenji*彭真文集) (Beijing: Renmin chubanshe, 1991): 255-269.

12 The Constitution of the PRC, September 20, 1954. http://www.npc.gov.cn/wxzl/wxzl/2000-12/26/content_4264.htm

13 Gong Pixiang, 1999: 165; also see Xin Chunying, 1999: 13.

come out than the CCP launched a campaign to promote it. Within a month, "close to 12 million copies of the law were published." In addition, the Party directed local Party committees to set up "constitution draft discussion committees in an effort to strengthen the "masses' patriotism." Anyone who questioned or criticized the constitution would be "quickly labeled class enemies."[14]

Another vital law, which passed one day after the constitution, was the OLC that specifically stated the roles, principles, and procedures of the people's court, which in many aspects were drastically different from its precursor in late 1951.[15] Like the constitution, Article 4 of the OLC reiterated judicial freedom from meddling by any government, social organization, or person. The law also endorsed public trials, people's juries, and defense lawyers. Defendants could defend themselves or ask lawyers to act on their behalf. This was important because the institution of attorneys was still embryonic at this time and qualified lawyers were few. All first-instance trials except minor civil and light criminal cases had to be jointly discussed and decided by judges and jurors. Lastly, the law stressed equality before the law with no regard to citizens' nationality, race, gender, profession, social status, or religion and no person had any special legal privileges.[16]

To be sure, the sincerity of the claims in both the OLC and the constitution that every citizen was equal before the law was rather questionable from the beginning. In June 1954, less than three months before the constitution and the OLC became effective, the Shanghai People's Court, apparently with the approval of the municipal government, issued a regulation allowing preferential treatment of whomever the CCP deemed to be important people or groups. The regulation stated that district court leaders could decide ordinary criminal cases with fixed-term sentences (*youqi tuxing*). Life or death sentences had to be sent to and approved by the district head or district Party secretary. The regulation said that if law was violated by any member of eight groups, the case should be sent first to either the military court (for volunteer army and PLA members) or the appropriate district government before it could be submitted to the municipal government for review. The eight privileged groups were: 1) Party and Communist youth members; 2) volunteer army and PLA; 3) cadres of governments, state-run enterprises, democratic parties, social organizations; 4) democratic party

14 Altehenger, 2018: 131-143.

15 See Chapter 3 for the Interim Organic Regulations of the People's Court.

16 1954 Organic Law of the Court, Tianjin People's Court, ed., "A Judicial Handbook (*sifa gongzuo shouce*司法工作手册)," November 1954.

members and people's representatives; 5) senior technicians or staff in private companies; 6) principals of elementary schools, teachers of middle schools and above; 7) renowned cultural people or performers and influential people in education, culture, and art circles; 8) important religious and minority leaders.[17] In October, a central law expanded the Shanghai regulation by requiring the death penalty for crimes against median-rank officials and important people such as college professors, engineers, renowned business, religious, and democratic party leaders, all individual cases to be determined by the central government.[18]

The preferential treatment of eight special groups of people in a Shanghai regulation endorsed by central law was strikingly reminiscent of the Eight Considerations, a covert or overt practice of law favoring certain privileged persons in most Chinese polities that could hark back to as early as the Warring States Era and was epitomized in the Tang Code.[19] Legal privileges for certain groups of people, especially members of the ruling class or minority nationalities, continued into the Qing period.[20] Although the regulation was supposed to be only "temporary" and the ensuing OLC renounced any legal privileges, such discriminatory practices persisted in Mao's China and beyond.[21]

2 Law Enforcement and Practice

Promulgating laws is one thing, enforcing them is another. Through recorded history, many if not most Chinese rulers failed to comply with laws even if some of them were aware that legitimate authority should take precedence over superior power.[22] The CCP leaders have certainly been no better enforcers of PRC laws than other erstwhile rulers. While both the constitution and the OLC championed judicial independence, impartial law, and certain legal systems and procedures, the actual practice of law in many people's

17 Archives of the Shanghai People's Court, June, 1954. B24-2-21.

18 *Comprehensive Gazette of Tianjin – Adjudicating Gazette* (*Tianjin tongzhi-shenpanzhi*天津通志-审判志) (Tianjin: Tianjin shehui kexueyuan chubanshe, 1999): 198.

19 Zeng Bingjun曾炳军, "The Eight Considerations in China's Feudal Criminal Law (*zhongguo fengjian xinglu zhongde bayi*中国封建刑律中的八议)" in *Faxue yanjiu*, 1981, Vol. 2, pp. 51-52; for the original law of *bayi* see Xue Yunsheng薛允升, *A Combination of The Tang and Ming Codes* (*tangminglu hebian*唐明律合编) (Beijing: Falü chubanshe, 1999): 3-4.

20 For legal privileges in the Qing see Pär Cassel, 2003: 156-180; Elliott, 2001: 198, 231.

21 For legal privileges in Mao's China see Chapter 6 on the 1957 Anti-Rightist Movement. The legal privilege of elites continues to exist in China today. See Fang and Li, 2017.

22 See Ibid., 2017: Introduction.

courts from 1954 to early 1955, the supposed "golden age" of PRC law, was not satisfactory.

In a summary report on judicial work in October 1954, the State Council pointed out some of the main achievements as well as some of the shortcomings of the people's court. The report first stated that all levels of the judicial system should serve the country in safeguarding economic construction and socialist transformation. In 1954, most cases were related to the economy. For example, in the first nine months of the year, all courts had accepted a total of 158,972 economic cases, 62% more than in 1953 and 115% more than in the previous year. The cause was the speedy development of state companies and industries that provided counterrevolutionaries, hoodlums, thieves, and some uneducated workers with good opportunities to sabotage and steal. In Shanghai, Tianjin, and Shenyang, resolved cases entailing economic crimes jumped around 11-15% and most criminals were unlawful capitalists. The State Council complimented the circuit courts, which were especially welcomed by peasants and township cadres for their convenience and accessibility. Because of their popularity, the number of circuit courts skyrocketed from 600 in early 1954 to 3795 by the year end. Equally fast-growing were the people's mediators and jurors who numbered over one million and 104,119 respectively, though many judges disrespected and/or refused to use jurors, an infringement of the provisions of the OLC.[23] Finally, the report noted that some judicial cadres still used torture to extract confessions, a practice that violated human rights and alienated the masses. Instead of telling local courts to punish law-breaking cadres, however, the State Council simply called for ameliorating cadres' political thought.[24]

Unlike the State Council's moderate summary, some local judicial reports were grimmer and more hostile to targeted classes. On April 30, 1954, the Shanghai Party Committee sent a directive to the judicial cadres of the city ordering them to heavily punish historical counterrevolutionaries without regard to the law. In its words, "All jobless but harmful [to social security] former hardened thieves, robbers, thugs, landlords, GMD officials, inspectors, and gendarmes should normally be sentenced to long-term labor camp even though their crimes are not serious." The directive stressed that district courts should be under the leadership of district Party committees and should report frequently to local party and government units. All grave cases

23 Article 36 of the OLC wrote that people's jurors had the same right as the judges. http://www.npc.gov.cn/wxzl/wxzl/2000-12/10/content_4267.htm

24 Shanghai Archives, August 8, 1955. B1-2-071-1697.

and unclear political problems should be reported to local governments.[25] Four months before promulgation of the constitution and the OLC, local Party officials still believed that the Party was above the law, consistent with the legal reform in 1952.

In October 1954, a report of the Shanghai Political and Legal Committee (*Zhengfawei*), which was in charge of the judicial system, stated that in the first nine months of the year it had taken a long stride forward by arresting 21,165 counterrevolutionaries and 10,171 violators of social security, already surpassing the goal of the whole year. Additionally, all courts had settled 68,914 cases, 4000 more than they had received up to October. The biggest problem of the courts was that many judges could hardly discern the line between counterrevolutionaries and breakers of social security and between migrants and criminals. As a result, the court had been unable to effect appropriate punishments. This report urged judicial cadres to learn about and propagate the new constitution and to understand that democratic development was a process designed to oppose privileged thought (*tequan sixiang*) as well as violations of the law.[26]

If the report of the Shanghai *Zhengfawei* was shy about the real problems within the judicial system, a summary of a local district court may allow us to pinpoint the problems more limpidly. On December 25, 1954, the annual review of the Shanghai Shuishang (lit. above water) District Court highlighted several errors made in the year. First, some judges cared more about the number of resolved cases than about the quality of the investigation into them. In counterrevolutionary cases, some judges assumed that the police had already interrogated the suspects and that there was no need for any further investigations. Even when judges discovered discrepancies between police reports and other documents, they often chose to end the cases anyway rather than conducting their own investigations. In addition, the *Zhengfawei* report seems to contradict a report of the Shanghai High Court on December 1, 1955, which said that before 1954, the police had been responsible for investigating counterrevolutionary cases, but starting from 1954 and before July 1955 the police were no longer involved in counterrevolutionary cases. Based on the crucial role and status of the police in the early PRC, we have reason to believe that the *Zhengfawei* report was more convincing and the police might have kept their power and duties in counterrevolutionary cases in 1954.[27]

25 Ibid., April 30, 1954. A38-2-9.

26 Ibid., October 21, 1954. A6-1-1.

27 Ibid., December 1, 1955. B2-1-14-36.

Another problem was that the punishments of certain thieves and counterrevolutionaries were not harsh enough because the boundaries between penalties were not clear. A third problem was judges' disrespect for defendants' rights and the continued use of torture and enticement by some judges to obtain confessions. Instead of making sufficient preparations before a trial, some judges merely used "reprimand and punish (*xun he zheng*训和整)" in trials and rarely or never considered defendants' views. In one case, for instance, a judge pressured a defendant named Shen Jinbao by repeatedly reminding him that he had "historical problems" (i.e. had been a GMD member or Republican official) rather than using persuasion to encourage him to tell the truth. Cornered and infuriated, Shen mounted resistance and refused to confess. The review also admitted that there were serious delays in the resolution of cases. Some cases lasted for over six months.[28] As I have argued in previous chapters, CCP's policy toward torture was not consistent despite the Party's claims of being against it.[29] Neither the new constitution nor the OLC mentioned torture, let alone banned it. In that regard, the new Communist judges could continue to use torture as most of them lacked legal education and training.

The district court's review of the problems of judges was corroborated by a report of the Shanghai People's Court on May 27, 1955. The report sharply denounced some judges' carelessness and dilatoriness in tackling cases. To cite one case, after one boatman's little finger was injured in a brawl, he sued the injurer to the local court. Yet the court had neglected the case for two years until the frustrated plaintiff asked the court in 1954 to drop the suit because his wounded finger had recovered, and he also did not want to pay the bus fares to go to the court. Due to extremely tardy trials, many suspects had to stay in prison for a long time awaiting a trial. Desperate and furious, some of them vented their anger to the government through noisy disturbances (*dachao danao*). Moreover, falsely charged prisoners and cases were rather prevalent. According to a prison account in Shanghai, more than 800 people had been wrongly judged or detained in 1954.[30]

In late 1954, at the request of the Supreme Court and the Ministry of Justice, the Shanghai People's Court held a judicial forum, which demanded that the people's court serve the CCP's ongoing missions of economic

28 Ibid., December 25, 1954. A80-2-18.

29 On September 21, 1956, Luo Ruiqin, Minister of Public Security, asserted that the CCP had always strictly opposed torture because torture could only make more mistakes and could not defeat enemies. See *Jiefang Daily*, September 21, 1956.

30 Shanghai Archives, May 27, 1955. B2-2-5-27.

construction and class struggle. That was an implicit abrogation of judicial impartiality. Regarding the question whether the law should be impartial and the court independent, the report clarified that only Communist China and not capitalist countries would have real equality before the law. When some cadres were baffled about the contradiction between independent adjudication and Party leadership, the report argued that, to better embody people's will and socialism, the people's court had to abide by Party policies and state laws. Therefore, the court should be under the leadership of the Party because "the independent judgment of the court does not mean that no one can control the court."[31] This report effectively undercut judicial independence ensured by the constitution and the OLC. It further indicates that the CCP did not intend to fulfill its constitutional pledges. That was not surprising because even Peng Zhen who played a "significant role in the post-Mao legal reform," insisted in the early 1950s that law should be subordinated to the Party.[32]

In early 1954, the Shanghai government had criticized many judges for prosecuting historical counterrevolutionaries more relentlessly than active counterrevolutionaries. Yet that problem was not solved because in February 1955 the Shanghai government again raised the same issue. Moreover, the government argued that some judges had no idea how to deal with capitalists. In some cases, judges treated capitalists leniently for the sake of the united front; in others, they would be harsher and criminalized capitalists for their normal withdrawal of funds. In conclusion, the government said that the judicial strike against enemies was not strong enough.[33]

The Shanghai government may have been right to allege that the court was lenient to capitalists in some cases. To cite one case, on January 16, 1954, the Shanghai Songshan District Court ruled on a dispute between a capitalist and his workers. A group of laid-off laborers sued the businessman Zhou Changlin to obtain unpaid wages. A judge rejected the workers' suit and sided with a previous decision of the labor bureau that asked the workers to understand the difficulty and inability of Zhou's company to pay them. Unlike in 1953, when judges could detain capitalists for failing to pay wages, the judge in 1954 tended to "understand" the capitalists' situation with more sympathy.[34]

31 Ibid., December 25, 1954. B2-2-5-20.

32 Potter, 2003: 64.

33 Shanghai Archives, February-April 19, 1955. A6-1-38.

34 Shanghai Songshanqu People's Court Verdicts, January 16, 1954. B128-2-1160-244.

However, if a capitalist committed any crimes, the court could still be relentless in punishing him or her. For example, in early 1954, workers in the Beiyang Glass Factory, together with the Jingan District Tax Bureau and the Shanghai Labor Bureau, lodged a collective suit against Jiang Geng, the former factory manager, in the municipal court. The plaintiffs alleged that Jiang's reckless mismanagement had resulted in the layoffs of forty workers in just two months. To cover the loss, Jiang resorted to fraud and blank checks that helped him swindle materials worth over 100 million *yuan*. By early 1954, the factory owed a total debt of 600 million *yuan*. Afraid of being punished, Jiang absconded. That abruptly halted factory production and aggravated the workers' plight. A judge decided that Jiang's actions were "extremely bad and should be harshly penalized." Jiang was arrested by the police, convicted by the court, sentenced to three years of imprisonment, and ordered to sell the factory to pay workers' wages and benefits.[35] With no civil law to conform to, the judge had to adjudicate using his "common sense" according to his own temperament.

If some judges expressed mercy to capitalists for the sake of the united front prior to the completion of socialist transformation in 1956, it would not be surprising that other judges treated workers less leniently. According to a report of the Shanghai People's Court in late May 1955, judges in at least one district court were inclined to impose heavier penalties on workers because, as the leadership of the PRC, workers should bear more punishment. In one case, after an employer had mistreated his apprentice, the apprentice beat and injured his employer, claiming self-defense. But a judge only trusted the employer's complaints about the poor performance of the apprentice and sentenced the apprentice to six months. While the ruling was corrected by an appellate court, it suggests that some judges were more likely to find fault with the workers at a time of relatively cordial state-capital relations.[36]

As the largest city in the PRC, Shanghai arguably had more qualified judges than most, if not all, other cities in this period. If judges in Shanghai courts violated laws or enforced laws haphazardly and unevenly, we can imagine that judges in smaller and more remote cities or counties might be even less professional. To cite one case, Chen Zhiqun, a former GMD member, became a teacher in a Guangdong elementary school after the CCP took power. In 1951, he lost his job for his past counterrevolutionary experience. In 1954, when the government tried to purchase grain from peasants, Chen allegedly "distorted" the government policy and said that

35 Shanghai Archives, October 7, 1954. B128-2-1076-165.

36 Shanghai People's Court, A80-2-297, May 27, 1955.

the government would "purchase" the grain but not actually pay for it. For that "rumor," Chen was sentenced by a county court to two years of forced control (*guanzhi*),[37] which was tantamount to working in a labor camp.[38]

3 Judicial Problems in Spring 1955

The practice of law or of the judicial system in the first half of 1955 was not much different from what it had been in 1954. On May 27, 1955, an internal report of the Shanghai Municipal Court on judges' implementation of policy and style of judging disclosed massive and sometimes shockingly unlawful and improper activities. The first problem was that some judges erroneously believed that only bad men would appear in court and accordingly inflicted punishment arbitrarily and unfairly. For instance, a young peasant who had no money to watch a street magic show took one of his brother's sweaters to sell. The local police detained him and accused him of theft. A court judge sentenced him to two years in prison without further investigation. One district court head in Shanghai even said that all persons with historical crimes should be imprisoned three years regardless of whether they had harmed people. Another problem was judges' failure to apply the laws evenly in similar cases. In divorce cases, some judges would approve a divorce if the marriage had been arranged and disapprove if it had been a free marriage. In cases of theft, judges were counterintuitively lenient toward hardened thieves but stringent on casual thieves driven by hunger and poverty. The report mentioned a case in which a peasant was sentenced to hard labor for stealing two pieces of clothing for his children to protect them from the cold weather.[39]

In addition, the court condemned some judges for their arrogance and privileged thought. A few district courts failed to respect their superiors and "seldom reported to the Party committee" because it was deemed to be

37 According to a judicial officer working at a government prison, both *guanzhi* and *laojiao* (started in 1957) are meant to punish working class people and not class enemies. The term of *guanzhi* normally is one to two years and the term of *laojiao* ranges from one to three years. Criminals sentenced to either of them will be sent to separate locations to do forced work with low compensations. The difference of the two is that *guanzhi* normally will be decided by police while *laojiao* has to be made by court. But in the 1950s, court often made decisions on *guanzhi*. Interview with a cadre at a provincial prison in central China. For the case of Chen, the month and date of the case were not mentioned in the case, see *Guangdong sifa tongxun*广东司法通讯, August 18, 1956, pp. 1-6; for the origin of *laojiao* see Hongda H. Wu, *Laogai: The Chinese Gulag* (Boudler: Westview Press, 1992): 17.

38 Dikotter, 1997: 149.

39 Shanghai People's Court, A80-2-297, May 27, 1955.

"troublesome [and] unnecessary" or because "the Party committee did not know the law." Other judges looked down upon judges from other cities and colleagues in the same court. Ironically, although the recent constitution and the OLC championed judicial independence, the report blamed some judges for their "fallacious belief that the court should make decisions independently so adjudication would be a lot easier [without the need to report to the Party committee]." This report suggests that the CCP from its very inception had no sincere intention to implement the constitution or to establish judicial independence. Some fundamental problems such as random detainments, indiscriminate incarceration, torture, and enticed confessions remained in 1954 and 1955. Believing in the "presumption of guilt" rather than the "presumption of innocence," some judges did not mind how many days a defendant had been in custody and some even felt "proud" to arrest people. One judge even used detainment as leverage to get information and solve cases, a violation of legal process.[40]

In Chapter 4, I have discussed the rampant torture during the 1952-1953 legal reform. This problem persisted beyond the reform. With neither criminal procedural law nor any conspicuous ban of torture in the constitution, many judges, like their counterparts in the past, counted on various forms of torture to extract confessions. The internal report of the Shanghai court entailed several cases of using torture and other illegal means in trials. One judge at the Zhabei district court used a trial to grill a defendant who had violated a local commercial law. The judge interrogated the defendant for a long time until he became so exhausted that he fell to the ground and hurt himself. In mediation cases, to force both parties to accept a mediation or to discourage them from appealing to the court, some court mediators/judges warned that the court ruling "would be the same as mediation." One judge went so far as to forbid both parties from going home before they accepted a mediation.

In some cases, it was not uncommon for judges to abuse litigants or to deprive them of their rights to appeal to appellate courts. One judge reportedly tried to prohibit litigants from speaking; another judge cursed his litigants as "profiteers, shrews, or bastards." When one disgruntled defendant attempted to appeal to an upper-level court, the judge thwarted him. One appeal to upper-level courts had been delayed by a lower court for more than six months, a brazen violation of legal process. To avoid trouble, a few judges chose to conceal the appellants' files in archives and refused

40 Ibid.

to send them to upper-level courts as the law required.[41] To discourage appeals, some district courts would use such pretexts as "the complaint letters were too long" or "the pencil-written appeal could not be accepted." In conclusion, the internal report admitted that the problems inside the courts were serious. According to one judicial cadre, had the inspection not been conducted in time the court per se would have become a venue full of law violators. Therefore, the report urged courts to implement the OLC and to strengthen democratic thought as well as legal principles among cadres.[42] It was contradictory and rather absurd for the internal court report to call on cadres to enforce the OLC while at the same time criticized some judges' "erroneous thought" of judicial independence, a core legal concept of the OLC.

In the spring of 1955, judges seemed to lean more toward supporting workers, though some of them were rather lenient toward businessmen. For example, on April 29, 1955, the Shanghai Jiangning District Court resolved a case in which a capitalist named Huang Xianzhong was accused by four workers of postponing the payment of wages. After Huang's hardware company had plunged into financial trouble, the workers had voluntarily proposed to cut their wages to help him to overcome the difficulties. When Huang refused to compromise and insisted he could not afford to pay any wages, the workers sued him in court. Without citing any laws, a judge ruled that Huang should be punished for his "mistake" of doing nothing to improve his business. The judge was aware of the inability of Huang's company to pay wages, however, and he ruled that Huang had committed "no crime." The judge finally sentenced Huang to four months in prison "for his error" and put him on probation for six months. Two workers were laid off to lessen the burden on Huang. This case suggests that the 1953 precedent of a penalty for capitalists who failed to pay workers' wages may have influenced the resolution of this case in 1955.

In both 1954 and the spring of 1955, there was a disparity in judges' treatments of capitalists in civil cases, but it was rare in criminal cases, especially those involving counterrevolutionaries. For example, after Ge Xionghua, a young worker at Shanghai Bike Factory, got a low score on his job evaluation in June 1953, he was furious. He vented his anger at his unit head by destroying machines and tools, resulting in a halt to production for

41 In the early PRC, most court verdicts would indicate that unsatisfied litigants could appeal to the appellate courts within ten days.

42 Shanghai Archives, May 27, 1955. A80-2-297.

two weeks. As with many civil case rulings in this period, the court did not cite any current laws and simply sentenced Ge to three years in prison.[43]

In another criminal case, judges at the Shanghai Zhenru District Court in April 1955 made a similar decision on the basis of government policies and personal reasons, not of law. The prosecutor of the case was a local policeman and the accused were Chen Baocheng and Duan Yugao. Duan was a former GMD soldier and interim unit head. Between 1952 and 1954, Chen had stolen about 250 pounds of copper and sold it for 500 *yuan*. He used the money to buy himself apartments and gold rings. But the state suffered a "big loss" of property and prosecuted Chen for theft. Invoking no law, the judge sentenced Chen to seven years and Duan to two years "in order to reform them."[44] In this case, while the second anti-counterrevolutionary campaign had yet to start, the court decision ostensibly considered the "historical crimes" (i.e. GMD membership) of both Chen and Duan that was in line with the CCP's longtime judicial policy dating back to the Jiangxi Soviet base.

The review of the PRC legislation, the Party's legal policies, and judicial practice from 1954 to the spring of 1955 tells us that the passage of important laws like the 1954 constitution and the OLC did not mean that the general legal situation after the 1952-1953 legal reform had improved. On the one hand, many judges, if not most, in China's largest and wealthiest city continued to abuse litigants, violate laws, and impose punishment at will. To obtain confessions from defendants, some judges still used unlawful torture or enticements. The CCP, on the other hand, exposed its hypocrisy as it required judges to report to and obey the leadership of local Party committees regardless of the principle of judicial independence pledged by both the 1954 constitution and the OLC. In that regard, the practice of law in this period of the PRC was little different from that in the post-legal reform era and therefore should not be called a golden age.

The Judicial System in a Political Storm, June 1955-May 1956

1 A Second Anti-counterrevolutionary Campaign

After establishing the PRC, central leaders generally maintained an amiable relationship among themselves and there was no major split in the Party. But

43 Shanghai Archives, June, 1954. A80-2-297.
44 Shanghai Archives, April, 1955. B108-2-29.

starting from late 1953, Gao Gang, the "Czar of Manchuria" whose excellent logistical efforts allowed China's army to continue its war in Korea until the end,[45] had lost the favor of Mao. Mao criticized Gao for his "unprincipled factionalism." In the summer of 1954, a frustrated Gao ended his life with a gun.[46] In the spring of that year, the Party Central had denounced both Gao and his "collaborator" Rao Shuoshi who led the Party in the Shanghai region as the "Gao-Rao anti-Party conspiracy," marking the first major split among the leaders of the CCP.[47]

In the fall, Hu Feng, a renowned writer and executive member of the Chinese Writers' Union, wrote a long letter to Party leaders calling for more freedom for writers and artists. The timing of Hu's letter could not have been less propitious as Party leaders were still purging cadres linked with Gao Gang. Before long, therefore, the Party launched a full-fledged attack on Hu and his associates. In the late spring of 1955, the witch-hunt escalated, and Hu was denounced as a counterrevolutionary. He was subsequently imprisoned until 1978. In the process, many of his friends and associates were "thoroughly discussed and assailed."[48]

When the summer came, the Party, haunted by fears of alleged enemies who were either internal "followers of Gao Gang" or external threats from the GMD in Taiwan (the 1954-1955 Taiwan Strait Crisis),[49] decided to launch a sweeping anti-counterrevolutionary campaign.[50] This campaign lasted until the spring of 1956 during which tens of thousands of people were reportedly detained and punished. In Canton, every government and Party unit was ordered to select at least 5% of its cadres as targets for further investigation. As a result, 34,670 targets were investigated in Guangdong province alone and among them 3670 (more than 10%) were pronounced to be counterrevolutionaries.[51] In Shanghai, a government report claimed that from the first quarter of 1955 through early 1957, over 4643

45 For the details of Gao Gang's role in the Korean War see Dai Maolin戴茂林 and Zhao Xiaoguang赵晓光, *A Biography of Gang Gang* (*Gao Gangzhuan*高岗传) (Shanxi: Shanxi Renmin chubanshe, 2016).

46 Short, 2000: 443-444.

47 Maurice Meisner, *Mao's China and After: A History of the People's Republic* (New York: The Free Press, 1999): 122.

48 Vogel, 1980: 135-136; also See Short, 2000: 454 and Meisner, 1999: 123-124.

49 For a detailed study on the Taiwan Strait Crisis see Bennett C. Rushkoff, "Eisenhower, Dulles and the Quemoy-Matsu Crisis, 1955-1955" in *The Political Science Quarterly*, Vol. 96, No. 3 (Autumn, 1981), pp. 465-480.

50 Meisner, 1999: 123. For the rising number of GMD agents who sneaked into mainland China see Shanghai Archives, January 3, 1957. B1-1-646.

51 Vogel, 1969: 136.

counterrevolutionaries and other criminals had surrendered to the government.[52] Between mid-1955 and early 1956, the Guangxi judicial system had dealt with 7704 counterrevolutionary cases in which 5751 criminals or 72.96% were served penalties ranging from over five years imprisonment to death.[53] According to Michael Schoenhals, the Party was so nervous about potential sabotage that it conducted a massive "Internal Elimination of Counterrevolutionaries," which assessed 18.5 million CCP and non-CCP personnel in a search for "GMD sleeper agents" or other enemies.[54]

Being a crucial weapon in the CCP's arsenal, the judicial system again acted as a "fear extinguisher" (i.e. defender of the state) in a political campaign whose mission was to violently assault counterrevolutionaries, further undermining legal principles such as judicial independence and due process. Just two months earlier, Fu Lei, a famous translator and member of the Shanghai Political Consultative Conference, had proposed a bill, noble but now anachronistic, suggesting that all Shanghai courts preserve their independence and focus only on the facts in handling cases, regardless of litigants' nationalities, classes, and properties.[55]

2 Toughening Court Policies

The campaign against counterrevolutionaries in 1955 and 1956 was triggered by the Gao Gang allegedly "anti-party" incident and deepened by Hu Feng's "counterrevolutionary" criticism of Party literary policy. On June 15, 1955, Mao blamed the arrogance and numbness of the revolutionaries for the infiltration of many counterrevolutionaries into the CCP. He pointed out that the only positive lesson of the Hu Feng incident was to "greatly enhance our [Communists] political consciousness and keenness, firmly repress all counterrevolutionaries, and consolidate our revolutionary dictatorship" through the ongoing "hair-raising (*jingxin dongpo*)" anti-counterrevolutionary campaign.[56] The new campaign against counterrevolutionaries occurred

52 "Report of the Shanghai People's Committee (Shanghai renmin weiyuanhui baogao)" in Shanghai Archives, B1-1-646, January 3, 1957.

53 *Guangxi difangzhi bianzuan weiyuanhui*广西地方志编纂委员会, *Gaungxi Gazette: The Adjudicatiion* (*Guangxi tongzhi*: *shenpanzhi*广西通志：审判志) (Guangxi: Guangxi renmin chubanshe, 2000): 197-198.

54 Michael Schoenhals, "The Intelligence Sleeper Who Never Was: Han Fuyin and Case 5004" in Leese and Engman, 2018, pp. 52-74: 53.

55 For Fu Lei's proposed bill see Shanghai Archives, L1-1-71-13. May 1955.

56 Mao Zedong毛泽东, "Introduction and Notes of Materials Regarding Hu Feng Counterrevolutionary Clique (*guanyu Hu Feng fangeming jituan decailiao de xuyan heanyu*关于胡风反

in the context of a crisis in the Taiwan straits and the PRC's first Five-Year Plan that aimed to speed up the socialist transformation. Mao and the Party might have hoped that the campaign could help minimize capitalist resistance and facilitate socialist transformation.[57]

In June 1955, the Ministry of Justice required all courts to closely collaborate with the procuracy and police in assaulting and eliminating counterrevolutionaries and other criminals.[58] At the beginning of the campaign, many judges continued to treat class enemies and criminals with lenience and did not take the Party's latest order seriously. This soon drew sharp criticism from the Party. Between July 10 and 12, the Shanghai High Court held a forum to study the directives of the Shanghai Party Committee. The forum reaffirmed the judicial system's role as one of the primary weapons of the people's dictatorship whose "spearhead" had to target counterrevolutionaries and criminals. But many judges still did not severely penalize class enemies and criminals. Moreover, contrary to the 1954 constitution and the OLC, the district court leaders told judges not to cite laws ("blindly") or deviate from Party policy (i.e. class struggle).[59] In other words, judges would be granted the discretion to sentence defendants to whatever punishments they liked. The right-leaning tendency among judges did not exist in Shanghai alone. It could be found in many other places as well. For example, a 1956 report of the Guangdong High Court admitted that the right-leaning deviation had persisted acutely for two months after the campaign against counterrevolutionaries had started in June 1955 and up to August of that year.[60]

Having been repeatedly censured by their superiors in the summer, "right-leaning" judges were forced to harden their stance against counterrevolutionaries. Lest others find fault with their lenience, many of them vied to inflict harsher penalties for minor, even trivial, offenses that could be construed as counterrevolutionary. On August 8, 1955, the State Council demanded that all judicial departments obey certain important orders. The first order required judicial and administrative cadres to implement the OLC and strengthen judicial thought, organization, and system so as to "guarantee economic development and socialist transformation and protect citizens' rights and lawful interests." The State Council also asked

革命集团的材料的序言和按语)" in *Selected Works of Mao* (Beijing: Renmin chubanshe, 1977): 5.160-167.

57 Vogel, 1969: 134-164.

58 Shanghai Archives, March 16, 1956. B2-2-41.

59 Ibid., July 10-12, 1955. B2-2-54.50-20; also see Shanghai Archives, December 17, 1955. B1-1-598-1.

60 Guangdong Provincial Archives, February 25, 1956. 250-1-28-1-10.

the judicial system to stringently punish all counterrevolutionaries and other criminals who "have disrupted and damaged rural cooperatives and public security." In the meantime, judges should "strictly" protect citizens' rights and lawful interests as described by the constitution and other laws. Finally, the State Council asked judicial cadres to learn Soviet legal practice and gradually enforce the formal legal process.[61] Obviously, the State Council saw no contradiction between "protecting citizens' rights" and harshly punishing class enemies as it believed that counterrevolutionaries or other class enemies were not citizens and thus there was no need to protect their rights under the aegis of the constitution. This was dangerous because in a political campaign even "good" citizens could easily be labeled and punished as counterrevolutionaries for merely speaking one "wrong" word or making one minor "mistake."

Prior to the OLC, it had been police and not courts that had interrogated criminals. Judges had based their decisions solely on police reports without bothering to meet with suspects. After the passage of the OLC in 1954, the court from then until May 1955 was supposed to carry out interrogations and render verdicts in accordance with the OLC. The police were now supposed to detain suspects and conduct preliminary interrogations, while the procuracy would make formal arrests and indictments.

In the summer of 1955, as the anti-counterrevolutionary campaign was deepening and expanding, the police in three Shanghai districts once again retrieved their old authority to interrogate suspects with the courts relegated to being puppets. By the end of the year, eight more districts followed suit. Consequently, the police would be in charge of most counterrevolutionary cases including arrest, interrogation, and punishment. According to a report of the Shanghai High Court, only about 7% of cases in this period that had undergone police preliminary interrogation would be transferred to the court, 0.2% were convicted by the procuracy, and 1% of cases would be tried publicly. In general, there were just two court verdicts: one did not specify the crimes and the other briefly mentioned them. With the police in charge, the courts in sixteen districts were unable to adjudicate any cases between January and October in 1955. To make sure that judges would be tough on class enemies, the Shanghai High Court even preset the number of counterrevolutionaries to be arrested during the first Five-Year Plan. From 1953 to 1955, each year the court should detain 40,000 counterrevolutionaries. The number would jump to 50,000 in 1956 due to the ongoing political storm and be slashed to 30,000 in 1957 when the campaign

61 Shanghai Archives, August 8, 1955. B1-2-071-1697.

receded. In the first nine months of 1955, Shanghai courts had already captured almost 40,000 people and settled 42,179 counterrevolutionary and other criminal cases. In the fourth quarter, the high court predicted that 7000 more counterrevolutionaries should be arrested based on recent district reports on mounting counterrevolutionary actions such as, inter alia, shouting reactionary slogans, stealthily cutting wires, sabotaging production, and writing reactionary banners.[62]

It may be inferred that if the preset number of arrests could not be reached, the court might have to detain people randomly so as to attain the quota. Despite enormous numbers of preset arrests of counterrevolutionaries and despite the fact that only few cases had gone through regular legal process, the high court, ironically or hypocritically, still ordered the police to show warrants of arrest in detaining any person, the procuracy to make indictment, the court to have open trial and adjudication, and defendants to have the right to appeal. It is highly plausible that the high court, like the State Council, did not think that counterrevolutionaries had legal rights.

In July 1955, when Shanghai leaders were scolding some judges for their right-leaning lenience toward class enemies, the police of the Jiangning District detained one Li Baogui, a progressive activist who had been falsely convicted as a "counterrevolutionary and bad element" based on documents fabricated by a household register. After the file went to the district court, judges were credulous of the police charge and sentenced Li to ten years of hard labor rather than conducting a serious investigation. Li's sister kept on appealing to the Shanghai Intermediate Court, which turned her down and sent Li to Xinjiang's labor camp where, in the words of Mühlhahn, only "very few inmates" could eventually return home.[63]

If violations of citizens' constitutional rights and legal process by law enforcers were overt in Shanghai, many other provinces and cities would find similar or even worse and bolder law infringements. Not only would people with historical crimes become an easy prey in the campaign, but people who had inadvertently said or done "bad things" would suffer severe penalties as well. For example, Zhang Keli from Foshan, Guangdong, was a former GMD party member and the vice head of a battalion. In the early PRC, Zhang allegedly spread rumors and sabotaged political movements. With no convincing evidence, the Foshan court sentenced Zhang to ten years in prison and reported to the local Party committee, which added five more

62 Ibid., December 1, 1955. B2-1-14-36.

63 Ibid., June 21, 1956. B2-2-41; for labor camp see Mühlhahn, 2007: 44.

years to Zhang's punishment.[64] This case shows that the ongoing political campaign pressed both cadres and judges to exert draconian penalties on just suspected counterrevolutionaries with little or no regard to evidence or the law.

In this campaign period, spurious charges and heavier punishments were unbridled. According to a report of the Zhanjiang region in Guangdong, a random check of 349 criminal cases in the second half of 1955 showed that as many as 59% were wrongly judged. In many cases, judges punished as counterrevolutionaries people who had simply complained about CCP policies. In one case, Qiu Qun was a former GMD member and district head. During the food shortage in 1955, Qiu allegedly observed that the government food ration was too meager for him to survive on. He complained that "Sooner or later, someone will die of hunger. Not only will I die, but also many other people will starve to death." For that grumble, the Maoming court imprisoned Qiu for ten years, a much longer sentence than those meted out to campaign victims in Shanghai.[65]

In a political campaign, no one was categorically secure. People with clean records could be punished for "erroneous or improper activities." A peasant named Su Mingxing had long been a law-abiding person whose history was unstained. When Guangdong province was hit by a severe drought in 1955, Su led a group of people to pray for rain, a hoary practice embedded in Chinese folk religion and culture. In all kinds of polities, Chinese rulers or the "sons of heaven" and sometimes officials would pray for rain in times of prolonged drought, a Confucian sign of heaven's displeasure.[66] Ostensibly because the CCP was a self-proclaimed atheistic polity, however, the Huaxian court sentenced Su to fifteen years in prison for his superstitious activity.[67]

While upper-level courts were supposed to correct false judgments or improper punishments made by the lower courts, they sometimes depended more on individual judges' self-discipline and professionalism than on the judicial system or law. In a political campaign, many appellate court judges turned derelict in their duty and did not burden themselves with punishments of class enemies. In June 1956, Deng Hanzhang, a judge from Hepu, Guangdong, accused the intermediate court of being careless and irresponsible. He cited a case in which one Chen Hua had committed

64 *Guangdong sifa tongxun*, December 30, 1955, pp. 5-7: 7.

65 Ibid., June 30, 1956, pp. 1-3.

66 For the custom of praying for rain in Chinese history and culture see Evelyn Rawski, *Early Modern China and Northeast Asia: Cross-Border Perspectives* (Cambridge: Cambridge University Press, 2015): 132.

67 *Guangdong sifa tongxun*, June 30, 1956, pp. 1-3.

counterrevolutionary crimes before 1949 and refused to confess in the early PRC. In late 1955, a county court accused Chen of spreading rumors, instigating people to butcher farm oxen, and sabotaging rural cooperatives. For both his new and old crimes, Chen was sentenced to twenty years in prison. When an intermediate court reviewed the case, the judge was unable to find any evidence that could justify the extremely harsh penalty imposed on Chen. Unfortunately, the judge simply reduced Chen's prison time to fifteen years rather than following the appropriate process and sending the case back to the county court for reinvestigation.[68]

The arbitrarily heavy penalty that Chen Hua had suffered in 1955 was highly common in many other counties. Between July 1955 and February 1956, the Xingning County Court in Guangdong had tried and punished 1031 counterrevolutionaries and other criminals. After the Shantou Intermediate Court reviewed 563 of them, it found that nearly half of the defendants were punished either falsely or too harshly. The primary causes were, as in the Hepu region, treating former GMD members who had made minor complaints or uttered improper words as active counterrevolutionaries or heavily punishing people for petty crimes. To cite one case, one middle peasant, Wu Lan, had raped four women in the Republican period and also had possessed such bad habits as gambling, taking drugs, and stealing. In the PRC, Wu focused on farming and had been faultless. In April 1955, when peasants were using bamboo containers to carry water to fight a drought, Wu allegedly said that "bamboo containers were too small to irrigate the land." For that harmless remark, Wu was accused of "discouraging people's enthusiasm in fighting drought" and he was imprisoned for seven years.[69]

The situation of historical counterrevolutionaries was no better in Shanghai. In late 1955, the Shanghai Penglai District Court indicted Shou Daqian for stealing state economic information and embezzling a "large amount" of state funds. A former GMD tax accountant and a person with a "corrupt" lifestyle, Shou in the early PRC opened a printing factory and needed funds. He used illegal means like blank checks to seize "untold" amounts of money from other people. Instead of investing the money in his factory, Shou had squandered a total of 7700 *yuan* in gambling, whoring, and feasting. To cover the loss, Shou bribed corrupt officials who helped him embezzle state funds totaling 7181 *yuan*. The district court found Shou guilty and sentenced him to life imprisonment based on his historical and current crimes. Although the penalty was quite heavy, it was milder than

68 Ibid., June 30, 1956, pp. 4-7.
69 Ibid.

that imposed on Qiu Qun and other victims in Guangdong province who had been imprisoned for from two to ten years for a simple complaint.[70]

3 The Rationale Behind Harsher Punishment

What was behind the courts' whimsical and excessively severe treatment of ordinary people or class enemies with minor complaints? Why did judges pay no or little attention to the constitution and the OLC? The Xingning County Court believed that judges had been compelled to become merciless especially after the nationwide denunciation of right-leaning judgments in the early summer of 1955. Since then, to avoid being accused of right deviation, judges developed an "erroneous thought" that they should be ruthless toward all detained persons. As a result, five years' incarceration or longer became the standard punishment imposed by judges.[71]

The worries of judges were evident in a case of one Lin Hancheng who had served in the GMD army between 1927 and 1949. In a military campaign against Communist guerillas, Lin avoided the battle by claiming sickness. In the early PRC, Lin tried to discourage his daughter from joining the Communist army. In 1954, Lin's daughter who was now working for a state-run factory, persuaded him to write a confession of his past "crimes" and she handed it in to her factory leaders. The local police obtained a copy of Lin's confession from the factory in 1955 and accused him of refusing to confess to a district court in the PRC. Although the judge knew that Lin had made his original confession a year before, he was "afraid of being labeled as right-leaning" if he questioned the police indictment or reported the truth to court leaders. To ward off any trouble to himself in a political campaign, the judge chose to denounce Lin for being "stubborn in the PRC and opposing any confession of his historical problems." Although Lin had not participated in a battle against Communist guerrillas due to his poor health, the judge claimed that Lin had fought the guerrillas and was thus an enemy of the people. The judge recommended five years of prison for Lin, but his superior changed it to four years. In this case, both the judge and his superior knew that Lin was innocent of the charge, but they accepted the police's false charge and Lin's heavy punishment in order to protect themselves.[72] After all, in a political storm, few judges were willing to care about the fate of a class enemy.

70 Shanghai Archives, late 1955. S40-4-301.
71 *Guangdong sifa tongxun*广东司法通讯, August 8, 1956, pp. 4-7.
72 Ibid., November 22, 1956, pp. 10-11.

No official source can tell us the number of judges who had been compelled to shift their "right-leaning" lenience toward class enemies. According to a report of the Guangdong Provincial Court, by the end of 1955, the court had "basically cleansed right-leaning" thought because in the first quarter of 1955, punishment of over five-year imprisonment constituted 17.14% of all counterrevolutionary cases and that percentage jumped to 53.37% in the second quarter. The percentage should be higher still in the political campaign after July 1955.[73]

If the fear of being accused of right-leaning forced judges to adopt draconian measures against class enemies and other criminals, the poor quality of many judges after the 1952-1953 legal reform was another important factor behind harsh punishments and the use of torture. To cite a few examples, in September 1955, while judge Yan Bingjie of the Shiqi City Court was adjudicating a counterrevolutionary case, he threatened a defendant, "[I]f you do not confess, I will kill you with a gun!"[74] In another Guangdong city court, about six or seven court cadres beat one litigant. One cadre was said to have struck a criminal with a bamboo. In one court, a group of judges led by a court leader continuously interrogated a criminal for two days.[75]

In the spring of 1956, the anti-counterrevolutionary campaign tapered off. But many courts kept on depriving defendants of their legal rights. In February, the Gaoyao County Court ruled in a civil case involving a dispute over the fare between the Gaoyao Transportation Station and the Gaoyao Marketing Cooperative. Dissatisfied with the court decision, the Transportation Station requested permission to appeal to the appellate court, which was rejected by the judge. Later, when two cadres from the Transportation Station went to the court asking for an appeal, one court cadre said, "[T]he ruling is there and no appeal is allowed. You may go home and follow the court decision." Infuriated, the two cadres appealed to the intermediate court. Unfortunately, the intermediate court did not respond to the appeal.[76] Both the county court's rejection of the litigants' appeal and the intermediate court's failure to respond violated the OLC in 1954. Such obstruction of justice was rare in civil cases in the early PRC.

73 Guangdong Provincial Archives, December 13, 1955. 250-1-1-14.
74 *Guangdong sifa tongxun*, February 20, 1956, p. 7.
75 Guangdong Provincial Archives, December 13, 1955. 250-1-1-14.
76 *Guangdong sifa tongxun*, August 18, 1956, pp. 12-13.

4 The Thaw in Spring 1956

Since early 1956, the Party had begun to rein in the excesses of the political campaign. The central government first ordered local judiciaries to allow counterrevolutionaries to appeal, a sign of policy change.[77] In late February, vice premier Chen Yi stated that, while judicial independence had to be under the Party's leadership, the Party would just provide the judicial system with principles rather than meddle in actual cases, a policy similar to that in Stalin's Soviet Union.[78] He pointed out several problems in the judiciaries. One of them was the blurred line between counterrevolutionary words/actions and normal complaints. Invoking Mao's words, Chen urged judicial cadres to reform most counterrevolutionaries and reduce the number of capital punishments. Furthermore, Chen wanted the people's court to moderate their policies toward retained GMD judges.[79] Chen Yi's talk lacked specific and detailed reform policies, but it hinted at a major change in Party policy in less than nine months: from relentlessness to mercy.

In contrast to Chen Yi's tacit tone, Zhang Dingchen, the Supreme Procurator, clearly articulated a shift of Party policy. While Zhang insisted that most of what the judicial system had done in the past year was right, he admitted the existence of many false arrests and penalties. In particular, Zhang cited two cases in which two innocent people were wrongly arrested and punished in Shanghai and Guangdong. A bigger problem was that some judges did not realize the gravity of their mistakes. "They [the judges] think that the number of wronged people is minimal," Zhang said, "but they do not know that any false arrest would inflict tremendous harm on the victim. Some victims have their production and lives affected, others even see death and the destruction to their family."[80]

On March 16, the Supreme Court issued a preliminary summary of all trials in 1955. The summary showed that after the Party chastised the right-leaning thought last July, the courts had accepted and adjudicated over 530,000 counterrevolutionary cases among which about 493,000 had been resolved. The ongoing political campaign acted as a double-edged sword. On the one hand, it "consolidates people's dictatorship and splits counterrevolutionaries;" on the other, after criticizing right-leaning thought inside the judicial system, some courts were unclear how to enforce Party

77 Shanghai Archives, January 10, 1956. B2-1-41-1.
78 See Cohen, 1968: 15.
79 Shanghai Archives, February 29, 1956. B2-2-41.
80 Ibid., March 2, 1956. B2-2-41.

policies. Owing to a "lack of universal standards in penalty calculation plus judges' subjectivism and carelessness," some courts turned to harsher punishments and even made false rulings. The summary listed a number of false or excessive penalties and admonished judges to bear in mind the following four issues in trials: 1) difference between counterrevolutionary and ordinary historical problems; 2) difference between common historical problems and active crimes; 3) reactionary historical problems should not be the primary or only basis for punishment; 4) difference between counterrevolutionary rumors/sabotage and some people's "backward" words and actions. The summary reveals that the Party central had begun to realize the detrimental fallout of the political campaign and attempted to contain it.[81]

Why did the Party suddenly soften its policy against class enemies in the spring of 1956, less than nine months after its first launch?[82] As late as December 1955, the head of the Shanghai High Court still reminded judges that any magnanimity toward people with historical crimes would be deemed as a right deviation.[83] Part of the CCP's change of policy might be attributed to Nikita Khrushchev's recent denunciation of Stalin's cruelty, dictatorial ruling, and personal cult. As Stephen Uhalley has pointed out, the denunciation was "the beginning of a concern on the part of the CCP to avoid some of the Soviet Union's more obvious problems."[84] Shen Zhihua asserts that Khrushchev's criticism of Stalin provided Mao and China with a chance to "surpass" the Soviet model and a confident Mao accordingly backed a more tolerant policy in early 1956.[85] On April 27, 1956, Mao argued that the number of counterrevolutionaries had "significantly" reduced and he ordered the curtailment of the arrests and killings of counterrevolutionaries. Next day, Mao called for the "Hundred Flowers Campaign", an old saying dating back to the Warring States Era, to encourage academic debate, signaling a more moderate policy.[86]

81 Ibid., March 16, 1956. B2-2-41.

82 In June, the Shanghai High Court and the Judicial Bureau told court cadres that the new leniency policy should not apply to every criminal. Only those who showed bona fide remorse could be exonerated. See Shanghai Archives, June 21, 1956. B2-2-41.

83 Ibid., December 17, 1955. B1-1-598-1.

84 Stephen Uhalley, *A History of the Chinese Communist Party* (Stanford: Hoover Press, 1988): 110.

85 Shen Zhihua沈志华, *Thinking and Choice: From Intellectual Meeting to Anti-Rightist Movement* (*sikao yu xuanze: cong zhishi fenzi huiyi dao fanyoupai yundong*) (Hong Kong: Hong Kong Chinese University Press, 2009): 217.

86 Mao Zedong毛泽东, "On Ten Relationships (*lun shida guanxi*)" in *Selected Works of Mao* (Beijing: Renmin chubanshe, 1977) 5. 267-88; also see Vogel, 1980: 190; Jia Zhangwang, *The Seventy*

However, the thaw did not happen instantly and the severity toward so-called enemies or criminals lingered into the summer. For instance, in the early summer, the Gaoyao Regional Intermediate Court in Guangdong had randomly selected 210 lower court cases from February through June to review. Most of the civil cases, about 78%, were correct. But the percentage of correctly dealt criminal cases was only 42%. Moreover, of the fourteen criminal cases sent by Gaoyao County, two were completely wrong. Of the twelve criminal cases judged by the Sihui county court, only one was right and all the others had their sentences either reduced or canceled.[87]

If the case of Gaoyao was too small to be representative, a State Council report would unveil an extensive and shockingly high percentage of false and harsh court decisions in 23 provinces in the first quarter of 1956. Of the 3555 death penalties reviewed by provincial high courts, only 26.9% were approved, 24.5% had to be revised, and as many as 48.8% were returned for retrial.[88]

In the spring, even if the central government allowed all first-instance death penalties involving counterrevolutionary and other criminal cases to be appealed, some local courts turned a deaf ear to the order and insisted on denying defendants' right to appeal.[89] In November 1955, a joint trial at the Lianjiang County Court in Guangdong suggested a two-year incarceration for Huang Chengzhen who had illegally traded 129 silver *yuan*. Two accomplices of Huang were released after being warned. After reviewing the case, a court leader tried to reduce the penalty to *guanzhi* because the crime was light. As soon as a local police head heard about the case, however, he admonished the court leader, "Huang Chengzhen's trading of the silver has indirectly assisted the imperialists (i.e. sabotaging state financial policies). [I think] your punishment is too generous." Scared, the court leader immediately increased Huang's sentence to eight years, six years more than in the original verdict. Each of Huang's accomplices would get three years. In March 1956, a frustrated Huang asked the court to review his case, but the court leader refused to budge. It was not until June that the county court eventually reinvestigated the punishment and released Huang after a brief reeducation. By the time Huang received his fourth court verdict within seven months,

Years of the New China under Mao Zedong (*Mao Zedong lingdaoxia dexin zhongguo qishinian*) (Beijing: Zhongguo wenshi chubanshe, 2014): 1. Ch. 11.

87 Also see *Guangdong sifa tongxun*, August 18, 1956, pp. 6-7.

88 Shanghai Archives, May 16-November 29, 1956. B2-1-001-36.

89 Both the 1954 constitution and the OLC did not mention the appeal for counterrevolutionaries. For the central order see Shanghai Archives, December 29, 1955. B2-1-41-1.

he had been in custody for over 200 days.[90] This case suggests that the court decisions remained quite arbitrary, unpredictable, and irresponsible even after a shift of central policy.

From mid-1955 to the early summer of 1956, the Party had first hardened its policy toward alleged counterrevolutionaries and later softened its tone due to both internal excessive punishments and, to some extent, the changing external situation, namely, the Soviet Union. In many regions, court penalties against class enemies were so merciless that they often went to extremes. A mere complaint could suffice to incur a sentence of several years or longer in prison. Additionally, constitutional principles such as judicial independence had been tweaked or neglected, and torture and arbitrary decisions including denial of appeals were as rampant as – if not worse than – in previous periods. In that regard, it is fair to argue that this period was anything but a golden age for the PRC judicial system.

A Limited "Golden Age"? May 1956-May 1957

1 More Tolerant since Mid-1956

Since the Party allowed counterrevolutionaries to appeal in early 1956,[91] the political campaign had begun to recede and certain previously condemned legal principles had come back.[92] On January 10, the Shanghai High Court criticized a district court for failing to cite laws in their verdicts, a common problem among judges in the campaign.[93] In March, although a Supreme Court review still acclaimed the political campaign, it nevertheless conceded that there had been widespread infringement of the laws by the courts, and it warned judges not to punish historical crimes.[94] From May 1956 through early 1957, it became increasingly explicit that the Party was trying to roll back its tough policy and to restore pre-campaign legal principles and legal professionalism.

90 *Guangdong sifa tongxun*, August 18, 1956, pp. 13-14.

91 But a February Central regulation stated that, if the counterrevolutionary cases had been settled and the defendants did not ask to appeal, the courts should not tell them to appeal to avoid "trouble." See Shanghai Archives, B2-1-001-41.

92 Unlike scholars who advocate a "Golden Age" in the 1950s, other scholars tend to go to another extreme by dismissing the 1950s law as completely arbitrary or adhering to "government policies." See Dikotter, 1997: 149, 154.

93 Shanghai Archives, January 10, 1956. B2-2-42-51.

94 Ibid., March 16, 1956. B2-2-41.

On May 22, 1956, the Shanghai *Zhengfawei* drafted some opinions on the main problems of the judicial system in the city. One opinion was that the police had amassed too much power and their decisions invariably neglected the distinctions that existed among provinces. In one example, the Ministry of Public Security had once made it a crime to steal two to three *yuan* which was improper when applied to richer regions such as Shanghai. Another opinion called for the abolition of the political and legal department and the transfer of some police duties such as managing prisons and labor camps and detecting crimes to the people's courts.[95] As I have mentioned, the police took charge of investigating suspected crime shortly after the campaign began. Now with the campaign on the wane, the courts tried to regain their authority over investigation so as to strengthen the standard legal process.

Meanwhile, the Ministry of Justice took solid steps to improve the attorney system by recruiting some judges, military veterans, and even former GMD lawyers. All lawyers would be treated as court cadres and could charge fees for service. To quell doubts about the political unreliability of retained lawyers, the department remarked that lawyers, unlike judges, would not make decisions.[96] The State Council also promised to create a number of law schools to train and improve the quality of local judges and procurators. Qualified law school students should have at least a middle school education and should also be politically reliable.[97] To restore court authority and legal professionalism, the NPC on November 16 proclaimed that in the future it would be the courts and not the police who should decide the *guanzhi* of all counterrevolutionaries.[98]

In late November, shortly after the Soviet Union's brutal suppression of the Hungarian revolt led by Imre Nagy,[99] the State Council highlighted some major problems inside the PRC judicial system. The first was the dearth of important laws such as the Criminal Procedure Law without which judges could hardly deal with cases properly. Another problem was the high percentage of falsely judged and harshly punished cases in the recent political campaign. The third was the poor quality of many judges. Some judges stressed "speed" rather than "legality" in settling cases and refused to follow legal procedures. The State Council ascribed these judicial problems

95 Ibid., May 22, 1956. B2-1-001-36.

96 Ibid., May 7, 1956. B2-1-001-38.

97 Ibid., June 7, 1956.

98 *Judicial Work Handbook* (*sifa gongzuo shouce*司法工作手册), Vol. 5, January 1957, p. 23.

99 For a good study on the Hungarian revolt see Paul Lendvai, *One Day That Shook the Communist World: The 1956 Hungarian Uprising and its Legacy* (Princeton: Princeton University Press, 2010).

partly to the lack of civil and criminal procedure laws and it prodded the central governments (i.e. the NPC) to quickly promulgate such laws.[100]

The poor quality of judges had been a major problem since the legal reform in 1952. Most new judges had little or no legal training. According to a report of the Shanghai High Court in late 1956, 40% of the city judges did not have college degrees.[101] If the credentials of Shanghai judges were low, we can imagine what were the credentials of judges in less prosperous regions. Indeed, due to judges' relatively low rank on the PRC political ladder, many cadres with higher education were loath to become judges. In Shanghai, for instance, the rank of most judges in the PRC was 20 (on a scale on which the lowest was 24), similar to that of a district cadre. To stimulate judges' ardor for hard work, the Shanghai court even proposed to reward them with public recognition and/or monetary incentives, elements of capitalism. Moreover, to enhance the "dignity of [the upholders of] the rule of law," the Shanghai court suggested that the central government consider making judicial uniforms.[102] In cities like Shanghai, many high-ranking judicial officials envisioned a more professional and formal judicial system consistent with a recent call by a vice head of the Supreme Court to learn from the judicial system of the Soviet Union.[103]

The CCP's softened stance and renewed tolerance of class enemies extended into spring 1957. On January 3, 1957, the Shanghai government issued a report on the current situation of the city's construction of laws. The report alleged that the number of GMD agents and spies discovered in Shanghai in 1956 was double that in 1955, but it did not call for a new crackdown against counterrevolutionaries. Instead, the report censured some judicial cadres for not "completely" adopting legal procedures in tackling cases. Interestingly, the tolerant policy was so vigorous that some judges balked at penalizing criminals who should have been punished, the reverse of what they had done barely a year earlier.[104]

On the next day, Wei Ming, the head of the Shanghai High Court who had ordered judges to punish people with historical crimes in late 1955, retreated from his previously tough stance against counterrevolutionaries. He first brought up a central policy of late 1956 that urged cadres to alleviate the severity in treating counterrevolutionaries. Then he said that

100 Shanghai Archives, May 16-November 29, 1956. B2-1-001-36.

101 Ibid., November 28, 1956. B2-2-38-43.

102 Ibid., 1956. B2-1-001-36.

103 In 1956, the vice head of the Supreme Court wanted Chinese courts to learn from the Soviet Union in writing verdicts and resolving cases. See Shanghai Archives, 1956. B2-2-42-16.

104 Ibid., January 3, 1957. B1-1-646.

Shanghai had reduced or absolved punishments of counterrevolutionaries who had ceased their nefarious activities and genuinely confessed. Next, he shifted his attention to the rising number of non-political crimes, such as hooliganism and theft, which stemmed from the remaining venom (*yidu*) of the "old society" (i.e. the ROC) rather than the PRC. Opposing blind lenience, Wei warned judicial cadres not to be unduly bound by the "more tolerant" policy and they should continue to punish "real" criminals.[105] As the court head, Wei Ming had to be cautious in finding a middle ground between the positive features of the political campaign and the excesses of the crackdown.

In mid-March, the focus of the judicial system seemed to have switched from counterrevolutionary cases to such "new crimes" as official corruption and mounting divorces. In the Shanghai courts, the number of criminal cases in 1956 was only one fifth of that in 1955. The main problems of the court were now the subjectivism, credulity, and hastiness of many judges resulting from "left-leaning" mistakes encouraged by court leaders during the anti-counterrevolutionary political campaign. Lesser problems entailed, among others, judges' ignorance of legal procedure, disrespect of jurors, use of torture to extract confession, and tardy adjudications.[106] The new situation faced by Shanghai courts reveals that, at least in big cities, the judicial system had started to look beyond the political campaign and to focus on reinstating part of the legal profession advocated by the 1954 constitution and the OLC.

On February 27, almost two months after Wei Ming's talk, Mao delivered one of his most important talks entitled "Correctly Handling Internal Contradictions among the People." After applauding the campaign's accomplishments and lashing out at any criticism, Mao acknowledged the existence of mistakes, but he dismissed them as being inevitable. In any case, he claimed that all errors had been corrected whenever they were found out. This may not have been true. As we have seen, many appellate courts had only randomly selected some cases from the lower court to review and their corrections were rather incomplete. Because China still had many counterrevolutionaries, Mao warned that it was wrong to discourage cadres who had made mistakes in the campaign. With the fresh Hungarian uprising in mind, Mao attempted to tell cadres that Hungarians who used force against their Communist government had largely been misled by the disingenuous ideas of Western democracy. He warned any Chinese who

105 Ibid., January 4, 1957. B1-1-647-1.
106 Ibid., March 19, 1957. B2-2-35.

might be sympathetic to the Hungarian rebels that the masses would not follow them. However fleetingly, it is clear that the Hungarian revolt had played an important role in goading top Party leaders to become more tolerant and conciliatory toward class enemies and intellectual criticism in early 1957.[107]

2 Tolerance in Cases

The shift of the CCP's policy from severity to magnanimity in early 1956 was evident in numerous court judgments. In one case, Wu Yaoting was the manager of the Fusheng Pharmacy in Beijing. After the government fined him in 1954 for evading taxes, he was furious and began cursing the CCP and Mao. He smeared Mao as a turtle spirit (*wangbajing*) and called him a "bastard." He also threatened to kill his workers who might have exposed his tax evasion to the local government. Had Wu been tried in the political campaign, any of his "abominable crimes" would be enough to warrant at least five years of imprisonment. But he was extremely lucky as his trial was in the midst of a political thaw. On May 21, 1956, the Beijing Intermediate Court sentenced him to only one year of prison with a probation period of one year. According to the judge, although Wu's smears and insults were crimes, he made them due to his "backward thought" and not out of any counterrevolutionary motives. Shortly after he was detained, Wu quickly admitted all his crimes. Accordingly, the judge did not charge him as a counterrevolutionary.

More important, even such a "light" punishment was questioned in late 1956 by Yan Shaoqing, a member of the Beijing Political Consultative Conference. Yan argued that the court punishment was harsh and problematic and would cause more grudges and complaints from Wu. Yan also noted that recently Wu's spirit was somewhat abnormal, and he was expressing pessimism and a desire to die. Yan asked the court to reconsider its "harsh" verdict.

In May 1957, the Beijing court responded to Yan's questions. It acknowledged that the court's previous decision on Wu might have been too light, but it was definitely not "wrong," given the solid evidence of Wu's crimes and his enmity toward the government. If there were anything inappropriate in the court ruling, it would have been the wording because Wu's crimes

107 Mao Zedong毛泽东, "Correctly Tackling the Internal Contradictions Among the People (*zhengque chuli renmin neibu maodun*正确处理人民内部矛盾)" in *Selected Works of Mao* (Beijing: Renmin chubanshe, 1977) 5. 363-402.

were rooted in his class animosity toward the CCP and not in his "backward thought."[108]

Like their Beijing counterparts, in 1957, Shanghai courts reviewed and corrected many cases of false or excessively harsh punishments. For example, in July 1955, the Shanghai Hongkou District Court had sentenced a businessman named Guo Caibao to five years in prison. Like Wu Yaoting, Guo's main crime was his tax fraud that came to light in the Five-Antis Movement in 1952. After Guo was punished by the government, his business had deteriorated and he vented his anger to the CCP. He allegedly ripped Mao's portrait and burned it in public. In addition, he had overtly objected to the government's taxes, bribed soldiers to join in stealing copper pipes, and issued blank checks. On January 25, 1957, the same court reviewed Guo's case and found that Guo's economic crimes were not serious and that the police had already "educated" him for destroying Mao's portrait. Accordingly, the court decided to free Guo immediately. By the time of his release, Guo had been incarcerated for over one and half years. Without the changing political wind, he could have stayed in prison for another three years.[109]

The nationwide review and rehabilitation of wrongly charged cases, known to Leese and Engman as "retractive justice,"[110] persisted until summer 1957 when the Party launched another campaign: The Anti-Rightist Movement. In April, the Shanghai Dongchang District Court revised an earlier "erroneous" punishment that involved Zhang Hekai, a former GMD member and thus a historical class enemy. In 1952, the police had detained Zhang for selling drugs. During the 1955 campaign, the court imprisoned Zhang for five years for gambling and for "breaking revolutionary order," a dubious crime coined in the early PRC that targeted minor social crimes. In early 1957, while looking into the case again, the court decided that what Zhang had committed was merely an "error" and not a "crime." Zhang regained his freedom, but his physical and psychological scars would no doubt linger for a long time.[111]

The judicial lenience manifested in these cases in Beijing and Shanghai was consistent with the CCP leaders' call for a tolerant policy toward class enemies and the "Hundred Flowers Campaign" to encourage criticisms since spring 1956. The pace of rehabilitation seemed to have accelerated after the revolt in Hungary. To be sure, the generosity was not applied evenly in the

108 Beijing Archives, May 20, 1957. 038-002-00566.
109 Shanghai Archives, January 25, 1957. B216-1-77.
110 Leese and Engman, 2018: 17.
111 Shanghai Archives, April 15, 1957. B205-2-29-12.

PRC. Many judges in interior China or particularly in remote county courts kept up draconian methods or penalties against alleged counterrevolutionaries. For instance, in late 1956 when the national political atmosphere was fairly mild, the Gaoling County Court in northern Shanxi province sentenced Liu Yujie, a former GMD member and agent, to seventeen years in prison for his counterrevolutionary rhetoric. In April 1954, Liu was unwilling to kill pests as required by the state, and he expressed dissatisfaction when a township secretary asked him to write a confession. In June 1956, Liu's father dug in his neighbor's land to look for water. When his neighbor criticized Liu for his father's activity, Liu allegedly replied, "I was unaware of it and you can do whatever you want." Although Liu did not say anything against the CCP or any leader, the county court, apparently taking into consideration Liu's historical crimes, accused Liu of "detesting the people's government, threatening a peasant, and encouraging his father's illegal action." Consequently, Liu was charged as a counterrevolutionary and would spend the next seventeen years in prison. That penalty was much heavier than that imposed on others in Beijing and Shanghai who had cursed Mao and burned his portrait.[112]

In another case that took place in September 1956, to justify a punishment of a person in a rumor case, a judge in Qingchuan County, Sichuan province, without even interrogating the defendant, fabricated the complete investigative report by himself. He wrote at the end that the "criminal has accepted all the charges."[113]

In spring 1957, about one year after the CCP reversed the course of its anti-counterrevolutionary campaign, longtime problems such as arbitrary adjudication, torture, and enticed confessions remained in many county courts. In a rape case, a judge at a county court in the region of Baoji, Shaanxi, ignored the contradictory confessions between two suspects (father and son) and lured the father into admitting his crime. Once the father "confessed" under pressure and enticement, the judge sentenced him to five years and his son to two years in prison with probation. When the appellate court found that the charge was incorrect and that both "culprits" were wronged and should be acquitted, the father had been in prison for over nine months. In other trials, county judges engaged in lewd language or threatened torture. For instance, one judge asked a sixteen-year-old girl who had been raped,

112 The Criminal Division of the Shaanxi Provincial High Court, "Opposing Subjectivism and Enhancing Trial Quality (*fandui zhuguan zhuyi tigao shenpan zhiliang*反对主观主义提高审判质量)" in *Shaanxi sifa tongxun*陕西司法通讯, Vol. 5, 1957, pp. 10-13.

113 *Sichuan Provincial Trial Gazette*, 2003: 318.

"When you were raped, what flowed from your lower body?" Another judge threatened to use shackles if a defendant did not confess.[114]

Since early 1956, the political climate had eased, and it continued to improve in the second half of the year. Many central and local judicial leaders had called for more clemency as well as the restoration of the legal profession that had been dramatically undermined in the second anti-counterrevolutionary campaign. The uprising in Communist Hungary in late 1956 prompted the CCP to further soften its severe and often illegal stance toward alleged class enemies. The generous policy in the spring 1957 was more conspicuous when numerous wrongly managed cases were rectified, including "crimes" that would have received harsher penalties just a year earlier. Yet the magnanimity or, to some extent, "the golden age" of law appeared only briefly and mainly in big cities. The inertia of arbitrary and harsh punishments and illicit methods such as torture or enticed confession carried on in many county courts.

A Short and Limited Golden Age

In the wake of the 1952-1953 legal reform and the tremendous chaos and infringements of law which it had unleashed, the CCP in 1954 made efforts to restore legal principles such as equality before law, judicial independence, and the jury and lawyer systems embodied in both the new constitution and the OLC. However, the Party's pursuit of legal professionalism was lukewarm and the legal principles failed to be followed in practice by many Communist cadres and judges. Even in Shanghai, the largest and most prosperous city in the PRC, many judges continued to break laws, abuse litigants, and employ arbitrary punishments, let alone smaller cities and counties in relatively poor and interior regions. After the CCP launched a second anti-counterrevolutionary campaign in July 1955, summary trials, severe punishments, and torture became unbridled and excessive. A mere curse or verbal disapproval of Party policies or leaders would suffice to incur sentences of years behind bars. Moreover, some local governments had set five years as the minimum imprisonment of historical counterrevolutionaries who had committed no crimes in the PRC. While the Party sensed the problems and attempted to scale back the crackdown in early 1956, tens of thousands of people had been harshly punished. Starting from the spring of 1956, with central calls for milder political and academic policies and

114 *Shaanxi sifa tongxun*陕西司法通讯, Vol. 6, 1957, pp. 35-36.

more tolerance toward counterrevolutionaries, many appellate courts had begun careful reviews of sentences imposed by local courts on minor "crimes" despite concomitant abuses of law in some county courts. In late 1956 and early 1957, probably alarmed by the incendiary political incidents in Hungary, the thaw of CCP's policies against class enemies was more obvious and effective. The Supreme Court began permitting counterrevolutionaries to appeal their convictions, and many falsely and heavily charged prisoners were rehabilitated and released. In stark contrast to some scholars' assertion that the period from 1953 to 1957 was a "golden age" in the Mao era, substantial evidence and cases in this chapter have shown that most of this period was not different from – and may have been worse than – the period between October 1950 and 1953. If there existed a so-called golden age, I would say it might have happened in big cities after spring 1956 when the political and legal severity eased. Still, rehabilitated prisoners were not compensated for their grievances and months or even years of imprisonment. In that regard, the golden age, if the term is appropriate at all, was short in time and limited in space. In comparison with tolerant periods in the early 1960s (see Chapter 6), the golden age was not even exceptional.

6 The Great Leap of Law

The Communist Judicial System in China, 1957-1965

Abstract

The role of the judicial system in the period from the Anti-Rightist Movement to the eve of the Cultural Revolution has been studied the least. Most scholarship has centered on the Anti-Rightist Movement, the Great Leap Forward, the 7000-Person Meeting, and the Four Cleanups. This chapter explores a leap forward of law in this period and how judicial cadres in the three principal law-enforcing agencies (i.e. police, procuracy, and court) coordinated and fulfilled their revolutionary missions. It also examines the Communist judicial system in the early 1960s after the Party scaled back its severity and unlawful activities. But the era after the Great Famine was highly volatile and the Party policies were inconsistent and sometimes contradictory. It is argued that the Communist judicial system swung between being a loyal Party instrument and honoring legal principles such as judicial independence and legal procedures.

Keywords: Anti-Rightist campaign, Great Leap of law, rather "left" than "right," retreat from the Great Leap, rehabilitation

No other institutions between the Anti-Rightist Movement (1957) and 1966, the eve of the Cultural Revolution (1966-1976), have received such limited coverage as the Communist judicial system. Most Western scholarship on this period tends to focus on political events such as the Anti-Rightist Movement, the Great Leap Forward, or the Four Cleanups.[1] Some Western

1 For Western studies see, for example, Lowell Dittmer, *China's Continuous Revolution: The Post-Liberation Epoch 1949-1981* (Berkeley: University of California, 1989); Julia F. Andrews, "Traditional Painting in New China: Guohua and The Anti-Rightist Campaign" in *The Journal of Asian Studies*, Vol. 49, No.3 (Aug. 1990), pp. 555-577; Maurice Meisner, *Mao's China and After: A History of the People's Republic* (New York: Free Press, 1999); Philip Short, *Mao: A Life* (New York: Henry Holt Co., 2000); Lee Feigon, *Mao: A Reinterpretation* (New York: Ivan R. Dee, 2002);

Fang, Qiang, *The Communist Judicial System in China, 1927-1976: Building on Fear.*
Taylor & Francis Group 2021
DOI: 10.5117/9789463729451_CH06

scholars who have studied the legal system in the early People's Republic of China (PRC), have merely summarized the roles of courts in this period and have not done any in-depth research due largely to the paucity of available resources.[2] For most, if not all, Chinese scholars, the history of law in the PRC has been taboo, and only a handful of researchers have studied the judicial system in the period from the Anti-Rightist Movement to the Four Cleanups.[3] Like their Western colleagues, none of them has done serious research on this period based on archival records. In 1984, Li Guangchan wrote that Chinese leaders based their legal principles on China's own situation and the Soviet Criminal Law. He claimed that PRC judiciaries followed this mode of operation until the outbreak of the Cultural Revolution in 1966. In other words, despite frequent political movements, crackdowns, arbitrary trials and imprisonments, and numerous summary executions between 1949 and 1966, the Chinese judicial system had been largely bound by such legal principles and practices.[4] Gong Pixiang is critical of the judicial system in this period and points out the combination of three judicial agencies into one after the Anti-Rightist Movement that eliminated the judicial system's mutual check. He also argues that Communist judges were reprimanded for "losing [socialist] ground" and "mistaking comrades for enemies." In his view, the judicial procedures were either simplified or abolished during political campaigns.[5]

Research into archival materials reveals that, as I will discuss in this chapter, the courts and related judicial agencies, such as the procuracy and police, experienced a roller-coaster period that was more complicated and

Ezra F. Vogel, *Canton under Communism: Programs and Politics in a Provincial Capital, 1949-1968* (Cambridge, Ma: Harvard University Press, 1980); Roderick MacFarquhar and Michael Schoenhals, *Mao's Last Revolution* (Cambridge, Ma: Harvard University Press, 2008); Frederick C. Teiwes, "The Purge of Provincial Leaders 1957-1958" in *The China Quarterly*, No. 27 (Jul-Sep., 1966), pp. 14-32; Stanley Lubman, *Bird in a Cage*, 2000: 79; Glenn Tiffert, *Judging Revolution: Beijing and the Birth of the PRC Judicial System, 1906-1958* (unpublished dissertation, University of California Berkeley, 2015).

2 For the Communist judicial system and its reforms see previous chapters in this book. Also see Cohen, 1968: 16; Mühlhahn, 2011: 249-269; Peerenboom, 2002: 45; Lubman, 2000: 79-80.

3 Many Chinese scholars whose interest is the PRC have paid little or no attention to the courts in this period. See, for instance, Lin Yunhui, *A Utopian Movement: From the Great Leap Forward to the Great Famine* (*wutuobang yundong: cong dayuejin dao dajihuang*) (Hong Kong: Hong Kong Chinese University Press, 2008); Zeng Xianyi, 2002; Ye Xiaoxin, 2002.

4 Li Guangcan李光灿, ed., *A Study on the Criminal Law in the PRC* (*Zhonghua renmin gongheguo xingfalun*中华人民共和国刑法论) (Jilin: Jilin renmin chubanshe, 1984): 1. 524-525.

5 Gong Pixiang, 1999: 203-217; for Lubman's view see Lubman, 1999: 79; also see Liu Lianjun 刘建军, "People's Judiciary in the Great Leap Forward (*dayuejin zhongde renmin sifa*大跃进中的人民司法)" in *Zhengfa luntan*, 2013 (September), Vol. 31. No. 5., pp. 142-153.

multifaceted than existing studies have recognized. Studies based on a single case study may be inadequate to grasp the dynamic internal struggles and quandaries of many judges who had to tack cautiously between the Scylla of legality and the Charybdis of Party leadership in a turbulent era.

Although the crackdown on so-called rightists began in May 1957, many judges continued to rectify cases of false charges in the summer. As the Anti-Rightist Movement deepened in the fall of 1957 and especially in 1958, judges, like their predecessors in the 1955 anti-counterrevolutionary campaign, resorted to harsher punishments on alleged counterrevolutionaries or "bad elements (*huaifenzi*)" lest any sign of lenience toward "enemies" risked being labeled a "rightist," a scary title for many people in this period.[6] After reaching its peak in 1958, the movement to penalize counterrevolutionaries gradually abated, albeit the political milieu remained tense and suffocating. The first sign of a real thaw came in 1961 when accused counterrevolutionaries in some provinces were allowed to appeal. In early 1962, with the 7000-people meeting that faulted Mao and the Great Leap Forward for the Great Famine, the Party Central ordered the judicial system to take up more moderate policies. Accordingly, the judicial system reinstituted legal processes and began to correct false or excessively draconian punishments. While the Party kicked off the Four Cleanups in late 1962, political tolerance and retroactive justice persisted in the cities. For instance, in 1965, some Shanghai courts still took legal and bold steps to right wrongfully imposed punishments.

The Anti-Rightist Movement and its Aftermath

In the spring of 1957, fearing that a crisis like the one in Hungary might happen in China and challenge the rule of the Chinese Communist Party (CCP), Mao stepped forward to encourage intellectuals and other people outside the Party to speak out and up. This liberal policy did not have the support of the powerful politburo.[7] In April, Mao quoted vice premier Chen Yi's words: "It is fine for people to curse us after we have governed for so

6 The term of *huaifenzi* was used both by the GMD and the CCP referring to people with vile actions and impure thoughts, but Mao made them criminals in 1957. They were not necessarily from the five bad types. See Yang Kuisong, "How a 'Bad Element' Was Made: The Discovery, Accusation, and Punishment of Zang Qiren" in Jeremy Brown and Matthew D. Johnson, eds., *Maoism at the Grassroots: Everyday Life in China's Era of High Socialism* (Cambridge, Ma: Harvard University Press, 2015): 19-50: 19.

7 Short, 2000: 462. Also see Feigon, 2002: 112.

many years."[8] After Mao's repeated calls, many initially hesitant intellectuals began to talk. Yang Zhaolong, a Republican legal specialist and official, blamed the legal reform of 1952 for forcing many non-Communist judges to leave courts and take jobs unrelated to law.[9] Like Mao, many local Party officials urged people to find fault with the Party. Xu Hongci, a student at Shanghai Medical College, questioned Mao's secret tours that might have missed chances to meet commoners.[10] Some professors complained about too much Party intervention in their promotions and many businessmen begrudged their unfair treatment by Party officials.[11]

As criticism of the Party soared, including personal attacks on Mao, Mao and some other Party leaders worried that the critiques could threaten the Party rule, an intrinsic fear that had long obsessed the CCP since reverses in the late 1920s. Backing off from his earlier support, Mao in mid-May told the Party to wait and let the rightists become unbridled (*changkuang*) so that the Party could lure them into open rebellion and destroy them altogether.[12] On June 8, 1957, the *People's Daily* accused the rightists of using the Rectification Campaign to isolate and overthrow the Party.[13] In another editorial on July 1, the *People's Daily* evinced a conciliatory tone toward notable rightists, writing that the government would merely paint them as rightists instead of punishing them.[14]

Ordinary rightists, however, would not escape penalties. In July, Mao equated rightists to counterrevolutionaries, and deemed them enemies of the Party. Mao also suggested that, with the exception of famous people, most rightists should be sentenced to education through labor (*laojiao*).[15] On August 3, the State Council made a regulation on *laojiao* ostensibly aiming to "reform idlers, law violators, and people not living from honest labor."

8 *Unofficially Published Works of Mao Zedong*, 1957, pp. 323-328.

9 Yang Zhaolong杨兆龙, "Between Party and Non-Party in the Legal Realm (*falujie dedang yufeidang zhijian*法律界的党与非党)" in *Wenhuibao*, May 8, 1957.

10 Xu Hongci, *No Wall Too High: One Man's Daring Escape from Mao's Darkest Prison* (New York: Sarah Crichton Books, 2008): 57. Similar personal tragedies in the Anti-Rightist Movement could also been found in Yue Daiyun, *To The Storm: The Odyssey of the Revolutionary Chinese Women* (Berkeley: University of California Press, 1987); Liang Heng and Judith Shapiro, *Son of Revolution* (New York: Vintage, 1984).

11 Vogel, 1980: 196-197.

12 Mao Zedong毛泽东, "Things Are Changing (*shiqing zaiqi bianhua*事情在起变化)" in *Unofficially Published Works of Mao Zedong*, Vol. 1, pp. 333-338.

13 Mao Zedong毛泽东, "What Has Caused This (*zheshi weishenme*这是为什么)" in *The People's Daily*, June 8, 1957.

14 *The People's Daily*, July 1, 1957.

15 For *laojiao*劳教 see Chapter 5. For Mao see *Unofficially Published Works of Mao Zedong*, Vol. 1, pp. 360-364.

But in actuality, the new "law" targeted rightists who were only politically untrustworthy but whose "crimes" did not warrant imprisonment.[16]

As a result of the Party crackdown, people, including many officials labeled rightists, lost their jobs or were penalized with years of *laojiao/laogai* without a court trial.[17] In the words of Frederick C. Teiwes, one of the most frequent targets was officials who had "supported criticisms of the Party by bourgeois rightists."[18] Not just officials but also many ordinary scholars and commoners were attacked and punished in the movement. Yue Daiyun, an instructor at Peking University, was sent to a county farm to do hard labor for two years after being indicted as a rightist. Xu Hongci, who had criticized Mao's secret tours, ended up in *laogai* for decades before his successful escape to Mongolia in 1972. According to Julia F. Andrews, when a sculptor refused to testify against Jiang Feng, director of the Central Academy of Fine Arts and "the No. 1 rightist in the art world," he was declared an "extreme rightist" and sent to a labor camp near the Soviet border.[19] Moreover, the State Council even made the incorrigibility of members of the "lumpenproletariat" in reeducation centers "a punishable offense" after August 1957, further demonstrating the wide and adverse consequences of the movement.[20]

In mid-August 1957, about two months after the Party rolled out the movement, there were an estimated 44,294 rightists nationwide and the number was ballooning as the movement accelerated.[21] While Mao initially claimed that around 10% of intellectuals were rightists, he admitted in 1961 that there were over 400,000 rightists. Mao's figure was dwarfed by that of Maurice Meisner who argues that more than one million Party members were purged in 1958.[22] In his study on labor camps, Klaus Mühlhahn argues

16 Lin Feng and Wang Shucheng, "The Transformation, Predicament, and Future of Reeducation Through Labor in China" in *Hong Kong Journal of Social Science*, Vol. 38, 2010 (Issue 1). https://www.sinoss.net/uploadfile/2010/0912/20100912100922160.pdf

17 While many civilian criminals still got *guanzhi* or *laogai* by a court, Party members like Xu Hongci, Yue Daiyun, and Dai Huang were treated differently as the Party could sentence them to *laogai* through Party discipline. Also see Dikotter, 1997: 149.

18 Teiwes, 1966: 19.

19 Andrews, 1990: 555-563.

20 Aminda M. Smith, "Thought Reform and the Unreformable: Reeducation Centers and the Rhetoric of Opposition in the Early People's Republic of China" in *The Journal of Asian Studies*, 2013, Vol. 72, No. 4 (Nov.) 2013: 937-958: 950.

21 Song Yongyi, ed., *Top Secret Documents of the Anti-Rightist Movement*, Vol. 3. 12-17 Issues, (New York: Guoshi chubanshe, 2015): 167.

22 A more convincing figure of the rightists labeled in 1957-58 was 550,000 made by a central document in 1978. For Mao's claim see *Unofficially Published Works of Mao Zedong*, Vol. 1, pp. 368-381: 368; and *Unofficially Published Works of Mao Zedong*, Vol. 6b, pp. 325-330: 326. January 18; for

that there were around 2000 camps at the turn of 1960 and a total number of twenty million prisoners in them. Many of them may have been rightists. In addition, the conditions in *laogai* camps were terrible. Inmates lacked space, food, water, fuel, clothes, and tools, and had to work as long as nineteen hours a day.[23]

Rather "Left" than "Right"

It was not until July 1957 that the judicial system actively engaged in the Anti-Rightist Movement. In April, Shanghai courts had still adopted a moderate stance toward criminals and had rehabilitated formerly wronged convicts. On April 26, the Dongchang District Court released one Zhang Hekai who had been sentenced to five years in the 1955 anti-counterrevolutionary campaign for his historical crimes before 1949 and for selling drugs and gambling in 1953. In fact, Zhang had been warned and punished in 1953 for his alleged crimes and had since been a lawful citizen. But during the 1955 campaign, the local court punished Zhang again for his "old" crimes, probably because his previous penalty was not severe enough. When the political atmosphere eased again in early 1957, the court set Zhang free on the grounds that his activities constituted only misconduct and not crime.[24]

In early July, even though the Anti-Rightist Movement had gathered steam, a Shanghai district court maintained its lenient stance and continued to rehabilitate victims who had been wronged in 1955. On July 10, the Yimiao District Court reversed the 1955 penalty meted out to one Xie Yanqiao. Xie had received eight years of imprisonment for criticizing China's involvement in the Korean War and praising Hong Kong newspapers as the only trustworthy media in China. The new court ruling stated that, while Xie's smears of the Party and labor union were false, they were products of Xie's "backward thought" and he should have been educated, not punished.[25]

The above two rehabilitations took place during a new round of political moderation after spring 1956. It reminds us that the PRC judicial system served the Party loyally but many judges endeavored to correct past false charges once the political wind shifted to permit it. Meanwhile, judicial

Meisner see Maurice Meisner, 1999: 188; for Party Central see *Yunnan Provincial Trial Gazette*, Vol. 55. (*Yunnan shengzhi shenpanzhi*云南省志审判志) (Yunnan: Yunnan renmin chubanshe, 1999): 238.

23 See Mühlhahn, 2009: 269, 249-268; Harry Wu, 1992; Xu Hongci, 2008: 95.

24 Shanghai Archives, April 1957. B205-2-29-12.

25 Ibid., July 10, 1957. B199-1-59.

leaders in Beijing also seemed to want to safeguard legality as embodied in the 1954 constitution. On July 2, 1957, Dong Biwu, the top supervisor of law, tried to downplay the threat of counterrevolutionaries, and he prodded judges to respect the law and legal principles. He argued that since 1956 counterrevolutionary crimes had dramatically diminished and most criminal cases in 1957 were perpetrated by ordinary toilers and not class enemies. An acute problem of the court was that many judges were unable to differentiate between two kinds of contradictions: the internal contradictions among the people and the contradiction between the people and their enemies. For instance, some judges purposely penalized such minor crimes as assault, gambling, and secretly butchering farm cattle so as to thwart future violators. Dong believed that those misjudgments, if not corrected, would alienate the people and worsen the internal contradiction among the people. Moreover, Dong wanted judges to adhere to both the constitution and the OLC in hopes of protecting right judgments. "Only decisions made in genuine compliance with the facts and law can be right ones," Dong remarked. For the relations among the three judicial agencies: police, procuracy, and court, Dong emphasized their separation and mutual supervision as the basis for fair trials.[26]

Had Dong waited for another couple of weeks, he might not have made so anachronistic a comment in support of the law and the shift of focus from anti-counterrevolutionaries to people's internal contradictions. In mid-July, just two weeks after Dong's talk, the Anti-Rightist Movement had shrouded the court. A report of the Dianbai County Court in Guangdong summarized the internal debate inside the court regarding the punishment of enemies and the role of law. The debate was about the relationship between the law and Party committee. With backing from some colleagues, judge Liu Jingdong scolded the Party for meddling in court trials and shielding criminals. But after other judges, especially court leaders, attacked Liu Jingdong and his "unprincipled" supporters, most cadres turned against Liu's view, advocated Party leadership in the court, and clarified law's role: to serve politics and strike enemies.[27] Judge Liu was more fortunate than many of his fellow judges in other courts who had been branded as rightists, stripped of jobs, or worse, sentenced to labor camps.[28] Nevertheless, the public denunciation and humiliation by his colleagues and superiors would effectively silence Liu.

26 Dong, 2001: 400-408.

27 Guangdong Provincial Archives, Dianbai County Court, 250-1-51-11-15. July 16, 1957.

28 To cite one of the cases, Han Shuzhi, deputy head of Shanghai High Court, was declared a rightist in 1958, deprived of his Party membership, and demoted to a lower position. Han's

In the following months, the central government stepped up pressure on the judicial system. On October 14, a *People's Daily* editorial chastised judicial cadres for only correcting falsely indicted cases in 1955 and not punishing enemies. The editorial warned judges against two proclivities: covering up enemies and neglecting Party leadership over law.[29]

The central policy forced more and more courts to wage interior crackdowns against "erroneous legal thoughts." In Shaanxi, all levels of courts had since July convened a series of meetings criticizing principles that had previously been deemed correct. For example, both the 1954 constitution and the Organic Law of the People's Court (hereinafter OLC) advocated judicial independence and lawful judgments, but during the Anti-Rightist Movement, these principles were condemned as "opposing Party leadership" or "using law to resist the Party." Additionally, emphasizing law and strictly following the law in tackling cases were dismissed as promoting "legal supremacy" or "legal omnipotence" without taking class enemies into account; the institution of lawyers was rebuked as "using lawyers' lawful identity to exonerate criminals;" and the following of legal processes was blamed for lacking a "right, timely, and class-struggle attitude." When the meetings ended in August 1958, seven court staff were declared rightists and all of them either lost their jobs or were demoted until 1979.[30]

In March 1958, the *People's Daily* injected more fear into the judicial system by uncovering an anti-Party clique inside the Anhui provincial court system. The head of the clique was Li Kenong, a vice governor of Anhui. Key members included the leaders of the provincial procuracy and the Party secretary of the provincial judicial department. Their main "crimes" were: 1) believing that judicial agencies should target ordinary criminals instead of counterrevolutionaries; and 2) holding that counterrevolutionaries should be pardoned because they had also done some revolutionary work. The editorial urged cadres to firmly oppose rightists who had ferociously attacked the Party in 1957.[31]

The Anti-Rightist Movement within the judicial system had adverse consequences. Glenn Tiffert notes that the number of judges in Beijing's

main "errors" were his opposition to Party intervention in trials, advocacy of GMD laws, and reinstitution of lawyer. See Song Yongyi, ed., *Verdicts and Internal Archives of nearly a Thousand of Rightists*, Vol. 2, (New York: Guoshi chubanshe, 2015): 182-184.

29 *The People's Daily*, October 14, 1957.

30 *Shaanxi Provincial Trial Gazette, Vol. 58.* (*Shaanxi shengzhi shenpanzhi*陕西省审判志) (Shaanxi: Shaanxi renmin chubanshe, 1994): 212-213.

31 *The People's Daily*, March 10, 1958.

courts dropped by 21.3% in late 1957.[32] Yet the biggest impact was "confusing judges' thought and blurring the boundaries between right and wrong." Because abiding by the law was condemned, judges tended to ignore the law in their future rulings. Many judges began thinking that the law was useless or at least inferior to Party policies. They became increasingly unwilling to cite the law in adjudicating cases. Worst of all, the "terror of the right" that many judges had experienced in the 1955 anti-counterrevolutionary campaign was resuscitated, and judges were forced to lean to the "left (the problem of method, *fangshi wenti*)" rather than to the "right (the problem of principle, *yuanze wenti*)." The result was numerous wrongly charged cases and victims.[33]

Like in Shaanxi, Yunnan's provincial courts also conducted internal checks and criticism of "erroneous" legal thoughts. According to the *Yunnan Provincial Gazette*, the provincial judicial system had 175 units and 1675 court police. From the outset of the movement, over 1400 cadres had participated. In October 1958, a report of the provincial high court revealed that 224 rightists, counterrevolutionaries, and "bad persons" had been dug out. Among them, 148 or 66% were rightists, including two leaders of intermediate courts and 23 heads of local courts. Most lawyers were rightists. Of all the rightists, 79 were dismissed from their posts and 27 had to do hard labor under supervision. The total number of rightists accounted for 10.57% of all participants in the movement. After many intellectuals, patriots, and cadres in Yunnan had been labeled and punished as rightists, there was a surge of leftism and both cadres and people dared not speak out.[34]

In Sichuan province, the movement was no less tense than in Shaanxi and Yunnan. The provincial court's criticism of many "correct" legal principles and "false" labeling of some rightists led to "unfortunate consequences." One of the consequences was, as in Shaanxi, that the movement sparked intellectual confusion among judges and allowed "erroneous thoughts and antipathy to law and the slogan "rather left than right" to prevail. Some judges "blatantly said that the law is useless and troublesome or that policies are the law." Under this overwhelming contempt for the law, judges no longer dared to speak and defend legal principles lest they should be declared as rightists or right-leaning.[35] The result was massive violations of law and falsely charged victims. In late 1957, cadres in most other provincial or city

32 Tiffert, 2015: 307.

33 *Shaanxi Provincial Trial Gazette, Vol. 58. Gazette of Trial*, 1994: 212-213.

34 *Yunnan Provincial Trial Gazette*, Vol. 55. *Gazette of Trial*, 1999: 238.

35 *Sichuan Provincial Trial Gazette*, 2003: 321.

courts, if not all, were facing similar situations and were prompted to turn left by ruthlessly punishing rightists and other "criminals."[36]

As shown in numerous cases, many courts in the late summer of 1957 began to feel the pinch of the Anti-Rightist Movement. Judges once again considered suspects' historical crimes or misconduct as grounds for harsher punishment and court verdicts became shorter and simpler. On August 23, the Shanghai Huangpu District Court sentenced Shen Jiancheng to three years in prison. Prior to 1953, Shen had been the manager of a manufacturing company. In 1956, the government helped Shen reopen his factory and let him renovate the Children's Home building. Using fabricated invoices, Shen requested more money than he needed from the government. Shen's illegal schemes were soon exposed, and he admitted all of them. The court ruled that Shen was a longtime speculator who during the Three-Antis and Five-Antis Movements (1951-1952) secretly did illegal business without license and cheated on labor and materials. Even after his crimes had been disclosed, Shen continued to deny them by all possible means. Because Shen was willing to return the money he had "stolen" from the state, the court sentenced him to only three years, a lesser punishment. With both lawyers and witnesses involved, the case generally followed the legal procedure of the OLC. It seemed that the court in the first couple of months of the Anti-Rightist Movement could still adhere to certain legal principles and procedures, albeit historical crimes again became an important factor in court decisions in the movement.[37]

Court Decisions under the "Left"

Since the people's court lumped many judicial principles and procedures into the scary category of "rightism," judges quickly leaned toward the "left" and handled criminal and counterrevolutionary cases with little or no regard to law or legal process. Some judges even applied their lawless whim to poor peasants, the so-called ruling class of the PRC. In Yunnan, for example, a poor female peasant named Li Laoshi had sold nine duck eggs and fourteen chicken eggs with prices below market level. Accusing Ms. Li

36 Due to the thought of "rather left than right" in the Anti-Rightist Movement, some Hunan judges sought to completely exterminate counterrevolutionaries by arresting more, trying more, and forcibly controlling more criminals. Many of the punishments were more severe and wrongly charged cases were not uncommon. *Hunan Provincial Gazette of Politics and Law*, Vol. 6 (*Hunan shengzhi diliujuan zhengfazhi*湖南省志第六编政法志) (Hunan: Hunan chubanshe, 1994): 259.

37 Shanghai Archives, August 23, 1957. B197-1-212-27.

of "frequently reselling eggs for illicit and excessive profits that is against state market price," the judge confiscated her eggs and basket. Although other judges disagreed with the ruling, they chose to remain silent for fear of being labeled as "rightists." Having lost her living, the poor peasant put on all her new clothes and hanged herself.[38]

If the court treatment of the poor peasant was harsh, the punishment of criminals, especially alleged counterrevolutionaries was harsher. In November 1957, more than four months after the beginning of the Anti-Rightist Movement, the Shanghai Xuhui District Procuracy charged one Huang Benren, a former accountant at a local factory, with "damaging revolutionary order." In fact, Huang's "crime" was sexual harassment at worst. On October 11, when Huang saw two women in the street, he went to chat with them and told them that his brother-in-law wanted to hire a maid. One of the women trusted Huang and accompanied him. When both of them were on a bus, Huang put his hands on the woman's shoulder and then touched her thighs, hip, and other sensitive areas. The court found evidence of Huang's former harassments of women. As recidivism, Huang's misdeeds were deemed by the court as "seriously hurting social order" and "violating revolutionary order." Without citing any specific law, Huang was sentenced to two years without probation.[39] By today's PRC law, Huang's punishment was quite draconian for alleged sexual harassment.[40] Yet, had he been convicted as a counterrevolutionary, his punishment would have been much worse.

In the early PRC, theft was regarded as a severe crime. From 1956 to May 1958, Wei Qun, a tax clerk, had stolen 300 *yuan* and two watches at a family building of the Shanghai Financial Cadre School where Wei was also living. The Shanghai Beijiao District Court found that Wei in 1954 took advantage of his post as a financial cadre to rape a saleswoman. The tax bureau where Wei was working simply educated and fired him without accusing him to the court. Apparently due to the loss of job and income, Wei chose to steal from his roommates at the dormitory. Although Wei confessed his crimes, his failure to correct his previous misconduct plus his new theft sufficed to warrant him five years in jail. The court verdict did not cite any contemporary laws and only mentioned that Wei's "relatively

38 *Yunnan Provincial Trial Gazette*, Vol. 55. *Gazette of Trial*, 1999: 239.

39 Shanghai Archives, November 16, 1957. B150-1-10-130.

40 According to Article 58 of the 2005 Protective Law of Women's Rights, sexual harassment is not a criminal case but at most a civil case in the court and/or is subject to administrative penalties by the police. See http://www.gov.cn/banshi/2005-05/26/content_980.htm

serious crimes directly affected his victims' normal life, study, and mutual harmony."[41] To be sure, a five-year incarceration for little more than 300 *yuan* was still quite severe. Wei's previous rape was surely a big reason for his long sentence.

In the Anti-Rightist Movement, there was a diffusion of law enforcement. Some non-judicial units such as schools or factories could convict and sentence alleged counterrevolutionaries, a clear violation of the OLC. On April 4, 1958, the Shanghai Financial Cadre School sued Xie Ying, one of its faculty members, to the court. The school claimed that Xie had joined a Nationalist Party (Guomindang, or GMD) youth league in 1939 and later became a GMD intelligence agent. In the Korean War, Xie listened to the Voice of America, a United States broadcasting program targeting Communist countries, and spread "rumors." In the 1955 campaign, the government temporarily detained Xie and released him the following year when the political situation was milder. "But the defendant (Xie) refuses to repent, remains haughty, and therefore his crime is serious," the district court noted. Citing the 1951 law against counterrevolutionaries, the court sentenced Xie to three years of *guanzhi* to "uphold state law and democratic dictatorship."[42]

Besides charging an employee in the court, the Shanghai Financial Cadre School, like many other governments, schools, and factories during the movement, seemed to assume the authority to sentence alleged counterrevolutionary employees to *laojiao*, further infringing the OLC provision that only the people's court had the authority to try a suspect. In March 1958, the financial school displayed a number of crimes committed by Xing Hairan, one of the school employees. According to the list, Xing helped the Japanese in the 1930s and joined the GMD in the 1940s. Since 1949, Xing had not only kept a mistress but also made "counterrevolutionary comments." He claimed that Soviet leader Stalin had sex with a woman almost every day during the war with the Nazis. After Luo Longji was denounced as one of the biggest rightists in the Anti-Rightist Movement,[43] Xing praised Luo as a talented writer. While Xing's reactionary comments and improper behaviors were not enough for the school to label him a rightist, school leaders still fired Xing and sentenced him to *laojiao*.[44] Unlike *guanzhi* (i.e.

41 Shanghai Archives, June 16, 1958. B117-1-21-1.

42 Ibid., April 4, 1958. B117-1-216.

43 For Luo Longji罗隆基 see Xie Yong谢泳, ed., *Luo Longji: My Experience and Rethinking of Arrest* (*Luo Longji: wode beibu dejingguo hefangan*罗隆基：我的被捕的经过和反感) (Beijing: Zhongguo qingnian chubanshe, 1999).

44 Shanghai Archives, March 24, 1958. B117-1-21-6.

forced labor), which could be decided by the police, *laojiao* had to be decided by a court. The financial school had no lawful right to sentence Xing to *laojiao* in normal times. But in the midst of the Anti-Rightist Movement nothing was impossible if the victim could be depicted as a reactionary or counterrevolutionary.

We have seen Shanghai judges in the movement who had not just ignored legal principles and process but also used alleged comments and petty/historical crimes to heavily punish so-called reactionaries or counterrevolutionaries. In contrast to their Shanghai counterparts, judges in poor and rural regions might have more discretion in making charges and imposing punishments. In early 1958, Liu Shiqing, a procurator of Jiaxing County in Zhejiang, accused Yu Qiuming, a sixteen-year-old student, of committing fraud and hooliganism. With no witnesses or tangible evidence, judge Zhang Qingrong stated that the teenage suspect had once stolen sundry articles such as an eraser, a pencil and a pound of copper from his classmates and aunt. In addition, Yu had joined a gang that targeted passengers near the railway station until he was caught on November 1. Alleging that "Yu has since childhood been a habitual thief," the county court adopted such campaign principles as "harsh penalty for active crimes" and sentenced Yu to three years in prison. The severe penalty was imposed on the underaged boy in the name of "protecting social security and severely punishing hoodlums and thieves."[45] With no existing criminal law to quote, the Jiaxing judge seemed to be able to misuse his "common sense" or "human sentiment" to mete out whatever punishments he wished to whoever was within his jurisdiction.

In Mao's China as in previous polities like the Qing, a few words against a ruler or the ruling party could result in heavy punishment or even death.[46] In the aforementioned case of Xing Hairan, an employee at Shanghai Financial Cadre School faced *laojiao* for just some "improper" complaints and gossip. But people in Jiaxing County suffered much more relentless punishment than Xing did for similarly poignant comments. One of the victims was Li Zhijian, who had been sentenced to five years of hard labor or *laogai* in the 1955 campaign for his alleged leadership in a former GMD youth league. While living in the labor camp, Li was accused of denying his evil deeds and asserting his innocence. He reportedly calumniated the labor camp as "a concentration camp" and cursed camp cadres and the Soviet Union but

45 Jiaxing County Archives, January 2, 1958. 94-1-301.

46 For the literary inquisition in the Qing see Jonathan Spence, *Treason by the Book* (London: Penguin Books, 2012).

praised the US.[47] Making matters worse, Li had rejected all charges against him and refused to confess. Based on Li's counterrevolutionary comments and actions plus his historical crime (i.e. youth member of the GMD), a judge added five more years on Li's *laogai* in early 1958.[48] Such severe punishment was normal during political crackdowns. Had Li been aware that a more violent political campaign was going on outside the labor camp, he might have refrained from making "reactionary" complaints or criticisms.

As we have seen, for class enemies or former GMD members and officials, life was rather precarious during the Anti-Rightist Movement. Even a slight misdemeanor could mean months if not years of *laogai* or imprisonment. In July 1958, one Zhou Dali, classified as a landlord (and thus as a member of an enemy class), was charged by the Jiaxing County Court with having "privately" (but not necessarily "illegally") cut down eleven trees in 1956. More recently, in July 1958, Zhou was found to have chopped down two more trees belonging to a cooperative. This was now considered to be a crime and he profited from it by selling the two trees for 22 *yuan*. Zhou allegedly committed another crime by spreading a rumor, but the court verdict was rather cursory and did not include any evidence or witness testimony. In the court decision, Zhou was identified as a landlord and his cutting down of public trees was deemed a "crime of damaging production." Ironically, the judge cited no law or regulation, but still ruled that Zhou should be sentenced to five years of prison "in compliance with the law."[49]

Adding to the plight of political victims in the movement was the poor quality of judges. Since the 1952 legal reform, the most valuable credential of judges was no longer their professional caliber but their political reliability. Consequently, many judges, especially those in county courts, had neither legal training nor qualified education. Court verdicts after 1953 had become less professional, sloppy, and short. Many judges still could not even write a formal verdict without miswritten characters. In one case, a former GMD official named Zhang Yuesheng was charged by the Jiaxing County Court with counterrevolutionary actions. The cursory court verdict contained several misspellings. For example, judge Zhang Qingrong wrote *jing* (well 井) in place of *jing* (police 警), a more complex character.[50] In another case, a judge wrote *ping* (flat (平) instead of *pin* (poor 贫) in his decision against

47 The US did not recognize the legitimacy of the PRC and was actively supporting GMD claims to authority over the islands of Quemoy and Matsu at this time.

48 Jiaxing County Archives, January 2, 1958. 94-1-301.

49 Ibid., 94-1-301, January 2, 1958.

50 Ibid., 94-1-301, March 20, 1958.

a poor peasant for participating in reactionary secret societies.[51] If a judge could not write formal verdicts correctly, it is rather doubtful that he could grasp the right meanings of laws and reports.

The cases I have discussed are just the tip of the iceberg of court verdicts in the Anti-Rightist Movement. Yet they help shed light on the relentless stance against alleged counterrevolutionaries taken by judges in major cities like Shanghai as well as rural areas in Zhejiang and Yunnan during this period. In extreme cases, some courts in Guangdong since 1957 had prohibited or at least discouraged criminals from appealing their cases. They also discontinued formal procedures such as juries, defenses, public trials, and the like.[52] The predominant cause behind judges' "leftist" and hostile attitudes in the movement was their fear of being branded as a rightist if their punishment of class enemies was lenient. After all, in a major political campaign that was characteristic of the PRC, suppressing all existing and potential class enemies was by far the most crucial political mission that outweighed anything else like legality or lawful procedure.

The Judicial System in the Great Leap

Shortly after Mao and his cohorts launched the Anti-Rightist Movement, they had another movement in mind: the Great Leap Forward. According to Vogel, the Great Leap was devised by Party leaders as "a shortcut on the path to modernity."[53] Mao's private doctor recalled that Mao had a good intention in the Great Leap but lacked modern education.[54] In other words, the Maoists were impatient to move quickly along the road to wealth and power as widely defined by the world in the third quarter of the twentieth century. In late 1957, Mao was inspired by Soviet leader Nikita Khrushchev's goal to catch up with or surpass the United States in wealth and power within fifteen years. Mao soon proposed that China should overtake Great Britain in a similar period. Like Mao's earlier call for a Hundred Flowers, his bold objective on the economic front initially won little support among top Party leaders. But after Mao reprimanded them for "frustrating 600 million people" and for coming "very close to being rightists," most leaders including

51 Ibid., 94-1-301, December 29, 1958.

52 In 1957 and 1958, most court verdicts allowed litigants to appeal to appellate courts. *Guangdong Provincial Trial Gazette* (*Guangdongsheng shenpanzhi*广东省审判志) (Guangdong: Guangdong renmin chubanshe, 1999): 66.

53 Vogel, 1980: 268.

54 Li Zhisui, *The Private Life of Chairman Mao* (New York: Random House, 1994): 351.

Liu Shaoqi, Zhou Enlai, and Deng Xiaoping finally threw in their lot with the Great Leap Forward.[55] As Jeremy Brown has argued, Mao's "views, whims, and policy judgments were extremely important in pursuing a revolutionary modernization project."[56]

The theoretic foundation for the Great Leap was "Continuous Revolution" coined by Mao at a meeting in early 1958. Mao believed that a "revolution has to be struck while the iron is hot and one revolution has to be ensued by another," which differed from Trotsky's Permanent Revolution which was more linear and irreversible. In the same meeting, Mao assured the Party that it was possible for China to surpass Great Britain in fifteen years.[57] For Mao, the Anti-Rightist Movement and the Great Leap Forward were stages and recurrent phases of the continuous revolution to keep the Party and the Chinese people moving forward to revolution, socialism, and communism. In the summer of 1958, as Mao gained more "assertive" power in the Party, he became increasingly enthusiastic and confident about the Great Leap. He was sure that China would overtake the Soviet Union even earlier than it would Western countries.[58]

At the height of the Great Leap, Mao, firmly believed in people's power to transform China and the world. Misled by exaggerated local reports of steel production and grain output, he slashed the length of time needed to outstrip the UK and the US by half, to seven years and fifteen years respectively.[59] Like officials, the masses were also mobilized to produce steel. According to Philip Short, 14% of the steel in September was made by small and local furnaces. In October, the figure was 41% percent. About 90 million people participated in steel production and abandoned their normal tasks.[60]

As a revolutionary movement, the Great Leap engulfed almost all social circles of the country, not just workers and peasants.[61] Inside the PRC judicial system, there was also a Great Leap of Law in coordination with the Party call. One of the methods utilized by many courts to attain the Great Leap

55 Other scholars such as Lowell Dittmer also believe that Mao was responsible for the Great Leap. Zhang Suhua张素华, *Change: Beginning and End of 7000-Men Meeting* (*bianju: qiqianren dahui shimo*变局：七千人大会始末) (Beijing: Zhongguo qingnian chubanshe, 2006): 133, 257-8; for Lowell Dittmer see Dittmer, 1989: 31.

56 Brown, 2014: 8.

57 *Unofficially Published Works of Mao Zedong, Additional Volumes of "Long Live Mao Zedong Thought" and other Secret Speeches of Mao*, 1958, Vol. 13, pp. 88-99: 96; also Meisner, 1999: 192; Dittmer, 1980: 33.

58 Dittmer, 1980: 31-32.

59 Zhang Suhua, 2006: 314-315.

60 Short, 2002: 487.

61 For the scope and scale of the Great Leap in the late 1950s see Lin Yunhui, 2008: 226-254.

of Law was to intensify the criticism of "fallacious" and "rightist" legal principles, albeit the Ministry of Internal Affairs disingenuously ordered provinces and cities to set up study of the Marriage Law and to "foster the custom of abiding by law."[62] In April 1958, Dong Biwu, the Supreme Court Justice who had asked judges to follow legal principles in the constitution and the OLC in the summer of 1957, was forced to back off from his previous legalist stance and to carefully cater to the new political wind. Dong now told judges to obey the order of the Party committees due to the existence of numerous counterrevolutionaries.[63] Despite his shift of stance to the left, Dong, according to one observer, was still chastised in a meeting in the summer of 1958 for opposing the merger of the three judicial agencies. In that meeting, Mao, the paramount leader in Deng Xiaoping's words,[64] reportedly downplayed the role of law. "Now we are rectifying judicial agencies," Mao said, "although law is useful, we have alternatives [...] [we] do not use the law to govern people [...] we mainly depend on [Party/central] resolutions and not civil or criminal laws to govern [the PRC]." A *People's Daily* editorial subsequently stated, "Why do we need law when a [mere] editorial [of the *People's Daily*] can be followed around the country?"[65]

Seeing contempt of law coming from the top, many central and local judicial leaders quickly followed suit and began attacking basic legal principles as "rightist". In a report on the Great Leap of the Guangdong judicial system, Li Lin, deputy head of the provincial court, denounced "judicial independence" and the "presumption of innocence" as nonsense. Li warned court cadres that their thoughts were still subject to several constraints. For example, some cadres were afraid of making mistakes because any one of their errors could be political. If a judge made 99 correct decisions and just one mistake, he might face grave consequences for the one mistake. Li Lin also criticized cadres' "blind faith" in legal textbooks, jurists, and legal principles such as the "presumption of innocence," the idea of the "law as paramount," and the citation of laws in all verdicts.[66]

Like Li Lin, Zhang Wenxiu, a leader at the Shanghai High Court, lashed out at "rightist views" such as "judicial independence" and "sitting in court

62 The reason that the government emphasized the marriage law might be that it was very unharmful in comparison to criminal and counterrevolutionary cases. For the Ministry of Internal Affairs see Altehenger, 2018: 163.

63 Dong, 2001: 411-418.

64 Dittmer, 1989: 33; also see Short, 2002: 494.

65 Xin Xiangdong辛向东, "Dong Biwu and Mao Zedong" in *Dangshi tiandi*, Vol. 5, 2009, pp. 7-8.

66 *The Great Leap of the People's Judicial Work* (*renmin sifa gongzuo dayuejin*人民司法工作大跃进) (Beijing: falu chubanshe, 1958): 73-85: 73.

to try cases." Zhang urged judges to go down to the factories and fields to deal with cases and assist the masses. The purpose of the court was to attack enemies and protect the Great Leap of production. Ironically, although Zhang wanted judges to discard legal principles and severely punish class enemies, he called on cadres to help enforce the socialist legal system and solidify mass legal consciousness to avert crimes. For Zhang and other Party leaders, law was a political instrument that the people (but not necessarily the Party) should abide by, a typical example of the rule by law.[67] One is reminded here of the hoary Chinese adage that the laws and punishments do not extend up to the elite, and the rituals do not extend down to the commoners (*xingbushang dafu, libuxiashuren*).

Li Yangling, head of the intermediate court in Xiangtan, Hunan, emphasized the importance of Party leadership over the judicial system. He argued that the court from 1955 to 1958 had witnessed a revival of bourgeois legal principles during which some judges only "partially understood" legal concepts such as "independent trials" and "obedience only to the law." Prior to 1958, judges usually sent their verdicts to Party committees after trials. Li rejected the practice as "nullifying the Party's leadership." Invoking Peng Zhen's order in October 1957, Li told judges to send their verdicts to Party committees before trials.[68]

In a national judicial meeting held in October 1958, one resolution formally denounced and jettisoned legal procedures stipulated in the OLC. It announced that judiciaries should be in line with the ongoing Great Leap Movement. Judiciaries should no longer mindlessly enforce legal processes and should adopt whichever methods would assist Party leadership and mobilize the masses. The free airing of views and mass debates would be the primary means of coping with internal contradictions among the people.[69]

In addition to condemning "rightist" legal principles, the judiciaries took some positive strides in improving the standard methods in order to make trials and other legal processes more convenient for the masses. In Zhejiang, for example, many judges who used to sit in the court to deal with cases now began to go out and connect with the masses. They held trials and solved cases in villages, lanes, and construction sites that were highly convenient to the masses. Some courts, under the slogan of "working hard for twenty days or a month," had resolved all pileup cases. In contrast to the spring of 1957, Zhejiang courts had reportedly elevated their efficiency

67 Shanghai Archives, October 31, 1958. B1-1-703-1.
68 *The Great Leap of the People's Judicial Work*, 1958: 1-6.
69 *Shaanxi Provincial Trial Gazette*, 1994: 215.

by four times with only two thirds the number of cadres.[70] Yet whether the quality matched the speed was unknown.

In Jiangxi, the provincial high court claimed that it had inspected 1834 cases from seventeen local courts in April and found that 92.26% of them, an unbelievable figure, were correct. Furthermore, a leader of the high court stressed the importance of high speed in tackling cases. "On the basis of ensuring quality," the court leader asserted, "many courts have increased their speed [in dealing with cases] by one or more times." In Shangrao County, the court finished 96% of its cases in two months among which more than 50% of cases had been solved within ten days. The court leader admitted that the Great Leap of Law was not without mistakes. One of them was that a few cadres merely cared about the number and speed of resolving cases without regard to quality. As a result, some cases that should not have been tried were adjudicated just to demonstrate the judicial system's hard work and efficiency.[71]

In certain aspects, however, the Great Leap of Law seemed to be rather radical and irrational, in some cases laughable. Since March 1958, there had been a nationwide campaign of "Ten 'Nos'" including: "no counter-revolutionaries," "no murder," "no robbery," "no theft" and the like. The point was to dramatize the goals of the judicial system which would ultimately be a communist society in which laws were no longer necessary. Some local governments and courts made unrealistic pledges and slogans. In one region, the local government promised that it would destroy all counter-revolutionaries in one day. It also displayed other preposterous slogans, such as that "big cases will be resolved in one day and small cases will be done in less than three hours."[72]

Another Great Leap plan was to combine all three judicial agencies and to simultaneously delete their no longer needed separate functions as articulated in the OLC in 1954. The Fourth National Judicial Conference in Zhengzhou, Henan, endorsed the merger of all three agencies. "The general trend of political and judicial departments is uniting and not splitting," the conference bulletin said, "insofar as police, procuracy, and court can sit together to clearly make their respective points, it is a [mutual] supervision. It is unnecessary for the agencies to do their individual work." The conference also stressed that law was made by men and was not something eternal. Whatever followed the Party policies was lawful. In light of the central

70 *The Great Leap of the People's Judicial Work*, 1958: 12.

71 Ibid., 1958: 25-31.

72 *Yunnan Provincial Trial Gazette*, Vol. 55, 1999: 239.

directive, most cities and counties combined police, procuracy, and court into one political and legal department (*zhengfabu*) or department of politics, law, and police (*zhengfa gong'anbu*).[73]

Many local courts speedily enforced the central directive. The Shaanxi Provincial High Court set out to overhaul its old procedure according to which the three agencies worked separately but in close coordination and with mutual checks. The new policy was that any head of police, procuracy, or court could from now on represent all three agencies. Moreover, any judge, procurator, or policeman could do whatever all three of them had to cooperate to do in the past. In other words, any cadre from the three agencies could conduct investigation, accusation, and adjudication altogether. While the new single procedure drastically improved the efficiency of the judicial system, it nonetheless eliminated the function of mutual checking among the agencies. As a result, some courts reportedly resorted to denunciation by the masses to tackle cases by condemning and threatening defendants. In some cases, once a person was singled out for criticism by the masses, the combined judicial system would charge and punish the person without further need of evidence. Torture and illicit interrogation were common.[74]

Such a merging of judicial agencies also took place in other provinces. In Inner Mongolia, the Great Leap of Law involved not only combining the three agencies but, in some localities, also replacing them with a political and legal department.[75] As in Inner Mongolia, the county government in Wanxian, Sichuan, integrated its three judicial agencies and allowed any head or cadre of the judicial agencies to do all the work. The previous three procedures – investigation, charge, and judgment – were streamlined into one organ. Only imprisonments for between five and ten years would be determined by the county Party committee; sentences for between three and five years would be discussed by the Party unit in the court; cases below three years would be decided by the head of the county court.[76] Given this discretion, court leaders or judges were granted a free hand in punishing defendants.

73 *Shaanxi Provincial Trial Gazette*, 1994): 216; also see Xu Lizhi, 2018: 37.

74 *Shaanxi Provincial Trial Gazette*, 1994: 215.

75 *Forty Years of the People's Court of the Neimenggu Autonomous Region* (*Neimenggu zizhiqu renmin fayuan sishinian*内蒙古自治区人民法院四十年) (Neimenggu: Neimenggu gaodeng renmin fayuan, 1993): 1-6.

76 *Wanxian County Court Gazette* (*Wanxian fayuanzhi*万县法院志) (Beijing: Fangzhi chubanshe, 2003): 114.

In the Great Leap of Law, some provinces adopted a policy that differed from that of Shaanxi, Inner Mongolia, and Sichuan. Although the Guangdong Provincial Court required one head of the three agencies to lead all of them, it continued to permit the three agencies to undertake their former separate functions. Police would still do preliminary investigation with procuracy lodging charges and the court trying cases. This made the union of the three agencies only nominal. That might have been because local Guangdong leaders disagreed with the "radical leftist" central and centralizing policy but also wanted to avoid trouble.[77]

The Great Leap of Law in Practice

While the official rhetoric of the Great Leap of Law portended a drastic deterioration of legal practices, the period, as we will see in numerous court cases, was in some respects actually not much different from – and not worse than – what we have seen in the previous PRC political movements of 1955 and 1957. For instance, the dire idiom that "a ready tongue is an evil" continued to draw severe punishments. In Dali, Yunnan, after a grand canteen, a showcase of communism, was built, a peasant came to the canteen and said that his child was still extremely hungry. The police detained the peasant who was later indicted for "active sabotage (*xianxing pohuai*)" and sentenced to six years in prison.[78] In the Great Leap as in the Anti-Rightist Movement, historical crimes or misdeeds would be considered in determining sentences.

On September 18, 1958, the Liangshan County Procuracy in Shandong accused one Zheng Pixian, a former poor peasant and village head, of pilfering 30 *yuan* from the commune in 1956 and 1957, stealing three animals (donkeys or cattle), and embezzling 200 *yuan* of public funds. In addition, Zheng refused to confess, a punishable misbehavior. On the same day, the Liangshan County Court tried the case and endorsed the procuracy charge that Zheng was a corrupt cadre. The judgment wrote, "To strengthen law and discipline and attain the goal of educating the criminal, Zheng would be sentenced to five years."[79] In this case, the county procuracy and court appeared not to be combined because the procuracy continued to be the prosecutor and the court still held the trial, though both the charge and

77 *The Great Leap of the People's Judicial Work*, 1958: 73-85.

78 *Yunnan Provincial Trial Gazette*, Vol. 55. *Gazette of Trial*, 1999: 241.

79 Liangshan County Archives, 1958. 53-3-647.

verdict were made on the same day. Also, had Zheng not been a poor peasant and low-level cadre, his punishment would have been much worse in a political campaign.

In the Great Leap, counterrevolutionaries, whether historical or active, were punished more harshly than were criminals from other social classes (e.g. cadres, workers, peasants). In July 1958, Wu Degen, a 26-year-old clerk at a local housing repair company, appealed to the Shanghai High Court seeking reduction of his ten-year incarceration made by an intermediate court. Wu had been accused of collaborating with a counterrevolutionary, Wang Jinting, in creating an illegal factory that secretly took orders from some local enterprises. Wu obtained illegal profit of as much as 500 *yuan* and squandered all of it. Unfortunately, the high court backed the original penalty of the lower court. Wang Jinting, the only counterrevolutionary in this case, refrained from appealing to the high court. Yet the high court discovered that Wang had helped the Japanese destroy thirty civilian homes and had conducted anti-CCP propaganda when he was a GMD committee member between 1939-1949. Combining Wang's old and new counterrevolutionary crimes, the high court augmented Wang's punishment from four to seven years' imprisonment.[80] Unlike crime mastermind Wu Degen, Wang was merely an accomplice. But Wang's historical counterrevolutionary crimes exacerbated his crime and denigrated his nature in a political movement.

If it was relatively "reasonable" for Wang Jinting, a historical counterrevolutionary, to suffer a heavier penalty for his fresh crime with Wu Degen, other historical counterrevolutionaries penalized with no new and "real" misconducts were not merely unlucky but also wronged. In July 1958, Li Tianshun, a mason, received a one-year *guanzhi* for nothing but his actions before 1949. According to the Jiaxing County Court, Li joined a local GMD security force and later was promoted to squad leader during which he allegedly had extorted people of twenty cartons of cigarettes, tobacco, and money. He had also beaten people and committed fornication. But Li had committed no new crime after 1949. In the Great Leap of Law, Li's historical crimes were exhumed, and he was punished.[81] In this case, none of Li's alleged historical crimes had been documented by the court. There is no doubt that the ongoing political campaigns compelled the court to prioritize the elimination of all likely enemies.

80 Shanghai Archives, July 18, 1958. B197-1-212-1.

81 Case of Li Tianshun, July 14, 1958; Jiaxing County Archives, January 2, 1958. 94-1-301.

In the process, the absence of evidence for old crimes and for new ones counted for little.

To be sure, not all cases in this period involved draconian penalties. Some Party lawbreakers were treated quite leniently. In one case, a production head in Luliang County, Yunnan, had allegedly beaten people many times and asserted that "the more people I have hit, the better my chance of getting a red flag (reward) and not a white flag (criticism) in a competition." He had reportedly beaten ten people to death and injured two other peasants in the movement. But the production head received only light punishment, probably because of his government post and Party membership.[82]

As in the Anti-Rightist Movement, charges in the Great Leap of Law could come from government units other than procuracy, the lawful prosecutor. But most charges against counterrevolutionaries came from local police. More important, according to the existing archival materials I have collected, none of them was wholly decided by any single agency of the "merged" judicial system, which was advocated by the central judicial meeting in the spring of 1958. In all cases, the adjudicator was the county court. Therefore, it is safe to argue that courts in many counties such as Jiaxing and Liangshan continued to follow certain basic legal procedures.

A new problem of the Great Leap of Law was the discrepancy in the number of days allowed to litigants to appeal to appellate courts. The 1954 OLC had specified that litigants would have ten days to appeal.[83] Yet, as early as June 1958, many judges in Jiaxing County gave random numbers of days for appealing to upper courts. For example, in the cases of Li Tianshun, Xu Xiaomei, and Ma Kang, the judges gave them ten days to appeal. But in some other cases, defendants got only five days to appeal.[84]

In most provinces and cities, the year of 1958 witnessed the greatest number of criminal/counterrevolutionary cases between 1950 and 1978, the year China initiated sweeping reforms. Undoubtedly, the politics-driven Anti-Rightist and Great Leap movements, the arbitrary use of law, and the poor quality of judges all lay behind the skyrocketing number of cases. The following two charts further demonstrate the abuses of law and the gargantuan number of criminal cases in the Great Leap (also see Chapter 7).

82 *Yunnan Provincial Trial Gazette*, Vol. 55. *Gazette of Trial*, 1999: 242.

83 *Guangdong Provincial Trial Gazette*, 1999): 66.

84 Case of Xu Wannian, July 14, 1958. Jiaxing County Archives, January 2, 1958. 94-1-301.

Table 6.1 No. of criminal cases in Guangdong province, 1949-1965[85]

Year	First Instance: Accepted/Resolved	Second Instance: Accepted/Resolved
1949	791	Not Available
1950	16974/11178	Not Available
1951	29374/30626	702/721 (appeal cases about 2.5%)
1952	35792/35443	Not Available
1953	19925/21255	577/635 (appeal cases about 2.5%)
1954	37940/35345	867/777
1955	61930/61990	2347/1866 (fewer appeals, about 3-4%)
1956	35644/34126	3320/3423
1957	47033/43870	4424/3909
1958	**110025/115377**	**4970/5601 (very few appeals, about 5%)**
1959	37232/37490	1295/1404 (appeal cases about 4%)
1960	29500/28843	566/518
1961	28997/28726	640/578
1962	17968/18073	858/848
1963	25465/24819	1434/1274
1964	12827/11750	792/907
1965	7483/7518	693/795

Table 6.2 No. of criminal cases in Shaanxi province, 1950-1965[86]

Year	No. of Criminal Cases	Counterrevolutionary Cases	Percentage of Total Cases	Solved Cases
1950	12345	610	4.87	11860
1951	25619	7895	30.82	25522
1952	18508	2954	15.96	18784
1953	18625	2730	14.64	19385
1954	23440	1219	5.20	22209
1955	27587	3831	13.87	27892
1956	17791	3944	22.17	19761
1957	16560	1501	9.06	15362
1958	**66981**	**23258**	**34.72**	**68063**
1959	12103	1692	13.98	12838
1960	12967	2939	22.67	12860
1961	13406	1453	10.76	12383
1962	13230	601	4.54	13553
1963	16801	907	5.40	16400
1964	10469	1594	15.23	9778
1965	11580	1137	9.82	11812

85 *Guangdong Provincial Trial Gazette*, 1999: 81.

86 *Shaanxi Provincial Trial Gazette*, 1994): 301-302.

In Table 6.1, the number of first-instance criminal cases in Guangdong that had been accepted and resolved in 1958 is the highest between 1949 to 1965. In Shaanxi province, both the total number of criminal cases and the percentage of counterrevolutionary cases in 1958 are significantly greater than in any other year between 1950 and 1965. The same scenario could also be found in cities like Tianjin and Jinhua (Zhejiang) and provinces like Yunnan and Sichuan.[87] Even if the numbers of 1957 were lower, they are still bigger than most other years. We could find an analogous situation in Tianjin in terms of its number of counterrevolutionary cases in 1958. In that year, the number was 3195, which was the highest from 1952 to 1963.

A Volatile Political Period, 1959-1965

From 1959 to the eve of the Cultural Revolution in 1966, Chinese politics was like a roller coaster. Frustration over the Great Leap began in early 1959 and turned into desperation in 1960 due to the Great Famine. In 1961, the radical revolutionary policies culminating in the Great Leap, the People's Commune, and the run for communism underwent a drastic reversal with the restoration of certain "capitalist elements" such as restoring peasants' private land, allowing peasants to have sideline business, and opening rural markets. In 1963, the country fell into another movement, the Four Cleanups. This movement featured a revival of class struggle and became a precursor to the Cultural Revolution.

Due to a polity-wide prioritization of steel production, the adverse consequences of the Great Leap surfaced in late 1958. Markets in cities like Shanghai were grappling with serious shortages of groceries and the problem worsened in the following spring. But local officials tended to conceal the problem because whoever spoke against the Great Leap could be denounced as a rightist.[88]

87 In Tianjin, the number of counterrevolutionary cases in 1958 was 3195, the highest from 1952 to 1963. See *Comprehensive Gazette of Tianjin – Adjudicating Gazette* (*Tianjin tongzhi-shenpanzhi* 天津通志-审判志) (Tianjin: Tianjin shehui kexueyuan chubanshe, 1999): 201; In Jinhua, the number of criminal cases in 1958 was 16,943, the highest since 1949. See *Jinhua Court Gazette* (*Jinhua fayuanzhi*金华法院志) (Beijing: Fangzhi chubanshe, 1999): 227-229; for Yunnan see *Yunnan Provincial Trial Gazette*, 1999: 55. 324.

88 Lin Yunhui, 2008: 431-454.

Studies have shown that Mao intended to slow down the Great Leap before the Lushan meeting.[89] However unfair, it seemed that Peng Dehuai, the Defense Minister and a hero of the Korean War, could be blamed for upending Mao's plan. Alarmed by the serious famine he had seen in the country, Peng wrote a 10,000-word private letter to Mao. In a meeting Peng criticized the empty pomp and asked the chairman to correct the left-leaning policies.[90] To Peng's surprise, Mao ordered that copies of his letter be passed to all attendees. Most cadres, especially central leaders such as Liu Shaoqi and Lin Biao, quickly sided with Mao and condemned Peng. Before the meeting was called off, Peng was declared the head of an "anti-Party" clique and he soon lost power.[91]

The unexpected letter of Peng Dehuai and the ensuing denunciation ostensibly messed up Mao's initial plan to roll back the Great Leap. On August 7, the Party central demanded that cadres at all levels oppose right-leaning thought and, at the same time, stimulate a new fervor of production. One week later, the Party neglected the serious problems of the Great Leap and urged all Party committees to focus on production in an effort to meet or exceed the Great Leap goal of the year. Anyone who opposed the Great Leap would be akin to countering socialism, a dire crime in Mao's China.[92] In early 1960, Mao reaffirmed his support of a "long-term" leap.[93]

In actuality, the shift of central policy was made in the midst of the largest famine in Chinese history. Since the spring of 1958, people in some localities had already suffered hunger.[94] Thousands of them fled their villages and entered cities like Shanghai. The situation turned bleaker in late 1959 as tens of thousands of famine victims flooded the streets of Shanghai, Tianjin, and other cities because they believed that "cities were better off than villages during the famine."[95] Scholars have tried different ways to fathom the numbers of famine victims. Cao Shuji estimates that around 32

89 See for example, Lee Feigon, 2002: 129. Lin Yunhui also writes that Mao told cadres to cool down when he was discussing the Lushan meeting. Lin Yunhui, 2008: 455.

90 Li Rui李锐, *A Veritable Record of Lushan Meeting* (*lushan huiyi shilu*庐山会议实录) (Henan: Henan renmin chubanshe, 1998).

91 Ibid.; also see Li Zhisui, 1996.

92 Lin Yunhui, 2008: 521.

93 *Unofficially Published Works of Mao Zedong*, Vol. 6b, 1991: 304.

94 Frank Dikotter, *Mao's Great Famine: The History of China's Most Devastating Catastrophe, 1958-1962* (New York: Walker & Co., 2010): 68-72.

95 During the Great Famine, many urbanities (in Tianjin) who had regular but reduced grain rations still suffered hunger. For Tianjin see Brown, 2014: 36, 53, 60-73; for Shanghai see Lin Yunhui, 2008: 552.

million people died as a result of the famine.[96] Yang Jisheng, a journalist whose father died in the famine, asserts that about 36 million people starved to death in the Great Famine.[97] Frank Dikotter estimates that around 45 million people "died unnecessarily between 1958 and 1962."[98]

To Mao, the supreme leader, the famine was a huge disgrace. According to Ezra Vogel, the chairman was "no longer sacred and invulnerable."[99] For a couple of years, Mao began "gloomily to implement his long-delayed promise to retire to the second front."[100] In May 1961, Liu Shaoqi who had enthusiastically backed the Great Leap three years before, now admitted that Party policies were the main culprit of the famine. This put him on a collision course with Mao who faulted natural disasters and the withdrawal of Soviet aid. In 1961, the Party finally retreated from the Great Leap and many other radical and leftist policies including the Great Leap of Law. Peasants were permitted to have an extension of their private plots and intellectuals could have more freedom in writing and art. Meisner likened China's policies between 1961 and 1965 to Vladimir Lenin's New Economic Policy in 1921. However limited in scale, the Party and judicial system also began to rehabilitate victims who had been wronged in the recent movements.[101]

The showdown among top leaders took place in two meetings in 1962. In early 1962, Mao, in the 7000-people meeting, made a self-criticism for the economic setback and famine owing to his lack of knowledge of industry and commerce.[102] Yet Mao remained the leader of the Party and the military. In the fall, upset by surging capitalism and maldistribution of wealth in rural areas, in another meeting Mao warned the Party of the problems.[103] In late 1962, to defend socialism in the country, Mao launched a new movement, the Four Cleanups, to "raise revolutionary vigilance and

96 Cao Shuji曹书基, *Great Famine: Chinese Population between 1959 and 1961* (*dajihuang: 1959-1961nian dezhongguo renkou*大饥荒：1959-1961年的中国人口) (Hong Kong: Shidai guoji chuban, 2005): iv, 284.

97 Yang Jisheng, *Tombstone: The Great Chinese Famine, 1958-1962* (New York: Farrar, Straus, and Giroux, 2012): 12-13.

98 Dikotter, 2010: x.

99 Vogel, 1980: 269.

100 Short, 2002: 505.

101 Only around 200,000 people out of 3.65 million rightists were rehabilitated in 1960 and 1961. See Meisner, 1999: 261; Lin Yunhui, 2008: 689-757.

102 Zhang Suhua, 2006: 190-191.

103 Qian Xiangli, *Historical Change: From Crisis Rescue to Opposing and Averting Revisionism, 1962-1965* (*lishi debianju: cong wanjiu weiji daofanxiu fangxiu*历史的变局：从挽救危机到反修防修) (Hong Kong: Hong Kong Chinese University Press, 2008): 272-289.

educate the masses on the benefits of socialism."[104] According to Maurice Meisner, the Four Cleanups aimed not only "to root out corrupt practices but to expose the collusion between Party cadres and rich peasants and their exploitation of the majority of the rural population."[105] While the nature of the Four Cleanups varied in different places, many places witnessed massive extralegal tortures, beatings, struggles, and suicides.[106]

The Retreat from the Great Leap of Law, 1959-1962

As a potent weapon of the Party, the Communist judicial system generally adhered to Party policies in this turbulent period. After the Party condemned Peng Dehuai in the Lushan Meeting and the ensuing new wave of Anti-Rightist Movement in the summer of 1959, the judicial system kept its leftist policies and its heavy punishment of class enemies. In the wake of the Great Famine and especially the change in the political atmosphere in early 1961, the pendulum of the judicial system shifted to restore legal processes by chastising radical leftism, separating police and procuracy, and correcting previously false or excessive punishments. Even though the Party adhered to leftism in the Four Cleanups, the judicial system largely preserved its lenience toward rightists and its resort to legal processes. The police were not as dominant in prosecuting counterrevolutionaries in this period as has sometimes been thought.[107]

According to some local gazettes, the moderate judicial policy seems to have been unevenly implemented. For example, the Guangdong Provincial Court stripped defendants of their right to appeal between 1957 and 1960. Legal procedures such as public trials, joint discussions, juries, and legal defense as pledged in the 1954 OLC were not restored until 1960, the year the provincial court started reinstituting all formal procedures in trials.[108] Jinhua in Zhejiang, however, claimed to have separated the three judicial agencies and restored legal procedures in the spring of 1959. In the fall, the

104 Frank Dikotter, *The Cultural Revolution: A People's History, 1962-1976* (New York: Bloomsbury Press, 2016): 18.

105 Meisner, 1999: 274.

106 Brown, 2014: 125-126; Qian Xiangli, 2008: 327.

107 The police did act as a major prosecutor on counterrevolutionary cases in the period, particularly during political movements. But the procuracy was the primary accuser in ordinary criminal cases, which along with some other government units could also file charges against counterrevolutionary cases during political movements. Stanley Lubman, 1999: 80.

108 *Guangdong Provincial Trial Gazette*, 1999: 66-67.

region followed the central policy of reducing the numbers of executions and arrests. In 1960, due to the influence of "the Great Leap of Law and erroneous leftism," many judges in Jinhua made decisions haphazardly with little regard to law.[109] In Shanghai, a deputy head of the procuracy asserted on June 4, 1959 that his agency had trusted only hard evidence rather than oral confessions and that "both the police and court rigorously follow the law and they are extremely serious and discreet in interrogation and trial."[110] Whether it was true or not, the deputy at least recognized that the judicial system in Shanghai was supposed to act lawfully even in a political movement.

Lingering severity against class enemies could still be found in the archival cases. In March 1959, after eighteen-year-old student Li Tongyu in Liangshan County, Shandong, failed to secure a living in Tianjin, he was so frustrated that he wrote slogans cursing Mao on the wall of a public bathroom. One slogan read: "Chairman Mao is a big bastard who is only qualified to monitor a bathroom." The county court subsequently sentenced Li to five years in jail for a few curses.[111] The harsh penalty was in tandem with others in major campaigns from 1951 to 1958. If a criminal in such cases was not a class enemy, the punishment would be light. In May 1959, the Liangshan County Procuracy accused Yan Keqin, a poor peasant, of cruelly beating his wife to death. After Yan discovered in March that his wife had committed adultery with another villager, he hanged her on a tree and brutally killed her. Because Yan "violates human rights and is an active criminal," the county court decided to imprison him for ten years.[112] Despite his cruelty in murdering his wife, Yan's penalty was fairly lenient in contrast to that of Li Tongyu who had merely cursed Mao. One reason behind the disparity was probably that Li was a counterrevolutionary and Yan was a poor peasant, nominally at least a member of the ruling class.[113]

Signs of more tolerant central policies arrived in 1960. In May, the Ministry of Public Security ordered that normal verbal complaints against the results of Party policies (e.g. famine) from rich peasants and ordinary people would be handled as internal problems among the people, namely by criticism and education. In November 1960, as the famine was intensifying, the Supreme Court prescribed local courts not to punish petty thefts and the clandestine

109 *Jinhua Court Gazette*, 1999: 227.

110 Shanghai Archives, June 4, 1959. B1-1-738-28.

111 Liangshan County Archives, June 1, 1959. 54-2-118.

112 Ibid., May 5, 1959. Y-3-746.

113 The same Yan Keqin was freed in 1962 by the court because of his good performance during *laogai*. See Liangshan County Archives, May 5, 1959. Y-3-746.

slaughtering of livestock driven by hunger. It scolded local courts that had abused their power in incarcerating people committing those crimes.[114] In the same year, the Guangdong High Court demanded that in most criminal trials legal procedures be implemented such as preliminary work (e.g. review files and set dates and places of trials), jury, public and on-site trials, and the like.[115] Although the central government in 1960 tried to soften tones and punishments amid the Great Famine, the fate of counterrevolutionaries remained the same. Dereliction of duties, abuse of power, resorts to torture, and false charges by judicial agencies were not uncommon. As the last hope for many defendants, especially those facing falsely imposed death penalties, the Supreme Court was supposed to be an incarnation of justice, though in some cases, the halo of the highest court could not always be taken for granted.[116]

According to a 1962 Supreme Court document, the Taishan County Police in Guangdong claimed in March 1960 that it had destroyed a counterrevolutionary "army" led by Huang Ruoying. Upon receiving the report from the police, the Taishan procuracy lodged a charge to the county court. Having discovered several problems such as a dubious source, reliance on a confession, use of torture, and a defendant's retraction of confession, the court returned the file to both the procuracy and police for reinvestigation. But the police sent the file back to the court and hinted with a caveat that the court might have been "leaning to the right." Hesitant but undeterred, some judges including court leaders chose to "safeguard judicial principles" and refused to back down even if it meant the "loss of their official posts." It is fair to say that the stamina of some court judges was laudable because 1960 was still at the peak of the Great Leap movement.

The deadlock between the court and police lasted until July 1961 when the county Party secretary convened a meeting for all three agencies to debate the case. While the Party secretary, a superior to the judicial system, advocated the police, court officials resisted the pressure and insisted that the evidence be deemed insufficient for a final judgment. The secretary told the court, "What else do you need to investigate? You must make a decision [on the case]." One court leader defiantly responded that he could not follow the order. Fortunately, the political ice in the summer of 1961 was already

114 *Yunnan Provincial Trial Gazette,* 1999: 243.

115 *Guangdong Provincial Trial Gazette,* 1999: 66.

116 In one case, after Pan Guohua, a peasant of Guizhou province, was wronged in a murder in early 1960, the Supreme Court became derelict in its duty by endorsing the death penalty without further investigation. It was the local court that saved Pan just days before his execution in a final review. See Liangshan County Archives, September 7, 1961. 53-2-8: 4-9.

melting and the secretary chose not to punish the court leaders. In August, an official from the Ministry of Public Security came to Taishan for a routine inspection. The court reported the case and won his support. The central official asked all three local agencies to form a work team to study the case. After twenty days of diligent reinvestigation, the truth finally surfaced that proved the court decision to be right. Huang Ruoying who had been coerced to confess under police torture gained his freedom. In a circular released on February 17, 1962, the Supreme Court extoled the Taishan court for its "audacity in defending legal principles." The circular also noted that all three judicial agencies had to coordinate and maintain mutual checking in battles against class enemies. More important, the circular stated, "the court is the last stage of handling a case and accordingly is responsible for both discovering and righting the wrong."[117]

This case tells us that not all local judicial agencies were combined in the Great Leap. While we do not know the number of courts that dared to do the same as the Taishan court in this movement, one thing is certain. At least some judges/courts could persevere in upholding basic legal principles and in acting independently by defying immense pressure from the police and Party leaders. Moreover, the case of Huang Ruoying reveals that the actual change in Party policy came no earlier than the fall of 1961 when the central government issued a directive correcting all false charges and purging all enemies.

The Supreme Court used another high-profile case to notify all courts to avoid similar mistakes. This case occurred in 1955 when one Bing Rui was falsely accused by the Yichun court in Heilongjiang and sentenced to eight years in prison. In the spring of 1955, a district government in Yichun found several "extremely reactionary" threatening letters and slogans. Based merely on handwriting verification, the local police arrested Bing Rui as the anonymous writer and sent him to the Yichun court. Although the court initially noticed problems in the charge and returned the case twice to the local procuracy and police for reinvestigation, in 1958 it chose to punish Bing Rui to avoid being branded as rightist. Bing Rui followed the legal procedure and appealed to the Songhuajiang Intermediate Court, which also disputed the police evidence and told the lower court to exonerate Bing Rui. This order was neglected by the lower court. It was not until April 1961 when the political strain was eased that Bing Rui was finally exonerated. By then, he had spent almost six years behind bars. The Supreme Court lambasted the Yichun court for not upholding its stance as the last stage of the three

117 Liangshan County Archives, April 6, 1962. 53-2-8-36.

agencies notwithstanding its first suspicion of the police handwriting verification. One of the reasons was Yichun court's fear of being criticized for being right-leaning. In a flat rejection to the dominant left-leaning since the Anti-Rightist Movement, the Supreme Court circular in 1961 stated that left-leaning was worse than right-leaning because "a falsely wronged person will damage the relationship between the Party and the masses, and the mistake will be more serious [than criminals who had received lenient penalties due to right-leaning thought]." Another reason for the false charge was the Yichun court's failure to consult with the local Party committee prior to making its decision.[118] This Supreme Court's argument was hardly credible because ever since the 1952 legal reform all courts had been required to obey Party committees. A more convincing explanation might have been that some local officials, like their predecessors in previous polities, were unwilling to review voluminous court files due to their lack of legal knowledge and training.[119]

In early 1962, less than four months after the Yichun court was criticized for not having consulted the local Party committee, the Supreme Court in no little irony ascribed a victim's grievance to the "intervention" of a local Party secretary in a court case. In both November and December of 1958, Wang Bin, an electrician in Guangshan County, Henan, was accused of conducting deliberate acts of "sabotage" during Party committee meetings. On the night of Wang's second alleged "sabotage," Ma Longshan, the head of the Party committee, immediately ordered the local police to arrest Wang Bin. The police inflicted torture and enticement to extract confession from him. With the "evidence" from police and the pressure from the Party committee, the local court did no independent investigation and simply sentenced Wang to eight years in prison. Aggrieved, Wang and his relatives managed to appeal to the Supreme Court, which ordered the Henan Provincial Court to review the case. The court finally rehabilitated Wang. In its report, the Supreme Court criticized local judges for failing to investigate the case and to stand up for legal principles. Instead, local judges had "blindly" meted out the order of Party secretary Ma Longshan and made cursory judgment.[120] Unlike in the case of Bing Rui, the grievance of Wang Bin was solely caused by the meddling of a local Party committee. The

118 Ibid., September 25, 1961. 53-2-8-23-24.

119 For magistrates' lack of legal training in Chinese history see Bao Yongjun, *A Study on Shaoxing Private Adviser Wang Huizu* (*Shaoxing shiye Wang Huizu yanjiu*) (Beijing: Renmin chubanshe, 2006).

120 Liangshan County Archives, January 5, 1962. 53-2-8: 27-28.

Supreme Court made no comment on the difference and the contradiction between its two reports.

The lenience and correction of erroneous charges in 1960 and 1961 were, in fact, concomitant with arbitrary and harsh punishments in some localities. In May 1961, Fang Dezhong, a starving peasant in E'shan County, Yunnan, stole two pounds of rice, one rabbit, and some beans. After being caught, Fang was beaten and hanged to death by leaders of a production team. No local law enforcement agencies were involved in this case of mass justice known elsewhere as lynching.[121] In another case, one Qin Zhaoxian, a student from Liangshan, Shandong, had since 1959 mailed six anonymous letters condemning Mao for the famine. The Liangshan County Court put Qin into five-year incarceration as an active counterrevolutionary, the same as what Li Tongyu received in 1959. Still, Qin Zhaoxian was more fortunate than Li due to the milder central policy in late 1961. Less than ten months later, while it was reviewing Qin's case, the court decided to free Qin on grounds that his "venomous" attacks on Mao mirrored the contemporary reality (i.e. popular anger at the famine). The court added that Qin was not a class enemy and his case should be resolved by mediation as it involved an internal contradiction among the people.[122]

Legal Rehabilitation after 1962

In the fall of 1962, two seemingly incompatible policies coexisted: The Four Cleanups and the ongoing retroactive justice. On the dark side, shortly after the CCP launched the Four Cleanups in late 1962 and early 1963, the Supreme Court demanded all courts to "timely and lawfully" penalize new counterrevolutionary activities "regardless of their social status and origin."[123] CCP's longstanding and fundamental fear of being overthrown was articulated more palpably by a deputy head of the Supreme Court in December 1963. He urged judiciaries to "unswervingly strike active counter-revolutionaries and thwart their conspiracy against the Party."[124] To many

121 *Yunnan Provincial Trial Gazette*, Vol. 55, 1999: 244.
122 Liangshan County Archives, January 1962. 54-2-185.
123 *Judicial Handbook* (*Sifa shouce*司法手册), Vol. 2., October 1964, pp. 62-80: 64; *Yunnan Provincial Trial Gazette*, Vol. 55. *Gazette of Trial*, 1999: 248.
124 Supreme Court Office, ed., *Judicial Handbook* (*sifa Shouce*), December 31, 1963.

victims who had survived several past movements, the Four Cleanups was like another nightmare.[125]

On the bright side, some central government offices and leaders issued more orders and directives in late 1962 in support of legal principles such as judicial independence and legal procedures. On November 27, 1962, the same Supreme Court promulgated the Provisional Methods of the People's Tribunal in which it reiterated that all trials should have one judge, two jurors, and one clerk.[126] Three days later, a tentative regulation enacted collectively by the Supreme Court, the Supreme Procuracy, and the Ministry of Public Security demanded a restoration of the separation and mutual oversight among the three judicial agencies.[127] At the Sixth National Judicial Work Meeting in early November, Xie Juezai, head of the Supreme Court, remarked that all people's courts had to make independent decisions and only follow the law. He criticized some local governments for allowing communes, work teams, or other government units to conduct trials and make rulings. Xie was right on this point. As we have seen, some schools and factories in Shanghai during political movements could sentence people to *guanzhi* or *laogai*.[128]

Fortunately, the Four Cleanups did not become another Great Leap of Law because its scope and scale of extralegal beating, torture, and killing were smaller. In this period, ordinary criminal cases were generally treated with lenience. In one case, Song Yifu, a peasant living in Liangshan, Shandong, had since June 1962 committed adultery with the wife of a fellow villager. On the night of June 29, 1962, when Song tried to sneak into the woman's home for sex, he was caught by people as a thief. To prove his innocence, Song admitted that his true intention was to see his mistress. Ashamed, the woman killed herself the next morning. The county procuracy accused Song of being responsible for the death of his sex partner. But the court ruled that, although Song's activity was unlawful, he should not be punished for the woman's death. This case largely followed legal procedure with the local procuracy as the prosecutor, one judge, and two jurors. The exception was

125 For the violence in the Four Cleanups see *Unofficially Published Works of Mao Zedong*, 1957, Vol. 10. 1991, pp. 364-367; Guo Dehong郭德宏 and Lin Xiaobo林小波, eds., *Personal Experiences in the Four Cleanups* (*siqing yundong qinliji*四清运动亲历记) (Beijing: Renmin chubanshe, 2008).

126 According to the court verdicts of Liangshan county court between 1958 and 1965, most, if not all, of them had already followed the procedure with two jurors and one clerk. For the supreme court document see Liangshan County Archives, December 20, 1962. 53-2-8: 100.

127 Ibid., November 30, 1962. 53-2-8: 53.

128 Ibid., November 2, 1962. 53-2-8: 92-98.

that Song was given only two days to appeal to the appellate court.[129] Even though Song did not need to appeal and did not do so, the two-day appeal time he was allowed attested to the poor quality and amateurishness of the judge.

In the PRC, the assumption was that Party members or cadres could enjoy certain legal privileges.[130] In some cases, however, Party members and cadres who were judged guilty of crimes would find their penalties more severe than those meted out to civilians. For instance, since 1954, Deng Mingsheng, a Party member and head of a local bank in Liangshan County, had taken advantage of his position by committing fornication with the wife of a man whose surname was Liu. That led Liu and his wife to divorce in 1957. Emboldened by the divorce, Deng and his mistress (now single) no longer had scruples in renewing their sexual relationship. On September 5, 1962, when Liu in a fit of fury tried to kill his ex-wife with a knife, Deng intervened to defend her and, in the process, hurt Liu. The frustrated Liu committed suicide. The county court ruled that Deng, a Party member and a cadre, had violated both state laws and social morality. More despicable was that Deng had split another family, caused the death of Liu, and left Liu's elderly parents untended. The court sentenced Deng to eight years in prison without citing any specific law or regulation. The punishment was rather harsh if compared with that of Song Yifu, the ordinary farmer.[131]

After 1962, the central government continued to rehabilitate people who had been falsely labeled rightists in the late 1950s. As part of this national reinvestigation, many local courts followed the policy and reviewed past cases. For example, in April 1963, the Lujiang Party Committee in Anhui claimed that it had reviewed 99.93% of the 26,480 cases in the county and had rehabilitated many rightists. To cite just one case, Zhang Xuefu, a former leader of the Bureau of Post and Telecommunication, was declared a rightist in the Anti-Rightist Movement for his alleged anti-Party talks. On September 20, the county government removed Zhang's rightist cap, restored his previous rank in the government, and allowed him to retrieve his Party membership and reputation.[132]

In 1964, although the central government flooded the media with articles on class warfare (e.g. Four Cleanups) and mass-line trials,[133] it also beefed

129 Court Verdict of Song Yifu in Liangshan County Archives, October 8, 1962. 54-2-295.
130 Peng Zhen, 1991: 257; also see Potter, 2003: 65-67; Dong, 2001: 236.
131 Liangshan County Archives, December 13, 1962.
132 Lujiang County Archives, September 20, 1963. 1-1-1-1963: 19/23.
133 Lubman, 1999: 80.

up the implementation of certain legal procedures and principles. In early 1964, the Guangdong High Court ordered local courts to restore public trials and the jury system. According to the order, three days before a trial, the court needed to inform the procuracy to attend and to lodge charges. After a trial, the court should deliver copies of the verdict to the defendant, the procuracy, and the police. In another regulation, the Guangdong high court demanded that all criminal trials follow the OLC and adopt public trials, juries, avoidance (*huibi*), joint discussion, and other legal proceedings. Minor criminal cases meriting the punishment of *guanzhi* could be decided by one judge. Prior to any public trial, the court should deliver copies with explanations to the defendant/s and also inform the procuracy. In addition, judges should render litigants the chance to defend and appeal.[134]

Like in Guangdong, the Yunnan High Court on April 23, 1964 circulated opinions of a recent central meeting on criminal trials. The gist of the opinions was to safeguard legal procedures and protect prisoners in the Four Cleanups. One opinion said that all courts should "correctly" handle all cases during the movement. Economic crimes such as corruption, larceny, and speculation of less than 300 *yuan* would not be punished. Falsely charged cases in the movement should be managed and corrected. It was imperative for courts to reduce the number of death penalties. To avert any wrong death sentences, all heads of local and intermediate courts had to directly interrogate defendants. In the high court judges should read each other's cases. Judges should try their best to go down to the masses, to the crime venues, and to interrogate defendants. When other evidence differed from that included in the confession and a defendant claimed to be wronged, the execution should temporarily be suspended, a practice dating back to earlier polities.[135] With Liu Shaoqi and Deng Xiaoping in charge after 1962, the central opinions on criminal cases were meant to avoid infringements of the laws and excessive punishments from 1957 to 1959.

During the last two years of the Four Cleanups, despite central efforts to rein in exorbitant judicial discretion, both historical and active counterrevolutionary cases received harsher punishments than those in 1962 but they were not as severe as in the Anti-Rightist and the Great Leap movements. Moreover, the rehabilitation that started in 1961 persisted through the eve of the Cultural Revolution. For example, in early 1964, the Liangshan County

134 *Guangdong Provincial Trial Gazette*, 1999: 67.

135 For the tradition of stopping execution after a defendant claimed grievance see Qiang Fang, 2013a: Ch. 1. For the Yunnan High Court see *Yunnan Provincial Trial Gazette*, Vol. 55. *Gazette of Trial*, 1999: 248.

Police discovered that Wang Zhiyu, a poor peasant, had engaged in a serious historical counterrevolutionary activity before 1949. For that crime, Wang was arrested and sentenced by the court to a three-year *guanzhi*. Had Wang been tried in 1958, his punishment would have been at least five years of incarceration. According to the verdict, Wang was a village head in 1949 who allegedly joined other GMD soldiers in burying eleven Communist cadres alive. The local government suggested in March 1963 that Wang be punished with severity. In November 1963, the provincial government ruled that, in compliance with the recent central document, it was better for the local court in Liangshan not to arrest Wang but to sentence him to work in his commune under *guanzhi*, which was better than in a labor camp.[136] Although the content of the 1963 central document was not available in the county archive, we can extrapolate from the verdict that it advocated a lenient treatment of historical counterrevolutionaries.

In some other cases, defendants with both historical and active crimes would receive terms of *guanzhi* similar to that of Wang Zhiyu. In Jiangjin, Sichuan, for example, one Hong Mingjin, a 39-year-old poor peasant, had served as a company commander in the GMD army before 1949. In 1962, when Hong served as a work-point recorder in the commune, he allegedly stole 600 pounds of red *lichi* seeds, used his power to add 800 points to himself, and illegally cut down three trees. The police charged Hong with both historical and active crimes and the local court, regarding him as an incalcitrant counterrevolutionary, sentenced him to a three-year *guanzhi*. Hong's historical crime was not as serious as that of Wang Yuzhi, but his active crime was much worse than Wang's. For that reason, Hong received a heavier penalty, which could have been more severe in 1955 and 1958.[137]

In this period, punishments mostly squared with the severity of crimes and the penalty would be more draconian if a defendant came from an enemy class. To cite one case, He Minmin and Lin Minggang were a wife and husband in Shanghai. He Minmin was born into a landlord and capitalist family and was therefore an enemy of the ruling working class. The procuracy charged the couple in 1964 with having abused Lin's mother since 1961, which resulted in the mother's suicide. The Shanghai Intermediate Court ruled that He Minmin still harbored a landlord mentality and collaborated with her husband in mistreating her mother-in-law. Although both wife and husband should have been equally faulted for the abuse of Lin's mother, He Minmin received a heavier punishment (seven years) due partly to her

136 Liangshan County Archives, January 25, 1964. Y-7-56.

137 Jiangjin County Archives, April 25, 1964. 0099-0002-00103: 2.

landlord class origins. Lin Minggang's family background was not indicated, but he was a cadre of the Shanghai Communist Youth Committee. He was sentenced to only four years in prison.[138]

On the eve of the Cultural Revolution, the people's court continued the 1961 policy to review past cases and to rehabilitate those people whose cases had been wrongly handled. For example, on October 18, 1965, the three judicial agencies of Yunnan issued a joint circular on the rehabilitation of one Li Guohua, a sewing worker in Yun county who had been charged with a counterrevolutionary murder in July 1963. On July 28, 1963, Yang Shaoyu, who lived beneath Li's room, suddenly died. The detective suspected that Li was the most likely suspect because he was Yang's close neighbor and because Yang was planning to disclose Li's corruption. Detained and tortured by the police, Li confessed his "crime." Taking the police report for granted, the local court sentenced Li to a death penalty. Li appealed to the intermediate court, but the court refused to reinvestigate the evidence. Desperate, Li appealed to the provincial high court. The high court found the evidence was rather opaque and sent the case back to the county court. Still the local judicial system refused to change their decision. It was not until January 1965 that a regional Party committee discovered that the case lacked evidence and reported their suspicions to the provincial high court. The high court decided to form its own work team to conduct an in-depth investigation. After weeks of hard work, the team found out that Li was innocent and Yang Shaoyu had actually killed himself for fear that his own corruption would be exposed. Having been in custody for two years, Li Guohua eventually won back his freedom, reputation, and job.[139] Without the question of a local Party committee, high court's intervention and meticulous work plus the moderate political and legal milieu, Li Guohua might not have been saved.

Conclusion

In hindsight, the historical pattern of the judicial system in this period from around mid-1957 to the eve of the Cultural Revolution in 1966 was similar to that of earlier periods, 1951-1952 and 1955-1956. Both periods began with a political storm that prompted all judiciaries to follow central policies by relentlessly punishing historical and active criminals. After six months at the shortest and several years at the longest, the Party central and soon the

138 Shanghai Archives, December 10, 1964. C21-5-1332-5.

139 *Yunnan Provincial Trial Gazette*, Vol. 55. *Gazette of Trial*, 1999: 250.

Supreme Court would scale back the severity of the movement and gradually start a process of rehabilitation. From the outset of the Anti-Rightist Movement in July 1957 to the peak of the Great Leap of Law in 1960, the campaigns were so big that they engulfed almost all courts and regions in the country. Fearing a rightist brand, most judges tended to impose harsh penalties on alleged counterrevolutionaries. Historical counterrevolutionaries with no active misbehavior would be put to short-term *guanzhi* or hard labor. In early 1961, a few words cursing Party leaders could earn one five years in prison. It was not until the end of the Great Famine and the ensuing 7000-people meeting (in 1962) that the Party reversed its radical leftist polices and adopted a more conciliatory stance toward campaign victims. Crimes or misdeeds that would have been rigorously punished in the movements were now treated with lenience or even rehabilitation. The largely milder central policy lasted even into the Four Cleanups in late 1962. Starting from 1961, the Supreme Court, though not impeccable, had circulated some high-profile cases to instruct local courts and judges to adhere to basic legal principles and process. In the words of the Supreme Court, "leftism" was more dangerous than "rightism," a straightforward refusal of the far left (*jizuo*) in the movements. Equally laudable was that some intermediate courts or high courts could diligently investigate cases and exonerate victims in a timely manner. Finally, central judicial leaders and agencies delivered talks and regulations emphasizing legal principles in the 1954 OLC such as judicial independence, the jury system, public trials, and proceedings. In this regard, the judicial pendulum that had gone to the left between 1957 and 1960 came back after 1962. While the overall judicial environment was tolerant after late 1961, victims' social class and historical record remained a crucial factor for judges in considering penalties. Criminals belonging to "black" classes or having historical stains would still receive heavier punishments.

7 Not the Worst Period of Law

The Communist Judicial System in the Cultural Revolution, 1966-1976

Abstract
This chapter focuses on the role of the judicial system in the Cultural Revolution, an era that is often reduced to political turmoil, lawlessness, Red Guard brutality, and mass killings. Little ink has been spilled on describing the day-to-day function and practice of the judicial system in this significant period. In the first two years, the Communist judicial system was clouded by inaction and revolutionary chaos as judicial cadres were involved in factional fights but stayed mostly free of street violence. Starting from early 1968, the military took over the judicial system. Unlike local gazetteers that tend to emphasize the harsh punishments of military-controlled courts, local archives offer a more moderate picture of courts that is consistent with the early years of the PRC. As had happened several times in the past, the judicial rehabilitation began as early as 1970 and it lasted until the spring of 1976. While judicial and official violations of the law were excessive, they were not as egregious as in some other periods of Mao's China.

Keywords: Cultural Revolution, six regulations of public security, military control committee of the police department, restoration of the People's Court, not the worst period

In 1966, Mao initiated his last revolution, the Cultural Revolution, ostensibly to counter the growing threat of capitalism since the 7000-people meeting in 1962 and also, as Elizabeth Perry remarks, "to cultivate 'revolutionary successors' by giving young people a taste of the hardship" of the aging revolutionary generation.[1] The movement lasted until Mao's death in 1976,

1 Bo Weihua卜伟华, *Smashing the Old World: The Upheaval and Havoc of the Cultural Revolution, 1966-1968* (*zalan jiushijie: wenhua dageming dedongluan hehaojie, 1966-1968*砸烂旧世界：文化

Fang, Qiang, *The Communist Judicial System in China, 1927-1976: Building on Fear.*
Taylor & Francis Group 2021
DOI: 10.5117/9789463729451_CH07

leaving untold death and trauma behind. For decades, scholars around the world have spilled much ink on the Cultural Revolution. From Yan Jiaqi's *Ten-Year History of the Chinese Cultural Revolution* to more recent studies authored or edited by Roderick MacFarquhar and Michael Schoenhals, Andrew G. Walder, Joseph Esherick, and Paul Clark, we have learned a lot about the movement.[2] Other scholars have concentrated on more specific aspects of the Cultural Revolution. For example, in *The Cultural Revolution at the Margins*, Yiching Wu centers the "voices and historical visibility" of people at the peripheries of the movement. Walder and Su Yang provide us with highly detailed pictures of the Red Guards in Beijing, the violence in the countryside, and the brutal mass killings in Guangxi during the Cultural Revolution; Jonathan Unger reveals the Cultural Revolution in areas such as high schools, factories, and villages; Elizabeth Perry and Li Xun unveil the Shanghai worker activism in the Cultural Revolution, Lowell Dittmer describes the role and tragic fate of Liu Shaoqi in the movement, Jin Qiu tries to reconstruct the history of Lin Biao's death, and Jeremy Brown describes the deportation to the country of people at the bottom including those said to belong to "bad types."[3]

The above studies along with many others have no doubt greatly enhanced our understanding of the Cultural Revolution. However, the lack of judicial archives and the draconian restrictions on sources by the

大革命的动乱和浩劫, 1966-1968) (Hong Kong: Hong Kong Chinese University Press, 2008): 6-7; Perry, 2012: 205.

2 Yan Jiaqi严家其, *Ten-Year History of the Chinese Cultural Revolution* (*wenhua dageming shinianshi*文化大革命十年史) (Hong Kong: Hong Kong Dagongbaoshe, 1987); MacFarquhar and Schoenhals, 2008; Joseph Esherick, Paul Pickowicz, and Andrew G. Walder, eds., *The Chinese Cultural Revolution as History* (Stanford: Stanford University Press, 2006); Paul Clark, *The Chinese Cultural Revolution: A History* (Cambridge: Cambridge University Press, 2008).

3 Yiching Wu, *The Cultural Revolution at the Margins* (Cambridge, Ma: Harvard University Press, 2014): xvi; Andrew G. Walder, "Factional Conflict at Beijing University, 1966-1968," *The China Quarterly*, No. 188, "The History of the PRC (1949-1976)" (Dec., 2006), pp. 1023-1047; Andrew G. Walder and Yang Su, "The Cultural Revolution in the Countryside: Scope, Timing, and Human Impact" in *The China Quarterly*, No. 173 (Mar., 2003), pp. 74-99; for the violence in the country also see Jonathan Unger, "Revolution Conflict in the villages" in *the China Quarterly*, No. 153 (Mar., 1998), pp. 82-106; Jonathan Unger, "The Cultural Revolution at the Grass Roots" in *The China Journal*, No. 57 (Jan., 2007), pp. 109-137; Elizabeth Perry and Li Xun, *Proletarian Power: Shanghai in the Cultural Revolution* (Boulder: Westview Press, 1997); Lowell Dittmer, *Liu Shaoqi and the Chinese Cultural Revolution* (Abingdon: Routledge, 2015); Jin Qiu, *The Culture of Power: The Lin Biao Incident in the Cultural Revolution* (Stanford: Stanford University Press, 1999); also see Jeremy Brown's study on the deportation of political outcasts from Tianjin in the first three years of the Cultural Revolution. Jeremy Brown, *City Versus Countryside in Mao's China: Negotiating the Divide* (Cambridge: Cambridge University Press, 2012): 137-168.

Chinese government have hindered serious scholarly research on the role and function of the Communist judicial system in the Cultural Revolution. After the Chinese Communist Party (CCP) promised to "thoroughly negate (*chedi fouding*)" the Cultural Revolution in 1981,[4] many Chinese officials and scholars swiftly began to criticize the movement. They "increasingly used the term 'lawlessness' to describe the violence, the breakdown of the legal system" in the Cultural Revolution.[5] For example, Li Rui, Mao's former secretary and a victim of the 1959 purge, denounced the Cultural Revolution as the "most complete annihilation of both democracy and the legal system."[6] Gong Peixiang asserts that the "wide spread of the rule of man, anarchism, and the legal nihilism" during the Cultural Revolution "recklessly destroyed" the constitution and the laws as well as citizens' faith in them.[7] Like their Chinese colleagues, some Western legal scholars have either ignored the period or simply made broad and brief remarks on the law and judicial system in the Cultural Revolution.[8]

Many local government gazettes have also echoed scholarly views and rhetoric after 1981 by denouncing the Cultural Revolution as lawless or filled with aggrieved cases. For instance, the *Shaanxi Provincial Gazette*, which in the words of Walder and Yang has the most coverage of the Cultural Revolution, has delivered ferocious assaults on the law in the movement. Instead of criticizing Mao, it blames Lin Biao and the "Gang of Four" for "recklessly destroying [the] socialist rule of law" and inciting a campaign to "smash all three agencies of the judicial system" that resulted in "unprecedented damage onto the organization, trial, and thought of the people's court."[9]

Recently, scholars such as Xu Lizhi and Jeremy Brown have called into question the conventional arguments that the Cultural Revolution was lawless or anarchical. Xu makes a macroscopic argument that the basic

4 Li Rui, "A Review of the Sixth Meeting of the Eleventh Plenary (*chongwen shiyijie liuzhong quanhui*)" in *Yanhuang Chunqiu*, No. 2., 2016; http://www.yhcqw.com/32/10086.html

5 See Altehenger, 2018: 172. For Chinese studies see Yan Jiaqi严家其, 1987: 84; Bin Liang, *The Changing Chinese Legal System, 1978-Present: Centralization of Power and Rationalization of the Legal System* (Abingdon: Routledge, 2008): 19-20; Yan Wang, 2004: 12; Tang Tsou, 1999): 315; Xin Ren, 1997: 57.

6 Li Rui李锐, *Selected Theses and Talks of Li Rui* (*Lirui lunshuo wenxüan*李锐论说文选) (Beijing: Zhongguo shehui kexüe chubanshe, 1998): 179.

7 Gong Pixiang, 1999: 287.

8 Teemu Ruskola, for example, argues that law in the Cultural Revolution was at its ideological nadir. Teemu Ruskola, *Legal Orientalism: China, the United States, and Modern Law* (Cambridge, Ma: Harvard University Press, 2013): 202.

9 *Shaanxi Provincial Gazette*, 1994: 221; also see *Sichuan Provincial Trial Gazette*, 2003): 323; *Inner Mongolian Autonomous Region Gazette*, 1993: 7.

legal principles, order, and sources persisted in the Cultural Revolution. In his study of a policeman who had been charged with rape, Jeremy Brown notes that, while criminal justice in the Cultural Revolution was flawed, it was a "complex system that evolved over time and sometimes functioned as it was intended" because the alleged rapist "had the opportunity to demand reinvestigation and reinstitution."[10]

Thanks to many newly available and rare court verdicts, police interrogations, and government documents,[11] this chapter seeks to conduct an in-depth and more nuanced study on the vicissitudes of the Communist judicial system in the Cultural Revolution. As we shall see from many archival cases and documents, although the judicial system was significantly undermined in this period by the military control committees and local revolutionary committees, the system managed to retain many of its staff, basic duties, and proceedings. In hindsight, the function of the Communist judicial system and the extent to which it had been adversely affected during the Cultural Revolution are mostly in line with or even less severe than during erstwhile political campaigns in 1951, 1955, and 1957-1960, which I have discussed in previous chapters.

Another issue that this chapter attempts to address is the length of the Cultural Revolution, scholars like Yan Jiaqi and Gong Pixiang as well as the Chinese government argue that it should be ten years.[12] Yet other scholars such as Jonathan Unger, Andrew Walder, and Bo Weihua contend that the real or violent Cultural Revolution lasted only two to three years.[13] In this chapter, I argue that, focusing on the judicial system, we can divide the Cultural Revolution into three periods: 1) 1966-1967 when the judicial system was under attack; 2) 1968-1972 when the judicial system was under military control; and 3) 1973-1976 (or 1978) when the judicial system was restored.

10 Xu Lizhi, "Beyond 'Destruction' and 'Lawlessness': The Legal System during the Cultural Revolution" in Daniel Leese and Puck Engman, 2018: 25-51; Jeremy Brown, "A Policeman, His Gun, and an Alleged Rape: Competing Appeals for Justice in Tianjin" in Leese and Engman, 2018, pp. 127-149: 128.

11 Some of the materials come from government archives and gazettes before 2012, others have been acquired through personal or private connections. Both archives and official documents are still under strict control by the government and the restriction apparently has become more severe since 2013.

12 For the orthodox view of the ten years Cultural Revolution see Yan Jiaqi, 1987; Gong Pixiang, 1999. For the Chinese government see "Resolution on Certain Party Issues Since the Establishment of the PRC," June 27, 1981, in http://news.xinhuanet.com/ziliao/2002-03/04/content_2543544.htm

13 Unger, 1998; Walder and Yang, 2003; Bo Weihua, 2008.

Opening a Pandora's Box

As MacFarquhar and Schoenhals have argued, the Cultural Revolution was the result of Mao's assessment of what was happening in both the Soviet Union and at home.[14] Indeed, China in the early 1960s was in an awkward and dangerous position confronting two superpowers. In the fall of 1964, when Premier Zhou Enlai led a Chinese delegation to Moscow intending to mend the relationship in the wake of the ouster of Khrushchev, the Soviet defense minister signaled to the Chinese that they should remove Mao Zedong. The insult came as a stunning reminder to Mao that someone in his inner circle could do the same to him, especially in light of the death of Stalin and his demonization in the Soviet Union.[15]

At home, Mao's relationship with his chief lieutenant and likely successor Liu Shaoqi soured after Liu blamed Mao in 1962 for the traumatic aftermath of the Great Leap.[16] Since 1962, Mao had largely absented himself from economic policy-making and suffered from a "growing sense of alienation from the Party and many of his old comrades."[17] In the meantime, Mao was increasingly worrying about the restoration of capitalism under Liu and Deng Xiaoping.

In 1965, Mao began a counteroffensive by targeting a Beijing opera entitled "Hai Rui Dismissed from Office" written by Wu Han, a historian and deputy mayor of Beijing. Seeing a parallel between Hai Rui and Peng Dehuai who had been dismissed by Mao in 1959 for scolding Mao's Great Leap,[18] Mao launched a media campaign against Wu Han's play and escalated it into a political struggle against Peng Zhen, Beijing's mayor and Liu Shaoqi's ally, who ended up being denounced as forming an anti-Party clique and subsequently purged.[19]

Meanwhile, Kang Sheng, a leader of the Central Organization of the Cultural Revolution (hereinafter COCR) secretly instigated Nie Yuanzi, the secretary of the Party committee in the Department of Philosophy at Peking University, to write China's first "Marxist-Leninist Big-Character" poster criticizing university leaders. In response, Liu Shaoqi dispatched work teams to universities to suppress Nie and her adherents. The conflict between the work teams and college radicals culminated in Mao's article entitled

14 MacFarquhar and Schoenhals, 2008: 8.

15 Ibid., 2006: 9.

16 Zhang Suhua, 2006: 317.

17 Yiching Wu, 2014: 19.

18 MacFarquhar and Schoenhals, 2008: 15-16. Also see Short, 1999: 528.

19 For Peng Zhen at the beginning of the Cultural Revolution see Potter, 2003: 102-103.

"Bombarding the Headquarters: My Big-Character Poster" on August 5. In Elizabeth Perry's words, Mao used this poster to "generate a fever of bombardment directed against Party and government cadres and agencies at all levels."[20] In the first couple of years of the Cultural Revolution, the Red Guards, formed largely by middle school students, became the staunchest supporters and weapons of Mao against his foes.[21]

Liu Shaoqi, now branded as "China's Khrushchev" and the primary target of the Cultural Revolution, was soon to be condemned and tortured in mass meetings and died in 1969 in Henan.[22] Backed by Mao and COCR leaders, the Red Guards quickly vented their revolutionary passion in attacking the Four Olds (old thought, old culture, old customs, and old habits), changing reactionary names, and attacking so-called capitalist roaders. Some studies and gazettes have shown that most of the violence in the Cultural Revolution occurred in the first two years.[23] Despite Mao's disingenuous calls in the summer of 1966 of lenience toward people with "serious mistakes,"[24] the "red terror" in Shanghai alone looted 84,222 homes of "bourgeois" families within three weeks.[25] A Peking University professor recalled that many university professors including famed writer Lao She lost their lives at the hands of the Red Guards.[26] In addition to raiding schools and governments, the Red Guards also stormed prisons and labor camps to attack guards or cadres for neglecting their duties.[27] After workers and peasants joined the movement in late 1966,[28] factional rivalries and violence were so intense

20 Roger Des Forges argues that the use of "bombardment" in the Cultural Revolution was in synchrony with the ongoing Vietnam War. Roger Des Forges, "Democracy in Chinese History" in Roger Des Forges, Luo Ning, and Wu Yen-bo, eds., *Democracy and the Crisis of 1989: Chinese and American Reflections* (Albany: SUNY POress, 1992): 42-43; for Perry see Perry, 1997: 9.

21 MacFarquhar and Schoenhals, 2008: 107.

22 For the details of Liu Shaoqi see Dittmer, 2015 and Bo Weihua, 2008.

23 For Gazette see *Yunnan Provincial Trial Gazette*, Vol. 55. (*Yunnan shengzhi shenpanzhi*云南省志审判志) (Yunnan: Yunnan renmin chubanshe, 1999): 256; for scholarly studies see Harry Harding, "The Chinese State in Crisis, 1966-1969" in Roderick MacFarquhar, ed., *The Politics of China: Sixty Years of the People's Republic of China* (Cambridge: Cambridge University Press, 2011): 149; Unger, 1998; Walder and Yang, 2003; Bo Weihua, 2008: 793.

24 Mao Zedong毛泽东, *Mao Zedong Works Since PRC Establishment* (*jianguo yilai Mao Zedong wengao*建国以来毛泽东文稿) (Beijing: Zhongyang wenxian chubanshe, 1990): 12. 87-88.

25 MacFarquhar and Schoenhals, 2008: 117.

26 Yue Daiyun, 1987; for more deaths in Beijing schools see Frank Dikotter, *The Cultural Revolution: A People's History, 1962-1976* (New York: Bloomsbury Press, 2016): 75-79.

27 Mühlhahn, 2011: 235.

28 Wang Hongwen, a leader of the labor movement in Shanghai, took power in Shanghai in early 1967, which became a model for the rest of the country. See Perry and Li, 1997: 36-50; also Meisner, 1999: 324-333.

that in some areas, such as Wuhan, Inner Mongolia, Hebei, Zhejiang, and Guangxi, hundreds of thousands of people had suffered arrests, torture, and death.[29] In Guangxi, as Walder and Yang have shown, mass killings, torture, mutilation, and even cannibalism appeared in several counties in 1968. The total number killed in the country during the Cultural Revolution could be between 750,000 and 1.5 million.[30]

The Judicial System in the Early Cultural Revolution, 1966-1967

In movements prior to the Cultural Revolution, the judicial system, one of the cornerstones of CCP authority, was speedily and actively engaged. But in the first years of the Cultural Revolution, the judicial system itself became a target. Many courts reportedly lost their intention and ability to deal with the violence in the country. In some cases, they became dysfunctional. According to the *Yushan County Gazette*, in Jiangxi, no sooner had the Cultural Revolution begun in May 1966 than the county court became involved. In November, it created its own "Cultural Revolution Leading Organization." In the following spring, after the seizure of power by Mao's followers and the founding of a revolutionary committee in Shanghai, the movement became widespread and rippled over other regions. All cadres in the Yushan county court became members of a newly formed "Fighting Squad with a Red Heart to the Party." When factional conflicts gained momentum in the summer of 1967, judicial cadres were split into two revolutionary factions. Conflicts ensued and the judicial system was reportedly paralyzed until the military took over in October and "supported the [revolutionary] Left."[31]

Similar actions were taken in other regions. In Shaanxi, the "Gang of Four," including Wang Hongwen, Zhang Chunqiao, Jiang Qing, and Yao Wenyuan, allegedly manipulated the revolutionary rebels in the courts and took over the court leadership. On January 16, 1967, the "Red Rebel Committee" of the provincial high court announced that it had seized the power of the high court from a small group of capitalist roaders. The Committee claimed that it was "another great victory of Mao Zedong's

29 For the violence in Wuhan and other places see MacFarquhar and Schoenhals, 2008: 211, 256-259.

30 Walder and Yang, 2003: 96; for Guangxi mass killings see Su Yang, *Collective Killings in Rural China during the Cultural Revolution* (Cambridge: Cambridge University Press, 2011).

31 On June 11, 1967, Mao wanted the leftists to be protected. For Mao see *Mao Zedong Works Since PRC Establishment*, 2006: 12. 183; also see Meisner, 1999: 333-334. For Yushan county see *Gazette of the Ji'an County People's Court* (Ji'anxian renmin fayuanzhi吉安人民法院志) (1985): 9.

thought." After the power seizure, three "new" functional units in charge of criminal, civil, and administrative cases would supersede the old criminal, civil, and administrative tribunals. Leaders of the three new units would be decided by the committee as opposed to the party secretary as in the past. In the following year, 1968, around 40% of the cadres in the high court including two leaders had been declared to be traitors, GMD agents capitalist roaders, or counterrevolutionary revisionists. Later they were interrogated and "struggled against". Some of them were sent to *niupeng* (lit. cowsheds) or camps to do hard labor.[32]

Before 1966, the only guidelines that judges could invoke to tackle criminal cases were the 1951 Regulations on Penalizing Counterrevolutionaries. However, as we have seen, many (or even most) judges in both regular and campaign periods often made perfunctory judgments and did not cite any laws as bases of convictions. On January 13, 1967, at the high tide of the Cultural Revolution during which Lin Biao had replaced Liu Shaoqi as Mao's new successor, the Party Central and the State Council promulgated several regulations as guidelines for local police and judges to handle new counterrevolutionary cases. The most notorious was "Certain Regulations to Strengthen Public Security Work in the Great Proletariat Cultural Revolution" or "Six Regulations of Public Security" (*gong'an liutiao*, hereinafter SRPS). According to Wang Li, a top official at the COCR, the regulations were decided by the politburo at Mao's request. The first regulation of the SRPS was a vow to punish any evidenced crimes such as homicide, arson, poisoning, robbery, stealing state secrets, and the like. The second one was most important and reportedly caused thousands of false charges and penalties. It said that any person who wrote and mailed counterrevolutionary letters, secretly or openly displayed or distributed counterrevolutionary handbills, wrote reactionary posters, or shouted reactionary slogans in order to "attack or calumniate the great leader Chairman Mao and his close comrade and friend Lin Biao" would be deemed an active counterrevolutionary and would be punished in accordance with this law. These regulations probably reflected Lin Biao's insecurity as Mao's heir apparent and signaled Lin's intention to preemptively crack down on any potential retaliation by Liu Shaoqi's supporters.[33]

32 *Shaanxi Provincial Trial Gazette, Vol. 58*. (*Shaanxi shengzhi shenpanzhi*陕西省审判志) (Shaanxi: Shaanxi renmin chubanshe, 1994): 221-222.

33 Cui Min崔敏, "The Disastrous Six Regulations of the Public Security (*weihuo canliede gongan liutiao*为祸惨烈的公安六条)" in *Yanhuang Chunqiu*, Vol. 12, 2012. http://www.yhcqw.com/32/8982.html

The rest of the regulations required officials to protect leftists and revolutionary organizations; to prohibit activities of people belonging to the "Five Black Categories (landlords, rich peasants, counterrevolutionaries, bad elements, and rightists);" to punish any of their acts of sabotage; to struggle people who capitalize on "great democracy" to spread reactionary words; and to discipline any Party, government, and public security cadre who "attempts to distort the regulations and fabricate facts" to repress revolutionary people.[34] According to Bo Weihua, the SRPS mainly aimed at protecting the "Headquarters of the Proletariat (i.e. Mao and Lin)" and the Cultural Revolution.[35]

Shortly after the SRPS, Xie Fuzhi, a key member of the COCR and head of the PRC's Public Security, speaking at a public security meeting, denounced the existing judicial system as perpetuating "old values" from the GMD, capitalism, and feudalism. "If the problem has not been solved in the past seventeen years (i.e. 1949-1966)," Xie noted, "it is now up to you (the police) to deal with it." In August, Xie reportedly spoke at a national public security meeting that all three judicial agencies had to be smashed. Xie hinted that the order came directly from Mao. Many scholars including Bo Weihua and Gong Pixiang are inclined to take Xie's threat at face value and to mistakenly believe that the judicial system had been "smashed" in the Cultural Revolution.[36] As we will find out in this chapter, apart from discontinuing the procuracy, the people's court and especially the police continued to function even after they lost or changed their names over several years.

From early 1967 to the military takeover of the court about a year later, many judges acted to enforce the SRPS. In Yunnan province, for instance, there were 820 "serious cases" between May 1966 and May 1967 that involved indictments of "criminals" who had attacked or slandered Chairman Mao, Vice Chairman Lin, and Mao's wife Jiang Qing. Some of the accused had simply chanted wrong slogans, written wrong words, or sat on Mao's portrait. Others had stained Mao's portrait or cursed Lin Biao and Jiang Qing and supported Liu and Deng. The punishments were harsh, including long prison terms and capital punishment. One ten-year-old child was reportedly punished for breaking the second regulation against slandering Mao or Lin.[37]

According to the *General Gazette of Tianjin*, a counterrevolutionary worker with the surname Shen, had allegedly since early 1967 given private

34 Ibid.

35 Bo Weihua, 2008: 597.

36 See Bo Weihua, 2008: 598; Gong Pixiang, 1999: 287.

37 *Yunnan Provincial Trial Gazette*, 1999: 252-253.

talks against Marxism, Mao Zedong thought, central leaders, and socialism. Shen had also mailed "counterrevolutionary letters" to more than twenty colleges and asked a friend to keep the drafts for "future reward once the CCP is toppled." The Tianjin Intermediate Court sentenced Shen to fifteen years in prison, a severe punishment apparently influenced by the SRPS as the incarceration was much longer than the average five years during the Anti-Rightist Movement. Yet the punishment was not exceptional if we compare it with similar punishments in the 1951 and 1955 campaigns.[38]

Unlike their counterparts in Yunnan and Tianjin, judicial cadres in Sichuan province appeared to be more negligent or lenient toward people violating the new SRPS. To cite one case, Li Jinyuan, a peasant of Qingchuan County, raised questions at a meeting in 1967. In Li's words, "Liu Shaoqi is legally elected as the state chairman, why is he ousted without justifications? If Chairman Liu is called a dog, aren't all Chinese dogs?" Although Li did not directly mention Mao and Lin, it was clear that he was supportive of Liu and critical of Mao and Lin, a punishable crime in the second SRPS regulation. But Li was lucky for the time being as he was not charged and punished until August 1968 when someone resumed the accusation.[39] The lenient treatment of people violating the SRPS in Sichuan shows that the regulations had not yet been strictly or evenly implemented in 1967 or even later.

It was not until the military took control of the judicial system that court decisions on regular crimes such as rape or homicide were consistent with those in the past. Criminals who had committed "historical crimes" continued to receive heavier penalties than did criminals in the present day. In Weinan County, Shaanxi, Zhang Guangmin, a former GMD officer, was a teacher at a local primary school. After the Communist victory, Zhang confessed about his past "crimes" to the new government and was exonerated. But between 1952 and 1953, Zhang allegedly had raped more than a dozen young women including underaged girls. Zhang's covert crimes were not exposed until November 1966 when the local county court charged him with rape and sentenced him to death.[40] Homicide cases continued to be dealt with harshly even if the culprits were local officials. In 1968, the Baoshan county court in Yunnan rendered a death penalty to Yang Feng, a production unit cadre, for murdering two fellow peasants in December 1967.[41]

38 *General Gazette of Tianjin – Trial Gazette*, 1999: 205. For similar harsh punishments see Chapters 3 and 5.

39 *Sichuan Provincial Trial Gazette*, 2003: 347-348.

40 *Shaanxi Provincial Gazette*, 1994: 364.

41 *Yunnan Provincial Trial Gazette*, 1999: 257.

The Military Takeover of the Judicial System, 1968-1972

Due to the "seizure of power" starting in early 1967 and the ensuing escalation of factional violence, many local governments including judicial agencies were said to be largely paralyzed and dysfunctional. To restore the judicial system's role as the CCP's "knife hilt," the Party in December decided to put the judicial system under military control. The military control kicked in on the first day of 1968 after which there were no longer people's courts or police. All county judicial agencies would be renamed as the "Military Control Committee of the Police Department under the Chinese People's Liberation Army." Similar military control committees/ units were also established in the intermediate courts, high courts, and the Supreme Court. The newly founded revolutionary committees at the local level also created the People's Security Unit (*renbaobu* or *renbaozu*) to coordinate with the military control committee. Former courts, procuracy, and police departments would be dissolved, and the judges, procurators, and police would be working under the dual governance of the military control committees and the people's security units. In Ji'an County, Jilin, the previous county court was reduced to be the Adjudicating Unit and would solely be in charge of criminal cases. Under military control, the court was reluctant to deal with civil cases, which were generally lumped into categories called "contradictions among the people" to be resolved via mediation.[42]

Many other provinces such as Sichuan and Shaanxi underwent comparable changes. In Sichuan, the military control committees ruled provincial courts in 1968 and adopted the SRPS guidelines for dealing with counterrevolutionary cases.[43] In Shaanxi, the military control committees failed to "reverse the misfortune of the court as one of the most disastrous places in the Cultural Revolution." On April 28, 1968, the *Shaanxi Daily* published an editorial titled "Thoroughly Smashing Our Province's Reactionary Police, Procuracy, and Court," claiming the existence of a reactionary clique inside the provincial judicial system and calling for a complete destruction of the judicial system. However antagonistic and menacing the tone of the editorial seemed to be, under military control the Shaanxi judicial system retained its past functions, though many former policemen and judges were superseded by military officers.[44] The

42 *Gazette of the Ji'an County People's Court*, 1985: 9.

43 *Sichuan Provincial Trial Gazette*, 2003: 323.

44 For military veterans turning to judges see He Weifang, 2002: 8-11.

provincial revolutionary committee contained four functional organizations and one of them was the "political and legal organization" whose principal duty was to collaborate with the military control committee in managing law-related issues. The "political and legal organization" had four sub-divisions – General Affairs, Political Work, Case Solving, and Approval (*shenpi*) – to take charge of all functions belonging to the previous judicial system. In that regard, the provincial judicial system experienced no major change after military control.[45] The following cases will further testify to this point.

Unlike the Ji'an County Court and Shaanxi province gazettes, the *Yunnan Provincial Gazette* does not mention the takeover of the provincial court by the military control committees in 1968. Instead, it asserts that the provincial courts were "replaced" by the people's security units of the revolutionary committees. And quite a few unit leaders emphasized the important function of the judicial system in handling cases of criminals who were class enemies. As a result of this preferential policy emphasizing criminal law, civil cases involving divorce, property, or debt in many localities were reportedly left unresolved. From 1967 through 1978, courts in Yunnan handled a total of 85,286 civil cases, accounting for merely 8.95% of all civil cases between 1949 and 1978, a period of significant paucity of civil cases. The average annual number of accepted civil cases in Yunnan in the Cultural Revolution was just 7753, the lowest since 1949.[46]

The disparities among local gazettes regarding the judiciaries under military control suggest that "thoroughly smashing the judicial system" touted in many records and editorials was an exaggeration to say the least. As some gazettes have put it, all judicial agencies continued to operate under military control in the Cultural Revolution. That corresponded to the precedence during the Great Leap of Law in 1958 when all three judicial agencies were supposedly combined into one unit. As the Ji'an *County Court Gazette* remarked, "[the judicial system under military control] repeated the erroneous method (combining the three agencies) [...] in the 1958 Great Leap Forward."[47] Furthermore, according to a former political commissar of the military control committee in the Shanghai Xuhui Police Bureau, most former judges and policemen were allowed to continue their judicial work while the military committee served only as a nominal watchdog. For the former commissar, there was little change before and after military

45 *Shaanxi Provincial Trial Gazette*, 1994: 223-224.

46 *Yunnan Provincial Trial Gazette*, 1999: 332.

47 *Gazette of the Ji'an County People's Court*, 1985: 9.

control.[48] One likely reason might be that most members of the military committee knew little about law.

To be sure, the minor change in the actual function of the judicial system after military control did not mean that it performed better than before. In previous chapters, I have shown that the judicial system as a whole had been undermined after the 1952 legal reform, if not ever since the 1950 anti-counterrevolutionary campaign. During most of the years under military oversight, the judicial system predominantly took a tougher stance than it had before against counterrevolutionaries or people who had breached the SRPS. But the judiciaries' handling of ordinary criminal cases remained unchanged. Like their predecessors in earlier campaigns, judicial cadres under military control were required to engage vigorously in political movements. For example, during the 1968 "Cleansing the Class Ranks" and the 1970 "One Strike and Three-Antis" movements, judicial cadres in many regions attacked, tortured, and punished hundreds of thousands of "class enemies." That was despite Mao's call on January 1, 1969 that cadres use lenient and lawful means to deal with counterrevolutionaries and people who had just made mistakes.[49] According to one account, during the "One Strike and Three-Antis" movement alone, the military-controlled judicial system adjudicated more than 100,000 counterrevolutionary cases. According to a later account after the Cultural Revolution was completed, some 80-90% of those cases involved spurious charges.[50] According to another official source, in Sichuan, the percentage of incorrect charges was as high as 90%.[51]

In the spring of 1970, the political wind appeared to shift to more tolerance. According to the case studies of Jeremy Brown and Wang Haiguang, an alleged police rapist in Tianjin and a counterrevolutionary schoolteacher in Jinlin province had their charges revised after 1970.[52] In July 1970, the

48 Author's interviews with a former commissar of the military commission in the Shanghai Xuhui Police Bureau in 2010; Xu Lizhi also argues that the basic judicial structure did not change under military control. See Xu Lizhi, 2018: 38.

49 Both movements aimed to strike at counterrevolutionaries. According to Zhang Ma, many Shanghai plants held their own brutal struggle classes to ferret out counterrevolutionaries that drove some to commit suicide. For the movements see Cui Ming, 2012; Dikotter, 2016: 183-191; for Mao's call see "Editorial (*shelun*社论)" in *The People's Daily*, January 1, 1969; for the struggle classes in Shanghai plants see Zhang Man, "From Denial to Apology: Narrative Strategies of a 'Perpetrator' after the Cultural Revolution" in Leese and Engman, 2018: 156.

50 See Bo Weihua, 2008: 598.

51 *Sichuan Provincial Trial Gazette*, 2003: 323.

52 Brown, 2018: 138; Wang Haiguang, "A Different Category of Life: The Counterrevolutionary Case of a Rural Schoolteacher" in Leese and Engman, 2018: 91-92.

judicial system rolled out a polity-wide rehabilitation campaign to review and correct cases involving false charges during two recent movements. In January 1971, probably because too much blood had been shed, Mao reportedly expressed concerns that "We do not rule [China] by killings" and "[we] should make some arrests and killings but not too many."[53] The new trend toward clemency continued beyond the abrupt end of military control of the judicial system in early 1972.

Trials under Military Control

To have a better and clearer picture of the role, status, function, and verdicts of the judicial system under military control between 1968 and 1972, we need to look into court cases in this period and find out the impact and dynamics of the SRPS on local courts and judges. There are three types of collected cases recorded in provincial gazettes, private sources, and court archives respectively.

1 Cases from Provincial Gazettes

Dozens of court cases appear in a number of provincial gazettes and the people involved were mostly violators of the SRPS who had disrespected Mao and Lin Biao. Moreover, almost all of the cases are simple in content with sketchy verdicts. For example, during the Cultural Revolution, local production cadres were supposed to erect Mao's portrait in fields where peasants were working. In 1968, a female peasant in Xichou County, Yunnan, saw that Mao's portrait had been blown down by the wind. Without thinking, she exclaimed: "Chairman Mao is down!" The county government and the county court quickly punished her as an "Active Counterrevolutionary." Fortunately, the upper intermediate court changed her crime to a "Serious Political Mistake," a lesser degree offense, and asked the local government to "criticize and educate" her. This case tells us that some judges in high-level courts with more legal experience or training might be more tolerant than their peers in county courts who were mostly military veterans or cadres with limited legal knowledge.

In Mao's China, disseminating religious ideas could be a serious crime. After Haitong county in Yunnan had an earthquake in 1970, a Muslim named Na Yuncheng held two seven-day Islamic rites among his followers to release the dead from purgatory. When a local military officer ordered him to stop,

53 *Hunan Provincial Gazette of Politics and Law*, 1995: 6. 263-264.

Na cursed the officer. For his religious activities and offense of a military officer, Na was branded an "active counterrevolutionary" and sentenced to five years in prison. This punishment was much lighter than the fifteen-year incarceration of Su Mingxing, a Guangdong peasant who made a similar religious worship for rain in a 1955 drought.[54] The case of Na Yuncheng shows that punishments in the Cultural Revolution of certain "crimes" or "misdeeds" could be less draconian than the punishment of similar crimes in the 1950s.

Some people who vented their anger over the downfall of Liu Shaoqi and Deng Xiaoping or spoke and wrote in their support could be punished more severely than other, more ordinary, offenders under the SRPS. To cite one case in Yunnan, after Zhao Shuhua, the Party secretary of a commune in Chenggong County, heard from the radio on October 13, 1969 that Liu Shaoqi had been permanently expelled from the Party and deprived of all his Party duties. Zhao immediately put Liu's pictures on the walls and said that "only after Liu Shaoqi becomes the chairman can peasants have new hope." The local judicial department under military control arrested Zhao and sentenced him to ten years behind bars.[55]

In 1969, Tang Dechang, a Buddhist scholar from Shitan County, Sichuan, wrote and sent 28 letters to central leaders such as Mao, Zhou Enlai, and heads of the National People's Congress (NPC) in which Tang advocated religious freedom and proposed to found a research forum on Mao Zedong's Buddhist thought. What Tang wanted was a unification of state and religion, an anathema to the atheistic CCP in normal times, let alone in the Cultural Revolution. The local government in June convicted Tang of "seeking to overthrow the proletariat regime" and jailed him for fifteen years. In another case, during a meeting of people belonging to the bad categories, Ding Guangxian, a former rich farmer, was so exhausted that he fell asleep and unconsciously dropped a book entitled *Selected Words of Mao* onto the floor. Ding was promptly denounced in the same meeting as being "disloyal to Chairman Mao" and was forced to confess that he "only loves Liu Shaoqi and Chiang Kai-shek and not Chairman Mao." For those fabricated charges, Ding was labeled an "active counterrevolutionary" and taken into custody for fifteen years. In comparison with similar cases in previous movements in the 1950s, Ding's case was punished much more heavily.[56]

54 For Su Mingxing see Chapter 5. For Nayuncheng see *Yunnan Provincial Trial Gazette*, 1999: 253.

55 *Yunnan Provincial Trial Gazette*, 1999: 266.

56 *General Gazette of Shanxi – Judicial Gazette* (*Shanxitonggzhi shenpanzhi*山西通志-审判志) (Beijing: Zhonghua shujü, 1998): 34. 126.

During the first two years of military control of the judicial system, the death penalty was often imposed on oral and literary critics, which had been rare in earlier campaigns.[57] The second regulation of the SRPS was specifically designed to target those violators. In one case, Deng Sijing, a teacher at a cadre training school in Taiyuan, the capital of Shanxi, was sentenced to death in 1970 for condemning Mao's wife and Lin Biao. Deng allegedly blamed Lin Biao and Jiang Qing for instigating factional violence, persecuting old cadres, and scuttling production. Furthermore, Deng went to Beijing three times in an effort to have his opinions heard by central leaders (i.e. Mao), a method reminiscent of aggrieved people in earlier polities seeking to bring their grievances to the attention of the ruler.[58]

Among the available provincial gazettes, only that of Hebei province contains a complete court verdict on a death penalty in early 1970. According to the verdict, the victim Wang Huaijing was an army veteran and a member of the Communist youth league in Yutian, Hebei. On February 3, 1970, the Ministry of Public Security accused Wang of being "extremely reactionary and insane" in his petitions to central governments and ordered the local government to punish him. The Yutian County Military Control Unit quickly detained Wang and sentenced him to death by summary execution. The verdict was soon approved by the provincial revolutionary committee. The verdict simply mentioned that Wang had "attacked the headquarters of the proletariat" (i.e. Mao and Lin) and it failed to provide the original content of Wang's letter. A subsequent reinvestigation in 1971, however, revealed that Wang had specifically accused Lin Biao of "opposing Mao's revolutionary and Marxist theories" and had suggested that the Party eradicate Lin Biao's venom as soon as possible. The review of Wang Huaijing's case became possible only after Lin Biao's disgrace and death on September 13, 1971. Wang was finally rehabilitated in November 1975, when the Hebei provincial government admitted that he had been wronged and ordered to have his reputation reinstated.[59]

57 For the literary inquisition in late imperial China see Spence, 2012.

58 *General Gazette of Shanxi – Judicial Gazette*, 1998: 34. 125; for aggrieved people went to state capital to complain see Jonathan K. Ocko, "I'll Take it All the Way to Beijing: Capital Appeals in the Qing" in *The Journal of Asian Studies*, Vol. 47, No. 2 (May, 1988), pp. 291-315; Qiang Fang, 2009.

59 For the national rehabilitation see Dai Huang戴煌, *Hu Yaobang and the Rehabilitation of Cases Involving Grievances and False and Wrong Charges (Hu Yaobang yu pingfan yuanjia cuoan*

2 Two Prominent Cases

Without the exposure of the deaths of more victims such as Deng Sijing and Wang

Huaijing in the Cultural Revolution by local gazettes, most people in China today would only remember a few prominent victims. One of them is Lin Zhao, both a Christian and a Communist, who attended Peking University in 1954. In the Anti-Rightist Movement, Lin was branded a rightist for her criticism of the Party. Refusing to succumb to the pressure, Lin continued to write poems that angered government officials. In the early 1960s, Lin was arrested. In prison, she wrote many letters to Shanghai leaders and the *People's Daily* to express her unorthodox political views. On April 29, 1968, due to her refusal to confess her "political crimes," the Shanghai High Court under the military control sentenced Lin to death.[60]

The official verdict was that Lin "stubbornly stuck to her counterrevolutionary stance" and wrote myriad counterrevolutionary diaries, poems, and articles that venomously cursed and smeared Chairman Mao and the socialist system. In the Cultural Revolution, Lin kept on composing her counterrevolutionary articles against the movement. Lin also stained Mao's portraits with her "dirty blood" and wrote and chanted counterrevolutionary slogans.[61] Like many other victims, Lin Zhao was eventually rehabilitated in 1980 when a revised criminal verdict from the same court ruled that Lin's former accusation and penalty were "evidently false" and should be corrected. The court affirmed that Lin was innocent.[62] Despite her final exoneration, she is still like a specter to the Party as she has become an icon of freedom to many people in China today.[63]

Another notable martyr of the Cultural Revolution was Yu Luoke, a young man whose parents were described as rightists in 1957.[64] Because Yu came from a "rightist" family, no university dared to accept him, a practice akin to the long-standing "collective responsibility and punishment."

胡耀邦与平反冤假错案) (Beijing: Zhongguo wenlian chuban gongsi and Xinhua Chubanshe, 1998); the case of Wang see *Hebei Provincial Gazette*, 1994: 73. 190-191.

60 Peng Lingfan彭令范, "My Sister Lin Zhao (*wode jiejie Lin Zhao*我的姐姐林昭)" in 1998, http://ywang.uchicago.edu/history/big5/linzhao4.htm; for a detailed study of Lin Zhao see Xi Lian, *Blood Letters: The Untold Story of Lin Zhao* (New York: Basic Books, 2018).

61 "The Criminal Verdict of Lin Zhao (*Lin Zhao xingshi panjueshu*林昭刑事判决书)" in http://jyushyur.blogspot.com/2015/05/blog-post_45.html (October 23, 2020).

62 Verdict of the Shanghai High Court on August 22, 1980 in https://zh.wikisource.org

63 For CCP's fear of Lin Zhao and people's love of her see Luo Siou, "Blood Papers in Prison: Why the CCP is Afraid of Dead Lin Zhao?" in the *New York Times*, February 13, 2019, in https://cn.nytimes.com/china/20190213/lin-zhao-blood-letters/

64 For a good study on Yu Luoke see Yiching Wu, 2014.

At the outset of the Cultural Revolution, Yu wrote a popular essay titled "The Theory of Class Origin" in which he challenged a common adage that "a heroic father will have a good son, while a reactionary father will only have a bastard son." Yu argued that social influence was more important than a family's influence in shaping a person's future character. Furthermore, Yu argued that those believing in the theory of family blood were not materialists. Yu's essay quickly won the support of many people who had similar family backgrounds. In April 1967, leaders of the COCR denounced the essay as a "poisonous weed" that not only distorted the Party's class line but also instigated youth from reactionary families to attack the Party. Hence, the Beijing police arrested Yu in early 1968 and a Beijing court sentenced him to death on March 5, 1970. Citing no laws, not even the SRPS, the court claimed that, since 1963, Yu had written and dispersed a good deal of reactionary words and essays "viciously tarnishing and slandering the proletarian headquarters." In the Cultural Revolution, Yu again wrote scores of reactionary essays in hopes of "propagating counterrevolutionary views." It was not until November 21, 1978 that the same court decided to restore Yu Luoke's reputation and rebuke its previous decision as false.[65]

From 1968 to 1970, apart from deaths caused by factional fights or torture, most victims, including Lin Zhao and Yu Luoke, still went through some kind of legal process and were sentenced by a court under a military control committee. As Leese and Engman have argued, "political campaigns in the PRC did not lead to the abandonment of procedure, however flawed."[66] At the same time, even carefully crafted verdicts in the absence of genuine due process could not add much to the legitimacy of the PRC judicial system. On the contrary, all too often the verdicts demonstrated that the judicial system was but a docile apparatus that the Party could use forcefully to achieve its political purposes.

3 Cases from Local Archives and Memoirs

Unlike provincial gazettes that mainly highlight victims who have suffered absurdly severe punishments for negligible "crimes" on flimsy evidence, the local archives I have gleaned tell a somewhat different story. According to them, in this period some people with comparable and even more "serious

65 "The Criminal Verdict of Yu Luoke (*Yu Luoke xingshi panjueshu*遇罗克刑事判决书)," March 5, 1970, in http://www.wailaike.net/news-1378383-0.html (October 23, 2020).

66 Leese and Engman, 2018: 12.

crimes" were sometimes treated quite leniently. Since 1970, many erstwhile "criminals" who had openly chastised Mao or intentionally tarnished his portraits have been released and not suffered any punishment.

To cite one case, Song Chaojun was a peasant living in Neixiang County, Henan, who had been a local official in the Republican period. From 1967 to 1968, he allegedly had cursed Mao and his wife Jiang Qing, a serious crime listed in the SRPS. Song had also "spread counterrevolutionary views" such as that today's China (the PRC) was not as good as in the past (the ROC) and he allegedly vilified socialism. The county court under military control noted that Song "has harbored reactionary thought for a long time" and has hated the socialist system and especially the CCP. More serious was his "vicious" attack on Party leaders and his cursing of the "great leader" Mao and "[our] beloved comrade" Jiang Qing. "To defend the great leader Chairman Mao" to the death and to comply with Article 2 of the SRPS as well as with the strong demands of the masses, the military control unit on March 5, 1969 sentenced Song to three years in jail and put him to work supervised by the masses. In contrast to provincial gazettes that recorded how minor errors could be described as counterrevolutionary and could earn one years of imprisonment and even capital punishment,[67] the archives contain primary documents that show that a strong critic of Mao like Song Chaojun got only three years of work under supervision of the masses and avoided spending any time in jail.[68] Undoubtedly, different judges in the Cultural Revolution could make different rulings and some seem to have had more room for individual choice than in more settled times. The case of Song Chaojun shows that punishment varied over space and time and local judges under military control could both cite laws in their decision and made relatively rational and clement punishments.

As I have mentioned, since the end of 1970, around six months after Yu Luoke's horrendous execution, punishments for "counterrevolutionary rhetoric" suddenly turned moderate and minimal. We can trace this trend in detail in the case of one Xiao Ruiyi, a middle school student in Xinhua County, Hunan, in 1968. Xiao secretly wrote three letters to Mao asking him to stop class struggle and to treat landlords and rich peasants the same as other peasants. Xiao also agreed with Liu Shaoqi's acceptance of a limited amount of private ownership. His most audacious suggestion to Mao was to eliminate his personality cult, which reached its zenith in the Cultural Revolution, and to allow for the liberation of other people's thought.

67 MacFarquhar and Schoenhals, 2008: 267.

68 Neixiang County Archives, March 5, 1968. Y-1-20.

"Some people are flattering Chairman Mao," Xiao wrote. "Today, with the exception of the chairman, who does not wear a Chairman Mao badge?" Xiao highlighted the defects of the personality cult as wasting human talent and material goods, ruining China's foreign relations as China's friends had to learn Mao's selected works, giving rise to dishonesty, and damaging educational quality because students only read Mao's selected works, making schools like churches. In addition, Xiao lashed out at the harsh and indiscriminate laws of the PRC. He invoked the Legalist Han Feizi's words that laws should be both strict and proper but should not be used to punish innocent people under any circumstances. During the famine in 1960, for instance, hungry people were compelled to steal, while other people plotted to create anti-government organizations. "Should the government kill all those thieves and dissidents [without taking their difficult situations into account]?" Xiao asked.

After a classmate discovered Xiao's critiques of CCP policies and Mao's personality cult, the student grabbed part of the letter and reported it to the local government. Xiao had to flee for his life and became a migrant worker in the next two years. The middle school issued a warrant for Xiao's arrest on August 20, 1968 and sent it to all local law-enforcement units. They charged Xiao with "lauding Liu Shaoqi" and "viciously attacking and reviling the great leader Chairman Mao and vice chairman Lin Biao."[69]

In May 1970, having absconded for two years, Xiao stealthily came home to see his parents. His uncle, a local cadre, immediately took him to the commune government. Based on Xiao's confession and people's accusations, the commune charged him with four crimes: 1) fiendishly attacking great leader Mao and his invincible thought; 2) viciously attacking the proletariat headquarter led by Mao and Lin; 3) recklessly striking at the socialist system and praising "bandit" Liu Shaoqi; and 4) manifesting extreme hostility to the proletarian dictatorship and opposing class struggle. Any of the alleged "crimes" should have sufficed to convict Xiao and to sentence him to death, just like Yu Luoke and Wang Huaijing had experienced in March 1970. After Xiao's case arrived in the county court, there were very heated debates among judges over his punishment. In this period, local judges under military control had the discretion to decide all penalties other than death.[70] Although

69 For Xiao Ruiyi's memoir see Yu Xiguang余习广, ed., *Daring not Forgetting to Worry about my Country: Collection of Appeals in the Cultural Revolution* (*weibei weigan wangyouguo: wenhua dageming shangshuji*位卑未敢忘忧国：文化大革命上书集) (Hunan: Hunan renmin chubanshe, 1989): 1-18.

70 The military representative of the Supreme Court in May 1969 rendered the decision of death penalty to the provincial governments and the Supreme Court would only have the right

most judges favored the death penalty, the head of the court and a deputy head of the military control unit disagreed. Peerenboom has argued that in some cases the Party's interference "may serve to ensure that the case is handled in accordance with the law."[71] Furthermore, this case is a repeat of what we have seen in Chapter 6 (e.g. Taishan court) that in a turbulent period some local judges and Party leaders could remain committed to basic legal principles or consciousness and refuse to blindly implement cruel laws against innocent victims. It is likely that both the excessive violence in the Cultural Revolution and Xiao Ruiyi's reasonable criticism had won the sympathy of some court leaders.

While the court was grappling with a final decision on Xiao, an unexpected windfall descended. According to Xiao's memoir, a central order demanded mercy in handling dissident intellectuals because too much blood (e.g. Lin Zhao's and Yu Luoke's) had been spilled. The court thus sentenced Xiao to work under mass supervision. Xiao later recalled that before he left the court, the deputy head of the military control unit who had opposed his death penalty praised Xiao as being "audacious in thought, talk, and action."[72] Unfortunately, the central order in Xiao's case could not be retrieved. Yet we can infer from Xiao's case that the political wind veered in the spring of 1970 when Mao called for reductions in sentencing the death penalty.

In this period, local archives indicate that the punishment of regular criminal cases did not witness a major change, even though all regular crimes now added a prefix of "counterrevolutionary." Robbers continued to receive harsh treatment as they had in the past. In one case, a group of robbers armed with guns in Neixiang, Henan, had since 1969 traveled to neighboring counties and looted people of money and goods worth thousands of *yuan*. After the police tracked down the group, they found a total of eight criminals, most of them around 20 years old. The leader was 22-year-old Zhang Jinjuan. The court verdict in September 1971 charged the group with being a "counterrevolutionary armed robbing clique" that had "seriously damaged economic development and social order." Citing Party policies instead of laws, the court sentenced the criminals in accordance with their individual crimes and confessions. The archive did not provide any evidence whether or not torture had been used. It reported only that the police had conducted an interrogation and the criminals had all confessed

to review. This was different from most of the period prior to the Cultural Revolution. *Guangdong Provincial Trial Gazette*, 1999: 69.

71 Peerenboom, 2002: 308.

72 Yu Xiguang, 1989: 1-18.

their misdeeds. In accord with long-time practice in China, the two leaders were put to death and the rest of the rebels received imprisonment ranging between five and twenty years.[73]

In another case, one Meng Qinghe, a poor peasant of Zhangqiu County, Shandong, had been sentenced to *laojiao* (i.e. hard labor, similar to *guanzhi*) several times for theft, profiteering, and escape. After his latest release in February 1966, Meng had no intention of rectifying his habitual crime. He went to Jiangsu and Anhui provinces and stole more than 500 *yuan* and many other valuable goods. The police arrested Meng in May 1971 and charged him with "gravely disrupting social order and being a habitual thief." The Zhangqiu County military control unit sentenced Meng to five years in jail in order to "strengthen proletariat dictatorship, to strictly strike hard against all criminal activities, and to defend the safety of people's property."[74] These two criminal cases, one involving social banditry and the other a lone robber, tell us that the punishments for armed robbery and theft were, unlike political crimes, generally consistent over the course of the PRC and were unaffected by the Cultural Revolution.

The People's Court Restored, 1972-1976

After judicial penalties against political critics and transgressors experienced a thaw in late 1970 and early 1971, a sweeping polity-wide review and rehabilitation of mishandled cases and wronged victims began in mid-1971. The most conspicuous sign of this policy shift was the restoration of the judicial system in late 1972. Withstanding several political headwinds in 1973 and 1974, the tolerant judicial policy was mostly preserved until the spring of 1976 when another major crackdown of critics was launched in the wake of the Tiananmen Incident on April 5th.

Shortly after Mao demanded less bloodshed in early 1971, premier Zhou Enlai, at the Fifteenth National Public Security Meeting, sharply denounced Lin Biao and Jiang Qing's "wholesale rejection" of all PRC legal practice from 1949 to 1966. Zhou remarked, "We cannot say that a 'black [anti-Party] line' had ruled the period before the Cultural Revolution, nor can we say that leaders of the public security in the past seventeen years were black-line leadership."[75] In July 1971, the newly moderate central administration started

73 Neixiang County Archives, September 23, 1971. Y-1-1-114.

74 *Zhangqiu County Archives*, 1971, 1976. Y-8-15.

75 *Shaanxi Provincial Trial Gazette*, 1994: 224.

to review counterrevolutionary cases in movements titled "Cleansing the Class Ranks (1968)" and "One Strike and Three-Antis (1970)." In the process they rehabilitated many falsely punished cases.[76]

The biggest incident in the Cultural Revolution that had shocked almost everyone was Lin Biao's alleged plot to assassinate Mao and his unsuccessful effort to escape to the Soviet Union.[77] The anticipated magnitude of the impact was so tremendous that the scandal was kept quiet by Party leaders for months. Lin's longtime followers in the army since the 1940s, including the commanders-in-chief of the navy and the air force, were summarily arrested or sent to clandestine concentration camps. Many military cadres were dismissed and stripped of their military titles and authority after years of service.[78]

To Mao, Lin's death was both embarrassing and shocking. The political blow to Mao's reputation was profound. According to Wang Haiguang, after the Lin Biao incident, some people turned from being Mao's fanatical adherents to being sober thinkers. They started to question the "rationality, necessity, and aftermath of the Cultural Revolution."[79] Mao gradually changed his indifference toward old cadres who had been attacked, humiliated, and tortured in the Cultural Revolution. On January 10, 1972, Mao suddenly appeared at the funeral for Chen Yi, former Shanghai mayor, marshal, and poet. Mao praised Chen as a good man in a talk with Chen's widow and expressed a positive view of Deng Xiaoping who was then in political exile in Jiangxi. Sensing the shift, Zhou Enlai in April 1972 ordered the *People's Daily* to publish an editorial that "all comrades, old and new, Party and non-Party, who have made mistakes" should be treated as contradictions within the people. In particular, the editorial lauded old cadres with years of revolutionary training as "important treasures" of the Party. In late 1972, Mao demanded that prisons abolish "fascist interrogation methods" or, in other words, treat old revolutionaries more humanely.[80]

76 *Hunan Provincial Gazette of Politics and Law,* 1995: 263-264.

77 For Lin Biao see Jin Qiu, 1999 and MacFarquhar and Schoenhals, 2008: Ch. 19.

78 For memoirs of key players in this purge see Wu Faxian吴法宪, *The Autobiography of Wu Faxian* (*Wu Faxian huiyilu*吴法宪回忆录) (Hong Kong: Beixing chubanshe, 2006); Li Zuopeng李作鹏, *The Autobiography of Li Zuopeng* (*Li Zuopeng huiyilu*李作鹏回忆录) (Hong Kong: Beixing chubanshe, 2011).

79 Wang Haiguang王海光, "The Movement of Criticizing Lin Biao and Confucius (*pilin pikong yundong*批林批孔运动)" in Zhang Hua张华 and Su Caiqing苏采青, eds., *Looking Back to the Cultural Revolution* (*huishou wenge*回首文革) (Beijing: Zhonggong dangshi chubanshe, 2000), pp. 1105-1121: 1105; Also see MacFarquhar and Schoenhals, 2008: 348-350.

80 Xi Xuan席宣 and Jin Chunming金春明, *A Brief History of the Cultural Revolution* (*wenge jianshi*文革简史) (Beijing: Zhonggongzhongyang dangshi chubanshe, 2006): 227-228.

The fallout of the Lin Biao incident helped the Party take another positive step to reinstate the judicial system, which had been in the grip of Lin's military for about four years. The judicial system, with the exception of the procuracy, generally resumed its functions in August 1972. According to the *Yushan County Gazette*, the Jiangxi provincial government issued a circular as early as August 26 that all counties should reestablish courts. Three months later, the Yushan County Court was reinstituted. In Yudu County, Jiangxi, judges of the "new" court at first had to work in the county government before a new court building was complete.[81] The pace of reestablishing courts varied among different provinces. Hunan, Shaanxi, and Tianjin, for instance, did not start rebuilding their courts until early 1973.[82] On February 26, 1973, about six months after Jiangxi, the Shaanxi Revolutionary Committee ordered the restoration of the provincial high court. Intermediate courts in Baoji and Shangluo regions were rebuilt in March and June respectively. In July, the provincial government terminated the political and legal unit and the military control committee, two key "judicial" organs since 1968. But the county courts in Xi'an, the provincial capital, were restored as late as 1975. The rebuilding of courts did not mean that they could function with real independence. As in periods before military control, the new courts continued to be an adjudicating tool of the provincial government. Before 1980, all cases had to be reported to the provincial government (i.e. the revolutionary committee) for review.[83]

The largest change in the "new" courts was their continued reluctance to enforce the SRPS. To cite one case, on June 26, 1972, a young woman called Zhong Xiangqun was arrested in Neixiang County, Henan, for her counter-revolutionary activities. According to the Neixiang county archive, Zhong was the head of a production unit harboring "serious capitalist thought." In the fall of 1970, while Zhong was stealthily eating sesame seeds inside the production team, Zhang Chenglin, a Party member and storekeeper, scolded her. Humiliated and infuriated, Zhong plotted a reprisal. On January 29, 1972, when all were having breakfast together, Zhong secretly wrote "Down with Chairman Mao" on the wall of the production team. On February 7,

81 *Yushan County Gazette* (*yushan xianzhi*玉山县志) (Jiangxi: Jiangxi renmin chubanshe, 1996): 16; *Yudu County Court Gazette* (*Yuduxian renmin fayuanzhi*于都县人民法院志) (Jiangxi: Jiangxi Yuduxian renmin fayuan, 1998): 85.

82 See *Hunan Provincial Gazette of Politics and Law*, 1995: 264; *General Gazette of Tianjin – Trial Gazette*, 1999: 205.

83 After 1980, courts had to report cases to the new people's government that replaced revolutionary committees. *Shaanxi Provincial Gazette*, 1994: 225.

as local cadres were probing into the "counterrevolutionary slogan," Zhong took out an old *People's Daily* and wrote "Down with Chairman Mao" on it along with curses of local cadres. Then she put the newspaper in a crack of wall close to Zhang's home. Zhong then accused Zhang's son of having authored the counterrevolutionary writings. Frightened and infuriated amid a heightened political storm, Zhang Chenglin reportedly went insane for over half a month.

The Neixiang police and the military control unit wasted no time in looking into the case. All the evidence, including the handwriting on the wall and in the old newspaper, indicated that Zhong was the key suspect. The local police detained Zhong who soon confessed her crimes. On July 22, the military unit indicted Zhong for "venting her dissatisfaction at Zhang Chenglin by plotting to frame him" (a counterrevolutionary crime), and for directing her venom against Mao, a crime punishable by SRPS. To solidify the proletarian dictatorship and with due consideration for Zhong's confession that mitigated the gravity of her offense, the military unit, without quoting any laws, sentenced Zhong to three years in prison with supervision by the masses. The punishment was considerably light in comparison to those meted out for similar crimes two years before. If those penalties had still been in effect, she could have been sentenced to ten or fifteen years behind bars. Both the county military control unit and the revolutionary committee endorsed the court decision. Like Xiao Ruiyi in 1970, Zhong was lucky to live in a time of a restored court and tolerant policies. In November, the intermediate court told the county court that Zhong Xiangqun should be exempt from the indictment. The intermediate court did not provide any detail of its extremely merciful treatment for an "active counterrevolutionary" who had deliberately used vicious words in a political movement abusing the great chairman. What we can infer is that local court leaders apparently noticed a novel political cue from the Party Central. On December 20, 1972, the military unit ruled on behalf of the nascent county court that Zhong would be pardoned due to her "good attitude" in making a full confession. More important, unlike all other court verdicts under military control before this one, this verdict no longer featured Mao's selected works on the first page, signaling a retreat from Mao's cult of personality.[84]

Shortly after the inception of the Cultural Revolution, Deng Xiaoping was denounced and exiled to a cadre labor camp for his association with Liu Shaoqi. The death of Lin Biao in 1971 opened the door for his return to

84 Neixiang County Archives, 1972. Y-1-1-129.

power. Since early 1973, Deng had been appointed as an assistant to premier Zhou in charge of economic and foreign policies. In August 1973, many allies of the "Gang of Four" were promoted to central posts at the Tenth Party Congress. Because of Mao's identification with Qingshihuang, China's first authoritarian centralizing ruler, and his critical view of Confucius, the late Zhou scholar who advocated a moral elite, Jiang Qing and others launched the "Anti-Lin [Biao] and Anti-Confucius Movement" in late 1973 to promote legalism, denigrate Confucianism, and indirectly oppose Deng Xiaoping and Zhou Enlai. The movement triggered new violence among different factions and many local Party committees were arguably paralyzed. After Zhou Enlai fell sick in June 1974, Mao appointed Deng Xiaoping to be the first vice premier, a rebuttal to the "Gang of Four."[85] In the Cultural Revolution, Mao's words had been more important than any law or policy. With Mao's backing, Deng had until spring 1976 been a key player in China whose primary missions were to maintain social order and develop the economy. Deng's reinstitution paved the way for more judicial tolerance and lenience.

From its restoration to early 1976, the judicial system generally carried on the rehabilitation of people who had been wronged by the judicial system during the Cultural Revolution. For example, in 1973, the Yushan county government corrected two major cases. One of them was the so-called "Yushan Anti-CCP Army" case, in which 4158 people had been charged with being counterrevolutionaries. The county reversed the verdicts on all of them, restored their jobs, and provided them with financial compensation. In another case, some men were arrested and punished in May 1968 for "raping female Red Guards." After the county government reviewed the case in February 1973, it decided that the case had been fabricated. All six living convicts/victims were accordingly set free, politically rehabilitated, and economically compensated.[86] In Yunnan, some courts were lenient toward people with petty "crimes." In one case, when one Wang Liqiao, a peasant in the Simao region, chanted a forbidden slogan, the county court sentenced him to incarceration for being an "active counterrevolutionary." The Simao Intermediate Court, however, adopted a much more forgiving stance by changing the charge to a "serious political error" and ordering Wang to be educated and not imprisoned.[87]

85 Wang Haiguang, 2000: 1108-1114.
86 *Yushan County Gazette*, 1996: 16.
87 *Yunnan Provincial Trial Gazette*, 1999: 260.

The wave of tolerance toward political offenders and rehabilitation of wronged victims moved on in 1974 and 1975 in Yunnan. For instance, after Fan Congying, an accountant of a local store in Fengqing County, exposed a cashier, Zhao Cuiju, who had lost 210 *yuan*, Zhao was resentful and tried to retaliate. During the "Cleansing the Class Ranks" in 1968, Fan's eight-year-old daughter accidentally defaced a portrait of Mao. Zhao immediately accused Fan of instigating her daughter to damage the chairman's portrait. Fan was thus declared an "active counterrevolutionary" and sentenced to three years of *guanzhi*. In 1974, the local court rehabilitated Fan and reinstated her in her previous job. The gazette did not say whether the false charger, Zhao, was punished. In another case in January 1975, the Simao Region Intermediate Court dismissed as unsubstantiated all charges against Zha Nu, a former Party secretary of Hongan county. In 1969, Zha had been sentenced to twenty years of imprisonment for having been a tyrant landlord involved in killing three revolutionaries. When Zha won back his reputation and previous job in 1975, the courts in Yunnan had reportedly corrected 1006 false charges against 1178 victims.[88]

In some other regions the judicial lenience seemed more ephemeral. In Yudu County, Jiangxi, the county began its review and rehabilitation of false charges as soon as its court resumed its functions. The Jiangxi High Court, however, followed a central directive in July 1973 demanding that local courts "strengthen criminal trials and unequivocally strike the sabotage of counterrevolutionaries and other crimes."[89] Like in Jiangxi, the Sichuan High Court in May 1973 asked all intermediate courts to implement central orders against the sabotage instigated by class enemies and to protect the young people sent down to the countryside during the Cultural Revolution.[90] In 1974, the provincial courts had tried 17,107 criminals; among them 141 were to be killed and more than 200 were sentenced to death with reprieve or life in prison. The executed criminals still included those who had distributed counterrevolutionary slogans. There was no evidence about whether the trials had used torture, forced confession, or other illegal procedures. It seems that in 1974 as in 1968, many people in Sichuan continued to receive harsh punishments, including death sentences for their dissident political views or slogans.[91]

88 Ibid.

89 *Yudu County Court Gazette*, 1998: 136-137; for the central order see Brown, 2018: 139.

90 After July 1968, over 16 million youth were sent down to the country or factories. See MacFarquhar and Schoenhals, 2008: 251; for a detailed study on sent-down youth and women see Michel Bonnin, *The Lost Generation: The Rustication of China's Educated Youth (1968-1980)* (Hong Kong: Chinese University Press, 2013).

91 *Sichuan Provincial Trial Gazette*, 2003: 324.

One of the most marked cases in Sichuan in this period was Tu Deyong, a Party member and a college teacher who had, since 1973, written "Ten Crimes of the Cultural Revolution." Tu accused the Cultural Revolution of, inter alia, causing spiritual, political, and physical suffering of over 60% of the population. That immensely dampened people's allegiance to the Party, allowed the "Gang of Four" to usurp state leadership, damaged the national economy, reduced people's living standards, and isolated China in the world. Tu was arrested in May 1975 and sentenced by court in 1976 to life in prison, which was ostensibly in compliance with the SRPS. Although Tu was not as lucky as Xiao Ruiyi, he was more fortunate than Yu Luoke and Deng Sijing. In 1978, having been jailed about two years, the Chengdu government rehabilitated Tu and restored his Party membership.[92]

Despite the restoration of the court and police in late 1972 and the largely consistent clemency toward political crimes in the following several years, the objective, function, and procedure of the judicial system were not much different from those of judiciaries prior to the Cultural Revolution. Moreover, the SRPS, although less forceful than before, remained a principal law for political crimes in many regions (e.g. Sichuan). The judicial system would always be a Party instrument as well as a formidable force to protect the Party's dominance.

In 1974, the Shanghai High Court convened a meeting in response to a central order and the ongoing "Anti-Lin [Biao] and Anti-Confucius Movement." The meeting alleged that both Liu and Lin had tried all means to seize control of the judicial system from the Party. For example, Liu had denounced the Party's absolute control of the judicial system as a left-leaning error and wanted to "use the law to resist the Party and to attempt to change the nature of the judicial system." In addition, Lin Biao and his adherents in Shanghai sought to "steal" judicial power and use investigation and the "ad hoc black task force" to collect "black materials" against central and Shanghai leaders. After the meeting, the high court stated that the proletarian dictatorship could only be implemented under the CCP's categorical leadership, which served as a yardstick to distinguish Marxism from revisionism. "As a knife of the proletarian dictatorship," the court report pointed out, "the court has to incessantly adhere to correct political direction in a struggle between two classes and two lines," namely proletarianism vis-à-vis capitalism. As a result, to avoid drifting off the right course, the court had to absolutely follow the CCP's leadership whatever it was.[93]

92 Ibid. Also see MacFarquhar and Schoenhals, 2008: 350-351.

93 Shanghai Archives, 1974. A102-2-4-37.

It seemed folly for the Shanghai High Court to criticize Lin Biao and Liu Shaoqi of opposing the Party's grip on the judicial system. During his tenure as a front-line leader between 1961 and 1965, Liu had never opposed the Party's control of the judicial system. What the judicial system had done in that period was, as in 1954 and 1956, to review and right cases which had been handled wrongly in the Anti-Rightist Movement. After Lin Biao became Mao's heir in the Cultural Revolution, the promulgation and implementation of the SRPS between 1967 and 1972 helped Lin use the judicial system to heavily punish his critics and defend Mao's impeccable status. In that regard, both Liu and Lin had done nothing to weaken the Party's control of the judicial system. Nor did they harbor any intent to do so. The accusation of the Shanghai High Court that Lin opposed the Party's control of the judicial system likely referred to his effort to put to the judicial system under the direct control of Mao or the "Gang of Four."

One of the missions of the court after its restoration in the 1970s was to penalize people (e.g. local cadres) who had abused sent-down youth. Most of those cases involved rape or sexual harassment of female youth. In one case, Luo Dingbang, a company commander of a military unit in Yunnan, reportedly had raped and harassed more than half of the 30 sent-down women in the company. In May 1974, the Yunnan High Court and the court of the Kunming Military Region co-organized an open trial in which they punished four military cadres, one of whom was sentenced to death for raping and tormenting female sent-down youth.[94]

In terms of the trial and punishment of ordinary criminals, there was little difference between restored courts and the previous military control units. On November 26, 1975, one year before the end of the Cultural Revolution, the Macheng County Court in Hubei punished Zhang Guixin, a 24-year-old student, with five years' incarceration and forced labor. The court accused Zhang of harassing and raping a sent-down woman in 1974 and early 1975.[95] Like court rulings before 1966 but not under military control, the above court verdict restored the ten-day period for litigants to appeal to appellate courts – further evidence of a return of the judicial pendulum to normalcy.[96]

As I have mentioned, civil cases had largely been deemed by military control committees as contradictions among the people which should be

94 *Yunnan Provincial Trial Gazette*, 1999: 260.
95 Hubei Macheng County Archives, 1975. 121-13-082-456-466.
96 Ibid., January 16, 1974. 121-13-082-426-436.

resolved through mediation. Starting from 1973, the "new" court began accepting more civil cases and most of them were concerned about marriage, a persistent focus since the 1950s.[97] According to a county gazette in Jiangxi, Li Daidi and Zhou Chunsheng were married by their own will in December 1973. In the first several months, the couple had enjoyed love and good relationship. Yet, due to his "serious patriarchal thought," Zhou Chunsheng started to "bluntly" meddle in his wife's social activities. For that reason, the couple often squabbled and fought. In September 1975, Zhou forcefully stripped off all his wife's clothes in a fight and coerced her to go see her parents. Outraged by the shame, Li Daidi sued Zhou to the county court demanding a divorce. After mediation failed, the court approved the divorce.[98]

In another case, the same county rejected a divorce request. Yi Longpan and Jin Shulan had been married since 1964 and their relationship was "very cordial." After Yi was promoted from a worker to a cadre (vice head of the labor union) in a mining factory, he had changed and demanded a divorce from his wife in July 1973. The county court turned down the request on grounds that the couple had originally married of their own volition. Owing to Yi's job promotion and his attempt to marry another woman after the divorce, his mind was obviously "immoral" and his action (e.g. divorce) erroneous. Once the plaintiff had rectified his attitude and restored his relations with his wife, the couple should be reunited. No law was cited in the second case including the 1950 Marriage Law.[99]

The rationale behind the court judge/s was at odds with Article 17 of the 1950 Marriage Law that permitted divorce if one party insisted.[100] More ironically, the judgment was made at an era of "Smashing the Four Olds" because it appeared to be akin to a post-Tang (618-907 CE) marriage norm of "seven outs and three exceptions" that a husband could not divorce his wife after he had turned from rags to riches.[101] For the Communist judge,

97 Philip C. Huang also argues that disputes over divorce made up the main content of Chinese civil litigation until the Reform period. See Huang, 2010: 36.

98 According to Philip C. Huang, PRC courts turned more stringent in the 1960s and 1970s requiring that all divorce cases first undergo high-pressure mediation by various levels of local governments. For the case see *Yudu County Court Gazette*, 1998: 136-137; for Huang's argument see Huang, 2010: 38.

99 Ibid. For the socialist ideology of the Marriage Law see Altehenger, 2018: 104.

100 The 1950 Marriage Law of the PRC, http://www.law-lib.com/law/law_view.asp?id=43205 (November 10, 2019).

101 For the post-Tang marriage norm see Glosser, 2003; Qin Fang, "Remembered and Forgotten: Discourse Changes of Qichu and Sanbuqu in Modern China" in *The Journal of Chinese Women's*

Yi's "immoral" behavior was likely due to his violation of a long-standing norm. In Hunan, similar divorce cases to that in Jiangxi between 1973 and 1976 would be dismissed by courts as being influenced by capitalist thought, a more orthodox rhetoric in the socialist PRC that deviated from tradition.[102]

Not the Worst Law Period

As many scholars around the world have correctly argued, the Cultural Revolution witnessed immense use of torture, many arbitrary punishments, and rampant violations of law. Millions of people were attacked, struggled against, and humiliated by Red Guards, the police, and officials in the first couple of years. Many victims had no chance to go through the already flawed and weakened legal process, let alone secure legal remedies. After the military took over the judicial system in 1968, numerous political critics and ordinary people were imprisoned and executed for their heterodox opinions or minor and unintentional offenses to the leaders. The situation was in some ways similar to Stalin's Russia when accidental errors could be defined as treason and punished accordingly.[103] But in China the court under military control at least followed certain legal processes and rendered formal verdicts to "active counterrevolutionaries." In some of the most infamous cases, such as the death sentences meted out to Lin Zhao and Yu Luoke, the military-controlled courts in Shanghai and Beijing announced their respective decisions in written verdicts. Despite a limited review and rehabilitation after 1970, most victims had to wait until late 1978 to redress their grievances.

However persuasive these scholarly arguments about law and justice in the Cultural Revolution are, I want to argue that the legal system and practice in this period were by no means a far cry from earlier periods in the PRC. As I have mentioned intermittently, with the exception of relatively harsher punishments between 1968 and 1970 and an addition of Mao's selected works on top of each verdict, legal process, court verdicts, and rehabilitation in the Cultural Revolution were comparable to those in the 1950s and early 1960s. Moreover, if we could read and compare all the first-instance criminal/

Studies, Nov., 2018, No. 6, Ser. No. 150.

102 *Hunan Provincial Gazette of Politics and Law*, 1995: 496.

103 Belova and Gregory, 2009: 466.

counterrevolutionary cases (most criminal cases were counterrevolutionary) from 1949 to 1976 in some provincial gazettes, we would easily find out that the total number of criminal cases during the Cultural Revolution was smaller than that in other periods. If the Cultural Revolution were a lawless period or worse than other periods, it would be difficult to answer the questions: Why were fewer people tried and punished for political and regular crimes during the Cultural Revolution than before in the PRC? Why were there fewer people sentenced to more severe punishments (e.g. life imprisonment and death) than those in some other periods? The following charts will help us better understand the actual function and practice of the judicial system and criminal justice in the Cultural Revolution. All the charts come from provincial and county gazettes published in the 1990s and early 2000s, a time when the central government still held a negative and hypercritical attitude toward the Cultural Revolution. Hence, there was no reason or impetus for the gazettes to purposely curtail the number of "criminal" cases or to make the judicial system in the Cultural Revolution seem less horrible than in previous periods.

Some local gazettes have indicated that many courts were dysfunctional due to internal power seizures and factional struggles at the outset of the Cultural Revolution, but the above chart of the Shaanxi provincial gazette tells a quite different story. The Shaanxi courts were able to deal with an average number of 6413 cases each year during the Cultural Revolution, which was much lower than in the periods before 1966. The only exceptional year was 1970 when the central government launched the "One Strike and Three-Antis" movement, resulting in mounting crackdowns. While the percentage of counterrevolutionary cases soared to almost 50% of all criminal cases after the military took over judicial system in 1968, the total number of counterrevolutionary cases remained considerably lower than that in previous years. From 1949 to 1976, the years having higher number of regular criminal and counterrevolutionary cases were all in the 1950s, especially in 1951, 1955, and 1958 when China was undergoing widespread political campaigns. Even in the early 1960s when the Party kicked off a general rehabilitation to correct falsely charged cases, the number of criminal and counterrevolutionary cases was still much bigger than that during the Cultural Revolution.

In Hunan province, the records of counterrevolutionary cases were missing from 1966 to 1969, the most violent period in the Cultural Revolution, probably because of the chaos inside the judicial system. But based on the number of accepted counterrevolutionary cases in the ten years of

Table 7.1 First-instance criminal cases in Shaanxi province, 1950-1978[104]

Year	Number of Cases Accepted	Number of Counterrevolutionary Cases	Percentage of Total Cases	Number of Cases Solved
1950	12345	610	4.87	11860
1951	25619	7895	30.82	25522
1952	18508	2954	15.96	18784
1953	18652	2730	14.64	19385
1954	23440	1219	5.20	22209
1955	27587	3831	13.87	27892
1956	17791	3944	22.17	19761
1957	16560	1501	9.06	15362
1958	66981	23258	34.92	68063
1959	12967	1692	13.98	12838
1960	12967	2939	22.67	12860
1961	13406	1453	10.76	12383
1962	13230	601	4.54	13553
1963	16801	907	5.40	16400
1964	10469	1594	15.23	9778
1965	11580	1137	9.82	11812
1966	8474	1855	21.90	8255
1967	3073	482	15.68	3435
1968	1904	604	31.72	1891
1969	3407	826	42.24	3528
1970	16844	7778	46.18	12332
1971	6716	1905	28.37	8659
1972	3809	581	15.25	7578
1973	3532	302	8.55	4091
1974	4909	277	5.64	4207
1975	5969	375	6.28	5884
1976	5498	549	9.99	5844
1977	6648	539	8.10	7591
1978	4907	220	4.48	4698

"upheaval,"[105] we can see a significant drop in the number of these cases from previous periods. The increase of counterrevolutionary cases in 1970 was still smaller than that in similar campaigns in the 1950s. In the first anti-counterrevolutionary campaign (1951), the number of counterrevolutionary cases was close to 100,000, almost five time as many as that in 1970. Another

104 *Shaanxi Provincial Trial Gazette*, 1994: 302.

105 *The People's Daily*, May 16, 2016; also Barbara Barnouin, *Ten Years of Turbulence: The Chinese Cultural Revolution* (Abingdon: Routledge, 1993).

Table 7.2 First-instance counterrevolutionary cases in Hunan province, 1950-1978[106]

Year	Cases Accepted	Cases Solved	More than Lifetime Sentence	Percentage of Accepted Cases	More than Five Years	Less than Five Years	*guanzhi*	No Charge	Innocent
1950	5350	3943	1135	21%	1310		52	506	1499
1951	96428	80478	26451	27%	15649		1965	26659	3845
1952	33571	38384	9636	28%	10025	10063	3171	4529	391
1953	7646	9607	1011	13%	3227	3054	322	417	114
1954	3548	3775	308	8%	1304	1463	96	188	28
1955	14069	12349	862	6%	7156	3396	326	362	44
1956	4189	4989	862	20%	1441	1607	354	298	72
1957	3080	2972	112	3%	606	1216	723	79	23
1958	29011	29131	817	2%	5415	4811	17867	145	13
1959	10353	10434	256	2.8%	2163	1529	6620	247	21
1960	5783	5781	279	4%	2079	1002	2855	106	6
1961	3046	3066	119	3.9%	1370	790	1358	226	14
1962	1162	1144	38	3%	463	317	420	175	23
1963	3572	3516	83	2%	1042	568	2125	352	8
1964	1264	1270	48	3%	513	203	660	256	5
1965	1088	1244	42	3.8%	526	178	487	194	77
1966	3866	3779	34	0.8%	450	218	3104	84	
1967	613	487	Not Available						
1968	3841	3484	Not Available						
1969	4500	4509	Not Available						
1970	24215	22099	376	1.5%	1572	1422	13708	6273	
1971	4497	7128	30	0.6%	732	487	4513	2118	
1972	1730	3283	24	1.3%	382	208	2158	1031	
1973	459	770	17	3.7%	168	106	466	124	
1974	425	383	18	4.2%	159	121	49	34	3
1975	698	660	61	8.7%	308	146	113	49	1
1976	882	782	67	7.5%	415	207	116	34	6
1977	1078	1060	115	10.6%	566	318	102	76	5
1978	327	466	31	9.4%	238	161	28	81	12

year that had more counterrevolutionary cases than the Cultural Revolution is understandably 1958, shortly after the CCP ignited the Anti-Rightist Movement. The number of accused counterrevolutionary cases in years other than 1970 was mostly smaller than those in the early 1960s, much less

106 *Hunan Provincial Gazette of Politics and Law*, 1995: 6. 269-271

than that in the 1950s. As far as severe punishments such as death sentence or life sentence are concerned, their percentage in the Cultural Revolution except the three missing years was lower than the rehabilitation period in the early 1960s and much lower than in the early 1950s. In 1970 and 1971, after Mao ordered the reduction in death penalties involving intellectual critics, the percentage of harsh punishments dwindled to around 1%.

In Table 7.3, the Shanxi provincial gazette has a very detailed and complete chart of the first-instance criminal cases from 1949 to 1978, but it does not contain a separate chart of the counterrevolutionary cases. Like in Hunan and Shaanxi, the number of the accepted first-instance criminal cases in Shanxi during the Cultural Revolution was much lower than almost all other preceding years. Although the number of imprisoned people in the ten "turbulent" years was higher than after 1977, it was lower than that in the 1950s.

Similar evidence can be found in other provinces such as Hebei, Sichuan, and Guangdong.[107] In those provinces, the numbers of accepted criminal/counterrevolutionary cases were also lower than – or close to – those in the 1950s and early 1960s. In the gazette of Wannian County, Jiangxi, the lowest numbers of criminal cases can be found in the Cultural Revolution (1969: 8; 1970: 4; 1971: 5). The years between 1953 and 1955 (1953: 125; 1954: 263; 1955: 219) had the highest numbers, but not 1958 (69), the year most other provinces saw the highest numbers.[108]

As evidenced in many provincial gazettes, the numbers of accused criminal cases and cases with severe penalties in the Cultural Revolution are significantly lower than those in 1950s movements. In contrast to the early 1960s, the Cultural Revolution still had relatively smaller or similar numbers of criminal cases. Why do existing local records of criminal cases not square with the stereotyped impression that the ten-year Cultural Revolution is arguably the darkest era for the Chinese people and for the law in the PRC? One possible answer is that most leaders ascending to power after 1976 had been attacked, struggled against, or dismissed in the Cultural Revolution. They more often than not tended to discredit the Cultural Revolution and overstress the internal chaos, false charges, incompetent judges, brutal penalties, and other dysfunctions of its legal system. In the

107 For those provinces see *Yunnan Provincial Trial Gazette*, 1999: 55. 324; *Sichuan Provincial Trial Gazette*, 2003: 349; *Hebei Provincial Trial Gazette*, Vol. 73 (Hebei shengzhi shenpanzhi河北省志审判志) (Hebei: Hebei renmin chubanshe, 1994): 204; *Guangdong Provincial Trial Gazette*, 1999: 88.

108 *Wannian County Court Gazette* (*Wannianxian fayuanzhi*万年县法院志) (Beijing: Fangzhi chubanshe, 2003): 149.

Table 7.3 First-instance criminal cases in Shanxi province, 1949-1978[109]

Year	Newly Accepted Cases	Solved Cases	Persons Judged	Declared Innocent	Death, Death with Reprieve, Lifetime, Prison Terms	Short-term Detainment	On Parole	*guanzhi*	No Charge
1949	6612	5052	6036	603	3279		103		1649
1950	23666	23272	27806	1362	1057		150		6593
1951	37191	37118	36976	886	5204				11383
1952	23882	22645	23628	837	11164	1024	337	520	8222
1953	24678	25726	25391	1702	11192	3902	266	165	6169
1954	30995	30988	33868	1309	15210	2257	427	113	9268
1955	40648	40816	40357	1399	21261	160	720	5578	8413
1956	17408	18653	14718	738	7772		455	168	4283
1957	20288	19516	17411	819	9235		666	764	3438
1958	47825	48980	47559		28524			15096	
1959	11790	11790	10486	235	5379		196	2182	769
1960	16025	15958	15802	71	8075		253	2865	432
1961	12302	12085	15073	117	5488		328	2629	1729
1962	10076	10114	12192	217	4157	690	323	445	2144
1963	10825	8348	10661	65	3037	1107	210	770	1980
1964	10419	10606	8664	88	2844	714	97	531	2570
1965	8151	10432	7536	145	3840	1256	116	816	1960
1966	7584	7567	7378	39	2890	18	104	934	173
1967	3851	4265	3779	86	1177	19	47	174	272
1968	1484	1416	1404	63	1297		3	43	48
1969	2381	2035	2210	16	3038		188	194	92
1970	4285	4207	5755	47	3396		369	422	652
1971	3290	3598	4709	315	7186		258	351	513
1972	2468	2927	3682	172	2335		128	242	346
1973	2152	2332	3408	243	2444		60	49	276
1974	3357	2978	2608	59	2064		58	33	318
1975	3880	3639	3774	135	3051		85	29	418
1976	2927	3026	3072	67	347		96	34	292
1977	4392	4223	4265	48	3631		164	34	245
1978	3279	3619	3410	69	2803		135	15	338

meantime, because the same leaders had been part of the leadership who were more or less directly involved in political campaigns in the 1950s,[110]

109 *General Gazette of Shanxi – Judicial Gazette*, 1998: 34. 196.

110 For example, Deng Xiaoping, the paramount CCP leader after Mao, was the Party secretary in 1957 who directly managed the Anti-Rightist Movement. Liu Shaoqi was behind the 1954

they "naturally" turned a blind eye to the Communist judicial system in the 1950s that presided over more expansive and serious violations of the law and wrongs inflicted on innocent people.

Conclusion

A fear of confrontations with both superpowers combined with anxiety about the erosion of socialism resulting from Liu Shaoqi's economic incentives after 1961 prompted Mao to launch the Cultural Revolution. In the first couple of years, an extralegal terror engulfed China and millions of people were reportedly attacked, tortured, or slain by the Red Guards or factional forces. Many scholars and gazettes have concurred that the violence and infringements of law reached their zenith in the 1960s. No doubt their arguments are credible and convincing. In the two years 1966-1967, no one, including Mao, felt safe.[111] Party leaders such as Liu Shaoqi, Peng Zhen, and Tao Zhu suffered brutal struggles and public humiliations in mass meetings by the Red Guards backed by Mao and other radical leaders.[112] In the face of a polity-wide ferocity, the regular judicial system found itself entangled in both internal chaos and external assaults and was unable to maintain order. Adding to the tumultuous era was the release of the SRPS in early 1967, which soon became a primary law justifying arrests and punishments of heterodox views and actions, however flimsily documented or unintentional, against top leaders (e.g. Lin Biao and Jiang Qing) who worried about losing their new power which they called a proletarian dictatorship.

By the time the military took control of the judicial system in early 1968, most criminal cases, if not all, would go through the flawed legal process, which neither cited existing laws nor included any time for appeals to upper courts. Although penalties in local gazettes appear to be harsher than those in the past, available archival cases show more generous punishments,

Gao Gang incident that was ensued by the 1955 Anti-counterrevolutionary campaign. For Deng Xiaoping see Ezra F. Vogel, *Deng Xiaoping and the Transformation of China* (Cambridge, Ma: Harvard University Press, 2013): 40-41; David Shambaugh, "Deng Xiaoping: The Politician" in *The China Quarterly*, No. 135, Special Issue: Deng Xiaoping: An Assessment (Sep., 1993), pp. 457-490: 468; and Michael Dillon, *Deng Xiaoping: A Political Biography* (New York: I.B. Tauris, 2014): 134; for Liu Shaoqi see Dai Maolin戴茂林 and Zhao Xiaoguang赵晓光, *Biography of Gang Gang (Gao Gangzhuan*高岗传) (Shaanxi: Shaanxi renmin chubanshe, 2011).

111 Jeremy Brown argues that the deportation of bad people to the country began in Beijing because Mao felt unsafe in 1966. See Brown, 2014: 142.

112 Vogel, 1980: 326-329; MacFarquhar and Schoenhals, 2008: 147-187.

which were mostly consistent with those in other periods. Some local judges and leaders were audacious enough to take lenient stances toward political dissenters. One year before the central government's decision to restore the people's court in late 1972, a polity-wide but limited review and rehabilitation had already begun. In many areas, this round of rehabilitation proceeded with and was followed by a restoration of the judicial system and certain legal processes. The new political and judicial moderation lasted several years until another crackdown occurred in the spring of 1976. In spite of its massive law infringement and judicial dysfunction, the Cultural Revolution does not stand out as worse than previous periods in the PRC in respect to the judiciaries. Statistics from many local gazettes palpably testify that both the number of criminal cases (including counterrevolutionary ones) and the percentage of harsh punishments in the Cultural Revolution were lower than those in most previous periods. In this regard, it would be unfair to single out the dysfunction of the judicial system in the Cultural Revolution as the worst in the history of the PRC.

Conclusion

From Party's Fear to People's Fear

Abstract
The conclusion focuses on law and legal practice in the post-Mao era after China reopened to the world and tried to embrace the West and world trade. As part of China's comprehensive reform, legal reform is one of the bright spots. The Chinese government has not only restored some legal institutions such as lawyers but also promulgated thousands of new laws. In 1997, Chinese leaders pledged that China would implement the rule of law. However, the fear of losing its power remains the top priority for the Chinese judicial systems. Whenever there is a threat to the Party rule, the judicial systems would quickly and resolutely punish the offender/s. After 2008, the Party reaffirms its firm control over the judicial systems and in a number of high-profiled cases, the judicial systems have convicted renowned critics such as Liu Xiaobo and Xu Zhiyong to long prison sentences. So long as the Party's fear of insecurity exists, the judicial systems will always be the loyal "Knife Hilt" of the Party.

Keywords: legalism, legal reform, party's fear, party's weapon

From its birth in the late 1920s to the end of the Cultural Revolution, the Chinese Communist judicial system had seen a coexistence of fear of losing power, legal instrumentalism, and legalism, albeit certain elements outweighed the others in some periods. Built on fear, the Communist judicial system was meant initially to be a violent and powerful instrument safeguarding CCP power and countering political enemies in the midst of life-and-death wars with the GMD, its foremost adversary. Having expelled the GMD to Taiwan and created the PRC, the CCP continued to fear for its security in the face of volatile and hostile domestic and international adversaries. That concern prompted the Party to launch intermittent campaigns (1950-1952, 1955-1956, 1957-1960, 1962, 1966) in which the judicial system

Fang, Qiang, *The Communist Judicial System in China, 1927-1976: Building on Fear.*
Taylor & Francis Group 2021
DOI: 10.5117/9789463729451_CONCL

(and military commissions in early years) acted as a coercive and faithful instrument of the Party. However, many Party leaders and judges at both high and local levels still adhered to basic legal principles and respected legal professionalism such as equality before the law, judicial process, and litigants' rights to defense or appeal. More important, the concomitant of the three crucial elements that has long accompanied the Chinese judicial system did not end in the post-1978 reforms. Rather, we can predict with assurance that all three elements will persist so long as the CCP survives.

Legalism and its Limitations

In the fall of 1976, Mao's death and the fall of the "Gang of Four" wrapped up the Cultural Revolution. The SRPS and the political and legal suppressions associated with it, however, did not end as many people had hoped. The legal hostility to political criminals lingered on for another couple of years until late 1978 in the wake of the Third Plenary of the Eleventh Party Congress. For instance, in October 1976, shortly after the central government under Hua Guofeng "smashed the Gang of Four," Jin Baofu, an elementary school teacher in Heshun County, Shanxi, inadvertently omitted the word "Smashing" in a slogan of "Warmly Celebrate the Great Victory in *Smashing* the Gang of Four," which completely reversed the meaning. For that mistake, Jin was indicted as being an "active counterrevolutionary" and sentenced to five years in prison.[1] The punishment was ostensibly based on the SRPS that was now inherited by the new CCP leader Hua Guofeng who vowed to follow whatever Mao had said and done.[2] According to the judicial gazette of Wanxian County, Sichuan, before the 1978 Third Plenum, a landmark of the beginning of China's latest reform, such Cultural-Revolution-era crime names as "vicious attacks [of Party leaders]" were still being used by judges, resulting in "many new false charges."[3]

1 *General Gazette of Shanxi – Judicial Gazette* (*Shanxitonggzhi shenpanzhi*山西通志-审判志) (Beijing: Zhonghua shujü, 1998): 34. 126.

2 For Hua Guofeng's "Two Whatevers" see Meisner, 1999: 428; Michael Dillion, *Deng Xiaoping: The Man who Made Modern China* (New York: I.B. Tauris, 2014): 221.

3 Recent studies show that local leaders continued to resist the review of false charges in the Cultural Revolution until 1984. For Wanxian see *Wanxian County Court Gazette* (*Wanxian fayuanzhi*万县法院志) (Beijing: Fangzhi chubanshe, 2003): 121; for similar arguments see *Shaanxi Provincial Gazette*, 1994: 227 and *Sichuan Provincial Gazette*, 2003: 325; for studies on the resistance of rehabilitation see Song Guoqing, "The Floating Fate of a Rebel Leader in Guangxi, 1966-1984" in Leese and Engman, 2018, pp. 174-200.

The legal reform was unveiled by the Party after 1979. Many of the new Party leaders such as Deng Xiaoping, Hu Yaobang, and Peng Zhen had been attacked in the Cultural Revolution. Against this historical backdrop, there was an urgent and strong call among top leaders to pursue a joint leadership and conduct a sweeping legal reform.[4] Prior to the Third Plenum, Marshall Ye Jianying, one of the few leaders who had not been attacked in the "Ten Turbulent Years," urged both Hua Guofeng and Deng Xiaoping to work together to strengthen the collective leadership. Ye believed that the mishap of the Cultural Revolution was the result of placing too much power in Mao's hands. Deng, on the other hand, emphasized the importance of "inner-Party" democracy and legal reform, which could prevent a single person, no matter how able, from becoming dominant.[5] In December 1979, Wan Li, the Party secretary of Anhui province and later the head of the National People's Congress (NPC), advocated a restoration of equality before the law pledged in the 1954 constitution. "All lawbreakers," Wan Li stated, "no matter how much revolutionary experience they have, how high their official posts are, and how much accomplishments they have made, will be brought to justice."[6]

Peng Zhen, a leading legal official behind the 1954 constitution, whose downfall had heralded the advent of the Cultural Revolution, returned to his previous role in charge of law and legal reform in 1978. His tragic experience in the Cultural Revolution reminded him of the need for "relatively formal and effective institutions and processes of law" that would confer legitimacy on the post-Mao regime."[7] On June 26, 1979, Peng Zhen remarked that all Chinese people "are [now] craving a healthy legal system." He also quoted Marshal Ye as saying that only a perfect socialist legal system could guarantee people's democratic rights and maintain political stability.[8] Despite his calls for equality before the law in accordance with the constitution, Peng Zhen, as Pitman Potter has noted, continued to view law as an instrument of the Party. It was not a "Diceyan set of overarching normative standards that governed the behavior of rulers and ruled alike, but rather a set of edicts enacted in pursuit of policy goals." In that sense,

4 Peerenboom, 2002: 55; Altehenger, 2018: 172.

5 Vogel, 2013: 240-243.

6 Wan Li万里, "Strengthening Socialist Democracy and Legal System (*jiaqiang shehui zhuyi minzhu hefazhi*加强社会主义民主和法制)" in Wan Li万里, *Selected Works of Wan Li* (*Wan Li wenxuan*万里文选) (Beijing: Renmin chubanshe, 1995): 146-147.

7 Potter, 2003: 117.

8 Peng Zhen, 1991: 368-369.

Peng Zhen did not see a conflict between the ideal rule of law and the practice of party leadership.[9]

To pave the way for a major legal reform, the official bulletin of the Third Plenum announced that citizens' democratic rights promised in the constitution had to be absolutely guaranteed so that no one could violate them. In order to protect people's democratic rights, China "must solidify its socialist legal system and make democracy systematic and legalistic." It was imperative for the PRC to draft laws and strictly implement them. For the first time since 1954, the Party suggested that both the judicial system and the procuracy preserve the "independence that they deserve" and "be loyal to law and legal practice, people's interests, and the truth." The bulletin also stressed the importance of equality before the law and that no one would be above the law.[10]

The full-scale legal reform marked a momentous period in lawmaking activities after the plenum.[11] In 1978, Party leaders restored the Procuracy (abolished in 1975) and in 1979 they reinstated the Ministry of Justice (canceled in 1959). Also, in 1979, both Beijing and Shanghai renewed their lawyer associations. Among major laws in this period, one was the Criminal Law, which was passed by the NPC on July 1, 1979. This long-awaited law was first proposed in the early 1950s, but its formal enactment had been interrupted by continuous political campaigns.[12] The law listed numerous crimes and the range of their respective punishments. Not ready to dispense completely with Mao's heritage, authors of the new law retained the name and category of "counterrevolutionary crime" and stipulated sentences ranging from ten years to life in prison. This made punishments less severe than in the 1951 Regulations on Punishing Counterrevolutionaries that had imposed the death penalty.[13]

Another statute, the Criminal Procedure Law, was even more important because it offered certain legal protections to litigants and put restrictions on judicial agents. Like the Criminal Law, the Criminal Procedure Law

9 Potter, 2003: 109.

10 "The Official Bulletin of the Third Plenum of the Eleventh Party Congress (*shiyijie sanzhong quanhui gognbao*十一届三中全会公报)," December 22, 1978. http://economy.caixin.com/2013-11-04/100598910.html (October 23, 2020); for the legal notions in the 1950s see Chapter 5 and Potter, 2003.

11 Ching Kwan Lee, *Against the Law: Labor Protests in China's Rustbelt and Sunbelt* (Berkeley: University of California Press, 2007): 18.

12 Chen Xingliang, "Forty Years Research of Chinese Criminal Law" in *The Journal of Wuhan University*, 2018, Vol. 2, pp. 31-41.

13 *The Criminal Law of the PRC* (Shandong: Shandong Provincial Police Bureau, 1979).

had not been enacted for almost 30 years.[14] Article 32 of the law allowed defendants to defend themselves. They could also ask a lawyer, relative, or persons recommended by their work units to defend people on their behalf. As I have mentioned in the Introduction, torture has a long history in China and has been used by officials/judges in dynasties, republics, and Mao's China alike to extract confessions thought essential to the legitimacy of the prosecution and to the defendant's rehabilitation as well as grounds for punishment. Although Communist Party leaders had banned torture many times, it remained a key method in local police interrogations in Mao's China. Many people had to "confess their crimes" in political campaigns due to their inability to stand torture. Article 53 once again outlawed torture, allurement, and coercion and required all law enforcement officers to abide by legal procedures and to verify crimes by using manifold evidence. Article 54 stated that all evidence collected by unlawful means such as torture and coercion would not be accepted. In particular, the law required the procuracy to corroborate evidence that they suspected to have been collected illegally.[15] Unfortunately, the law has not been fully implemented since then. As shown in other studies, torture continues to be used by police in China today.[16]

The 1982 constitution was reminiscent of its 1954 counterpart in terms of its content on law-related provisions. For instance, Article 37, which protected citizens' personal freedom and prohibited unauthorized arrest of citizens, was almost the same as Article 89 in the 1954 constitution. Like the 1954 law, the new constitution stipulated judicial and procuracy independence, open trials, a people's jury system, and litigants' right to defense. One noticeable difference in the new constitution was Article 5, which stated that the PRC would construct the rule of law while the 1954 law emphasized suppression of all traitors and counterrevolutionaries. Another difference was its large number of articles (138), more than in any former constitutions back to the 1949 Common Principles. According to Altehenger, soon after the enactment of the new constitution, the Party, as it had done in the 1950s, launched a propaganda campaign to propagate the law among the masses. Yet a dilemma ensued among the public security

14 Susan Trevaskes, *Courts and Criminal Justice in Contemporary China* (Lanham: Lexington Books, 2007): 46-47.

15 The Criminal Procedure Law of the PRC, July 1, 1979. http://www.gov.cn/flfg/2012-03/17/content_2094354.htm (December 20, 2019).

16 See for example, Qiang Fang, "The Case of Virgin Prostitute: Chinese Media and Legal Reform" in *Stanford Journal of East Asian Affairs*, Vol. 2, pp. 26-40, 2002; Qiang Fang and Xiaobing Li, 2017.

cadres who were supposed to run the campaign but tended to oppose legal education lest people with more legal knowledge would challenge the illicit actions of the police.[17]

In the Mao era, people could lodge complaints to almost all government agencies against official violations of their rights. The disputes between the masses and the cadres were viewed as internal "contradictions among the people" that should be resolved through mediation. In that period, courts and police were to handle external cases involving contradictions between the people and class enemies and criminal cases.[18] In the 1980s, as China was stepping up its legal reform and embracing what it considered to be a "modern" regime of the rule of law, the central government moved to legalize its complaint system. In 1989, the NPC promulgated the Administrative Litigation Law, which opened the court to aggrieved people who were now allowed to sue official lawbreakers.[19]

In the 1990s, and especially after the Fourteenth Congress of the CCP (in 1992) proposed to establish a "socialist market economy," the legal reform gained more momentum. As some scholars have argued, to build up a market economy would require the rule of law.[20] The law would play a pivotal role when the Chinese economy was merging with the world economy.[21] Consequently, both national and local congresses had enacted thousands of laws. Many crucial laws such as the Judge Law, the Procurator Law, the Constitution, and the Criminal Procedure Law were either promulgated or revised in the 1990s. With the enactments of both the Administrative Litigation Law and the Regulations Regarding Letters and Petitions (*xinfang tiaoli*) in 1995, the CCP seemed to have completed the reinstitution of all six GMD laws it had abolished in the early PRC.[22] The culmination of the legal reform discourse, as opposed to actual operation, was in 1997 when President Jiang Zemin formally announced that the PRC would "use the

17 Altehenger, 2018: 199; for the 1982 constitution see The Constitution of the PRC, December 4, 1982; http://www.people.com.cn/GB/shehui/1060/2391834.html (January 20, 2020); for the 1954 constitution see http://www.npc.gov.cn/wxzl/wxzl/2000-12/26/content_4264.htm (October 23, 2020).

18 For a complete study on China's complaint history see Fang, 2013.

19 The Administrative Litigation Law of the PRC, April 4, 1989. http://www.npc.gov.cn/wxzl/wxzl/2000-12/05/content_4519.htm (October 23, 2020).

20 Xia Yong 夏勇, *Ruling the Country With Law: State and Society* (*yifa zhiguo-guojia yu shehui* 依法治国-国家与社会) (Beijing: Shehui kexue wenxian chubanshe, 2004): 99.

21 Lubman, 2000: 123.

22 The Regulations Regarding Letters and Petitions in 1995 is similar in form but not in nature to the 1932 Republican Petition Law (*suyuanfa* 诉愿法). See Qiang Fang, 2013a: Ch. 4.

law to rule the nation."[23] In 1999, constructing the rule of law in China was added to the national mission under the constitution. By 2003, the NPC alone had passed 430 laws or relevant regulations. The State Council and local people's congresses had promulgated or passed a total of 900 and 9000 laws respectively.[24] According to one statistic, about 69% of laws passed by the NPC have been revised at least once and 19.7% of laws have been revised twice.[25]

As the legal reform deepened, the number of judges and lawyers increased sharply. In 1979, there were only 58,000 judges, but that figure rose almost five times to 250,000 in 1997, though the quality of judges was problematic.[26] Lawyers who had not been seen since 1957 reemerged in the legal reform. The number of lawyers jumped from virtually none in 1979 to 50,000 in 1992 and 200,000 in by early 21st century.[27] As Harold M. Tanner notes, lawyers also saw their role strengthened in defense of criminal suspects.[28] In 1990, just one year after the Administrative Litigation Law, over 2400 administrative tribunals were created.[29] In this period, people greatly expanded their legal consciousness resulting from massive coverage of law-related reports by national and local public media.[30] In contrast to the past, Chinese people in the reform period are more willing to use the law to solve disputes. In 1990, for instance, all Chinese courts had dealt with a total of 2.9 million

23 *The People's Daily*, September 22, 1997.

24 *The People's Daily* (Overseas Edition), January 3, 2003; for a more detailed account of the laws passed by the NPC see Guoli Liu, "Political Culture and Legal Reform" in *American Review of China Studies* 1 (Winter 2000): 1-25.

25 Li Lin李林, "Main Experiences of China's Legislation in the Thirty-Year Open Policy (*Kaifang sanshinian zhongguo lifa zhuyao jingyan*开放三十年中国立法主要经验)," *Xuexi shibao*, August 2008.

26 In 1998 the outspoken legal scholar He Weifang pointed out the problem that about half of the judges were military veterans who, like many judges after the 1952 legal reform, had little legal knowledge and training. See He Weifang贺卫方, "Military Veterans Enter the Court (*fuyuan junren jin fayuan*复员军人进法院)" in *The Southern Weekend*, January 2, 1998; also see He Weifang贺卫方, *The Method of Conveying Justice* (*yunsong Zhengyi defangshi*运送正义的方式) (Shanghai: Shanghai sanlian shudian, 2002): 8-11.

27 For the number of judges see Lubman, 2000: 253; for lawyers see Weixing Chen and Yang Zhong, *Leadership in a Changing China* (London: Palgrave Macmillan, 2004): 72.

28 Tanner, 1999: 19.

29 Ren Jianxin任建新, "Working Report of the Supreme People's Court (*zuigao renmin fayuan baogao*最高人民法院报告)" in *The People's Daily*, April 10, 1990.

30 Qiang Fang, "Chinese Media and the Rule of Law: The Case of the China Youth Daily, 1979-2006" in Xiaobing Li and Qiang Fang, eds., *Modern Chinese Legal Reform: New Perspectives* (Lexington: University Press of Kentucky, 2013): 27-58.

cases. By 2006, the number of cases accepted by Chinese courts had almost quadrupled.[31]

However significant the progress the legal reform attained after 1978, the role of PRC judicial system remains an instrument of the Party and legal instrumentalism has recently been beefed up. It is true that Party leaders were aware of the importance of law after Mao's death, and it is also true that the Party has made serious and significant efforts to develop a legal system in line with the economic reform and restore legal principles first propounded in the 1950s. But the Party, haunted by a fundamental fear of insecurity and losing power as well as the immense benefits associated with its power, has no intention of taking the risk of crossing the Rubicon to construct what Peerenboom has called a "thick" rule of law based on liberal democracy and other relevant beliefs.[32] Instead, the Party insists on its dominance and only tolerates a legal reform insofar as it will not challenge its one-party rule. In 1979, Deng Xiaoping, who backed legal reform to avert concentration of power, laid out four cardinal principles to guarantee CCP's leadership.[33] Peng Zhen, the advocate of equality before the law since the 1950s and the mastermind behind the 1982 constitution, envisioned a law being the "instrument of rule through which the Party state articulated its policies and exercised its political authority."[34] While Jiang Zemin vowed in 1997 to construct a rule of law whose many features were "central to a thin theory of rule of law," he saw the rule of law "as a tool for strengthening Party rule" that could rein in increasingly independent local governments and ensure that central policies would be meted out.[35]

Not only have Party leaders set a boundary on legal reform, but most, if not all, supreme court justices have also conceded Party supremacy over law. In his report to the NPC in April 1986, Supreme Court justice Zheng Tianxiang noted that all courts "must serve the general aims and objectives of the Party state as well as socialist construction."[36] In the spring of 1990, about nine months after the Tiananmen massacre, Ren Jianxin, the Supreme Court justice, ordered all judicial cadres to uphold the Party's four cardinal

31 "How do Courts Deal with the Rigorously Rising Litigations? (*guansi xunmeng pansheng, fayuan ruhe yingdui*官司迅猛攀升，法院如何应对)" *Jiaxing ribao*, July 24, 2007.

32 Peerenboom, 2002: 71.

33 Vogel, 2011: 262.

34 Potter, 2003: 109.

35 According to Peerenboom, the thin theory of rule of law promises some degree of predictability and at least some limitation on arbitrariness. See Peerenboom, 2002: 60.

36 Zheng Tianxiang郑天翔, "Report of the Supreme People's Court (*zuigao renmin fayuan baogao*最高人民法院报告)" in *The People's Daily*, April 18, 1986.

principles and oppose capitalist liberalization. He reaffirmed the court's instrumental role for the Party and said that the people's court was "one of the key parts of the people's dictatorship and thus all adjudicating works are directly connected with safeguarding social stability."[37]

In 2000, after China incorporated the rule of law into its constitution and joined the World Trade Organization, its judicial system was supposed to be more independent than in the past. Yet, Xiao Yang, the Supreme Court justice, continued to stress courts' subordination to the Party. In his words, the "smooth and healthy development of adjudication will be impossible without CCP leadership, NPC's supervision, [and] administrative support" at all levels.[38] As though the promises made by supreme court justices to be loyal to the party were not sufficient, Party leaders sometimes would openly stress the instrumental role of the Communist judicial system. For example, while attending a meeting on Chinese law in early 2014, President Xi Jinping emphasized that the Party had to firmly control the judicial system. "Being a state organ, legal departments [i.e. the judicial system, police, procuracy, prison, etc.] must be placed under the Party's absolute leadership (*juedui lingdao*)." Xi added, "All levels of legal units should align themselves with a steadfast political stance, a high-degree political soberness, and a strong political consciousness to the Party central."[39] One year later, Xi revived the Mao-era term "knife hilt" to refer to the judicial system and ordered the Party to tightly control it.[40] Indeed, Xi's words are consistent with the Party's basic legal policy since the base period: that judicial system and law are instruments which the Party uses to strengthen its rule.

Fear of Losing Power

As this book has shown, the Communist judicial system in China was born amid bloody and lethal wars and therefore its vital mission has ever since been to safeguard the Party's survival and suppress its internal

37 Ren Jianxin, 1990.

38 Xiao Yang肖扬, "Report of the Supreme People's Court (*zuigao renmin fayuan baogao*最高人民法院报告)" in *The People's Daily*, March 20, 2000.

39 "Xi Jinping Delivers Important Speech at the Central Political and Legal Work Meeting (*Xi Jinping chuxi zhongyang zhengfa gognzuo huiyi bingfabiao zhongyao jianghua*习近平出席中央政法工作会议并发表重要讲话)" in *The People's Daily*, January 29, 2014.

40 "Important Directives of Xi Jinping on Political and Legal Work (*Xi Jinping jiuzhengfa gognzuo zuochu zhongyao zhishi*习近平就政法工作作出重要指示)" in *The People's Daily*, January 21, 2015.

enemies. Even after the Party defeated the GMD and established the PRC, such an intrinsic and constant fear of losing power and insecurity was so overwhelming that the Party had launched numerous political campaigns from 1950 till 1976. The end of the Cultural Revolution and the beginning of the open policy in 1978 did not alleviate the Party's fear. Rather, this fear continues to haunt the Party, which will take preemptive and often aggressive measures against any real or imagined threats no matter how small or insignificant they may seem. For example, in 1979, when Wei Jingsheng, a former soldier, took a bold step criticizing the PRC political system and urged the Party to add democracy or "a fifth modernization" to its ongoing modernization plan, the government accused Wei of counterrevolutionary crime and sentenced him to fifteen years in prison, a harsh punishment not inferior to those made during the anti-counterrevolutionary campaigns in the 1950s and the Cultural Revolution.[41]

The 1989 Tiananmen demonstration proved to be one of the biggest challenges to the CCP's legitimacy. Initially hesitant to take on the protesters, the Party soon moved to brutally suppress the student movement when its fear of losing power was aggravated. As the loyal "knife hilt" of the Party, the judicial system wasted no time in cracking down on "counterrevolutionaries" and the punishments were often severe and relentless, albeit the scope and scale were smaller and more tolerant than in the Mao era. To cite just one case, on May 23, 1989, three men from Hunan vandalized Mao's giant portrait on Tiananmen. They subsequently received highly severe penalties. Yu Zhijian, the head of the three, was sentenced to life in prison. The other two got sixteen and twenty years' imprisonment.[42]

The 1979 Criminal Procedure Law explicitly outlawed torture. Yet torture remained a regular practice by police in handling politically charged cases. A good example is the massive crackdown of Falun Gong practitioners after the 1999 protest, which was deemed by the Party as an ominous threat to its "monopoly on power." Newspapers have reported that many believers of the semi-religious sect whose followers range from 3 to 6 million have been tortured for their belief.[43]

41 For Wei Jingsheng case see Vogel, 2013: 254-256.

42 Luo Si'ling,罗四鸰 "In 1989, Why Did They Throw Eggs on Mao Zedong's Portrait? (*1989nian, tamen weihexiang Mao Zedong huaxiang rengjidan* 1989年他们为何向毛泽东画像扔鸡蛋)" in *The New York Times* (Chinese Version), May 23, 2017. https://cn.nytimes.com/china/20170523/egging-mao-tiananmen-square/

43 John Pomfret and Philip P. Pan, "Torture is Breaking Falun Gong" in *The Washington Post*, August 5, 2001.

In the 2000s, although China was deepening its economic reform as well as legal reform, the CCP has not loosened its grip on power and tolerated political dissidents. To some degree, political sanctions have intensified after 2008. In 2008, Liu Xiaobo who had formally been imprisoned for his active involvement in the 1989 demonstration, was punished again with eleven years' incarceration for leading the 2008 Charter Movement, which asked for more political freedom and democracy. For his peaceful political resistance, Liu won the Nobel Peace Prize in 2010. In the same year, Chen Guangcheng, Hu Jia, and Gao Zhisheng, three prominent political dissidents, were incarcerated for criticizing China's one-child policy, helping AIDS victims,[44] and defending Falun Gong practitioners respectively.[45] The primary reason behind their punishments was the Party's fear that their activities could stoke social discontent and disorder that could eventually threaten Party rule.

In 2014, the Party kicked off a more expansive assault on human rights lawyers and political activists. A total of around 300 lawyers had been in custody and renowned lawyers such as Gao Yu, Xu Zhiyong, and Cao Shunli were sentenced by courts for different crimes. Gao Yu, a Beijing journalist whose articles were highly critical of the Party, was indicted for "leaking state secrets," a dubious crime often used by the Party against political dissenters, and not for her critiques of the state. Gao, at the age of 71, was sentenced to stay in prison for seven years.[46] The CCP's fear of political dissent was best expounded by Xu Zhiyong, one of the rights lawyers who received four years imprisonment in 2014. For years, Xu, a renowned social and political activist, had strived for social justice. In 2013, he founded the New Citizen Movement, a non-government organization aiming at promoting political reform in China. Xu and his supporters had staged many street protests that had perturbed the Party and resulted in his arrest. In a closed-door trial, which had been illegal since the 1950s, Xu refused to accept the charges that he had "disrupted public order" and instead, he pointed out a "profound problem" of the CCP. "A more profound problem is the fear deep in your heart," Xu stated, "your fear of an open

44 In the 1990s, many peasants in Henan rushed to donate their blood for money. But due to the poor quality of hospitals, official cover-up, and lax check of blood donors, tens of thousands of peasants had been infected with AIDS. See Gao Yu, "Blood Disaster: Walking Visit to Henan 'Aids Village' (*xuehuo: zoufang henan aizicun*)" in *Salian shenghuo zhoukan*, September 5, 2001.

45 "Human Rights Movements After June 4th" in *Human Rights Watch*, May 30, 2019. https://www.hrw.org/zh-hans/news/2019/05/30/330635 (November 23, 2019).

46 Sui-Lee Wee, "China Jails Journalist for Seven Years for 'Leaking State Secrets'" in *Reuters*, April 16, 2015.

trial in which citizens can freely participate and listen, your fear that my name will appear on the internet, and your fear of a coming free society." In a message to his peer lawyers and judges, Xu told them that it was their duty to exercise their faith in law and conscience in defending the bottom line of social justice and the rule of law.[47] Xu might have been too naïve in thinking that his lofty words of social justice would move the judicial cadres. In a state where its judicial system was a key political weapon of the ruling Party, few, if any, judges (most are Party members) would dare challenge the Party in defense of the rule of law.

Since 2015, the Party's fear of losing power has prompted crackdowns on dissidents that extend beyond mainland China. As a result, many political activists in Hong Kong, Taiwan, and overseas scholars have been detained or imprisoned. As I have shown in the Introduction, a Taiwan democratic activist named Lee Ming-cheh was arrested by Chinese police while traveling in the mainland. A Chinese court sentenced him to five years in prison for "subversion of state power." In June 2020, the NPC passed the Hong Kong National Security Law that is believed to effectively curtail the protest and freedom of Hong Kong people. The law will also have a devastating impact on the Hong Kong judicial system as any person opposing the policies of the Hong Kong government and China can be punished.[48]

In a bolder move, the Chinese security officials in the fall of 2019 arrested professor Nobu Iwatani, a Japanese historian at Hokkaido University for "possessing a forbidden book." It was not until Japanese Prime Minister Shinzo Abe hinted to Chinese leaders that the detention would affect President Xi Jinping's scheduled visit to Japan in 2020 that the Chinese government finally decided to release Iwatani. While many people are wondering what harm a banned book could cause, one thing is clear: the Party is so worried about its political insecurity and power that it cannot even allow a dissident book to enter its territory.[49]

47 Amy Qin, "Suffering and Hardship Belong to Me: Chinese Dissidents Recounts Prison Years" in *The New York Times*, September 19, 2018; for Xu's words see Xu Zhiyong, "For Freedom, Justice, and Love: My Court Remark (*weile ziyou gongyi ai: wode fating chenci*)," https://www.hrichina.org/chs/gong-min-yan-chang/xu-zhi-yong-zai-fa-ting-shang-de-zui-hou-chen-shu (October 23, 2020).

48 Grace Tsoi and Lam Cho Wai, "Hong Kong Security Law: What is it and is it Worrying?" in *The BBC News*, June 30, 2020. https://www.bbc.com/news/world-asia-china-52765838

49 Shaun O'Dwyer, "China's Growing Threat to Academic Freedom" in *The Japan Times*, November 25, 2019. https://www.japantimes.co.jp/opinion/2019/11/25/commentary/japan-commentary/chinas-growing-threat-academic-freedom/

From Party's Fear to People's Fear

Max Weber once argued that there are three types of authority: charismatic, traditional, and legal-rational. Among them, the legal-rational or bureaucracy that is based on law and not on a charismatic or traditional leader fits a modern capitalist society with a dominance of Protestantism.[50] In the PRC, there may exist another type of authority – fear. As the history of the Chinese Communist judicial system has told us, the CCP built its judicial system as a loyal, powerful, and violent instrument to attack its enemies and consolidate its rule. Unlike its military that has been deemed as "the barrel of a gun," its judicial system is referred to as "a knife hilt." Both are the power bases of the Party in both periods of revolutionary wars (prior to 1949) and socialist construction (i.e. the PRC). Due to its intense fear and persistent insecurity, the CCP has maintained complete control over its judicial system to an extent beyond that of its comrades in the former Soviet Union. During political crises and campaigns, the Party would open a green light and allow its "knife hilt" to arbitrarily arrest and harshly punish alleged counterrevolutionaries or dissenters. In so doing, the Party has embraced the politics of fear by gradually instilling apprehension among ordinary Chinese people who accordingly have to conduct self-censorship by not doing and expressing anything that may offend the Party state/leaders and cause trouble to themselves. To amplify people's fear, the Party has adopted myriad methods such as public trials, parades of criminals, publicization of high-profile cases, torture, and ruthless penalties (including death) of any challengers. Recently, the public security has also used televised confessions broadcast on CCTV to humiliate and deter political critics.[51]

To be sure, stoking fear to deter potential critics and dissidents was not invented by the CCP. Nor is it limited to China. The King of Zhouli (890-828 BCE) was arguably the first Chinese ruler to place secret agents to spy on critics in the streets. That practice had given rise to tremendous apprehension

50 For Max Weber see Max Weber, *Economy and Society: An Outline of Interpretive Sociology* (Guenther Roth and Claus Wittich, eds.) (Berkeley: University of California Press, 1978): 212, 956; for the relationship between Protestantism and capitalism see Max Weber, *The Protestant Ethic and the Spirit of Capitalism* (New York: Courier Corporation, 2012).

51 For example, in 2016, after Gui Minhai, one of the Hong Kong booksellers involved in the Causeway Bay case, was kidnapped by Chinese agents in Thailand, he was seen on CCTV making a televised confession about his "crime" of illegally shipping sensitive books to the mainland. Austin Ramzy, "Hong Kong Bookseller Confesses on TV to Evading Rules on Shipping to Mainland" in *The New York Times*, March 1, 2016.

among the people who dared not speak to each other on the streets.[52] Since then, many dynastic and Republican rulers have adopted the "fear tactics" to warn opponents and strengthen their rule. "Fear tactics" experienced a revival in Mao's China. In both the 1957 Anti-Rightist Movement and the Cultural Revolution, a petty mistyping or unintentional action (see Chapter 7) could result in years of imprisonment. Intimidated, most people were afraid to discuss politics, much less to criticize Party policies. It was because they were aware that the Party was ready to "kill some 'chickens' to warn the monkey."

Since the bloody end of the 1989 Tiananmen demonstrations, the political atmosphere has seen a steady decline, which worsened after 2008. The fear among Chinese people and especially scholars in their comments on and criticism of government policies has intensified. The government often takes speedy and forceful actions against outspoken critics. In order to tighten its grip on universities, the Party has appointed student spies and installed surveillance cameras in classrooms to monitor professors' lectures. Some professors who have criticized Party policies or leaders are stripped of their right to teach or even fired by their universities. To cite just one case, You Shengdong, a popular professor at Xiamen University, was fired in 2018 after students in his class reported to university administrators about his criticism of President Xi Jinping's polices. As Professor You has pointed out, "Everyone feels they are in danger" because of tougher government crackdown on criticisms, whether made on the internet or in classrooms.[53]

Adding to the pains of political dissenters is their inability to file suits in the courts, one of the CCP's powerful weapons, to reinstate their jobs and lift restrictions. The chilling effect caused by the Party's suppression and the dire prospects of losing their jobs and income prompt most teachers to shut their mouths. Moreover, the Party's rash detainments and harsh penalties of political dissenters have stimulated more intense fear among potential critics both inside and outside China. At least for the moment and perhaps for some years to come, the tactics of transferring fear from the rulers to the people works. Although the Party in the future may return to a more tolerant policy, its fundamental insecurity and fear of losing power will remain an obsession as long as the Party is in power. Unfortunately, the Communist judicial system in China seems likely to remain a coercive and faithful Party instrument whose overriding mission is nothing but to safeguard the Party's rule.

52 Zuo Qiuming, 2015: Ch. 3.

53 Hernandez, 2019.

Bibliography

Primary Sources

Archives

Shanghai Archives (*Shanghai dangan*上海档案), 1949-1973
Beijing Archives (*Beijing dangan*北京档案), 1950-1955
Liangshan County Archives (*liangshanxian dangan*梁山县法院档案), 1949-1976
Neixiang County Archives (*neixiangxian dangan*内乡县档案), 1949-1976
Jiangjin County Archives (jiangjinxian fayuan dangan江津县档案), 1964
Jiaxing County Court Archives (jiaxingxian dangan嘉兴县法院档案), 1949-1958
Lujiang County Archives (lujiangxian dangan庐江县档案), 1963
Zhangqiu County Archives (Zhangqiuxian dangan章丘县档案), 1976
Hubei Macheng County Archives (*Hubei machengxian dangan*湖北麻城县档案)
Red China (*hongse zhongguo*红色中国), 1931-1935

Others

1950. Central Legal System Committee, ed., *Repressing Counterrevolutionaries* (*zhenya Fangeming* 镇压反革命, October 26.

1952. The Joint Inspection Group of the Central Political and Legal Organs, edited, *Compendium of Judicial Investigation Report* (*sifa diaocha baogao huibian* 司法调查报告汇编), June (An Internal Edition).

1952. Studying Documents of the People's Judicial Construction (*renmin sifa jianshe xuexi wenjian*人民司法建设学习文件). Beijing: Zhongyang sifa jiguan sifa gaige bangongshi.

1952. Fujian Provincial People's Court (Fujian sheng renmin fayuan福建省人民法院) (Internal Report).

1952. *Studying Documents of Constructing People's Judicial System* (*renmin sifa jianshe xuexi*人民司 法建设学习).

1952. The Investigation Unit of the Central Political and Judicial Organs (*zhongyang zhengfa jiguan lianhe shichazu*中央政法机关联合视察组), *Compendium of Judicial Investigation Report* (*sifa diaocha baogao huibian*司法调查报告) (Classified Internal Report).

1954. Organic Law of the Court, Tianjin People's Court, ed. 1954. "A Judicial Handbook (*sifa gongzuo shouce*司法工作手册)," November.

1955. The Judicial Work News Agency (*sifa gongzuo tongxunshe*司法工作通讯社), *Opposing Objectivism in Judging Work* (*fandui shenpan gongzuozhong dezhuguan zhuyi*反对审判工作 中的主观主义). Beijing: Judicial Work News Agency.

1955-1956. Guangdong Judicial Circular (*Guangdong sifa tongxun*广东司法通讯).

1958. *The Great Leap of the People's Judicial Work* (*renmin sifa gongzuo zaiyuejin*人民司法工 作在跃进). Beijing: Falü chubanshe.

1963. Supreme People's Court Office, ed., *Judicial Handbook* (*sifa Shouce*司法手册), Dec 31.

1985. *Gazette of the Ji'an County People's Court* (Ji'anxian renmin fayuanzhi吉安县人民法院 志).

1993. *Forty Years of the People's Court of the Neimenggu Autonomous Region* (*Neimenggu zizhiqu renmin fayuan sishinian*内蒙古自治区人民法院四十年). Neimenggu: Neimenggu gaodeng renmin fayuan.

1994. *Shaanxi Provincial Trial Gazette* (*Shaanxishengzhi shenpanzhi*陕西省审判志). Shaanxi: Shaanxi renmin chubanshe.

1994. *Hebei Provincial Trial Gazette*, Vol. 73 (Hebei shengzhi shenpanzhi河北省志审判志). Hebei: Hebei renmin chubanshe.

1994. *Hunan Provincial Gazette of Politics and Law*, Vol. 6. *Gazette of Politics and Law* (*Hunan shengzhi zhengfazhi*湖南省志-政法志). Hunan: Hunan chubanshe.

1995. Wan Li万里. *Selected Works of Wan Li* (*Wan Li wenxuan*万里文选). Beijing: Renmin chubanshe.

1996. *Yushan County Gazette* (*yushan xianzhi*玉山县志). Jiangxi: Jiangxi renmin chubanshe.

1998. *Yudu County Court Gazette* (*Yuduxian renmin fayuanzhi*于都县人民法院志). Jiangxi: Jiangxi Yuduxian renmin fayuan.

1998. *General Gazette of Shanxi – Judicial Gazette* (*Shanxitonggzhi shenpanzhi*山西通志-审判 志). Beijing: Zhonghua shujü.

1999. *Yunnan Provincial Trial Gazette*, Vol. 55. *Gazetter of Trial* (*yunnansheng shenpanzhi* 云南省志审判志). Yunan: Yunnan renmin chubanshe.

1999. *Jinhua Court Gazette* (*Jinhua fayuanzhi*金华法院志). Beijing: Fangzhi chubanshe.

1999. *Guangdong Provincial Trial Gazette* (*Guangdongshengzhi shenpanzhi* 广东省志审判志). Guangzhou: Guangdong renmin chubanshe.

1999. *Comprehensive Gazette of Tianjin – Adjudicating Gazette* (*Tianjin tongzhi-shenpanzhi*天津通志-审判志). Tianjin: Tianjin shehui kexueyuan chubanshe.

2000. *Gaungxi General Gazette – Trial Gazette* (*Gaungxi tongzhi: shenpanzhi*广西通志-审判志). Guangxi: Guangxi renmin chubanshe.

2003. *Wanxian County Court Gazette* (*Wanxian fayuanzhi*万县法院志). Beijing: Fangzhi chubanshe.

2003. *Wannian County Court Gazette* (*Wannianxian fayuanzhi*万年县法院志). Beijing: Fangzhi chubanshe.

2003. *Sichuan Provincial Trial Gazette* (*Sichuan shenpanzhi*四川审判志). Sichuan: Dianzi keji daxue chubanshe.

2006. *The PRC Criminal Procedural Law* (*zhonghua renmin gognheguo xingfa*中华人民共和国 刑法). Beijing: Zhongguo fazhi chubanshe.

2006. Original Archives of President Chiang Kai-shek's Biographical Account (*Jiang Zhongzheng zongtong dangan shilue gaoben*蒋中正总统档案史略稿本). Taibei: Guoshiguan yinxing.

2015. Amnesty International Report, "China: Torture and Forced Confessions Rampant amid Systematic Trampling of Lawyers" in https://www.amnesty.org/en/latest/news/2015/11/china- torture-forced-confession/

Ai Shaorun艾邵润, ed. 2007a. *A Collection of Laws and Regulations of the Shanganning Border Area* (*Shanganning bianqu Falü fagui huibian*陕甘宁边区法律汇编). Shaanxi: Shaanxi renmin chubanshe.

Ai Shaorun艾邵润, ed. 2007b. *Selected Cases of the Precedent Cases of the Shanganning Border Area* (*Shanganning bianqu panli anlixuan*陕甘宁边区判例案例选). Shaanxi: Shaanxi remin chubanshe.

Chen Minshan陈敏珊. 1950. "How to Accurately Enforce the Policy of 'Mutual Benefit between Capitalist and Labor' (*zenyang laizhunquede zhixing Laozi liangli zhengce*怎样来准确执行劳资两利政策)" in *Shanghai Commerce and Industry*, March 7.

Dong Biwu董必武. 2001. *Collected Law Articles of Dong Biwu* (*Dong Biwu faxue wenji*董必武文集). Beijing: Falü chubanshe.

Han Fei韩非. 1992. translated by Zhang Jue, *Han Feizi*韩非子. Guizhou: Guizhou renmin chubanshe.

Hubei Provincial Government. 1950. *Hubei Political Report* (*hubei zhengbao*湖北政报).

Jiangxisheng danganguan江西省档案馆, 1982. *Selected Historical Sources of the Central Revolutionary Base* (*zhongyang geming genjudi shiliao xuanbian*中央革命根据地史料选编). Nanchang: Jiangxi renmin chubanshe.

Lenin, Vladimir. 2014. *The State and Revolution*. Chicago: Haymarket Books.

Li Rui李锐. 1998. *Arguments of Li Rui* (*Lirui lunshuo wenxuan*李锐论说文选). Beijing: Zhongguo shehui kexue chubanshe.

— *A Veritable Record of Lushan Meeting* (*lushan huiyi shilu*庐山会议实录) (Henan: Henan renmin chubanshe, 1998).

— 2016. "A Review of the Sixth Meeting of the Eleventh Plenary (*chongwen shiyijie liuzhong quanhui*重温十一届六中全会)" in *Yanhuang Chunqiu*, No. 2., 2016; http://www.yhcqw.com/32/10086.html (November 20, 2019).

Li, Xiaobing. 2012. *China at War: An Encyclopedia*. Santa Barbara: ABC-CLIO.

Li, Zuopeng. *The Autobiography of Li Zuopeng* (*Li Zuopeng huiyilu*). Hong Kong: Beixing chubanshe.

Liang, Heng and Shapiro, Judith. 1984. *Son of Revolution*. New York: Vintage.

Lord Shang商鞅. 2018. *Book of Lord Shang* (*shangjunshu*商君书). Shanghai: Shanghai sanlian shudian.

Luo Ruiqing罗瑞卿. 1994. *Luo Ruiqing's Comments on People's Public Security Work* (*Luo Ruiqing lunrenmin gongan gongzuo*罗瑞卿论人民公安工作). Beijing: Qunzhong chubanshe.

Mao Zedong毛泽东. 1990. *Mao Zedong Works Since PRC Establishment* (*jianguo yilai Mao Zedong Wengao*建国以来毛泽东文稿). Beijing: Zhongyang wenxian chubanshe.

— 2001. *Articles of Mao Zedong* (*Maozedong wenji*毛泽东文集). Beijing: Renmin chubanshe.

— 2019 [1927]. *An Investigation Report on Hunan Peasant Movements* (*Hunan nongmin yundong kaocha Baogao*湖南农民运动考察报告), http://cpc.people.com.cn/GB/64184/64185/66615/4488900.html (November 23, 2019).

Pan Zhenqiu潘振球, ed. 1936. *A Draft of Historical Compendium of the Republican China Town* (*Zhonghua minguo shishi jiyao-chugao*中华民国史实纪要初稿). Taiwan: Guoshiguan.

Peitian Zhang and Hua Zhang, eds., *China Southwest Archives: The Material of Judicial Reform* (*1950-1952*) (Australia: International Culture Press, 2007): 1-4.

Peng Zhen彭真. 1991. *Selected Works of Peng Zhen* (*Peng Zhen wenji*彭真文集). Beijing: Renmin chubanshe.

Ruijinxian renmin fayuan, ed., *Selected Trial Materials of the Chinese Soviet Republic* (*Zhonghua suweiai gongheguo shenpan ziliao xuanbian*) (Beijing: Renmin fayuan chubanshe, 1991): 208-10.

Rushkoff, Bennett C. 1981. "Eisenhower, Dulles and the Quemoy-Matsu Crisis, 1955-1955" in *The Political Science Quarterly*, Vol. 96, No. 3 (Autumn, 1981), pp. 465-480.

Shaanxi sifa tongxun bianji weiyuanhui, ed. 1957. *Shaanxi sifa tongxun* (Judicial News Report of Shaanxi).

Shaanxisheng danganguan and Shaanxisheng shehui kexueyuan, eds., 1987. *Selected Documents of the Shanganning Border Government* (*Shanganning bianqu zhengfu wnejian xuanbian*) Beijing: Dangan chubanshe.

Sima, Qian. 2014. *Historical Record* (*shiji*). Beijing: Zhonghua shujü.

Song, Yongyi, ed. 2015. *Top Secret Documents of the Anti-Rightist Movement*, Vol. 3, 12-17 Issues. New York: Guoshi chubanshe.

Song, Yongyi, ed. 2015. *Verdicts and Internal Archives of nearly a Thousand of Rightists*, Vol. 2. New York: Guoshi chubanshe.

Sun, Yirang. 2015. annotates. *The Ritual of the Zhou Dynasty* (*zhouli zhengyi*). Beijing: Zhonghua shujü.

Unofficially Published Works of Mao Zedong, Vol. 8, May 15, 1951, 1991.

Wu, Faxian. 2006. *The Autobiography of Wu Faxian* (*Wu Faxian huiyilu*). Hong Kong: Beixing chubanshe.

Xie, Juezai谢觉哉. 1984. *Diary of Xie Juezai* (*Xie Juezai Riji*谢觉哉日记). Beijing: Renmin chubanshe.

Xu, Hongci. 2008. *No Wall Too High: One Man's Daring Escape from Mao's Darkest Prison*. New York: Sarah Crichton Books.

Xue, Yunsheng. 1999. *A Combined Edition of the Tang and Ming Codes* (*tangminglu hebian*). Beijing: Falü chubanshe.

Yu Xiguang余习广, ed. 1989. *Daring not Forgetting to Worry about my Country: Collection of Appeals in the Cultural Revolution* (*weibei weigan wangyouguo: wenhua dageming shangshuji*位卑未敢忘忧国：文化大革命上书集). Hunan: Hunan renmin chubanshe.

Yue, Daiyun. 1987. *To the Storm: The Odyssey of the Revolutionary Chinese Women*. Berkeley: University of California Press.

Zhang, Guotao. 1966. *My Memoir* (*Wode huiyi*). Hong Kong: Minbao yuekan.

Zhangsun, Wuji. 1999. *Tang code with commentaries* (*Tanglu shuyi*). Beijing: Falü chubanshe. State Council and Supreme Court (zhengwuyuan政务院, zuigao renmin fayuan最高人民法院), "*Directives Regarding Counterrevolutionaries* (*guanyu zhenya fangeming huodong dezhishi* 关于镇压反革命活动的指示)," July 23, 1950. see zh.wikisource.org/wiki/政务院、最高人 民法院关于镇压反革命活动的指示

Zhu, Xi, ed. 1998. *Collective Connotation of the Four Books* (*sishu zhangju jizhu*) *Analects* (*lunyu*). Liaoning: Liaoning jiaoyu chubanshe.

Zuo, Qiuming. 2015. *Discourses of the States* (*guoyu*). Shanghai: Shanghai guji chubanshe.

Secondary Sources

1944. "The Adjudicating Method of Comrade Ma Xiwu (*Ma Xiwu tongzhide shenpan fangshi*马锡武同志的审判方式)" in the *Jiefang Daily*, March 13.

1981. "Resolution on Certain Party Issues Since the Establishment of the PRC," June 27. http://news.xinhuanet.com/ziliao/2002-03/04/content_2543544.htm

1990. *Repression in China Since June 4, 1989*. New York: Human Rights Watch.

2007. "How do Courts Deal with the Rigorously Rising Litigations? (*guansi xunmeng pansheng, fayuan ruhe yingdui*官司迅猛攀升，法院如何应对)" *Jiaxing ribao*, July 24.

2014. "Xi Jinping Delivers Important Talk at the Central Political and Legal Work Meeting" in *The People's Daily*, January 29.

2015. "Important Directives of Xi Jinping on Political and Legal Work (*Xi Jinping jiuzhengfa gongzuo zuochu zhongyao zhishi*习近平就政法工作作出重要指示)" in *The People's Daily*, January 21.

2016. "2 Chinese Activists Sentenced to Over 10 Years on Subversion Charges" in *The New York Times*, June 20, 2016.

2017. "China: Democratic Voice Liu Xiaobo Dies in Custody" in *Human Rights Watch*, July 13. https://www.hrw.org/news/2017/07/13/china-democratic-voice-liu-xiaobo-dies-custody

Alford, William P. 1995. *To Steal a Book is an Elegant Offense: Intellectual Property Law in Chinese* Civilization. Stanford: Stanford University Press.

— 1984. "Of Arsenic and Old Laws: Looking Anew at Criminal Justice in Late Imperial China" in *California Law Review*, Vol. 72, No. 6 (Dec.), pp. 1180-1256.

Altehenger, Jennifer. 2018. *Legal Lessons: Popularizing Laws in the People's Republic, 1949-1989*. Cambridge, Ma: Harvard East Asian Monograph.

Andrews, Julia F. 1990. "Traditional Painting in New China: Guohua and The Anti-Rightist Campaign" in *The Journal of Asian Studies*, Vol. 49, No. 3 (Aug.), pp. 555-577.

Baker, Hugh D.R. 2015. *Chinese Family and Kinship* (London: The Macmillan Press.

Bao Yongjun鲍永军. 2006. *A Study on Shaoxing Private Adviser Wang Huizu* (*Shaoxing shiye Wang Huizu yanjiu*绍兴师爷王辉组研究). Beijing: Renmin chubanshe.

Barnouin, Barbara. 1993. *Ten Years of Turbulence: The Chinese Cultural Revolution*. Abingdon: Routledge

Belova, Eugenia and Gregory, Paul. 2009. "Political Economy of Crime and Punishment under Stalin" in *Public Choice*, Vol. 140, No. 3/4 (Sep.), pp. 463-478: 466.

Bo Weihua卜伟华. 2012. *Smashing the Old World: The Upheaval and Havoc of the Cultural Revolution, 1966-1968* (*zalan jiushijie: wenhua dageming dedongluan hehaojie, 1966-1968* 砸烂旧世界：文化大革命的动乱和浩劫). Hong Kong: Hong Kong Chinese University Press.

Bonnin, Michel. 2013. *The Lost Generation: The Rustication of China's Educated Youth (1968-1980)*. Hong Kong: Chinese University Press.

Bourgon, Jerome. 2004. "Rights, Freedoms, and Customs in the Making of Chinese Civil Law, 1900-1936" in William C. Kirby, ed., *Realms of Freedom in Modern China*. Stanford: Stanford University Press, pp. 84-112.

Brook, Timothy, Bourgon, Jerome, and Blue, Gregory. 2008. *Death By a Thousand Cuts*. Cambridge, Ma: Harvard University Press.

Brown, Jeremy. 2014. *City Versus Countryside in Mao's China: Negotiating the Divide.* Cambridge: Cambridge University Press.

— and Pickowicz, Paul, eds. 2007. *Dilemmas of Victory: The Early Years of the People's Republic of China.* Cambridge, Ma: Harvard University Press.

Buckley, Chris. 2017. "Chinese Activist Sentenced to 8 Years in Prison for Shaming Officials" in *The New York Times*, December 26.

Butler, William E. 1983. *Soviet Law.* London: Butterworths.

— ed. 1983. *The Legal System of the Chinese Soviet Republic, 1931-1934.* New York: Transnational Press.

Cao Shuji曹书基. 2005. *Great Famine: Chinese Population between 1959 and 1961 (dajihuang: 1959-1961nian dezhongguo renkou*大饥荒：1959-1961年的中国人口). Hong Kong: Shidai guoji chuban.

Cassel, Pär. 2003. "Excavating Extraterritoriality: The 'Judicial Sub-Prefect' as a Prototype for the Mixed Court in Shanghai" in *Late Imperial China*, Vol. 24, No. 2 (Dec.), pp. 156-180.

Chen Guangzhong陈光中 and Zeng Xinhua曾新华. 2009. "A Review of the Legal Reform Movement in the Early PRC (*jianguo chuqi sifa gaige yundong shuping* 建国初期司法改革运动述评)" in *Faxuejia*, No. 6, pp. 1-8.

Chen, Jian. 1994. *China's Road to the Korean War.* New York: Columbia University Press.

Chen, Shouyi. 1980. *A Review of the Thirty-Year Jurisprudance in New China* (*xin-zhongguo faxue sanshinian huigu*) in *Faxue yanjiu*, No. 1, pp. 1-10.

Chen, Weixing and Zhong, Yang. 2004. *Leadership in a Changing China.* London: Palgrave Macmillan.

Chen, Xingliang. 2018. "Forty Years Research of Chinese Criminal Law" in *The Journal of Wuhan University*, Vol. 2, pp. 31-41.

Clark, Paul. 2008. *The Chinese Cultural Revolution: A History.* Cambridge: Cambridge University Press.

Cohen, Jerome A. 1968. *The Criminal Process in the People's Republic of China, 1949-1963: An Introduction.* Cambridge, Ma: Harvard University Press.

Cong, Xiaoping. 2016. *Marriage, Law and Gender in Revolutionary China, 1940-1960.* Cambridge: Cambridge University Press.

— 2009. "Zuo Run suing Wang Yinsuo: Women, Marriage, and State Building in the 1940s Shanganning Border Area (*Zuorunsu Wang Yinsuo: ershi shiji sishi niandai Shanganning bianqude funu hunyinyu guojia jiangou*)" in *Kaifang shidai*, Vol. 10.

Conner, Alison W. 2010. "Training China's Lawyers: Enduring Influences and Disconnects" in Albert Chen and John Gillespie, eds., *Legal Development in East Asia: China and Vietnam Compared.* Abingdon: Routledge, pp. 276-298.

Creel, Herrlee G. 1980. "Legal Institutions and Procedures during the Chou Dynasty" in Cohen, Jerome A., Edwards, R. Randle, and Chen, Fu-mei Chang, eds. *Essays on China's Legal Tradition* (Princeton: Princeton University Press, pp. 26-55.

Cui, Min崔敏. 2012. "The Disastrous Six Regulations of the Public Security (*weihuo canliede gongan Liutiao*为祸惨烈的公安六条)" in *Yanhuang Chunqiu*, Vol. 12. http://www.yhcqw.com/32/8982.html (October 30, 2019).

Dai Huang戴煌. 1998. *Hu Yaobang and the Rehabilitation of Cases Involving Grievances and False and Wrong Charges* (*Hu Yaobang yu pingfan yuanjia cuoan*胡耀邦与平反冤假错案). Beijing: Zhongguo wenlian chuban gongsi and Xinhua Chubanshe.

Dai Maolin戴茂林 and Zhao Xiaoguang赵晓光. 2016. *A Biography of Gang Gang* (*Gao Gangzhuan* 高岗传) (Shaanxi: Shanxi Renmin chubanshe).

Dardess, John. 2002. *Blood and History in China: The Donglin Faction and its Repression, 1620-1627*. Honolulu: University of Hawaii Press.

— 2015. *Liu Shaoqi and the Chinese Cultural Revolution*. Abingdon: Routledge.

Dikotter, Frank. 2002. *Crime, Punishment and the Prison in Modern China*. New York: Columbia University Press.

— 1997. "Crime and Punishment in Post-Liberation China: The Prisoners of a Beijing Gaol in the 1950s" in *The China Quarterly*, No. 149 (Mar.), pp. 147-159.

— 2010. *Mao's Great Famine: The History of China's Most Devastating Catastrophe, 1958-1962*. New York: Walker & Co.

— 2016. *The Cultural Revolution: A People's History, 1962-1976*. New York: Bloomsbury Press.

Dillion, Nara. 2007. "New Democracy and the Demise of Private Charity in Shanghai" in Brown and Pickowicz, 2007, pp. 80-102.

Dillon, Michael. 2014. *Deng Xiaoping: A Political Biography*. New York: I.B. Tauris.

Dirkes, Emile and Cook, Sarah. 2019. "China's Surveillance State Has Tens of Millions of New Targets" in *Foreign Policy*, October 21. https://foreignpolicy.com/2019/10/21/china-xinjiang-surveillance-state-police-targets/

Dittmer, Lowell. 1989. *China's Continuous Revolution: The Post-Liberation Epoch 1949-1981*. Berkeley: University of California.

Dutton, Michael. 2005. *Policing Chinese Politics: A History*. Duke: Duke University Press.

Eastman, Lloyd E. 2002. *Seeds of Destruction: Nationalist China and Revolution, 1937-1949*. Stanford: Stanford University Press.

— 1986. "Nationalist China during the Nanking Decade, 1927-1937" in John K. Fairbanks and Albert Feuerwerker, eds., *The Cambridge History of China, Vol. 13, Republican China 1912-1949, Part 2*. Cambridge: Cambridge University Press, pp. 116-167.

Elliott, Mark C. 2001. *The Manchu Way: The Eight Banners and Ethnic Identity in Late Imperial China*. Stanford: Stanford University Press.

Esherick, Joseph, Pickowicz, Paul, and Walder, Andrew G. eds. 2006. *The Chinese Cultural Revolution as History*. Stanford: Stanford University Press.

Fan, Daren. 1999. The Rise and Fall of the Royal Pens in the Cultural Revolution: The History of Liangxiao (*wenge yubi chenfulu: liangxiaowangshi*文革御笔沉浮录：梁效往事). Hong Kong: Mingbao chubanshe.

Fang Lizhi方励之. 2013. *Autobiography of Fang Lizhi* (Fang LIzhi zizhuan方励之传) (Taiwan: Tianxia yuanjian chubanshe).

Fang, Qiang. 2002. "The Case of Virgin Prostitute: Chinese Media and Legal Reform" in *Stanford Journal of East Asian Affairs*, Vol. 2, pp. 26-40.

— 2009. "Hot Potatoes: Chinese Complaint Systems from Early Times to 1898" in The Journal of Asian Studies, Vol. 68, No. 4 (Nov.): 1105-1135.

— 2013a. *Chinese Complaint Systems: Natural Resistance*. Abingdon: Routledge.

— 2013b. "Chinese Media and the Rule of Law: The Case of the China Youth Daily, 1979-2006" in Xiaobing Li and Qiang Fang, eds. *Modern Chinese Legal Reform: New Perspectives*. Lexington: University Press of Kentucky, pp. 27-58.

— 2013c. *A Short History of Chinese Petition* (*zhongguo shangfang zhidu shihua*). Beijing: China Youth Press.

— and Li, Xiaobing. 2017. *Power Versus Law in Modern China: Cities, Courts, and the Communist Party* (Lexington: University Press of Kentucky): Ch. 1.

— and Roger Des Forges. 2007. "Were Chinese Rulers Above the Law? Toward a Theory of the Rule of Law in Chinese History" in *Stanford Journal of International Law*, Vol. 44.1.

Feigon, Lee. 2002. *Mao: A Reinterpretation*. New York: Ivan R. Dee.

Fenby, Jonathan. 2009. *Chiang Kai-shek: China's Generalissimo and the Nation He Lost*. Cambridge: Da Capo Press.

Feng Jie冯杰. 2015. "A Brief Study on Xie Juezai's Thought on Legal Development (*Qianxi Xie Juezai fazhi jianshe sixiang*浅析谢觉哉法制建设思想)," April 3, http://www.npxfy.gov.cn/dcyj/125.html (November 30, 2019).

Forsythe, Michael. 2016. "If China Meant to Chill Hong Kong Speech, Booksellers' Case Did the Job" in *The New York Times*, November 7.

Friedman, Lawrence M. 2005. *A History of American Law*. New York: Simon & Schuster.

Gao Hua高华. 2000. *How Did the Red Sun Rise: The Entire Course of the Yan'an Rectification Movement* (*Hongtaiyang shizenyang shengqide: Yan'an Zhengfeng yundong shimo*红太阳是怎样升起的：延安整风运动始末). Hong Kong: Hong Kong Chinese University Press.

Gao Yu高昱. 2001. "Blood Disaster: Walking Visit to Henan 'Aids Village' (*xuehuo: zoufang henan aizicun*血祸：走访河南艾滋村)" in *Salian shenghuo zhoukan*, September 5.

— 2019. "Human Rights Movements After June 4th" in *The Human Rights Watch*, May 30. https://www.hrw.org/zh-hans/news/2019/05/30/330635 (October 23, 2020).

Gillespie, John, Chen, Albert, and Chen, Hongyi, eds. 2010. *Legal Reforms in China and Vietnam: A Comparison of Asian Communist Regimes*. Abingdon: Routledge.

Glosser, Susan L. 2003. *Chinese Visions of Family and State, 1915-1953*. Berkeley: University of California Press.

Gong, Pixiang公丕祥, ed. 1999. *China's Current Legal Revolution* (*dangdai zhongguo de falü geming*当代中国法律革命). Beijing: Falü chubanshe.

Gong Tingtai龚廷泰 and Wang Jianguo王建国. 2008. "Lenin's Thought on the Judicial Right and its Contemporary Value (*Leningde sifaquan sixiang jiqi shidaijiazhi*列宁的司法权思想及其时代价值)" in *Falü kexue*, Vol. 6, pp. 9-17.

Goodman, David S.G. 2000. *Social and Political Change in Revolutionary China: The Taihang Base Area in the War of Resistance to Japan, 1937-1945*. New York: Rowman & Littlefield.

Griffin, Patricia. 1976. *The Chinese Communist Treatment of Counter-Revolutionaries, 1924-1949*. Princeton: Princeton University Press.

Guo Dehong郭德宏, ed. 2014. *Chronicle of Wang Ming* (*Wang Ming nianpu*王明年谱). Beijing: Shehui kexue wenxian chubanshe.

— and Lin Xiaobo林小波, eds. 2008. *Personal Experiences in the Four Cleanups* (*siqing yundong qinliji*四清运动亲历记). Beijing: Renmin chubanshe.

Hao Zaijin郝在今. 2006. *The Precedent History of the Cultural Revolution: A True Record of the Rescuing Movement in Yan'an* (*"wenge" qianshi: Yan'an qiangjiu yundong jishi*文革前 史：延安抢救运动纪实). Hong Kong: Liwen chubanshe.

Harding, Harry. 2011. "The Chinese State in Crisis, 1966-1969" in Roderick MacFarquhar, ed., *The Politics of China: Sixty Years of the People's Republic of China*. Cambridge: Cambridge University Press.

Harris, James. 2016. *The Great Terror: Stalin's Terror of the 1930s*. Oxford: Oxford University Press.

He Bing何兵. 2014. "Lei Jingtian, the Person who Founded the Red Judicial System but had no Legal Values (*meiyou Falü guandiande hongse sifa dianjiren Lei Jingtian*没有法律观点的红色司 法奠基人雷经天)" in *Nanfang dushibao*, July 20.

He Qinhua何清华. 2012. *A History of Chinese Jurisprudence* (*Zhongguo faxue shigang* 中国法 学史纲). Beijing: Shangwu yinshuguan.

He Weifang贺卫方. 1998. "Military Veterans Enter the Court (*fuyuan junren jin fayuan*复员军 人进法院)" in *The Southern Weekend*, January 2.

— 2002. *The Method of Conveying Justice* (*yunsong Zhengyi defangshi*). Shanghai: Shanghai sanlian shudian.

Heale, M.J. 1998. *McCarthy's Americans: Red Scare Politics in State and Nation, 1935-1965*. Georgia: University of Georgia Press.

Heberer, Thomas and Gobel, Christian. 2011. *The Politics of Community Building in Urban China*. Abingdon: Routledge.

Hernandez, Javier C. 2019. "Professors, Beware. A 'Student Information Officer' Might be Watching" in *The New York Times*, November 1.

Horton, Chris and Buckley, Chris. 2017. "China Charges Activist from Taiwan with 'Subverting State Power'" in *The New York Times*, May 29.

Hou Songtao侯松涛. 2008. "Legal Reform Movement in the Early PRC: Retrospect and Thinking (*jianguo chuqide sifa gaige yundong: huigu yusikao*建国初期司法改革运动：回顾与思 考)" in *Zhidu jianshe*, Vol. 1, pp. 93-96.

Hua, Shiping. 2018. *Chinese Legal Culture and Constitutional Order*. Abingdon: Routledge.

Huang Dong黄东. 2003. "A Study on the Reform of the Marriage Law in the Red Soviet Base (*hongse suqu hunyin gaizao shulun*红色苏区婚姻改造述论)" in *The Journal of Capital Normal University*, 3.

Huang, Philip C. 1994. "Codified Law and Magisterial Adjudication in the Qing" in Kathryn Bernhardt and Philip Huang, eds., *Civil Law in Qing and Republican China*. Stanford: Stanford University Press.

— 1998. *Civil Justice in China: Representation and Practice in the Qing*. Stanford: Stanford University Press.

— 2010. *Chinese Civil Justice, Past and Present* (Lanham: Roman & Littlefield Publisher): 4.

Huang Wenzhi黄文治. 2016. "Conflict among Local Officials and Judicial Interference in the Great Leap Forward: Centering on the Case of Fang Shixin in Feixi County (*dayuejin shiqi jiceng ganbu chongtu jisifa jieru: yi Feixixian Fang Shixin anwei zhongxin*大跃进时期基层 干部冲突及司法介入)" in *Anhui shixue*, Vol. 2, No. 22.

Jia Zhangwang. 2014. *The Seventy Years of the New China under Mao Zedong* (*Mao Zedong lingdaoxia dexin zhongguo qishinian*毛泽东领导下的新中国七十年). Beijing: Zhongguo wenshi chubanshe.

Jiang, Yonglin. 2010. "In the Name of 'Taizu': The Construction of Zhu Yuanzhang's Legal Philosophy and Chinese Cultural Identity in the 'Varitable Records of Taizu'" in *T'oung Pao*, Second Series, Vol. 96, Issue 4, pp. 408-470.

— and Wu Yanhong. 2007. "Satisfying Both Sentiment and Law: Fairness-Centered Judicial Reasoning as Seen in Late Ming Casebooks" in Charlotte Furth, Judith Zeitlin, and Ping- chen Hsiung, eds., *Thinking with Cases: Specialist Knowledge in Chinese Cultural History* (Seattle: University of Washington Press): 31-61.

Jiao, Guocheng焦国成. 1989. "An Evaluation of Yang Zhu School's 'Egoism' (*Yang Zhu xuepai 'weiwo zhuyi' bianxi*杨朱学派'唯我主义'辨析)" in *The Journal of China People's University*, Vol. 6, pp. 88-95.

Jin Qiu. 1999. *The Culture of Power: The Lin Biao Incident in the Cultural Revolution*. Stanford: Stanford University Press.

Kaiman, Jonathan. 2014. "China Upholds Four-year Sentence of Activist Xu Zhiyong" in *The Guardian*, April 11.

Kim, Ilpyong J. 1973. *The Politics of Chinese Communism: Kiangsi under the Soviets*. Berkeley: University of California Press.

Kong, Xue. 2004. "The Origin of Lingchi and its Development in the Song Dynasty (*lunlingchi zhixing deqiyuan jizai songdai defazhan*)" in *Shixue yuekan*, Vol. 6, pp. 38-47.

Lai Chengzuo来承祚. 1936. *A Tiny Complete Book of Chinese Six Laws* (*xiuzhen zhonghua liufa quanshu*袖珍中华六法全书). Beijing: Zhonghua shujü.

Lee, Ching Kwan. 2007. *Against the Law: Labor Protests in China's Rustbelt and Sunbelt*. Berkeley: University of California Press.

Leese, Daniel and Engman, Puck. 2018. *Victims, Perpetrators, and the Role of Law in Maoist China: A Case Study*. Berlin: Walter de Gruyter GmbH & Co KG.

Leggett, George. 1981. *Lenin's Political Police: The All Russian Extraordinary Commission for Combating Counter-revolution and Sabotage*. Oxford: Clarendon Press.

Lei Jingtian雷经天. 2004. "The Judicial System of the Shanganning Border Area (*Shanganning bianqu desifa zhidu*陕甘宁边区的司法制度)" in Zhang Shibin 张世斌, ed., *The Historical Traces of the High Court in the Shanganning Border Area* (*Shanganning bianqu gaodeng fayuan shiji*陕甘宁边区高等法院史迹). Shaanxi: Shaanxi renmin chubanshe.

Lendvai, Paul. 2010. *One Day That Shook the Communist World: The 1956 Hungarian Uprising and its Legacy*. Princeton: Princeton University Press.

Leng, Shaochuan. *Criminal Justice in Post-Mao China: Analysis and Documents*. Albany: State University of New York Press.

Li Guangcan李光灿, ed. 1984. *A Study on the Criminal Law in the PRC* (*Zhonghua renmin gongheguo xingFalün*中华人民共和国刑法论). Jilin: Jinlin renmin chubanshe.

Li Lin李林. 2008. "Main Experiences of China's Legislation in the Thirty-Year Open Policy (*Kaifang sanshinian zhongguo lifa zhuyao jingyan*开放三十年中国立法主要经验)," *Xuexi shibao*.

Li Lu李露. 2014. "Rethinking the Situation and Policy of the 'Coordination of Repression and Magnanimity' (*zhenya yu kuanda xiangjiehe xingshi zhengce fansi*镇压与宽大相结合刑事 政策反思)" in *Renmin luntan*, Vol. 3, pp. 33-38.

Li Rui李锐. 1998. *Selected Theses and Talks of Li Rui* (*Lirui lunshuo wenxüan*李锐论说文选). Beijing: Zhongguo shehui kexüe chubanshe.

— 1998. *A Veritable Record of Lushan Meeting* (*lushan huiyi shilu*庐山会议实录). Henan: Henan renmin chubanshe.

— 2016. "A Review of the Sixth Meeting of the Eleventh Plenary (*chongwen shiyijie liuzhong quanhui*重温十一届六中全会)" in *Yanhuang Chunqiu*, No. 2. http://www.yhcqw.com/32/10086.html (December 20, 2019).

Li Yixia李宜霞. 2004. "Liang Botai and the Construction of the Judicial System in the Chinese Soviet Republic (*Liang Botai yuzhonghua suweiai gongheguo sifa zhidu zhijianshe*梁柏台与中华苏 维埃共和国司法制度之建设)" in *The Journal of the Central CCP Party School*, Vol. 3.

Li Yusheng李玉生. 1999. "Comments on the Legal Reform Movement (*sifa gaige yundong shuping* 司法改革运动述评)" in *Nanjing shehui kexue*, Vol. 9, pp. 49-54.

— 1999. "Legal Reform Movement (*sifa gaige yundong*司法改革运动)" in *Faxue yanjiu*, September, pp. 49-54.

Li, Zhisui. 1994. *The Private Life of Chairman Mao*. New York: Random House. (*Kaifang sanshinian zhongguo lifa zhuyao jingyan*开放三十年中国立法主要经验)," *Xuexi shibao*.

Lian, Xi. 2018. *Blood Letters: The Untold Story of Lin Zhao*. New York: Basic Books.

Liang, Bin. 2008. *The Changing Chinese Legal System, 1978-Present: Centralization of Power and Rationalization of the Legal System*. Abingdon: Routledge.

— and Lu, Hong, eds. 2015. *The Death Penalty in China: Policy, Practice, and Reform*. New York: Columbia University Press.

Lichtman, Robert M. 2012. *The Supreme Court and McCarthy-Era Repression: One Hundred Decisions*. Urbana: University of Illinois Press.

Lin Feng and Wang Shucheng, "The Transformation, Predicament, and Future of Reeducation Through Labor in China" in *Hong Kong Journal of Social Science*, Vol. 38, 2010 (Issue 1). https://www.sinoss.net/upload-file/2010/0912/20100912100922160.pdf (November 30, 2019).

Lin Jiaqi林家祺 and Liu Junlin刘俊麟. 2017. *Civil Procedural Law* (*minshi susongfa*民事诉讼法). Taiwan: Shuquan chubanshe.

Lin Qian林乾. 2013. *Power and Law in Traditional China* (*chuantong zhongguo dequan yufa*传 统中的权与法). Beijing: Falü chubanshe.

Lin Yunhui林蕴晖. 2008. *A Utopian Movement: From the Great Leap Forward to the Great Famine* (*wutuobang yundong: cong dayuejin dao dajihuang*乌托邦运动：从大跃进到大饥 荒). Hong Kong: Hong Kong Chinese University Press.

Liu Fengjing刘风景. 2009. "Ringing out the Old and Ringing the New in Legal Concepts: Using the Criticisms of the 1952 Legal Reform against Old Legal Concepts (*sifa liniande chujiu buxin: yi 1952nian sifa gaige duijiufaguandian* *depipan weisucai*司法理念的除旧布新：以1952 年司法改革对旧法观点的批判为素材)" in *Beifang faxue* (Northern Jurisprudence), Vol. 1, pp. 96-105.

Liu Hengwen刘恒妏. 2008. "Revolution and Counterrevolution: A Study on the GMD Law in the Period of Nanjing Nationalist Government (*geming/fangeming: Nanjing guomin zhengfu shiqi guomindang deFalü lunshu*革命/反革命：南京国民政府时期国民党的法律论述)" in Wang Pengxiang王鹏翔, ed., *Legal Thoughts and Social Vicissitudes in 2008* (*2008 falü sixiang yushehui bianqian* 2008法律思想与社会变迁) (Taiwan: Academia Sinica, 2008) , pp. 255-304.

Liu Lianjun刘建军. 2013. "People's Judiciary in the Great Leap Forward (*dayuejin zhongde renmin Sifa*大跃进中的人民司法)" in *Zhengfa luntan*, (September), Vol. 31, No. 5, pp. 142-153.

Liu Shouchu刘受初. 1995. "The Legal Construction of the Chinese Soviet Republic (*zhonghua suweiai gongheguo defazhi jianshe*中华苏维埃共和国的法制建设)" in *The Journal of Ji'an Teachers College*, Vol. 16, No. 4, Nov.

Liu, Sida. 2011. "With or Without the Law: The Changing Meaning of Ordinary Legal Work in China, 1979-2003" in Margret Y.K. Woo and Mary E. Gallagher, eds., *Chinese Justice: Civil Dispute Resolution in Contemporary China*. Cambridge: Cambridge University Press.

Locke, John. 1768. *An Essay Concerning Human Understanding*. London: H. Woodfall.

Lötveit, Trygve. 1979. *Chinese Communism 1931-1934: Experience in Civil Government*. Lund: Studentlitteratur.

Lü Shilun吕世伦. 2000. *History of Lenin's Legal Thought* (*Liening falü sixiangshi*列宁法律思想史). Beijing: Falü chubanshe.

Lubman, Stanley. 2000. *Bird in a Cage: Legal Reform in China after Mao*. Stanford: Stanford University Press.

— 2012. *The Evolution of Law Reform in China: An Uncertain Path*. New York: Edward Elgar.

— ed. 1996. *China's Legal Reform*. Oxford: Oxford University Press.

Luo Si'ling罗四鸰. 2017. "In 1989, Why Did They Throw Eggs on Mao Zedong's Portrait? (*1989nian, tamen weihexiang Mao Zedong huaxiang rengjidan* 1989年他们为何向毛泽东画像扔鸡蛋)" in *The New York Times* (Chinese Version), May 23. https://cn.nytimes.com/china/20170523/egging-mao-tiananmen-square/

— 2019. "Blood Papers in Prison: Why the CCP is Afraid of Dead Lin Zhao?" in *The New York Times*, February 13.

Macauley, Melissa. 1998. *Social Power and Legal Culture: Litigation Masters in Late Imperial Chinq*. Stanford: Stanford University Press.

MacFarquhar, Roderick and Schoenhals, Michael. 2008. *Mao's Last Revolution*. Cambridge, Ma: Harvard University Press.

Meisner, Maurice. 1967. *Li Ta-Chao and the Origins of Chinese Marxism* (Cambridge: Harvard University Press.

— 1999. *Mao's China and After: A History of the People's Republic*. New York: The Free Press.

Miao Tijun苗体君. 2012. "The Exploration and Contribution of He Shuheng to the Rule of Law Enterprise of the Central Soviet Base (*He Shuheng duizhongyang suqu fazhi shiyede tansuo yugongxian*何叔衡对中央苏区法制事业的探索与贡献) in *The Journal of Hunan First Normal University*, Vol. 2, No. 2 (Apr.), pp. 76-81.

Mühlhahn, Klaus. 2011. *Criminal Justice in China: A History*. Cambridge, Ma: Harvard University Press.

— 2007. "Repaying Blood Debt: State Violence and Mass Crimes During the 1950s in China" in Mechthild Leutner, *Rethinking China in the 1950s*. Berlin: Lit.

Myers, Steven Lee. 2019. "A Crackdown on Islam Is Spreading Across China" in *The New York Times*, September 23.

Needham, Joseph. 1975. *Science and Civilization in China*, Vol. 2, "History of Scientific Thought." Cambridge: Cambridge University Press.

Nie Xin聂鑫. 2010. "The Transition of the Judicial Grade System in Modern China: Concept and Reality (*Jindai zhongguo shenji zhidude bianqian: linianyu xianshi* 近代中国审计制度变 迁：理念与现实)" in *Peking University Law Journal*, Vol. 22, No. 2, pp. 246-261: 252-253.

O'Dwyer, Shaun. 2019. "China's Growing Threat to Academic Freedom" in *The Japan Times*, November 25. https://www.japantimes.co.jp/opinion/2019/11/25/commentary/japan- commentary/chinas-growing-threat-academic-freedom/

Ocko, Jonathan K. 1988. "I'll Take it All the Way to Beijing: Capital Appeals in the Qing" in *The Journal of Asian Studies*, Vol. 47, No. 2 (May), pp. 291-315.

Peerenboom, Randle. 2002. *China's Long March toward Rule of Law*. Cambridge: Cambridge University Press.

Peng Lingfan彭令.范1998. "My Sister Lin Zhao (*wode jiejie Lin Zhao*我的姐姐林昭)", http://ywang.uchicago.edu/history/big5/linzhao4.htm (October 30, 2019).

Pepper, Suzanne. 1999. *Civil War in China: The Political Struggle, 1945-1949*. Lanham: Roman & Littlefield.

Perry, Elizabeth J. 2012. *Anyuan: Mining China's Revolutionary Tradition*. Berkeley: University of California Press, 2012.

— and Xun, Li. 1997. *Proletarian Power: Shanghai in the Cultural Revolution*. Boulder: Westview Press.

Pomfret, John and Pan, Philip P. 2001. "Torture is Breaking Falun Gong" in *The Washington Post*, August 5.

Potter, Pitman B. 2003. *From Leninist Discipline to Socialist Legalism: Peng Zhen on Law and Political Authority*. Stanford: Stanford University Press.

Qian, Xiangli. 2008. *Historical Change: From Crisis Rescue to Opposing and Averting Revisionism, 1962-1965* (*lishi debianju: cong wanjiu weiji daofanxiu fangxiu*). Hong Kong: Hong Kong Chinese University Press.

Qin, Amy. 2018. "Suffering and Hardship Belong to Me: Chinese Dissidents Recounts Prison Years" in *The New York Times*, September 19.

Qin, Fang秦方. 2018. "Remembered and Forgotten: Discourse Changes of Qichu and Sanbuqu in Modern China (beijizhude yubeiyiwangde: jindai youguan qichu sanbuqu dehuayu yanbian 被记住的与被遗忘的：近代有关七出三不去的话语演变)" in *The Journal of Chinese Women's Studies*, Nov., No. 6, Ser. No. 150.

Qin Ouyang秦欧阳. 1982. "A Report on the Central Soviet Region (*zhongyang suweiai quyu baogao*中央苏维埃区域报告)" in Jiangxisheng danganguan, 1982: 1. 385.

Qiu, Xue. 2015. *The Declaration of China in the 21st Century: World Section*. Salt Lake City: American Academic Press.

Ramzy, Austin. 2016. "Hong Kong Bookseller Confesses on TV to Evading Rules on Shipping to Mainland" in *The New York Times*, March 1.

Rawski, Evelyn. 2015. *Early Modern China and Northeast Asia: Cross-Border Perspectives*. Cambridge: Cambridge University Press.

Ren Jianxin任建新. 1990. "Working Report of the Supreme People's Court (*zuigao renmin fayuan baogao*最高人民法院报告)" in *The People's Daily*, April 10.

Ren, Xin. 1997. *Tradition of the Law and Law of the Tradition: Law, State, and Social Control in China*. New York: Praeger.

Robin, Corey. 2006. *Fear: The History of a Political Idea*. Oxford: Oxford University Press.

Ruskola, Teemu. 2013. *Legal Orientalism: China, the United States, and Modern Law*. Cambridge, Ma: Harvard University Press.

Ryan, James. 2012. *Lenin's Terror: The Ideological Origins of Early Soviet State Violence*. Abingdon: Routledge.

Schoenhals, Michael. 2018. "The Intelligence Sleeper Who Never Was: Han Fuyin and Case 5004" in Leese and Engman, eds., pp. 52-74.

Schram, Stuart R. "The Chinese Soviet Republic: Some Introductory Reflections" in W.E. Butler, ed., 1983, pp. 7-21: 8-11; John N. Hazard, "The Experience with Constitutionalism" in Butler, ed., 1983, pp. 21-45.

Schrecker, Ellen. 2004. "McCarthyism: Political Repression and the Fear of Communism" in *Social Research*, Vol. 71, No. 4, Fear: Its Political Uses & Abuses (Winter), pp. 1041-1086.

Shambaugh, David. 1993. "Deng Xiaoping: The Politician" in *The China Quarterly*, No. 135, Special Issue: Deng Xiaoping: An Assessment (Sep.), pp. 457-490: 468.

Shen Jiaben沈家本. 1976. *Factual Study of the Past Criminal Laws* (*lidai xingfakao* 历代刑法考). Beijing: Zhonghua shujü.

Shen Weiwei沈玮玮 and Han Wei韩伟, "An Overview of the Studies on the Legal Construction of the Central Soviet Base (*zhongyang suqu fazhi jianshe yanjiu zonglun*中央苏 区法制建设研究综论)" in *The Journal of China Executive Leadership Academy Jinggangshan*, Vol. 5, No. 4, July 25, 2012.

Shen Zhihua沈志华. 2009. *Thinking and Choice: From Intellectual Meeting to Anti-Rightist Movement* (*sikao yuxuanze: cong zhishi fenzi huiyi dao fanyoupai yundong*思考与选择：从知 识分子会议到反右派运动). Hong Kong: Hong Kong Chinese University Press.

Sheridan, James E. 1966. *Chinese Warlord: The Career of Feng Yu-hsiang*. Stanford: Stanford University Press.

Sherman, Dennis and Salisbury, Joyce. 2006. *The West in the World: A History of Western Civilization*. New York: McGraw Hill.

Shi Shui石水, "The Social Protection Law in the Central Soviet Base (*zhongyang suqude shehui baozhang lifa*中央苏区的社会保障立法)" in *The Circular of the Labor Protection*, Vol. 7, P19, 2001.

Short, Philip. 2000. *Mao: A Life*. New York: Henry Holt Co.

Simons, William B. "Reflections on State Administration in the Chinese Soviet Republic and the Soviet Union" in Butler, ed., 1983, pp. 47-52: 48.

Smith, Aminda M. 2013a. "The Dilemma of Thought Education: Beijing Reformatories and the Origins of Reeducation Through Labor, 1949-1957" in *Modern China*, 39 (2) , pp. 203-234.

— 2013b. "Thought Reform and the Unreformable: Reeducation Centers and the Rhetoric of Opposition in the Early People's Republic of China" in *The Journal of Asian Studies*, Vol. 72, No. 4 (Nov.), pp. 937-958.

Smith, William H.C. 2007. *The Bonapartes: The History of a Dynasty*. London: A & C Black.

Solomon, Peter H. 1996. *Soviet Criminal Justice Under Stalin*. Cambridge: Cambridge University Press.

Song Guoqing. 2018. "The Floating Fate of a Rebel Leader in Guangxi, 1966-1984" in Leese and Engman, eds., pp. 174-200.

Spence, Jonathan. 1982. *The Gate of Heavenly Peace: The Chinese and Their Revolution*. London: Penguin Books.

— 2012. *Treason by the Book: Traitors, Conspirators and Guardians of an Emperor.* London: Penguin Books.

Strauss, Julia. 2006. "Morality, Coercion and State Building by Campaign in the Early PRC: Regime Consolidation and After, 1949-1956" in *The China Quarterly*, No. 188. The History of the PRC (1949-1976) (Dec.), pp. 891-912: 894.

Su Yang. 2011. *Collective Killings in Rural China during the Cultural Revolution.* Cambridge: Cambridge University Press.

Sun, Guangyan and Yu, Yisheng. "A Review of the Influence of the Soviet Law on the Development of the Chinese Legal System (*sulianfa yingxiang zhongguo fazhi jianshe Jincheng zhihuigu*)" in *faxue yanjiu*, Vol. 1, 2003.

Tanner, Harold. 1999. *Strike Hard: Anti-Crime Campaigns and Chinese Criminal Justice, 1979-1985*. Cornell: Cornell University Press.

Teiwes, Frederick C. 1966. "The Purge of Provincial Leaders 1957-1958" in *The China Quarterly*, No. 27 (Jul.-Sep.), pp. 14-32.

Tiffert, 2015. *Judging Revolution: Beijing and the Birth of the PRC Judicial System, 1906-1958* (unpublished dissertation, University of California Berkeley).

Trevaskes, Susan. 2007. *Courts and Criminal Justice in Contemporary China*. Lanham: Lexington Books.

Tsoi Grace and Wai, Lam Cho. "Hong Kong Security Law: What is it and is it Worrying?" *The BBC News*. June 30, 2020. https://www.bbc.com/news/world-asia-china-52765838

Tsou, Tang. 1999. *The Cultural Revolution and Post-Mao Reforms: A Historical Perspective*. Chicago: University of Chicago Press.

— 1963. *America's Failure in China, 1941-1950*. Chicago: University of Chicago Press.

Turner, Karen. 1993. "War, Punishment, and the Law of Nature in Early Chinese Concepts of the State" in *Harvard Journal of Asiatic Studies*, Vol. 53, No. 2 (Dec.), pp. 285-324.

Tuttle, William M. Jr. 2001. "Red Summer, Red Scare" in William Graebner and Leonard Richards, eds., *The American Record: Images of the Nation's Past*, Vol. II, Boston: McGraw Hill.

Unger, Jonathan. 1998. "Revolution Conflict in the villages" in *The China Quarterly*, No. 153 (Mar.), pp. 82-106.

— 2007. "The Cultural Revolution at the Grass Roots" in *The China Journal*, No. 57 (Jan.), pp. 109-137.

Vladimirov, Peter. 2004. *Yan'an Diary* (*Yan'an riji*延安日记). Beijing: Dongfang chuabnshe.

Vogel, Ezra F. 1980. *Canton under Communism: Programs and Politics in a Provincial Capital, 1949-1968*. Cambridge, Ma: Harvard University Press.

— 2013. *Deng Xiaoping and the Transformation of China*. Cambridge, Ma: Harvard University Press.

Wang Celai王策来. 2002. *The Case of Yang Naiwu and Xiao Baicai* (*Yangnaiwu yu xiaobaicaian*杨乃武与小白菜). Beijing: Zhongguo jiancha chubanshe.

Wang Chaobin王朝彬. 1992. *An Authentic Record of the Three-Antis Movement* (*sanfan shilu* 三反实录). Beijing: Jingguan jiaoyu chubanshe.

Wang Haiguang王海光. 2000. "The Movement of Criticizing Lin Biao and Confucius (*pilin pikong Yundong*批林批孔运动)" in Zhang Hua and Su Caiqing, eds., *Looking Back to the Cultural Revolution* (*huishou wenge*回首文革). Beijing: Zhonggong dangshi chubanshe.

Wang Pengxiang王鹏翔, ed. 2008. *Legal Thoughts and Social Vicissitudes in 2008* (2008 *Falü sixiang yushehui bianqian*法律思想与社会变迁). Taiwan: Academia Sinica.

Wang Shirong汪世荣. 2010. "The Accomplishments of the Shanganning High Court (*Shanganning bianqu gaodeng fayuande chengjiu*陕甘宁边区高等法院的成就)" in *The Journal of Southwest University of Politics and Law*, Vol. 12, No. 6 (Dec.), pp. 10-17.

— ed. 2011. *The Cornerstone of the New China Judicial System* (*Xinzhongguo sifa zhidude jishi*新中国司法制度的基石). Beijing: Shangwu yinshuguan.

Wang Tianyou王天有 and Xu Daling许大龄, *Sixteen Emperors of the Ming Dynasty* (*mingchao shiliudi*明朝十六帝). Beijing: Zijincheng chubanshe.

Wang, Yan. 2004. *Chinese Legal Reform: The Case of Foreign Investment Law*. Abingdon: Routledge.

Wang, Zheng. 2014. *Never Forget National Humiliation: Historical Memory in Chinese Politics and Foreign Relations*. New York: Columbia University Press.

Wakeman, Frederic Jr. 1995. *Policing Shanghai, 1927-1937*. Berkeley: University of California Press.

— 2003. *Spymaster: Dai Li and the Chinese Secret Service*. Berkeley: University of California Press.

— 2007. "'Cleanup': The New Order in Shanghai" in Brown and Pickowicz, 2007, pp. 21-58.

Walder, Andrew G. "Factional Conflict at Beijing University, 1966-1968," *The China Quarterly*, No. 188, The History of the PRC (1949-1976) (Dec., 2006), pp. 1023-1047.

— and Su, Yang. 2003. "The Cultural Revolution in the Countryside: Scope, Timing, and Human Impact" in *The China Quarterly*, No. 173 (Mar.), pp. 74-99. Beijing: Falü chubanshe.

Weber, Max. 1978. *Economy and Society: An Outline of Interpretive Sociology* (Guenther Roth and Claus Wittich, eds). Berkeley: University of California Press.

— 1998. *Confucianism and Daoism* (*rujiao hedaojiao*). Beijing: Shangwu yinshuguan.

— 2012. *The Protestant Ethic and the Spirit of Capitalism*. New York: Courier Corporation.

Wee, Sui-Lee. 2015. "China Jails Journalist for Seven Years for 'Leaking State Secrets'" in *Reuters*, April 16.

Wu, Harry. 1992. *Laogai: The Chinese Gulag*. Boulder: Westview Press.

Wu Jue吴珏. 2014. *A Veritable Record of the Three-Antis and Five-Antis Movements* (*sanfan wufan yundong jishi*三反五反运动纪实). Beijing: Dongfang chubanshe.

Wu, Yiching. 2014. *The Cultural Revolution at the Margins*. Cambridge, Ma: Harvard University Press.

Xi Xuan席宣 and Jin Chunming金春明. 2006. *A Brief History of the Cultural Revolution* (*wenge jianshi*文革简史). Beijing: Zhonggongzhongyang dangshi chubanshe.

Xia Yong夏勇. 2004. *Ruling the Country with Law: State and Society* (*yifa zhiguoguojia yu shehui*依法治国-国 家与社会). Beijing: Shehui kexue wenxian chubanshe.

Xiao Shu笑蜀. 1999. *Precursor of History: Solomon Pledges Made a Half Century Ago* (*lishi dexiansheng: bange shiji qiande zhuangyan chengnuo*历史的先声：半个世纪前的庄严承 诺). Shantou: Shantou daxue chubanshe.

Xiao Yang肖扬. 2000. "Report of the Supreme People's Court (*zuigao renmin fayuan baogao*最高人民法院报告)" in *The People's Daily*, March 20.

Xiao Zhoulu肖周录. 2014. "A Study on the Compiled Book of Legal Cases in the Shanganning Border Area (*Shanganning bianqu panli huibian kaolue*陕甘宁边区判例汇编考略)" in *Faxue yanjiu*, Vol. 1, pp. 190-208.

Xie Xiangjing谢祥京. 2015."Li Mu'an: CCP's First Constitutional Advocator (*Li Mu'an: zhonggong xianzheng diyiren*李木庵：中国宪政第一人)," February 5 in http://www.mingjingnews.com/MIB/News/news.aspx?ID=N000075073&Page=2 (October 23, 2020).

Xie Yong谢泳, ed. 1999. *Luo Longji: My Experience and Rethinking of Arrest* (*Luo Longji: wode beibu dejingguo hefangan*罗隆基：我的被捕的经过和翻案). Beijing: Zhongguo qingnian chubanshe.

Xin Chunying信春鹰. 1999. *Chinese Legal System and its Reform* (*zhongguode Falü zhidu jiqi gaige*罗隆基：我的被捕的经过和翻案). Beijing: Falü chubanshe.

Xin Xiangdong辛向东. 2009. "Dong Biwu and Mao Zedong" in *Dangshi tiandi*, Vol. 5, pp. 7-8.

Xu, Lizhi. 2018. "Beyond 'Destruction' and 'Lawlessness': The Legal System during the Cultural Revolution" in Leese and Engman, eds., pp. 25-51.

Xu, Xiaoqun. 2008. *Trial of Modernity: Judicial Reform in Early Twentieth-Century China, 1901-1937*. Stanford: Stanford University Press.

Xu Zhiyong许志永. 2019. "For Freedom, Justice, and Love: My Court Remark (*weile ziyou gongyi ai: wode fating chenci*为了自由公益爱：我的法庭陈词)," https://www.hrichina.org/chs/gong-min-yan-chang/xu-zhi-yong-zai-fa-ting-shang-de-zui-hou- chen-shu (October 23, 2020).

Yan Jiaqi严家其. 1987. *Ten-Year History of the Chinese Cultural Revolution* (*wenhua dageming shinianshi*文化大革命十年史). Hong Kong: Hong Kong Dagongbaoshe.

Yang Bojun杨伯峻, ed. 2018. *The History of Zuo* (*zuozhuan*左传). Beijing: Zhonghua shujü.

Yang, Jisheng. 2012. *Tombstone: The Great Chinese Famine, 1958-1962*. New York: Farrar, Straus, and Giroux.

Yang, Kuisong. 2015. "How a 'Bad Element' Was Made: The Discovery, Accusation, and Punishment of Zang Qiren" in Jeremy Brown and Matthew D. Johnson, eds., *Maoism at the Grassroots: Everyday Life in China's Era of High Socialism.* Cambridge, Ma: Harvard University Press, pp. 19-50.

Yang Musheng杨木生. "The Judicial System in the Soviet Base (*lun suqude sifa zhidu* 论苏区 的司法制度)" in Qiushi, http://www.zhlzw.com/qx/fxlw/683882_5.html (October 23, 2020).

Yang Yonghua杨永华 and Fang Keqin方克勤. 1987. *Historical Materials of the Shanganning Border Area* (*Shanganning bianqu fazhi shigao*陕甘宁边区法制史稿). Beijing: Law Press.

Ye Xiaoxin叶孝信. 2008. *History of Chinese Legal System* (*zhongguo fazhishi*中国法制史). Shanghai: Fudan daxue chubanshe.

Yu Ming于明. 2015. *Ruling a State in Accordance with Law: Political History of English tribunals, 1154-1701* (*sifa zhiguo: yingguo fatingde zhengzhishi, 1154-1701*司法治国：英国 法庭的政治史, 1154-1701). Beijing: Falü chubanshe.

Zeng Bingjun曾炳钧. 1981. "The Eight Considerations in China's Feudal Criminal Law (*zhongguo fengjian xinglu zhongde bayi*中国封建刑律中的八议)" in *Faxue yanjiu*, Vol. 2, pp. 51-52.

Zeng Shaodong曾少东. "The Land Law System of the Central Soviet Base (*zhongyang suqu tudi falü zhidu*中央苏区土地法律制度)" in *Agricultural Archeology*, Vol. 3, 2010.

Zeng Xianyi曾宪义. 2002. *History of Chinese Legal System* (*zhongguo fazhishi*中国法制史). Beijing: Beijing daxue chubanshe.

Zhang Bo张波. 2016. "An Analysis of the Argument of 'Discourse Milieu' in the Shanganning Border Area (*Shanganning bainqu sifa zhidude 'yujinglun' fenxi*陕甘

宁边区司法制度的语 境论)" in *Lilun daokan*, Vol. 9. http://www.mingjingnews.com/MIB/News/news.aspx?ID=N000075073&Page=2 (October, 2020).

Zhang Hongmou张宏谋. 1988. "Yifeng Judicial System in the Democratic Revolutionary Period (*minzhu geming shiqi yifeng renmin sifa zhidu*民主革命时期宜丰人民司法制度)" in *Yifeng wenshi ziliao*, pp. 86-97.

Zhang Jinfan张晋藩, ed. 2004. *History of Chinese Judicial System* (*zhongguo sifa zhidushi*中国司法制度史). Beijing: Renmin fayuan chubanshe.

Zhang, Man. 2018. "From Denial to Apology: Narrative Strategies of a 'Perpetrator' after the Cultural Revolution" in Leese and Engman, eds., pp. 150-173.

Zhang Min张慜. "A Tentative Study on the 1952 Legal Reform Movement (*shilun 1952 sifa gaige yundong*试论1952年司法改革运动)" in *Falü shiyong yuekan*, 2004/8, pp. 55-58.

Zhang, Qianfan. 2012. *The Constitution of China: A Contextual Analysis*. Oxford: Hart Publishing.

Zhang Shibin张世斌, ed. 2004. *The Historical Traces of the High Court in the Shanganning Border Area* (*Shanganning bianqu gaodeng fayuan shiji*陕甘宁边区高等法院史迹). Shaanxi: Shaanxi renmin chubanshe.

Zhang Suhua张素华. 2006. *Change: Beginning and End of 7000-Men Meeting* (*bianju: qiqianren dahui shimo*变局：七千人大会始末). Beijing: Zhongguo qingnian chubanshe.

Zheng Tianxiang郑天翔. 1986. "Report of the Supreme People's Court (*zuigao renminfayuan baogao*最高人民法院报告)" in *The People's Daily*, April 18.

Index

For Product Safety Concerns and Information please contact our EU representative GPSR@taylorandfrancis.com
Taylor & Francis Verlag GmbH, Kaufingerstraße 24, 80331 München, Germany

www.ingramcontent.com/pod-product-compliance
Ingram Content Group UK Ltd.
Pitfield, Milton Keynes, MK11 3LW, UK
UKHW020020200926
475702UK00014B/1974

* 9 7 8 1 0 4 1 1 8 7 4 8 6 *